An Introduction to Personal and Social Adjustment

The Search for Self

Joseph Simons
Santa Rosa Junior College

D. C. HEATH AND COMPANY
Lexington, Massachusetts   Toronto

Cover Photograph by Cary Wolinsky/Stock, Boston

CHAPTER OPENING PHOTOGRAPH CREDITS

Page 1, Frank Siteman/Stock, Boston; page 27, © Nancy Bjornson/West Stock; page 53, Peter Vandermark; page 77, Frank Siteman; page 103, Ken Heyman; page 131, Frank Siteman; page 155, Marion Bernstein; page 181, © Susan Lapides; page 209, Anestis Diakopoulos/Stock, Boston; page 233, Terry McKoy; p. 259, © Joel Gordon; page 281, Karen R. Preuss/Jeroboam; page 305, Ken Heyman; page 327, Los Alamos Scientific Laboratory; page 347, Peter Vandermark

Copyright © 1980 by D. C. Heath and Company.

All rights reserved. No part of this publication may be reproduced or transmitted in any form or by any means, electronic or mechanical, including photocopy, recording, or any information storage or retrieval system, without permission in writing from the publisher.

Published simultaneously in Canada.

Printed in the United States of America.

International Standard Book Number: 0-669-02570-4

Library of Congress Catalog Card Number: 79-84741

PREFACE

The Search for Self presents the psychology of adjustment from several vantage points and theoretical positions. The goal of this approach is to help students develop their own personal attitudes toward adjustment, rather than expect them simply to adopt a ready-made position. In my experience, students with no previous exposure to psychology as well as those with an elementary background will find this approach exciting and accessible.

The book is organized with two purposes in mind. First, the structure gives students a logical overview of the personal and social adjustment field. Second, it helps students gradually understand themselves as they read. The first chapter introduces the concept of the *Self* and the way professional psychologists understand that concept. A discussion on *Personality* (2) offers students a further understanding of their uniqueness. The *Learning* (3) chapter examines how psychologists see us develop and change as we interact with our environment. And the discussion of *Motivation and Emotion* (4) also helps students discover their uniqueness by explaining how they might react to the various circumstances of life.

Since the development process never runs smoothly and inevitably creates periods of conflict, the book then presents a discussion of *Anxiety and Stress* (5), their roots, and the way such tensions can lead to *Conflict, Anger, and Aggression* (6). A chapter on *Psychotherapy* (7) gives students an understanding of that process and its potential value during periods of conflict and stress.

The chapter on *Attitudes and Values* (8) helps students understand why their own attitudes are so unique. Because such uniqueness can both help and hinder communication, a chapter on *Communication* (9) gives students not only pertinent theories but also personal help in their attempts to communicate adequately. A discussion of *The Individual and the Group* (10) also helps students understand their place in the social atmosphere. A chapter on *Love and Friendship* (11) gives students an opportunity to understand better the process that leads to friendship. Ignorance about

Sex (12) still abounds, and a frank discussion of the basic facts continues to be important. A chapter on *Marriage and Family* (13) is written to help both married and single students understand that intimate relationship better. The discussion of *Work and Leisure* (14) can give students an opportunity to learn more about themselves by examining their present work attitudes as well as their career goals. And finally, the chapter on *Life Cycles* (15) will help students understand how passage through the various stages of life will affect their personality.

To help stimulate student interest, I have included many excerpts from primary sources. Freud, Skinner, Rogers, and others are introduced in short, easily understood quotes. In addition, examples illustrating the role of research in psychology help students understand the value of research methods in self-assessment. Quizzes, which were given to over 500 randomly selected college students, appear throughout the book. Although these quizzes lack strict scientific validity for personality assessment, they do allow students to measure their own psychological attitudes and encourage them to become personally involved with the material.

- An *outline* and *learning objectives* to give students an overview of the entire chapter.
- *Bold-faced key terms,* highlighted in the text and listed at the end of the chapter, to emphasize the important material.
- *Case studies* to provide students with applications of pure theory and to give the material a more personal feel.
- *Overviews* and *summaries* to unify each chapter.
- *Study questions* to help students become involved with the subject matter and gain insights into their personal experiences.
- A list of *additional readings* that relate to the topics in the chapter.
- Numerous *photographs* and *illustrations* to bring the world of theoretical psychology into the students' everyday lives.

In addition, a glossary of important psychological terms appears at the end of the book for easy reference.

Briefly put, the book will help students search for themselves. The search, using the personally involving approaches provided by this book, will give students a grasp of psychological principles. It will also help them begin to understand themselves better.

I would like to acknowledge the assistance provided by Jack W. Bradley (West Valley College), Virginia C. Chancey (Southern Methodist University), W. Malcolm Flanagan (University of Missouri-Columbia), Valda Robinson (Hillsborough Community College), R. A. Staneski (Chaffey College), and Robert S. Tomlinson (University of Wisconsin-Eau Claire). Their comments helped make this a better book.

JOSEPH SIMONS

CONTENTS

Chapter One

THE SELF — 1

Our Search for Self — 4
Psychology Can Help / Disagreement Among Psychologists

The Psychoanalytic Approach — 6
Early Personality Development / The Freudian Personality System / The Defense Mechanisms

The Behavioristic Approach — 11
A Look at the Self / A Focus on Behavior / Rewards and Learning / Prediction and Control

The Humanistic Approach — 17
Our Subjective World / Free Choice / Growth and Potential

Conclusion — 23

Chapter Two

PERSONALITY — 27

The Psychoanalytic Approach — 31
The Oral Stage / The Anal Stage / The Oedipus Complex / The Electra Complex

The Behavioristic Approach — 37
Environmental Formation / Reward and the Personality / Extinction and the Personality

The Humanistic Approach — 44
Personal Choices / Emotional Experiences / Honest Relationships / Self-Actualization

Conclusion — 50

Chapter Three: LEARNING — 53

The Behavioristic Approach — 56
Further Discoveries / Operant Conditioning / Behavior Shaping

The Cognitive Approach — 63
Chimpanzee Insight / Sign Learning / Latent Learning / Controversy and Resolution

The Humanistic Approach — 69
Blocks to Learning / Discovery Learning / Real Teachers

Conclusion — 73

Chapter Four: MOTIVATION AND EMOTION — 77

The Psychoanalytic Approach — 80
Extraverts and Introverts / Homeostasis / Psychological Balance / Individuation

The Behavioristic Approach — 88
Emotional Byproducts / Turning Adjectives into Nouns / The Behaviorist Explanation

The Humanistic Approach — 93
Embarrassment / Balancing Conflicting Emotions / Self-Trust

Conclusion — 100

Chapter Five: ANXIETY AND STRESS — 103

The Psychoanalytic Approach — 107
The Anxiety Experience / Reality Anxiety / Neurotic Anxiety / Moral Anxiety

The Behavioristic Approach — 115
Sinfulness / Generalization / Thoughts and Anxieties

The Humanistic Approach — 119
The Roots of Anxiety / The Meaning of Life / Facing Anxiety

Conclusion — 127

Chapter Six

CONFLICT, ANGER, AND AGGRESSION   131

The Psychoanalytic Approach   134
The Death Instinct / Our Destructive Nature / The Inevitability of Human Aggression

The Behavioristic Approach   138
Frustration and Aggression / Social Learning / Obedience to Authority

The Humanistic Approach   145
Anger and Violence / Healthy Aggression / The Fair Fight

Conclusion   152

Chapter Seven

PSYCHOTHERAPY   155

The Psychoanalytic Approach   158
The Talking Cure / Dream Interpretation / Freudian Slips / Transference

The Behavioristic Approach   166
Social Learning / Assertiveness Training / Learned Helplessness

The Humanistic Approach   173
Effective Concern / Trust / Emotional Maturity

Conclusion   177

Chapter Eight

ATTITUDES AND VALUES   181

The Psychoanalytic Approach   184
The Archetypes / The Shadow / Anima and Animus

The Behavioristic Approach   193
Manipulating Propinquity / First Impressions / Shared Values

The Humanistic Approach   198
Self-Actualization and Values / Psychology Implies Values / The Highest Values

Conclusion   205

Chapter Nine

COMMUNICATION 209

The Psychoanalytic Approach 213
Repression / Projection / Reaction Formation

The Behavioristic Approach 217
The Space Between Us / Touch Talk

The Humanistic Approach 224
Congruence / Passing Judgments / Listening

Conclusion 230

Chapter Ten

THE INDIVIDUAL AND THE GROUP 233

The Psychoanalytic Approach 237
Karen Horney / Harry Stack Sullivan / Erik Erikson

The Behavioristic Approach 243
Leadership Styles / Group Pressure / The Risky Shift

The Humanistic Approach 250
The Encounter Group / Feeling Expression / Encounter-Group Dangers

Conclusion 256

Chapter Eleven

LOVE AND FRIENDSHIP 259

The Psychoanalytic Approach 262
Learning an Art / Practicing an Art / The Art of Loving

The Behavioristic Approach 269
Plain People / Love Is the Answer / Hard to Get

The Humanistic Approach 273
The Sounds of Silence / The Risk of Loving / Peace

Conclusion 278

Chapter Twelve

SEX 281

The Psychoanalytic Approach 284
Sex Roles / Sexual Conflict / Homosexuality

The Behavioristic Approach — 290
The Kinsey Results / Masters and Johnson / The Masters and Johnson Results

The Humanistic Approach — 295
Sex Without Love / The New Puritanism / Eros

Conclusion — 302

Chapter Thirteen — MARRIAGE AND FAMILY — 305

Open Marriage — 308
The Open Marriage / Open Relationships / Jealousy

Between Parent and Child — 313
Praise and Criticism / Self-Defeating Patterns / Discipline and Permissiveness

Creative Divorce — 321
Memories / Growth Through Mourning / The Creative Effect

Chapter Fourteen — WORK AND LEISURE — 327

Work Theories — 330
Trait-and-Factor Theory / Need-Drive Theory / Developmental Theories / John Holland / Work-Motivation Theory / Theories of Management

Leisure — 340
Playful Work / Other People

Chapter Fifteen — LIFE CYCLES — 347

Industry — 350
Inferiority

Identity — 352
Role Confusion

Intimacy and Isolation 355
Genitality

Generativity and Stagnation 357

Ego Integrity and Despair 358

Death and Dying 361
Denial and Anger / Bargaining and Depression / Acceptance and Hope

Notes 367

Glossary 375

Index 381

The Search for Self

Chapter One

The Self

OUTLINE

Our Search for Self
    Psychology Can Help
    Disagreement Among Psychologists

The Psychoanalytic Approach
    Early Personality Development
    The Freudian Personality System
    The Defense Mechanisms

The Behavioristic Approach
    A Look at the Self
    A Focus on Behavior
    Rewards and Learning
    Prediction and Control

The Humanistic Approach
    Our Subjective World
    Free Choice
    Growth and Potential

Conclusion

LEARNING OBJECTIVES

After reading this chapter, you should be able to:

1. Explain the role of the unconscious.
2. Understand Freud's attitude toward early childhood development.
3. Discuss the interaction between the id, the ego, and the superego.
4. Explain the role of the defense mechanisms in the personality.
5. Discuss how behaviorists link reward and behavior.
6. Explain the primary distinction between behaviorism and humanism.
7. Understand the role of free choice in the humanistic philosophy.

Chapter One

Debbie, a nineteen-year-old sophomore, chatted with me recently in the school cafeteria. About midway into our conversation Debbie said, "I have trouble deciding who I am. When I am with my parents, I am usually quiet and reserved. I hardly say a word. Then, when I get together with my friends, I become loud and love to joke around."

"And this confuses you?" I asked sympathetically.

"You bet! I want to know which of those Debbies is the real one. Is the real Debbie loud and outgoing?" Debbie looked down into her coffee cup. "Or am I quiet and reserved like I am when I am with my family?"

Debbie went on to tell me about the many other people she becomes. She said she is one person when she and her boyfriend are together. She becomes another person when she is alone. The fact that she becomes many different people does not often cause her turmoil. Yet, the day she talked to me, she was obviously troubled by her confusion.

Debbie is far from alone. Jack, the basketball captain, is alive and excited when the tension mounts before a game, but he becomes passive when listening to a chemistry lecture. Anne, a successful lawyer, can become a totally fresh personality when she unwinds at a cocktail party after a hard day at work. Some teachers go unrecognized by their students in the informal atmosphere of a pizza parlor. The difference in behavior between students in a large lecture hall and in a small discussion class can be dramatic.

Different experiences of ourselves can also occur without changing settings. During the course of one conversation, people can be angry and hostile just minutes before turning warm and loving. Many people discover—right after declaring to a friend that they feel calm and relaxed—that they actually have been anxious for most of the day. Such sudden shifts in mood are common to all of us. The various examples cited here remind us that we experience ourselves differently during the course of a day, week, or year. We sometimes talk of ourselves as if we were one concrete, easily defined person. Then we recall experiences of ourselves as flowing and changing. At such moments we become confused about our identity as a person.

OUR SEARCH FOR SELF

Many people want to know more about the dramatic changes they experience within themselves. They wonder why discussions with the supermarket checker leave them feeling so different from their conversations with the bank teller, for example. They continue to puzzle over why they feel so relaxed with George, a close friend, but not with Paul, a friend who puts them off in some undefinable way. They become curious about their relaxed feelings when engaged with one person in conversation and their anxiety whenever they enter a group of three or more.

Some people become so interested in these dramatic changes in their experiences of themselves that they try to study their emotional reactions in some systematic manner. They isolate a troubling emotion, for example, and see if they can discover the cause of that anger, loneliness, or anxiety. This curiosity about themselves and their reactions often leads people to books, articles, and classes in psychology. The majority of students in any psychology course, then, are searching to understand themselves and their many differing emotional reactions.

Psychology Can Help

People have been curious about the causes of their conduct for many years. "Since 1860 when psychology officially became a science," Hall and Lindzey said in their classic work, *Theories of Personality*, "the question of a psychic agent which regulates, guides, and controls man's behavior has been repeatedly raised and discussed." (1) Psychologists try to study the self in a systematic way. They conduct experiments, tabulate surveys, and even philosophize as they attempt to clarify the elusive concept we call the **self**. The study becomes so complex and varied that psychologists specialize in one of the separate disciplines of clinical psychology, counseling psychology, industrial psychology, learning theory, personality theory, or educational psychology, to mention a few categories.

Besides wondering about the self and how it operates, psychologists search for practical results. In therapy, clinical psychologists help troubled people to cope better with their lives. Learning theorists search for practical ways to help people learn faster and understand more clearly. Industrial psychologists feel successful only when they make conditions better for workers and improve work production. Psychologists, then, are people dedicated to gaining insights with practical impact.

One interesting study took place at the University of Michigan. A ten-week Test Anxiety Program was introduced on that campus by James D. Papsdorf, a psychology professor. Papsdorf designed counseling and "self-coaching strategies" to help students reduce test-related tensions. The program is so successful that between 85 and 90 percent of the students who complete the exercises report decreased anxiety.

Counseling is one of the many disciplines in which psychologists can specialize. (© Frank Siteman, 1979)

Dr. Papsdorf's work has led him to speculate about the personality of students with high test anxiety. Such students apparently cannot take tests one item or question at a time. "They start with the task of chopping down a single tree," the Michigan psychologist explains. "It works all right, but then they look up and see the whole forest, and it overwhelms them." Once students peek at the entire test, they feel helpless. Papsdorf also believes anxious students have a tendency to think in "musts" and "shoulds"—"I must learn everything. I should do well." The training program helps them relax in the face of such pressures. (2) Studies such as Papsdorf's Test Anxiety Program give psychologists a better understanding of people in general and also produce specific practical results.

Disagreement Among Psychologists

At first glance, we might expect to find easy answers to our questions when we turn to a field dedicated to systematic studies of the person. Unfortunately, quick answers are not available. Although psychological studies occasionally produce clear insights, their results are more often contradictory and confusing. The best efforts to capture some element of truth about the self often fail. Even those studies that give us a feeling of accomplishment are like one small piece of a giant jigsaw puzzle.

More discouraging for those who look to psychology for answers is that the various schools of psychology often disagree on the proper approach to the study of the self. One school of thought, the *psychoanalytic*, suggests we look into our unconscious in order to understand our self. Another important school of psychology, the *behavioristic*, studies only the observable, measurable behavior of people. Behaviorists believe the person will be best understood by looking only at what that person *does*. Finally, a third approach to psychology, the humanistic, considers that the

From *Non-being and Somethingness: Selections from the Comic Strip "Inside Woody Allen,"* by Woody Allen, drawn by Stuart Hample. Copyright © 1978 by IWA Enterprises and Hackenbush Productions, Inc. Reprinted by permission of Random House, Inc.

behavior of people reflects their emotions, attitudes, and feelings. Humanists look to this inner part of people to understand them.

Many writers tie themselves to one or another of the various schools of thought. They then set out to explain the experience of the self from that particular vantage point, but I feel such an approach limits understanding. I am convinced each school of psychology contributes important truths to our understanding of ourselves. Therefore, this text will look at the various important psychological concepts—personality, stress, love, sex, friendship, and others—from several vantage points. By passing back and forth from the psychoanalytic, the behavioristic, and the humanistic schools of psychology, we can achieve greater insight into these concepts. And this process, when repeated, can bring us a more complete understanding of ourselves than any other approach can.

THE PSYCHOANALYTIC APPROACH

A variety of different theories fall under the general heading of the psychoanalytic approach, which stresses the importance of the unconscious. Though Freud founded the school, many psychoanalytic theorists sharply disagree with Freud's theories. Throughout this book, we will discuss Freudian and neo-Freudian theories; however, we will begin our discussion by talking about Freud's outlook.

Sigmund Freud's greatest contribution to psychology may well have been his theories on the **unconscious**. He decided that forces we cannot even be aware of direct our actions and even our emotions (CASE 1:1). According to the Freudian scholar Calvin S. Hall:

> Freud likened the mind to an iceberg in which the smallest part showing above the surface of the water represents the region of consciousness while the much larger mass below the water level represents the region of unconsciousness. In this vast domain of the unconscious are to be found

the urges, the passions, the repressed ideas and feelings—a great underworld of vital, unseen forces which exercise an imperious control over the conscious thoughts and deeds of man. From this point of view, a psychology which limits itself to the analysis of consciousness is wholly inadequate for understanding the underlying motive of man's behavior. (3)

Freud's theory of the unconscious only began his exploration into the self. Once he decided the mind has a storehouse for lost thoughts and feelings, he began to describe the effects of that unconscious region on the personality. To one degree or another, Freud said, we all push our consciousness of sexual drives, troubling memories, and other disturbing psychic elements into our unconscious. People are more than their conscious world—the unconscious also molds their personality.

While working on his master's degree at the University of Texas, the psychologist Roger Bennett became fascinated with one way the unconscious intrudes into the daily life of us all. He carefully read about the work of two West Coast psychologists, Paul Ekman and Wallace Freisen, who were studying body language. They had written that when people attempt to lie they give themselves away with "micromomentary" facial expressions. Bennett became convinced that such fleeting intrusions of the unconscious into the conscious world could be recognized by trained observers. Such a skill could help news reporters, tax investigators, law officers, and many others. His hunch proved correct. His training methods have become well known, and he is in demand for his workshops in "lie detection." (4)

● Case 1.1

Freud's theory of the unconscious helps to explain the problems that Norman, a thirty-year-old bank teller, experienced. No one would have ever guessed hidden forces directed Norman's life until the day he witnessed a tragic suicide. On his way home from work one evening he came upon a grotesque scene: a young woman had just jumped from a fourteen-story building. The incident triggered a series of nightmares for Norman. At first, he assumed the nightmares were nothing more than a reaction to the suicide. However, the nightmares not only persisted, but became increasingly upsetting. They finally disturbed his sleep so much that he could no longer function adequately in his job.

As a last resort, Norman visited a psychiatrist to see if his trouble might be psychological. The psychiatrist used hypnosis to probe Norman's unconscious in search of a cause for his persistent nightmares. In time, Norman and the psychiatrist came upon an incident buried deep in Norman's unconscious. When he was only four, Norman's mother, a woman with fanatical religious attitudes, forced him to kiss his dead grandmother at her wake. The scene so revolted Norman that he repressed it in his unconscious, along with feelings of hatred for his mother. The suicide scene somehow triggered those long-repressed feelings. Once Norman recognized his hatred for his mother, he and the psychiatrist were able to work toward a resolution of the feelings so long repressed.

Early Personality Development

Freud was one of the first theorists to stress the importance of early childhood development on the adult personality pattern. He believed that the adult personality is established very early in life, and almost completely formed by the age of five. (5) The earliest experiences of life with its mother, for example, teach the child how much to trust the world. Toilet training and similar experiences determine how much independence the child carries into later life. The same training, if traumatic, can leave the child with guilt feelings permanently fixed in the personality. Early sexual explorations—and parental reactions to them—can also influence adult attitudes toward sexuality.

Not all psychoanalytic theorists accept Freud's belief that personality is fixed quite so early. However, they all recognize the critical importance of early childhood on later personality development. Thus, no wonder Freudian and neo-Freudian therapists attempt to help emotionally troubled people by probing their early experiences. Such understanding, psychoanalytic schools of thought claim, is the key that unlocks the personality.

Freud believed our adult personalities are shaped by early childhood experiences. (© Joel Gordon, left; Peter Vandermark, right)

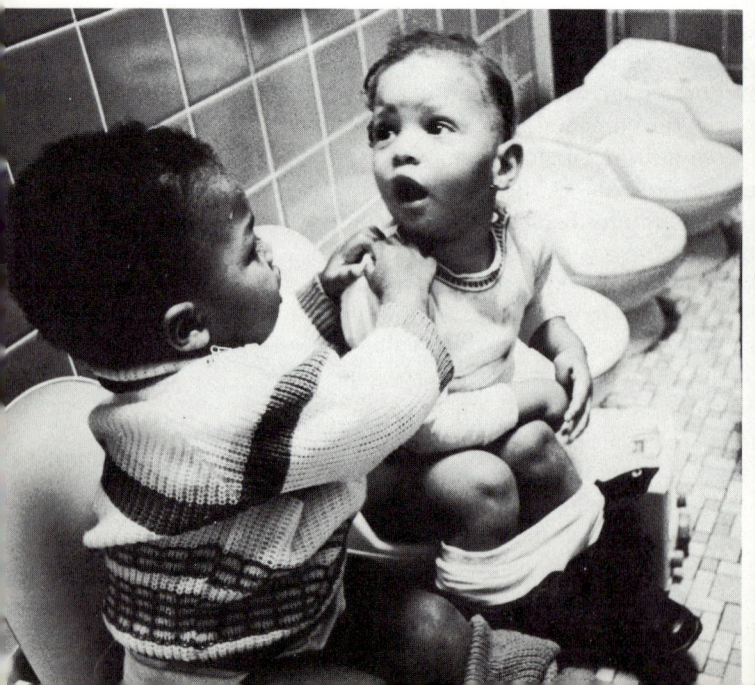

"Darling, what do you suppose they're going to tell their psychiatrists about us?"

Reprinted by permission of Chronicle Books.

● Case 1.2

The impact of an early childhood experience on later life was significant for Martha, a middle-aged woman who worked with me in therapy some years ago. Though Martha felt trapped in a loveless marriage, she had trouble breaking from her husband, Garth. Every time she felt the strength to tell Garth she wanted a divorce, she found herself overcome by guilt feelings. She kept asking me, "What would happen to Garth if I left him?" These feelings of responsibility tied Martha to Garth.

Finally, after several weeks of therapy, Martha had an important dream. In it she saw herself leave Garth. But as she left home, she glanced back only to see Garth on the floor dead. We worked together to help Martha see that dream image of Garth as clearly as she could. In a burst of emotion, Martha discovered the dead man in her dream was not Garth but her father. It seems that Martha, as a child, was with her father when he suffered a fatal heart attack. She was only four at the time, and the incident had a permanent effect on her. The emotional turmoil grew over the years even though she had repressed it. Martha buried that incident from childhood in her unconscious in such a way that it disturbed the rest of her life. Only when it was uncovered did she begin to understand the turmoil it had caused her. In time, therapy helped free Martha of the results of her destructive repression.

The Freudian Personality System

The **id,** the **ego,** and the **superego** are the abstract terms Freud used to explain the personality. We can understand Freud's concept of the self by understanding the struggle among the three.

10   The Self

The id is filled with unconscious drives that press us to satisfy our most primitive needs for sexual and aggressive pleasures. The id is a strong drive that would gratify its pleasure-seeking desires at any cost. For this reason, Freud talked about the id operating according to the **pleasure principle.** The ego, by contrast with the id, sees the reality that exists in the world. It understands that not all the id impulses can be satisfied immediately. The hunger drive, for example, cannot be satisfied until food becomes available. Social and personal restrictions make it necessary for us to delay gratification of the sex drive. Consequently, Freud talked about the ego operating according to the **reality principle.**

The superego interacts with the ego and the id to further complicate these personality dynamics. The superego operates as a conscience, telling us what it considers wrong, and also punishes us with guilt feelings for ignoring its orders. The superego also operates as an ego ideal, as it suggests ideal goals to strive for. The superego offers us a series of rewards for striving to achieve the good our superego suggests.

At first it seems that the three functions of id, ego, and superego are three different personalities struggling against one another. They are, in fact, three interrelated processes within the total personality; they complement as well as struggle with one another.

To illustrate the interaction of these three functions of the personality system, we might look at the young man who notices an attractive young woman on a downtown street corner. His id reacts immediately. The id wants the young man to respond to his aroused sexual instincts and satisfy his strong desire for pleasure. He no more than experiences this sexual drive, however, when his ego points out reality. If he seeks immediate sexual pleasure, he may wind up in prison. To further complicate the young man's life, his superego, in the form of a conscience, reminds him of his parent's warnings against the evil of sex. Simultaneously, that same superego reminds him of the ideal of his parent's warnings—he must always stay pure by remaining in control of his animal nature. Just such struggles proved to Freud and many of his followers the complex interaction between the various parts of the total personality.

The Defense Mechanisms

Freud gave us another important clue to understanding the self when he explained the way we defend ourselves against unpleasant reality. The id can become filled with an upsetting drive—a disturbingly strong sexual drive, for example. In order to cope with the drive for sex and the disturbance that drive causes simultaneously, the ego must do something to satisfy the conflict. One such resolution is a defense Freud called *repression*. The person simply represses, or hides from, the upsetting sexual drive. By forcing the conscious sexual drive into the unconscious, the ego uses a mechanism to defend itself from the upsetting results of the conflict between the id and the ego. Thus, Freud called this process and similar ego-defending processes **defense mechanisms.**

Defense mechanisms such as repression have two important characteristics: 1) they deny, distort, or falsify reality, and 2) they operate unconsciously. When we repress the reality that might overwhelm the ego, we are not aware of using a defense mechanism. Because repression is unconscious, it is important to investigate carefully the psychoanalytic theory if we hope to understand the way we cope with reality.

A recent study of auto accident victims suggests that people in extreme danger employ defense mechanisms. A research team of four psychologists questioned 102 automobile accident victims who did not lose consciousness during their crash. Over 30 percent of the victims experienced a period when they felt a loss of control, a detachment from reality, a perception that events were moving in slow motion, and a feeling of detachment from their body. In that way, it appears, they psychologically defended themselves from the fear that seemed too much to bear. In Freudian terms the ego, overwhelmed by fear, used a defense mechanism to shut out the frightening experience. (6)

THE BEHAVIORISTIC APPROACH

Most historical perspectives on behaviorism, the study of observable, measurable behavior, begin with the work of the Russian physiologist Ivan Pavlov (1849–1936). Pavlov showed that a dog could be trained to salivate at the sound of a bell. Any time a bell was rung, the dog was given meat. Once this ritual had been repeated often enough to lead the dog to know that when the bell rang he could anticipate the food, the bell alone caused the dog to salivate.

This experiment and its implications so excited John Watson (1878–1958), a famous behavioral psychologist, that it became a turning point in his career. Watson believed that psychology created its own problems by paying too much attention to the intangible elements of the mind such as sensation, perception, and emotion. Experiments like Pavlov's could, he felt, lead to a science of the mind that would only study those observable things that stimulate us and our observable responses to such stimuli.

Modern behaviorism has taken in various directions since Watson. Many behaviorists today sharply disagree with one another, and their theoretical work is diverse. Much of our discussion of behaviorism will center on the work of B. F. Skinner, a leading contemporary theorist. Skinner's work is emphasized not only because he has a large following among psychologists, but also because he writes well and is easily understood.

A Look at the Self

Most behaviorists would not want their studies used to bring insight into the self because they consider their entire approach to psychology to be an attempt to escape from such untestable concepts as the self and the emotions. In fact, behaviorism emerged as a separate approach to psychology largely because so many psychologists reacted against systematic attempts to study intangible concepts. Love, for example, can be neither weighed, measured, touched, nor seen. Consequently, behaviorists remain convinced that psychologists can study the emotion of love only in the most subjective way. B. F. Skinner argues with the critics of behaviorism.

> It is often said that a science of behavior studies the human organism but neglects the person or self. What it neglects is a vestige of animism, a doctrine which in its crudest form held that the body was moved by one or more indwelling spirits. (7)

Behaviorists are often criticized for refusing to admit that emotions and feelings exist. Some people accuse them of claiming there is no such thing as love. Most behaviorists would probably deny such charges. They are well aware that people experience feelings, but they claim that feelings are far too subjective for systematic study. Behaviorists point to attempts to understand love and note how little we have learned from a scientific standpoint about that emotion after study. Psychologists should use their energy to perform scientific studies of the behavior they *can* measure.

A Focus on Behavior

Behaviorists begin their study of the person with those aspects of the person that can be observed and measured. They can see how far a person walks, measure how long he talks, notice that he stops talking after a companion raises her voice. It is much better, say the behaviorists, to spend out time observing and measuring such behavior. Edward C. Tolman stated over fifty years ago in the *Psychological Review:*

> We behaviorists, whatever else our divergences, are agreed in viewing overt behavior as the primary datum for psychology. It is from a study of such overt behavior and its environmental settings that we believe we will obtain our causal understanding both of the grosser activities of the lower animals, and of the higher conscious activities of human beings. (8)

Does this approach mean behaviorists entirely ignore the emotional world of the person? Hardly. There are machines to measure the emotional turmoil a person experiences by measuring heart beat, pulse rate, galvanic skin response, and similar bodily functions. The lie detector, or polygraph, records a series of physical responses that help operators draw conclusions about whether or not an individual experiences emotional reactions. But a lie detector cannot make any certain statements about whether or not a person is lying. Nor can any machine make conclusive statements about emotions such as love, anger, or loneliness.

One study that translated external behavioral clues into a practical understanding of people was conducted by market research firm. Consumer Response Corporation of New York became disturbed over the results of their telephone customer surveys. Though people said they preferred one particular brand of cereal, for example, sales did not indicate they followed their declared preferences when they shopped. So the reseachers began to use a device called Volpan (voice pitch analyzer) to detect false statements. When people lie, their voice pitch usually goes up. Volpan measures variations in the voice pitch, and Volpan operators make inferences about the truth of the statements. In one instance, researchers discovered 49 out of 100 people apparently lying about their preferred brands. By using Volpan, Customer Response Corporation now predicts sales with far greater accuracy. (9)

Rewards and Learning

Even though behaviorists have engaged in scientific study of behavior for only a short period of time, they have made some important discoveries. The most important conclusion they have drawn is that people tend to repeat behaviors that lead to **rewards**. B. F. Skinner tells us:

> A **positive reinforcer** strengthens any behavior that produces it. A glass of water is positively reinforcing when we are thirsty, and if we then draw and drink a glass of water, we are more likely to do so again on similar occasions. (10)

The child who occasionally receives a reward for playing quietly will more likely continue to play that way than if no reward were given at all. So the adult, when properly rewarded, will repeat behavior patterns.

Many of the discoveries made by behaviorists center on their reward theory. Their experiments with people and with animals have become more and more complicated as they systematically alter the timing and amount of reward. The goal for the behaviorists is to help people better understand their behavior. And if we can all gain insights into what makes us behave one way rather than another, the behaviorists say, we will live much healthier and more productive lives.

• Case 1.3

This discussion of reward and learning reminds me of David, a premed student I knew some years ago. After a lecture on reward and behavior, David told me, "I think I used rewards to help me stop smoking last year."

"How did you do that?" I asked.

"Well, I remember thinking to myself how much I wanted to give up cigarettes. I even figured out how many times I tried to quit smoking and couldn't." David looked away.

"Nicotine forms a strong habit," I said sympathetically.

"I know. Anyway, I decided I needed to do something good for myself if I were to take away such strong pleasure." David smiled. "The thing I love to do more than anything else is ride my motorcycle. But I don't get much time on it because of my studies. So I figured I would give myself one point for each cigarette I passed up. And once I accumulated enough points I could spend an hour on my motorcycle."

Children who are occasionally rewarded for desirable behavior will most likely repeat that behavior. (Peter Vandermark)

"And that was enough of a reward to help you quit smoking?"

"It was. Every time I reached for my cigarettes, I thought about delaying my time on my bike and I put the pack away again. Before I knew it I was off cigarettes." David grinned with unrestrained pride.

Not everyone can end such a strong habit by promising themselves rewards. However, many people are able to find pleasures strong enough to end long-term habits in just this manner.

Prediction and Control

Behaviorists believe that behavior is determined by inherited and environmental factors, not by the will of the individual. As B. F. Skinner writes:

> A scientific analysis of behavior must, I believe, assume that a person's behavior is controlled by his genetic and environmental histories rather than by the person himself as an initiating, creative agent. We cannot prove, of course, that human behavior as a whole is fully determined, but the proposition becomes more plausible as facts accumulate. (11)

Besides the belief that our behavior is determined by forces outside ourselves, the behaviorists also think we will some day be able to control behavior. Many people, when they hear that prediction, immediately think of a science fiction future where a small group uses **behavior control** to dominate the masses. This is *not* what the behaviorists mean by ultimate behavior control. They do not foresee investing the power for control in the hands of a few people. Rather, they hope to teach everyone the principles of prediction and control. They want us to learn what determines the amount of reading we do, the amount of leisure time we enjoy, the amount of time we spend drinking and smoking. About the most common plea I hear as a psychologist is, "I wish I could cut down on my smoking," or, "I wish I didn't spend so much time in front of the television set." These people, if they knew the principles of control, might be able to fulfill their wishes. Behaviorists have already helped many people learn to improve control over their behavior.

An interesting study that increases our understanding of behavior and our ability to predict and control it took place at the University of Wyoming, where Marianne W. DeVoe administered a self-concept scale to 290 ten-year-olds. She then let the children play competitive games together. She discovered that those children with high self-esteem (self-concept) became the most competitive and the least cooperative. By contrast, the children with lowest self-esteem became the least competitive and the most cooperative. Her strategy was to place children scoring high in self-esteem with children possessing low self-esteem. Playing the same games, the mixed pairs were more competitive than the low self-esteem children and less competitive than children with high self-esteem. (12)

Pairing children with high and low self-esteem can help both kinds of children develop a healthy attitude toward competition and cooperation. (Peter Vandermark)

The study suggests an educational strategy that could benefit all children. If children with high and low self-esteem were mixed for part of the school day, they could all develop a more balanced attitude toward competition and cooperation. The strategy need not involve manipulation. The children could be told of the reason for such pairing and even freed from the need to cooperate if they desired. The contact would still be effective for those involved.

● Case 1.4

The behavioristic belief that we will one day predict and control behavior may strike some of you as quite improbable. However, the evidence that psychologists are moving closer to that goal mounts daily. Scientific journals are filled with studies of how psychologists have improved the lives of people through the use of control techniques.

One young woman who was helped by such techniques spent most of her life in a mental hospital. When Alice first came to the attention of a psychiatrist who had experience in behavior therapy, she was in a deep depression. At that time Alice spent most of her day sitting limply in a rocker near a window that overlooked the hospital grounds. Regularly, she suffered acute anxiety attacks and screamed, "I want love!" During such periods she could not be consoled.

Traditional therapy did not seem to help Alice. So the psychiatrist decided to use a form of behavior modification (a systematic use of rewards to produce desired behavior) to encourage her to leave her rocker and become more social. The psychiatrist explained to Alice that each time she engaged in a conversation with another patient she would be rewarded with a stated number of points. The further she moved from her rocker the more points she gained. Before long she began to visit the hospital grounds and even started to take short bus rides. Soon Alice was working toward a 100-point reward contract with her psychiatrist.

The first 100-point contract offered Alice a trip to a nearby shopping center with the psychiatrist. She completed this contract in six months and began immediately to work on another. The second contract overtaxed her and Alice tore it up in a fit of anger. The psychiatrist feared for her progress, but soon convinced Alice to begin work on a third contract. This contract took about six months to complete and involved social contact with the entire hospital staff. Her success with this contract gave everyone, including Alice, reason to be hopeful about her future.

THE HUMANISTIC APPROACH

No two groups could be more divergent than the behaviorists and the humanists. In sharp contrast to the behaviorists, for example, the humanists focus their attention on **emotions** and feelings. They believe emotions reveal people far better than behavior. If we watch someone attend a specific movie at a given time of day, we might make certain guesses about that person's motives. But, according to the humanists, only when we enter the thoughts and feelings that motivate our moviegoer can we really begin to understand his or her behavior (Self-Quiz 1.1).

Humanists are particularly insistent on their approach when dealing with people who have emotional difficulties. They believe people have trouble coping with their lives specifically because they lose touch with their feelings one way or another. Either they try to hide from their own feelings, or else they let themselves be dominated by their feelings. Humanists believe that emotions, not behavior, are most significant in any psychological difficulty. In his book *On Becoming a Person* Carl Rogers says that his clients in therapy

> gradually come to express more fully, to members of their families as well as to others, feelings which might be thought of as positive — tenderness, admiration, liking, love. It is as though the client discovers in therapy that it is possible to drop the mask he has been wearing, and become more genuinely himself. A husband finds himself becoming furiously angry with his wife, and expressing this anger, where before he had maintained — or thought he had maintained — a calm and objective attitude toward her behavior. It is as though the map of expression of feelings has come to match more closely the territory of the actual emotional experience. Parents and children, husbands and wives, come closer to expressing the feelings which really exist in them, rather than hiding their true feelings from the other person, or from the other person and themselves. (13)

Self-Quiz 1.1 — Ideal Self/Real Self

In his book *Client-Centered Therapy*, Carl Rogers talks about a technique he uses to evaluate the effectiveness of therapy. The technique involves asking clients to compare their image of how they see themselves with their image of their perfect self. The closer a person's two images match, according to Rogers, the more likely it is that that person is well adjusted. You can develop a sense of how closely your real and ideal self compare by completing the following exercise.

In the column labeled *Real Self*, place the number 1, 2, 3, 4, or 5—depending on how characteristic each statement is of you. Continue the process for each of the statements. Then fill in the *Ideal Self* column. A glance at the differences between the numbers in the two columns will give you an idea of how closely your real self and ideal self match.

5 strongly characteristic of me
4 moderately characteristic of me
3 neutral
2 moderately uncharacteristic of me
1 strongly uncharacteristic of me

Ideal Self / Real Self

1. I am worthless.
2. I am likable.
3. I often feel humiliated.
4. I am a hard worker.
5. I have a feeling of hopelessness.
6. I am self-reliant.
7. I am a good mixer.
8. I put on a false front.
9. I am relaxed and nothing really bothers me.
10. I am intelligent.
11. It is difficult to control my aggression.
12. I understand myself.
13. I tend to be on my guard with people who are somewhat more friendly than I had expected.
14. I am satisfied with myself.
15. I am assertive.
16. I have initiative.
17. I feel apathetic.
18. I am tolerant.
19. I am poised.
20. I try not to think about my problems.
21. I am no one. Nothing seems to be me.
22. I make strong demands on myself.

___ ___ 23. I am sexually attractive.
___ ___ 24. I am liked by most people who know me.
___ ___ 25. I am confused.
___ ___ 26. My hardest battles are with myself.
___ ___ 27. I can usually live comfortably with people around me.
___ ___ 28. I have a horror of failing in anything I want to accomplish.
___ ___ 29. Self-control is no problem to me.
___ ___ 30. I feel insecure with myself.
___ ___ 31. I am a responsible person.
___ ___ 32. I have a warm emotional relationship with others.
___ ___ 33. I am responsible for my troubles.
___ ___ 34. I have few values and standards of my own.
___ ___ 35. I usually feel driven.
___ ___ 36. My decisions are not my own.
___ ___ 37. I am a hostile person.
___ ___ 38. I am ambitious.
___ ___ 39. I don't trust my emotions.
___ ___ 40. I am a rational person.
___ ___ 41. I have the feeling I am not facing things.
___ ___ 42. I am contented.
___ ___ 43. I despise myself.
___ ___ 44. I just don't respect myself.
___ ___ 45. I am afraid of full-fledged disagreement with a person.
___ ___ 46. I am a failure.
___ ___ 47. I usually like people.
___ ___ 48. I really am disturbed.
___ ___ 49. I have to protect myself with excuses, with rationalizing.
___ ___ 50. I am unreliable.

Our Subjective World

Behaviorists insist on making objective observations of people. The scientist, they claim, sees life as it truly exists. Humanists respond by arguing that the world people live in is **subjective.** Ask the police about the contradictory stories that come from eyewitnesses to an accident. One person, shocked by the sight of blood, will look right at the accident and see practically nothing. Another person, identifying with the woman taken away in an ambulance, will claim her to be totally without blame for the accident. Still a third person, fearful of becoming involved, will be unable to remember any part of the incident.

When two or more people listen to the same piece of music, look at the same painting, view the same movie, or even watch the same sporting

Humanists say our reactions to individual events can be entirely unique. (Richard Kalvar/Magnum)

event, they have different emotional experiences. The humanists claim that such subjectivity makes so-called scientific observation of behavior impossible. The person, say the humanists, can only be properly understood when we focus our attention on the emotional world that is part of us all.

Free Choice

What separates behaviorists sharply from humanists is the issue of human freedom. Unlike the behaviorists who believe that behavior is determined by forces outside the self, the humanists believe we are free to make personal choices. "Human beings have the capacity to make choices," Hadley Cantril states in *Challenges of Humanistic Psychology*, "and the desire to exercise this capacity." (14) Our freedom to choose our behavior is a central truth for the humanists, who disagree with the behaviorist claim that freedom is only an illusion. Humanists believe that the freedom to choose is a pivotal point.

To the humanists, freedom is an important goal for any person in therapy. The freedom to function unrestricted by the limiting factors of guilt, resentment, and defensiveness is a humanistic goal in the therapeutic relationship. Only when patients in therapy can find their way out of their restrictive behavior and experience freedom of choice will humanists feel the patients are psychologically healed.

● Case 1.5

This discussion of freedom and choice reminds me of John, a young man who attended my introduction to psychology class a number of years ago. John's eyes, in particular, told me that he knew what suffering meant. After a few casual conversations helped him trust me, John told me he was once committed to a mental hospital. He also admitted he had experienced several splits in his personality. At various times he would lose control of his identity and become Angie, a precocious six-year-old girl. On other occasions he would become Arthur, a middle-aged business man, or Chip, a motorcycle buff. Because he lacked control, his identity delusions became more and more severe. The second time he was committed to a mental hospital he felt his fate was determined.

Fortunately for John, he met Nan, a young therapist who truly cared about him. She convinced John that he still had a choice. John told me he remembered sitting at a bare wooden table in the hospital trying to gain the courage necessary to believe in himself again. He finally did. His own efforts combined with those of Nan helped John overcome the forces that pressed him toward life in a mental hospital. Even later, when I met him, John still had to take special care of his health, not let himself become run down, and make sure he spent plenty of time with people. Otherwise, his delusions could return. But he had begun the long road to recovery. Even during the darkest period of his life, John retained his choice to have control over his life, and, fortunately for him, he chose to become sane.

Growth and Potential

The humanists believe our goal as human beings is to grow and expand toward our **potential,** the best we can be. That faith remains one of the most appealing aspects of their psychological approach. James Bugental tells us in *The Nature and Task of Humanistic Psychology:*

> We sense the fantastic potential in human thought, imagination, and communication, and become aware of the dizzying vastness of possibility that can keep pace with the universe's immensity, for only man's thought can hope to match that incredible range. (15)

Rather than look at people as objects to be manipulated by the environment, the humanists see them as growth-centered and in charge of their environment. Thus, according to the humanists, a person's primary goal is growth. As we experience and acknowledge the attitudes, feelings, and emotions that restrict our free enjoyment of life, we expand our ability to learn about ouselves and live life to the fullest.

Humanists stress the importance of the "prizes" that people traditionally hope life will offer them—openness to life, trust in personal abilities, potential to grow through experience—to name only a few. These goals are sought directly by humanist therapists. And the humanists, as well as those who have completed humanistic therapy successfully, claim that the direct encounter with personal thoughts and feelings brought them closer to the emotional joys of life than they ever thought possible.

Humanists search to release the potential in each person. (Ulrike Welsch)

CONCLUSION

The various psychological approaches to studying the self remind me of the old fable about the three blind men who attempted to describe an elephant. The first man positioned himself at the tail of the elephant; the second man, at the trunk; and the third one, at the leg. Each man described what he observed to the other two. The descriptions were so contradictory the three men could never gain any consistent picture of the elephant.

In our approach to the self, we can be compared to those blind men. We begin with no consistent concept of the self. So we describe the various functions of the self without any insight into how those functions work together to create a unity. To make our task even more difficult, our approaches are quite diverse. The behaviorists only look at measurable behavior. The humanists restrict their focus to the emotions and feelings. The psychoanalysts attend to the unconscious and its role in life. No wonder we don't end up with a unified description of the self.

Many psychologists spend a great deal of time refuting one another's theories, pointing out how a rival theory cannot possibly be true. Unfortunately, they do not spend a proportionate amount of time attempting to reconcile the different theories. It would be better if psychologists devoted more time to discovering how the various theories about the self can work together to provide us with a clearer understanding of ourselves. Most of us forget, in our attempts to understand the self, that no single theory is necessarily correct. In fact, because of the many approaches, there is a good chance that various parts of all the theories are valid. We can look at several theories to find the elements of each that give us insight into ourselves.

A natural question for any student about to study the various theories of the self is, What is the best way to approach such diversity? My own answer to that question came to me from a friend who had a similar problem when he studied the various religions of the world. He wondered how he could gain insight into religion in general through his study of so many separate religions.

My friend's answer came to him in a flash of insight. He had been studying each religion as if it must be correct or incorrect. More important, he had been looking at each religion as a critic from the outside. Then he decided he should look at religion from the inside out: thus, to study Buddhism, he assumed the mind of a Buddhist; to study Judaism, he mentally became a Jew; to study Christianity, he adopted the mind of a Christian. Only through this perspective could my friend gain insight into the religions that seemed to contradict each other so dramatically.

John Dunne called the process he brought to the study of religion "passing over," which indicated a passing over from one culture to another.

Passing over is a shifting of standpoint, a going over to the standpoint of another culture, another way of life, another religion. It is followed by an equal and opposite process we might call "coming back," coming back with new insight to one's own culture, one's own way of life, one's own religion. (16)

Our study of the self should follow the same process. We cannot study the various schools of thought from the outside. Instead, we must adopt the mentality of a psychoanalyst to gain insight from psychoanalytic theories. To understand behavioristic theories, we must see them from a behavioristic point of view. Only when we become humanists can we understand the humanists' ideas.

We need not become uncritical when we immerse ourselves in the various theories. Yet a person prepared only to criticize cannot gain much from any theoretical view. If we immerse ourselves in a theory, we can catch a glimpse of our own experience and a better understanding of ourselves from that theory—without losing sight of its shortcomings. When we learn all we can in this way about several theories, we will surely understand ourselves better.

SUMMARY

1. In each of life's situations, we experience ourselves differently. The confusion these experiences cause leads many people to try to understand or at least systematically to study themselves more carefully. Quite often, we turn to psychologists for help in our attempts to gain such understanding. Ironically, however, psychologists often disagree with one another on the proper approach to the study of the self.
2. The psychoanalytic school of thought believes unconscious forces direct the personality. These psychologists also think that childhood experiences permanently affect the personality. Once we understand the struggle taking place between the id, the ego, and the superego, say the Freudians, we will understand ourselves.
3. The behaviorists claim the only proper study of the self is based on behavior. Their studies of such behavior lead psychologists to believe that our behavior occurs because we were once rewarded for it and thus repeat it. They further believe that we will one day be able to predict and control behavior.
4. The humanists, instead of concentrating on observable behavior, focus their attention on emotions and feelings. This approach leads them to believe that our behavior is subjective and that people remain free to make choices. Possibly the most appealing aspect of this philosophy is its belief that our goal is growth toward our greatest potential.
5. These three separate approaches to the self seem too diverse ever to be reconciled. Yet that attitude grows from the false notion that all aspects

of one approach must be correct and the other approaches totally wrong. But if we look at all approaches and explanations as offering us some parts of a total truth, we can gain significant insights into ourselves.

KEY TERMS

self
unconscious
id
ego
superego
pleasure principle
reality principle

defense mechanisms
reward
positiver reinforcer
behavior control
emotion
subjective
human potential

STUDY QUESTIONS

1. Try to think of some ways in which the unconscious has an influence on your daily life.
2. Explain the fundamental reason that makes you either agree or disagree with Freud's attitude that the adult personality is completely formed by the age of five.
3. Do you agree with the many behaviorists who believe psychologists waste their time when they try to study intangible concepts like love, fear, or loneliness? Explain.
4. How much of your own behavior do you believe you learned through the use of rewards? Give an example.
5. What would be some of the objections humanists would raise to the behaviorist's theory that we learn only through rewards?
6. If you were in need of some professional therapy, would you tend to choose someone with a psychoanalytic, behavioristic, or humanistic background? Why?

ADDITIONAL READING

Bry, Adelaide. *A Primer of Behavior Psychology*. New York: New American Library, 1975.

Clark, K. E., and Miller, G. (Eds.) *Psychology*. Englewood Cliffs, N.J.: Prentice-Hall, 1970.

Freud, Sigmund. *New Introductory Lectures on Psychoanalysis*. Translated by James Strachey. New York: W. W. Norton, 1965.

Hall, Calvin. *A Primer of Freudian Psychology*. New York: New American Library (Mentor), 1965.

May, Rollo. *Man's Search for Himself*. New York: New American Library (Signet), 1967.
Murphy, G., and Kovach, J. K., *Historical Introduction to Modern Psychology* New York: Harcourt Brace Jovanovich, 1972.
Norby, V. J., and Hall, C. S. *A Guide to Psychologists and Their Concepts*. San Francisco: W. H. Freeman, 1974.
Rogers, Carl. *On Becoming a Person*. Boston: Houghton Mifflin, 1961.
Skinner, B. F. *About Behaviorism*. New York: Vintage, 1976.

Chapter Two

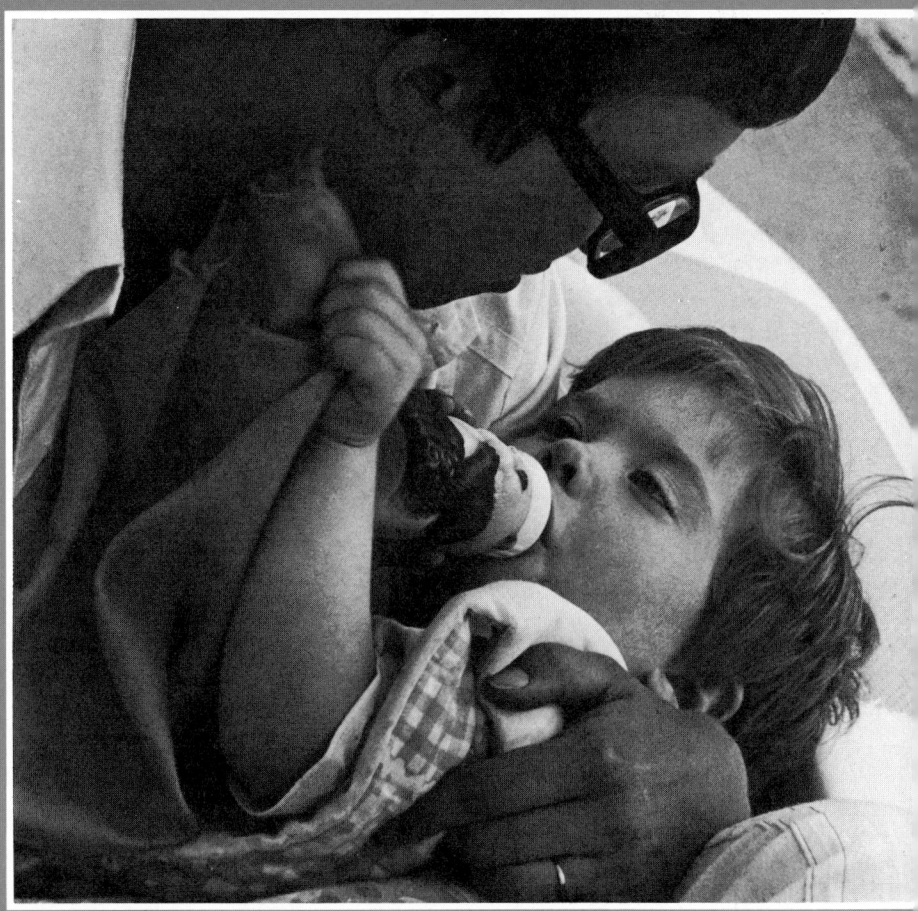

Personality

OUTLINE

The Psychoanalytic Approach
    The Oral Stage
    The Anal Stage
    The Oedipus Complex
    The Electra Complex

The Behavioristic Approach
    Environmental Formation
    Reward and the Personality
    Extinction and the Personality

The Humanistic Approach
    Personal Choices
    Emotional Experiences
    Honest Relationships
    Self-Actualization

Conclusion

LEARNING OBJECTIVES

After reading this chapter you should be able to:

1. Explain the oral, anal, and phallic stages in Freud's psychoanalytic theory.
2. Discuss the differences between the Oedipus complex in boys and the Electra complex in girls.
3. Discuss what factors the behaviorists claim create personality differences in individuals.
4. Explain the role of reward and extinction in the development of the personality.
5. Discuss the factors the humanists feel contribute most to personality development.
6. Understand the goal humanists set for the individual personality.

Chapter Two

Jeff, a high school sophomore, spent hours in front of the mirror making sure his hair looked just right. He sometimes fretted about what he should wear on a given occasion. He never forgot the time he wore his blue slacks to a basketball game only to discover all his friends wearing jeans. More important, whenever he joined a group of friends, he assumed the casual manner that they seemed to have. If the topic was professional football, he knew just what degree of enthusiasm to display for the local team. In fact, he could respond correctly to almost any topic his friends might choose to discuss.

Jeff knew how to react to make certain he remained friends with his high school buddies. What he did not realize was that his personality, because of his effort to conform, became based on elements originating from sources outside of himself. He hid from his uniqueness because he didn't want to be "different." He did not reveal some parts of his personality because those parts embarrassed him. He knew he tended to be far more sensitive to sunsets, flowers, and lovely landscaped lawns, for example, than any of his friends. Yet, he feared that if they discovered that sensitivity, they would laugh at him. So it was with everything that made Jeff unique. He feared letting others see his individuality.

When people like Jeff finally do decide they want to begin a search for themselves, they must first look for a means or a method. The early professional psychologists who began serious studies of such journeys into the self quickly saw that various paths are possible. As we saw in the first chapter, the psychoanalysts show us a path that involves looking at our unconscious and our early childhood. The behaviorists suggest we come to know ourselves best when we confine our study to our behavior and its consequences. Finally, the humanists suggest we might better focus our attention on our emotions, our growth potential, and our free choices. A reflective look at these three approaches to the self suggests we should consider all three attitudes before we draw any definite conclusions about ourselves.

As we start our self-exploration, our initial look at the various attitudes toward the self tells us about what we have in common with all people. Everyone wonders how free our choices are and how much we are determined by outside factors. We commonly look at our behavior to find out more about ourselves. As we look more closely, we discover the qualities

Our search for ourself begins when we try to discover the uniqueness in our personality. (Eric Kroll/Taurus)

that are unique to us. We begin to see what outside factors make us more apt to be outgoing than shy, why we experience fear during occasions when everyone else seems calm, why we grow close to one person rather than another. We start to look at our personality—the uniqueness of our self (Self-Quiz 2.1).

Each of the three psychological schools of thought emphasizes different ways to look at ourselves and our experiences to discover what makes us unique. The psychoanalysts say we must carefully study our childhood to determine how our development differs from that of everyone else. This involves remembering experiences that can be difficult and even painful to recall. The behaviorists want us to look objectively at our experiences. Again, we might want to resist the study we are asked to make. For instance, it can be painful to see how much we are manipulated by people and events. The humanists ask us to notice those emotions we might rather hide, to accept the weaknesses we do not want to admit, and even to express openly the most embarrassing things about ourselves. All three of the approaches, then, demand self-exploration that can be painful or uncomfortable, but in the end, enlightening.

Each school of thought demands courage from us in our search to see our personality development clearly, because what makes us unique can be embarrassing. Most people want to be inconspicuous—a part of the crowd. That tendency presses us to conform to other people's standards rather than to stand out as individuals. We can have true knowledge of ourselves only if we have the courage to accept our personalities as unique and to face ourselves with honesty.

As a therapist, I enjoy watching people as they begin to explore themselves. Most of the people who come to me find it difficult at first to talk about the things that set them apart from others. One young woman thinks she talks far too much for anyone to enjoy being with her. A middle-

Self-Quiz 2.1 — Word Association

Psychoanalytical psychologists sometimes use word-association tests to gain insight into the personality. Ask a friend to read the following list of words to you, one word at a time, and time how long it takes you to make an association with each word. For example, to the word *black*, you might respond *white*. To the word *up*, you might respond *down*. By looking at your associations and the length of time it takes you to respond to each word, you can learn something about yourself. Some psychologists suggest that people being tested hesitate longest when they try to make associations with words that have special emotional meanings.

1. tree
2. mother
3. kiss
4. paper
5. mouth
6. fish
7. breast
8. sex
9. apple
10. ocean
11. father
12. fire
13. rain
14. death
15. chair
16. barn
17. anger
18. love
19. infant
20. bathroom

---

aged man feels that he is too shy and withdrawn to attract friends. I recall a sad-faced truck driver who thought no one could ever like him because he laughed so loudly. A young bank clerk suffered serious anxiety because she constantly worried someone would notice her slight tendency to stammer.

The therapy process helps such people accept their uniqueness. Sometimes the path to self-acceptance is filled with obstacles, and people often fear nothing more than the discovery of their own personality. But as therapy progresses, such anxieties fade, and individuality becomes acceptable. In time, the uniqueness that once caused so much pain can become a source of pleasure, even pride.

THE PSYCHOANALYTIC APPROACH

The Oral Stage

According to Sigmund Freud, children begin to develop their personalities immediately after birth. Beginning with their first day of life, infants gradually discover that they are totally dependent on their mothers for all their needs, including nourishment. Infants can only cooperate in sustaining their life by sucking. This sucking process is so important in infants' lives that Freud believed it must give them some fundamental pleasure, similar to sexual pleasure, because they are assuring their survival and the survival of the race. Freud called the period of early infancy the **oral stage.**

Erik Erikson, a well-known neo-Freudian, elaborated on Freud's theory. He noted that this dependence of children on their mothers is so total that it determines how much or little they will trust the world as adults. If the mother is nurturing and responds to the need for food quickly, the infant learns to trust the world. If the mother neglects cries of hunger or punishes the infant for the cries, the infant learns to mistrust the world. How much or how little we trust others and ourselves later in life, Erikson felt, depends to a great extent on how we were treated during those first months of life

> Mothers create a sense of trust in their children by sensitive care of the baby's individual needs and a firm sense of personal trustworthiness. This forms the basis in the child for a sense of identity which will later combine a sense of being "all right," of being oneself, and of becoming what other people trust one will become. (1)

Freud also saw strong connections between infants' experiences in the oral stage and later personality characteristics. He labeled one particular effect of poor early experience "oral aggression." Those children who lack proper affection at the oral stage, Freud thought, can become orally aggressive later in life. A study by Bonnie W. Camp of the University of Colorado School of Medicine suggested one way in which oral aggression might be reflected in behavior. Camp tested 95 first- and second-grade boys and separated them into two groups she labeled normal and unusually aggressive. She noticed that the aggressive boys mumbled, rambled, and whispered in patterns designed to provoke hostility. The speech patterns of the nonaggressive boys, by contrast, showed that they developed mature patterns characterized by consideration and self-control. (2)

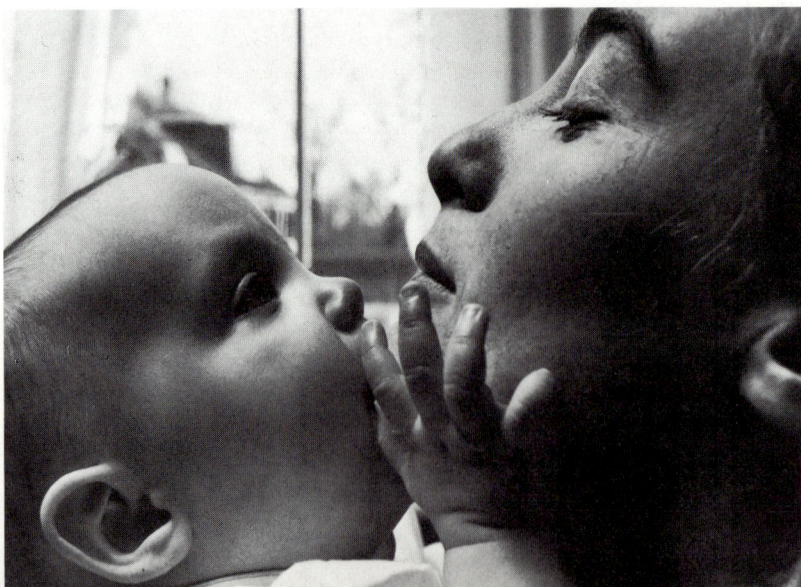

As infants we depend entirely on others for our survival. (Burk Uzzle/Magnum)

Smoking is one way Freud thought that adults satisfy their oral needs. (© Joel Gordon)

The Anal Stage

Most parents know only too well about the "terrible twos" and the struggle they have with children of that age as they grow anxious to express themselves and become independent. Just as Freud saw the mouth as a source of pleasure during the first stage of life, he also saw the anus as a pleasure source during the scond stage, called the **anal stage**. Children experience the buildup of feces at the anus and feel great relief when they release that pressure. If parents attempt to control this instinctively pleasurable experience during the toilet training years, the two-year-old child may react with great resistance. J. Langer writes in his book *Theories of Development:*

> Freud maintained that in the second psychosexual stage (from about one to three years of age) the child's instinctual urges shift to the anal erogenous zone and its functions of retention and evacuation. These modes of functioning require the child to attempt actively to master his own impulses. They also presumably occasion the first direct parental attempts to teach the child to inhibit his natural tendencies by toilet training. The importance of this stage for later development lies particularly in the fact that it marks the initial appearance of ambivalence between impulsive and inhibitory tendencies. At the anal stage the primary observable ambivalence is the child's indecision whether to be active (outgoing, intruding upon the world and exploring it) or to remain passive. (3)

According to Freud, parents who initiate harsh measures during toilet training can leave children with feelings of shame that remain with them for the rest of their lives. Children who are punished or shamed for their inability to control their bowels may suffer permanent doubts about all their abilities. By contrast, parents who help their children discover their ability to control their bowels can build feelings of confidence and autonomy in their children. The proper parental approach during the toilet-training period, then, can lead the child to independence. Harsh punishment during this period can create self-doubt that remains a permanent part of the child's personality.

The Oedipus Complex

Freud called the third stage of childhood development the **phallic stage.** For the male child, this stage marks the beginning of the **Oedipus complex,** named after King Oedipus from Greek tragedy who, through a bizarre set of circumstances, unwittingly killed his father and married his mother. In parallel fashion, Freud thought, each male child develops strong sexual feelings for his mother and hostility toward his father and begins to think of himself as a rival with his father for his mother's attention (Case 2.1). Hall and Lindzey tell us in their book *Theories of Personality:*

> The boy's incestuous craving for the mother and his growing resentment toward the father bring him into conflict with his parents, especially the father. He imagines that his dominant rival is going to harm him, and his fears may actually be confirmed by threats from a resentful and punitive father. His fears concerning what the father may do to him center around harm to his genital organs because they are the source of his lustful feelings. He is afraid that his jealous father will remove the offending organs. Fear of castration or, as Freud called it, **castration anxiety,** induces a repression of the sexual desire for the mother and hostility toward the father. (4)

Momma by Mell Lazarus. Courtesy of Mell Lazarus and Field Newspaper Syndicate.

During the phallic stage the child also realizes that he has no chance of defeating his father as a rival. So he learns to identify with his father in hopes that he will learn how to gain similar power. How well or poorly the male child resolves the Oedipus conflict will permanently affect his sexual attitudes for the rest of his life. Freud saw unresolved Oedipal struggles as the primary source of sexual conflict in all males.

Freud never spelled out all of the ways in which the unresolved Oedipus complex created sexual aberrations later in life. He did say, however, that sexuality can become confused with anger, fear, and powerlessness. A striking example of such a distortion was found recently in a study done with males convicted of rape. A. Nicholas Groth and Ann Burgess investigated the sexual functioning of 170 men convicted of sexual assault. One-third of them, it turned out, experienced sexual dysfunction, or malfunction, most often in the form of impotence or retarded ejaculation during rape. The researchers also reported that among a sample of 69 women who had been victims of rape, sperm were found in less than half the cases. Even among 23 victims who had been raped by more than one man, only one-half showed traces of sperm.

The most obvious Freudian application of their findings appears in the courtroom. Juries remain reluctant to convict rapists unless sperm is found in the victim's vagina, believing that rape is an act of sexual aggression. Groth and Burgess, however, are convinced that "rape is not simply a normal extension of the sexuality of the male but that it is much more a use of sexuality for nonsexual needs and symptomatic of a defect in personality and development." (5) Freud might have defined rape in the same way.

- Case 2.1

If it is not successfully resolved, the Oedipus complex can cause conflict indefinitely. A young man's rivalry with his father, for example, is sometimes never resolved.

Such unresolved conflicts caused Allen unreasonable turmoil long after his thirtieth birthday. Everyone who knew Allen assumed he would never be anything but a failure. His high IQ seemed to be of no help to him in his schooling. Every time he took an examination, his mind went blank and he wound up failing more exams than he passed. In the end, he was fortunate to receive his high school diploma. Allen's failures were particularly painful for his father, who held a prominent teaching position at a state university.

When he finally entered therapy, Allen was working as a clerk in a shoe store. That job was the ninth position he held in thirteen years. His failure in the world of work matched his poor record at school. Nothing went well for him. Only after painful months of therapy did Allen discover his unresolved feelings toward his father. As far back as he could remember, he resented his father because he always felt a sense of competition in their relationship. The feelings that finally emerged in therapy were bitter and hateful. In a fit of anger, Allen once said, "I cannot even remember a time when I did not hate my father."

Once his feelings came to light, however, Allen could see them more objectively. With much patience and understanding from his therapist, Allen gradually began to cope with his anger. In time, he talked to his father about his feelings of competition and anger. Though they never became close to one another, at least Allen made peace with his father and stopped wasting so much emotional energy on destructive inner conflicts.

The Electra Complex

Freud called the phallic struggle for females the **Electra complex.** The sequence of events that leads to its development and resolution is more complicated than that of the Oedipus complex. First of all, the female must turn from her first love, her mother, to a new love, her father, when she discovers that she doesn't possess a penis. To use Sigmund Freud's own words:

> The castration complex of girls is started by the sight of the genitals of the other sex. They at once notice the difference and, it must be admitted, its significance too. They feel seriously wronged, often declare that they want to "have something like it too," and fall a victim to "envy for the penis," which will leave ineradicable traces on their development and the formation of their character and which will not be surmounted in even the most favorable cases without a severe expenditure of energy. The girl's recognition of the fact of her being without a penis does not by any means imply that she submits to the fact easily. On the contrary, she continues to hold on for a long time to the wish to get something like it herself and she believes in that possibility for improbably long years. (6)

According to Freud, because the female holds her mother responsible for the loss of her penis, she turns to her father who has the valued organ. Unfortunately, her love for her father, as well as her love for other men, becomes tainted with feelings of envy. Like the young male, the female becomes preoccupied with the penis. Rather than fear her penis will be cut off, however, she feels she has already lost this valued possession.

The Electra complex for girls parallels the Oedipus complex for boys. The young woman wants to take her mother's role as wife and lover to her father. The need to repress her feelings, however, never becomes as acute for her as for young men. Boys do not feel free to be physically affectionate. Though the girl represses her desire for sexual intercourse with her father because of obvious restrictions of reality, she is allowed to be much more free with her demonstrations of affection. This difference between male and female approaches to sexual feelings accounts, Freud says, for many of the different sexual attitudes between men and women.

Many people, not just feminists, object to Freud's chauvinistic **penis-envy** theory. The roots to such objections are not new. Karen Horney, the eminent psychoanalyst and theoretician, took strong objection to Freud's

Freud believed that society allows little girls a great deal of freedom in showing affection for their fathers. (Peter Vandermark)

theory of the penis envy. In its place she proposed, in a 1927 paper, a theory of womb envy. The theory suggests men envy women their power to bear children. Her argument from a feminine perspective seems every bit as convincing as Freud's masculine standpoint. Unfortunately, we may overlook some basic Freudian insights by totally dismissing his theory as sexist.

THE BEHAVIORISTIC APPROACH

Behaviorism grew as a psychological force because so many psychologists thought theories of personality were not based on any facts. The Freudian explanation of the sexual stages of development, for example, struck behaviorists as nothing more than a series of sophisticated guesses. The behaviorists saw a certain irony in theories that claimed to "explain" behavior. More often than not the theories needed to be explained themselves. And no matter how hard theorists attempt to explain their theories, they seldom have any conclusive evidence. B. F. Skinner, one of the best-known behaviorists, did not believe theory was valuable to psychology. Hall and Lindzey tell us:

> It would be difficult to find a theorist who was less enthusiastic about being cast in the role of theorist than Skinner. In spite of his enormous theoretical influence he has until recently questioned the contribution of theory to scientific development and has looked on his own work as illustrating an informed and systematic empiricism that operates without theoretical derivation. He has consistently opposed any attempt to fill in the gap between observed events with inferred or hypothesized variables. His intent has been to gather behavioral data and organize them into a

systematic framework of behavioral laws with no "explanatory fictions" at all. (7)

Behaviorists think theories of personality can become problems in themselves. For example, once we decide how a **schizophrenic** ought to act, we tend to expect that behavior of anyone labeled schizophrenic. Therapists, once they believe one or another theory of schizophrenia, begin to look for certain symptoms. Patients may learn to respond to such expectations and acquire the symptoms to please their therapists and, in the process, upset themselves more. The same holds true of any label we might apply to a person suffering emotional turmoil.

It is better to abandon all preconceptions of the person and only observe behavior, say the behaviorists. Whenever we observe and measure how long a person talks, how shrill his voice becomes, how long her silent periods persist, how often he engages in physical activity, how early she retires in the evening, we begin to see the person clearly, and we have supporting evidence for conclusions about his or her personality. Then our theories do not stand between us and the people we would like to understand.

Ironically, labels apparently also distort our understanding of behaviorism. An interesting study, conducted by psychologists Anita Woolfolk, Robert Woolfolk, and G. Terence Wilson, demonstrated the power of psychological labels. They asked 144 college juniors and 50 graduate students to view a teaching approach used in a special-education class. The tape included three ten-minute segments showing a teacher working with emotionally disturbed second graders. Two different sound tracks were attached to the same videotape picture. In one case, the teaching strategy was described as an example of behavior modification. Phrases such as "appropriate stimuli," "control of disruptive behavior," and "selective attention" were used. The other sound track labeled the same visual scenes as examples of humanistic and affective education. In this second case, "self-awareness," "secure environment," and "self-esteem" were some of the phrases used.

The group of students who saw the videotape with the behavioristic-oriented sound track did not like the teacher and technique nearly as much as those who heard the humanistic description. Those who thought they had witnessed a humanistic approach perceived the teacher as more competent, more personally attractive, more flexible, and the method more attractive. Apparently, the verbal labels distorted the students' perception of what they saw. (8)

Environmental Formation

Although behaviorists reject the notion of a theory of personality, theories do emerge from their work. The first thing that strikes most people who look at the work of the behaviorists is their attitude toward the child at

The Behavioristic Approach 39

birth. Because the behaviorists think we are formed almost completely by our **environment,** they believe the newborn infant is nearly free of any psychological content. Granted, they admit some innate responses in the most primitive sense. However, for practical purposes, we can think of the infant the behaviorists see as a piece of clay waiting to be formed by the environment.

Another image sometimes used to illustrate the behavioristic view of the infant is the **mechanical mirror.** The child enters the world like a mirror without much content of its own, and like the mirror, the infant reflects what happens around it. Whatever the child sees, hears, smells, or tastes has an immediate impact on the formation of that infant's personality in one direction or another. As J. Langer tells us:

> The child is born empty of psychological content into a world of coherently organized content. Like a mirror, however, the child comes to reflect his environment; like an empty slate he is written upon by external stimuli; like a wax tablet he stores the impressions left by these stimuli; and like a machine he may be made to react in response to stimulating agents. The contemporary mechanical mirror formulation adheres closely to such images. (9)

"Early on, Ed, I learned never to forget that these numbers are honest-to-God flesh-and-blood human beings."

Reward and the Personality

Though the behaviorists believe the infant begins life with only a few behavioral characteristics or innate responses, they also believe children are immediately influenced by their environment. The infant who is rewarded with a warm hug from its mother for producing a broad smile quickly learns to repeat that smile. Cries, children soon learn, bring parents running to discover the cause of the cry. The infant will repeat the slightest behavior that is rewarded. Early in life, then, the child begins to develop a personality based on the reward patterns that have been reinforced by parents and others in the environment (Case 2.2). B. F. Skinner explains this behavioristic concept:

> When a given act is almost always reinforced, a person is said to have a feeling of confidence. A tennis player reports that he practices a particular shot "until he feel confident;" the basic fact is that he practices until a certain proportion of his shots are good. Frequent reinforcement also builds faith. A person feels sure, or certain, that he will be successful. He enjoys a sense of mastery, power, or potency. The infant is said to acquire a sense of infantile omnipotence. Frequent reinforcement also builds and maintains an interest in what a person is doing. In all this the behavior is erroneously attributed to the feelings rather than to the contingencies responsible for what is felt. (10)

Behaviorists believe that reinforcement is crucial in the development of our personality. (Peter Vandermark, far left; Harry Wilks/Stock, Boston, left)

Modern behaviorists do not totally deny the role of genetics in personality development. Rather, they emphasize the more significant contribution of reward to personality development. Children rewarded for bursts of emotion are likely to repeat those outbursts provided they continue to find rewards in such behavior. Another child, sometimes in the same family, finds rewards for repressing emotional displays. Such a child will probably develop an entirely different set of personality characteristics.

The effect of reward on child behavior was demonstrated in an interesting study done by James Kauffman, Russell Grieger, and Tanya Grieger. First they observed the amount of aggressive behavior and cooperative play among 90 children in two combined kindergarten classes. They observed the children for several days before introducing a daily ten-minute "sharing time" into the school schedule. During "sharing time," the children were given an opportunity to tell the class about classmates who had been friendly to them during the play period that day. The children named were allowed to reward themselves with a happy-face badge from a hook prominently displayed on the wall. As might be expected, the number of aggressive acts per day dropped from an average of 42 to 9. Even after the happy-face badges were gradually dropped from the program, the level of aggression remained low so long as "sharing time" remained an integral part of the day. (11)

• Case 2.2

Behaviorists believe that a careful use of reward can help people overcome most serious problems. Rather than attempt to find the mental or emotional cause of the difficulty, as many other psychologists do, the behaviorists begin to reward desired behavior. At times the results can be amazing. Take, for example, Cheryl who began to lose a great deal of weight during her last year in grade school. At first, the weight loss improved her figure. Her friends complimented her, and Cheryl liked how she looked. Before long, however, weight loss became a compulsive drive. Even after her friends stopped complimenting her and began to express concern, Cheryl could not stop her dramatic dieting. Cheryl started to experience periods of depression; her moods became sober, at times even hostile. She embarrassed her friends with sudden bursts of uncontrolled emotion and also worried those same friends with periods of isolation.

Finally, her moods frightened even Cheryl. She made an appointment with a school counselor. He talked to Cheryl at some length about her moods and also about her weight loss. The counselor suggested to Cheryl that her weight loss was not only physically but also mentally dangerous. Cheryl replied that her diet was now so much a part of her she doubted she could change. He suggested she begin slowly, only asking her to gain one pound during the following week. When Cheryl returned to the counselor's office, she reported good news about a one-pound weight gain. The psychologist gave her strong positive reinforcement by telling her how much better she looked with even the one pound of extra weight. Before long, Cheryl replaced five lost pounds. With the extra weight and the psychologist's sincere encouragement, Cheryl not only gained the lost weight but also found relief from the depressing moods that plagued her.

Extinction and the Personality

How often rewards are given as well as when those rewards are given are among the many factors that influence the development of the personality. In particular, it is important to note that if a person is regularly rewarded for a given behavior, he comes to need those rewards. Without the reward, **extinction** occurs. Behaviorists use the term extinction to refer to quickly ended behavior. For example, the child who receives a "treat" every time she cleans her room will come to rely on the treat. If the treat stops, and no other reward such as praise is begun, her willingness to clean her room stops also. B. F. Skinner explains extinction:

> When reinforcement is no longer forthcoming, behavior undergoes "extinction" and appears rarely, if at all. A person is then said to suffer a loss of confidence, certainty, or sense of power. Instead, her feelings range from a lack of interest through disappointment, discouragement, and a sense of impotence to a possibly deep depression and these feelings are then said—erroneously—to explain the absence of the behavior. For example, a person is said to be unable to go to work because he is discouraged or depressed, although his not going, together with what he feels, is due to a lack of reinforcement—either in his work or in some other part of his life. (12)

Peanuts. © 1958 United Feature Syndicate, Inc.

Behavior that receives only occasional rewards is much more difficult to extinguish than regularly rewarded behavior. For example, if a child who knows he must go to bed at ten o'clock every night is permitted on one particular evening to stay up late to watch television, he may never forget that reward. The child may pester parents for months, even years, to be allowed to stay up late again.

Most behaviorists believe parents unwittingly set personality characteristics in their children. Without intending to, they reward behavior they might actually deplore. Behaviorists think such an unaware approach to child rearing is unfortunate. They believe a more scientific approach to child care can help parents form healthier and happier personalities in their children (Case 2.3).

● Case 2.3

Many parents find that the reward approach can help them deal with the normal difficulties we expect from every child. In this context, I remember when Anne, a neighbor, stopped me on my walk to school one day and said, "You're a psychologist. Maybe you can help me. My son, Tommy, must be about the most troublesome four-year-old in the world."

"I'm not sure I know what you mean," I replied.

"He expects me to spend my entire day playing with him. I can't leave him for five minutes without him making some big scene. He starts to fuss and cry the minute I turn to work that just has to get done."

"It sounds to me like you reward all his crying and fussing," I said hesitantly.

"Oh, no! I spend a great deal of time scolding him, telling him why I can't play with him, and even punishing him." Anne was angry.

"That's what I mean. All the time you talk to him, even when you might be punishing him, you pay attention to him. Many children would rather be punished than ignored."

"Now I'm the one who doesn't understand," Anne replied.

"Tommy may just want your attention. He may also know only one way to get it — kick up a fuss. Then, even though he might receive punishment, he at least has your attention."

"So what can I do?" Anne's eyebrows pulled together with concern.

"One thing you can do is begin to reward Tommy when he acts the way you hope he will. Any time you see him playing quietly alone, give him a little hug and tell him what a fine boy he is."

"And the times he creates a fuss?" Anne interrupted.

"That's the hardest part. Ideally, you should ignore him when he tries to get such attention from you. That can be impossible at times. But the less you pay attention to that behavior the more quickly it will disappear."

When Anne saw me about three weeks later, she was glowing. She could not believe the change in Tommy. While he still did not qualify for any "child of the year" award, he spent much more of his day playing quietly by himself and less time creating conflict.

THE HUMANISTIC APPROACH

Unlike the psychoanalysts or the behaviorists, the humanists do not focus their attention on childhood or on reward. Instead, they center their study on the person as an **organism.** Like other organisms that follow a process toward fulfillment—animals, trees, and flowers—people have the purpose of growing to their full potential. Just as the flower becomes fully itself by reaching maturity, so people become fulfilled by becoming fully human (Case 2.4).

Humanists make special note of the difference between other organisms and the person—**free choice.** This freedom, psychologist Rollo May says,

> is man's capacity to take a hand in his own development. It is our capacity to mold ourselves. Freedom is the other side of consciousness of self: if we were not able to be aware of ourselves, we would be pushed along by instinct or the automatic march of history, like bees or mastodons. But by our power to be conscious of ourselves, we can call to mind how we acted yesterday or last month, and by learning from these actions we can influence, if ever so little, how we act today. (13)

People can be actively involved in their growth toward personal fulfillment. Naturally, with free choice, they can also flee the difficult decisions that would help them grow. They can blame their parents for not making it possible for them to function fully; they can blame society, their spouse, their children, their friends—almost anyone and anything. People who are fulfilled, however, have had to make difficult personal choices along the way. Such difficult choices, say the humanists, lead responsible people toward their own unique personalities.

● Case 2.4

Every time I think about the humanist's theory that we bring living organisms to fruition by nurturing them properly, I recall Cindy. She was a beautiful five-year-old child, but unfortunately, sadness dulled her eyes most of the time. Her mother, a nervous woman, worried about Cindy almost constantly. In her need to help Cindy, she kept the little girl in a state of turmoil. And the more her mother hovered over Cindy and tried to help her emerge from her sadness, the less Cindy seemed to respond. Finally, a neighbor's urging pressed Cindy's mother to seek the aid of a psychiatrist.

The psychiatrist, skilled in play therapy, diagnosed the situation immediately. He saw the suffocating effect Cindy's mother had on her, so he directed his play therapy to giving Cindy maximum freedom when they were together. He and Cindy remained, for the clinical hour, in a room filled with toys, games, and dolls. Cindy sat in the middle of the floor and made no move to play with any of the toys or talk to the psychiatrist. The psychiatrist let Cindy have this freedom, and his approach paid large dividends. Before the end of the first session, Cindy began to talk with him.

The psychiatrist permitted Cindy the same freedom every session they spent together. Some days Cindy used the freedom to play and only incidently talked to the psychiatrist. Often her play symbolized her home conflicts. She sometimes played with a mother doll and a child doll, for example, and talked about their relationship. The stories usually gave Cindy a chance to express indirectly her inner turmoil; they also gave the psychiatrist an insight into how she coped with her mother's overprotectiveness. On other days, Cindy talked directly to the psychiatrist about her problems.

Cindy spent many months coming out of her turmoil, but the psychiatrist's patience and his belief in Cindy were finally successful. She responded to his trust in her and started to grow again as children do when allowed to be spontaneous.

Personal Choices

Humanists insist that growth only occurs through proper choices. We, of course, want to know what those choices are and how we should make them. Humanists believe that the important choices for us are those we make for ourselves; in other words, we should make choices that seem right to us and not choices that other people tell us we should choose. One young person makes a personal choice when he decides he must leave home now rather than waiting for the time his parents feel would be right. The young mother who decides, in the face of her husband's disagreement, that she must return to college even before her children are grown is making an important personal choice (Case 2.5). Such choices are the proper choices to help us grow toward our fulfillment as a person. Carl Rogers says:

> In choosing what course of action to take in any situation many people rely upon guiding principles, upon a code of action laid down by some

group or institution, upon the judgment of others (from wife and friends to Emily Post), or upon the way they have behaved in some similar past situation. Yet as I observe the clients whose experiences in living have taught me so much, I find that increasingly such individuals are able to trust their total organismic reaction to a new situation because they discover to an ever-increasing degree that if they are open to their experience, doing what "feels right" proves to be a competent and trustworthy guide to behavior which is truly satisfying. (14)

This process of choosing by our own inner sense of right and wrong leads us, say the humanists, to a value system. They do not claim our choices will always be correct. Using our own sense of logic and following our emotions may lead us astray at times. We might well make choices that will prove destructive to ourselves and others, but those mistakes will help us make better future choices. In the process, we develop for ourselves a well-tuned sense of personal value and, ultimately, personal fulfillment.

• Case 2.5

The humanists tell us we grow only when we make proper choices. The proper choices, they say, are those we make for ourselves. Many times, those personal choices are opposed by others, even those we love, because they appear to be illogical.

Linda was a person who made such a choice. That young mother, by her own admission, had everything. Her husband could not have been more devoted. Their children, though they loved to be "into everything," were healthy and happy. Though the budget became strained at times, the financial situation usually worked out. So no one could have been more surprised than Linda when she went into a depression. At first, she and her husband simply explained away the small bursts of sadness that overcame her from time to time. A weekend camping trip or a special night out usually lifted her spirits until the depression periods grew more intense.

Linda thought of seeking professional help until one night she had a vivid dream. In the dream, she found herself in the top room of a high tower doing nothing. From her turret window she could see beauty all around her, but inside the tower she was alone and lonely. In interpreting the dream to her husband later, she told him she felt as if she had no value. She never finished college. Her friends did not talk about anything she considered serious. She had no career possibilities if something should happen to him. She felt she must, now that the children were both in school, return to college and begin to develop some interests and skills.

Linda's husband, as well as most of her friends, tried to discourage her from her plans. They said it would take her forever to finish college on a parttime basis and pointed out that she had no real need for a degree. Everyone but Linda thought her move made no sense at all. In spite of the extra work college meant and in the face of so many objections, however, Linda returned to college. The first semester proved more difficult than she ever imagined, and she found herself embarrassed to be in a classroom with so many young people. Her memory skills had faded some, and study time was hard to find while running a household. But Linda was so busy she forgot all about ever having been depressed. Her routine soon smoothed out, and her enthusiasm grew. The decision to return to college not only relieved her depression, but also finally gave her a new sense of confidence in herself and her abilities.

Emotional Experiences

The humanists believe that most human emotions are valuable to experience. Not only are the emotional expressions of love, joy, and warmth good, the humanists also see anger, loneliness, and sadness as integral to our growth as a person. They ask people to pay attention to their anger, experience their loneliness, and be aware of their sadness, because the worst thing a person can do with unpleasant emotions is to deny them. Repressed anger grows turbulent and dangerous. People who try to deny lonely feelings only give those feelings time to become painful and grow out of perspective. Repressed sadness can cause depression and permanent pain. Instead of repressing, denying, and hiding from feelings that cause us pain, Carl Rogers and other humanists want us to experience those feelings and integrate them into our personality.

> In our daily lives there are a thousand and one reasons for not letting ourselves experience our attitudes fully, reasons from our past and from the present, reasons that reside within the social situation. It seems too dangerous, too potentially damaging, to experience them freely and fully. But in the safety and freedom of the therapeutic relationship, they can be experienced fully, clear to the limit of what they are. They can be and are experienced in a fashion that I like to think of as a "pure culture," so that for the moment the person *is* his fear, or he *is* his anger, or he *is* his tenderness, or whatever. (15)

The humanists place great emphasis on the **acceptance of feelings,** especially painful feelings. We do not have to like our loneliness, sadness, or anger, but we do need to accept them as part of our total personality. We come closer to our potential by letting ourselves be lonely at times, get down in the dumps for periods, and get good and angry at someone or something. Once we air our feelings, we have a better chance of having them pass through our system and free us to turn our attention elsewhere.

A study that demonstrates the value of an open and honest display of anger was done by W. Doyle Gentry and two of his colleagues. They examined what they termed "descriptive anger." Their study suggests that if you're angry with people you should tell them, and tell them why.

The three psychologists based their conclusions on an experiment they

The humanists suggest we should accept our feelings, particularly painful feelings such as loneliness and sadness. (© Susan Lapides 1979)

conducted with 60 undergraduate males. These students were led to believe they were participating in a study of competition. After they were paired with their opponents (actually research confederates) and placed in rooms separate from those opponents, they played a simple game to measure reaction time. The winner of the game would be allowed to administer a mild shock to the loser, the strength of which he could vary at will.

After a few trials, the winners began to increase the shock intensity indicator until they heard cries from the losers. The shouts were examples of descriptive anger in which the "opponents" described how painful the shock was that angered them. These experimental subjects who heard the shouts immediately began to lower the intensity indicator. Another group of students playing the same game, who did not hear the descriptive cries, continued to increase the shock level as the experiment continued. Gentry and his colleagues feel the descriptive bursts of anger actually lowered tensions in the subjects who heard the descriptive anger as compared to those who heard nothing. (16)

Honest Relationships

When we suppress our true feelings, we not only harm ourselves but also our relationships with other people. Humanists believe we should strive for openness with others to allow us to share not only our love with friends, but also our anger. Growth in a friendship means we can gradually tell our friends even the most embarrassing things about ourselves (Self-Quiz 2.2).

Self-Quiz 2.2 — Self-Disclosure

Next to each statement place the number 1, 2, 3, 4, or 5—depending on how characteristic each statement is of you. Continue the process for each of the statements. Then total your score.

- 5 strongly characteristic of me
- 4 moderately characteristic of me
- 3 neutral
- 2 moderately uncharacteristic of me
- 1 strongly uncharacteristic of me

____ 1. I would rather risk losing a friendship than ever lie to a friend.
____ 2. I can be enthusiastic about a movie, television show, or book with friends even though my friends do not share my enthusiasm.
____ 3. If I am depressed, I do not try to cheer up to avoid depressing others.
____ 4. I enjoy using the word love when it seems appropriate.
____ 5. When others express affection for me, I rarely become embarrassed.
____ 6. I would rather express my anger than hold hostile feelings inside myself.
____ 7. When an intimate friend makes me jealous, I let that person know my feelings.
____ 8. I can only cherish friendships in which I can express most of my feelings.
____ 9. I would find it difficult to think of loving someone who does not allow me to express anger openly.
____ 10. I believe people who can rid themselves of frustration by crying are fortunate.

____ TOTAL SCORE

42–50   Few students who took this quiz scored in this high range. Such high scores indicate an ability to be open emotionally with others.
32–41   The vast majority of students scored in this range. Such scores suggest you exhibit the same degree of openness as most people who took this test.
Below 32   Scores in this range fall below the norm for those who have taken the inventory. Such a score indicates you are ill at ease with an open expression of feeling.

One of the most valuable things people can do for themselves and for their relationships is to take chances. The humanists believe individuals and relationships both grow when the partners gradually become more willing to risk hurting their friends and being hurt by them. Friends who open themselves to such pain realize they can be misunderstood and even rejected. Yet it is far better to let a friend know how angry certain remarks make us than to "play it safe" and let the anger grow. Trust and growth in a relationship are possible only when painful and angry feelings are exposed. We cannot expose our anger to a friend without a great trust that the friendship can survive the honesty.

Self-Actualization

Abraham Maslow, an important humanist, felt psychologists spent far too much time studying the maladjusted person, so he devoted much of his study to the unusually well-adjusted person. He called such people **self-actualized,** or fully human. He discovered people began achieving self-actualization late in life, usually in their sixties. This finding confirms the humanists' notion that growth is part of an entire life process. The characteristics common to such self-actualized people also support this humanistic philosophy of growth.

In his book *A Third Force,* Frank Goble lists some of the characteristics Maslow found to be common to self-actualized people.

1. They can see life clearly, that is, see the world as it really is and not as they wish it would be.
2. They listen carefully to other people and can admit when they are wrong.
3. Their perception is less distorted by desires, anxieties, and fears.
4. They are dedicated to some work, duty, or vocation they consider important.
5. They suffer less internal conflict so that they have more energy for productive purposes.
6. They have a healthy respect for themselves and their ability.
7. They are highly independent and quite social.
8. They have a religious sense of a meaningful universe and an attitude toward life that could be called spiritual.
9. They form deep personal friendships, but only with a few people. These relationships do not exploit, but rather enhance all concerned.
10. They experience far less fear than the average person.

CONCLUSION

Each theory presented in this chapter helps us understand the development of our personality. If we take time to look at our childhood development from a psychoanalytic point of view, for example, we can see how much that period influenced us. A careful look at the behavioristic notion that we become who we are because of how our environment affects us helps us gain further insights. Finally, the humanists add a different perspective when they suggest we are free to make choices, and those choices determine just how our personalities will develop.

We must remember, however, that we will never gain insight into a theory if we stand outside that theory as critics. We must allow ourselves to become absorbed by the theory, the viewpoint, and the attitude that make the theory unique. There are rewards for using this open approach to studying the theories. If you are inclined to be sympathetic toward humanistic ideas, but take time to understand the behaviorist point of view, you will gain insights that would be impossible from studying the humanistic perspective alone.

As you study the different theories in this book, it would be valuable to keep a notebook or journal to record your insights. Many students find that after they have studied a theory that seems quite foreign to them, they experience a period when they feel especially unbound by conventional attitudes. This period offers them a chance to look clearly at themselves and their personalities. These important insights may be attributed to one theory or another, but often are not.

You may find it difficult to record persistent thoughts that seem silly, unimportant, or embarrassing, but my experience shows that some of the most significant and valuable insights at first seemed trivial or embarrassing.

SUMMARY

1. Freud believed children develop a sense of trust or mistrust during the first, or oral, stage of life. During their toilet-training years they form permanent attitudes toward independence and shame. The male child then begins to experience, according to Freud, the Oedipus complex. During this conflict he develops sexual feelings for his mother and begins to view his father with hostility. The female experiences a parallel crisis during the same years—called the Electra complex by Freud.
2. The behaviorists believe we will best understand the person if we abandon all theories of personality development. They would rather have us watch as the child reacts and responds to the environment. Behaviorists emphasize the importance of the rewards and punishments that cause people to respond one way rather than another. Such careful observation gives them, they claim, a better understanding of what makes people respond the way they do.
3. The humanists focus their attention on the role of free choice in the personality of the individual. They claim we become the people we are by choosing for ourselves and not making important choices because we want to please others. Humanists further feel we discover our true personalities by giving our emotions their proper expression. Particularly in our relationships with others, we find our true personality by being open and honest. The goal toward which we should strive was most clearly described by Abraham Maslow in his work with self-actualized people.

KEY TERMS

oral stage	Electra complex	extinction
anal stage	penis envy	organism
phallic stage	schizophrenic	free choice
Oedipus complex	environment	acceptance of feelings
castration anxiety	mechanical mirror	self-actualization

STUDY QUESTIONS

1. Of Freud's three stages explained in this chapter—oral, anal, and phallic—which makes the most sense to you and which seems the most preposterous? Explain.
2. Does Freud's theory of the Electra complex seem like an example of male chauvinism to you? In what way?
3. What would a behaviorist such as B. F. Skinner probably say about the Oedipus and Electra complexes? In what specific ways might he try to disprove these theories?
4. Do you believe you would be most likely to break a bad habit by being offered a series of rewards or by being subjected to a series of punishments? Explain.
5. Think of a specific thing you do every day which you believe to be an example of free choice. To what extent do you think you might be influenced, even in that act, by outside factors?
6. Do you believe that accepting your feelings is always the best course to take? Name a specific time and place where you feel you did the best thing by hiding your feelings.

ADDITIONAL READING

Byrne, D. *An Introduction to Personality: Research Theory and Application.* Englewood Cliffs, New Jersey: Prentice-Hall, 1974.

Erikson, Erik H. *Childhood and Society.* New York: Norton, 1963.

———. *Identity: Youth and Crisis.* New York: Norton, 1968.

Goble, Frank. *A Third Force: The Psychology of Abraham Maslow.* New York: Grossman, 1970.

Hall, Calvin S., and Lindzey, Gardner. *Theories of Personality.* New York: John Wiley, 1970.

Jourard, Sidney M. *The Transparent Self.* New York: Van Nostrand, 1971.

Maddi, S. *Personality Theories: A Comparative Analysis.* Homewood, Ill.: Dorsey, 1972.

Mischel, W. *Introduction to Personality.* New York: Holt, Rinehart, and Winston, 1976.

Rychiak, J. F. *Introduction to Personality and Psychotherapy: A Theory-Construction Approach.* Boston: Houghton Mifflin, 1973.

Skinner, B. F. *Walden II.* New York: Macmillan, 1948.

Chapter Three

Learning

OUTLINE

The Behavioristic Approach
    Further Discoveries
    Operant Conditioning
    Behavior Shaping

The Cognitive Approach
    Chimpanzee Insight
    Sign Learning
    Latent Learning
    Controversy and Resolution

The Humanistic Approach
    Blocks to Learning
    Discovery Learning
    Real Teachers

Conclusion

LEARNING OBJECTIVES

After reading this chapter you should be able to:

1. Understand the distinction between classical and operant conditioning.
2. Explain what is meant by shaping behavior.
3. Discuss the cognitive structure and its implication for learning.
4. Explain what is meant by latent learning.
5. Understand the distinction between the humanistic and behavioristic approaches.
6. Discuss what humanists mean by discovery learning.

Chapter Three

Some of the most difficult questions students ask me concern learning theories. The difficulty with these questions is in the student expectations behind them. Their questions usually contain a search for better ways to study, to understand, and to avoid the work of learning. Most students would like to read, comprehend, and retain books with ease and to understand complex relationships without strain. They would like to achieve high grade point averages without sacrificing so much of their social life.

I understand these motivations behind student questions about learning, because I have the same desires to improve my ability to learn. I often hope that we are just on the brink of a new breakthrough in learning theory that will help people learn with much more ease. In fact, however, psychologists have only begun to understand how we learn. More important, their approaches are not well integrated with one another, but rather have separate and distinctly different vantage points to the learning process.

The behaviorists concern themselves with our observable behavior, paying close attention to the minute details of the learning process. They notice, for example, that when we are rewarded for performing a given action, we are more likely to repeat that action. We will also see that the behaviorists do not agree as they try to describe just how the learning process operates. Some claim we learn one minute detail after another until we are capable of complex thought processes. Others, such as cognitive theorists, think we learn to make patterns or maps in our minds as we try to solve problems. Even the few behavioral theories we will study here will give us a sense of their diversity.

The humanists think the behaviorists' microscopic studies of learning behavior yield little significant information. Instead, the humanists look at the learning atmosphere of the school. They point out that, although we know that fear hinders learning, our educational system tends to promote a fear of grades and examinations. The system trains teachers to expect little from students, and consequently students respond with very little learning. The humanists would rather have us turn to what they call "discovery learning," believing that the student who is free to discover answers will learn more quickly, retain more effectively, and make school only the beginning of a lifetime of learning.

THE BEHAVIORISTIC APPROACH

Most of us only need to reflect momentarily on our daily experiences to realize some of our reactions occur spontaneously. We smell bread baking and we salivate. A bug flies too close to our eyes and we blink. Because no one had to teach us to blink or to salivate under such conditions, the behaviorists refer to such involuntary responses as unlearned, or **unconditioned responses.** The stimulus that causes the unconditioned response—the smell of bread, the bug—is termed the **unconditioned stimulus.**

As mentioned earlier, Ivan Pavlov made an important discovery concerning unconditioned responses. He found out in his study of the salivary response in dogs that stimuli other than food could cause salivation. Even before the dogs could see or smell the food, the sound of someone approaching with food would cause them to salivate. When footsteps rather than food caused the salivation, the footsteps became the stimulus. The footsteps under these circumstances are termed the learned, or **conditioned stimulus.** The salivation under such circumstances is called the **conditioned response.** And such learned conditioning is labeled **classical conditioning.**

A familiar, everyday example can make these terms easier to remember. The first time you eat a juicy hamburger at a fast-food chain it might make your mouth water. We could refer to the salivation as the unconditioned, or unlearned, response. No one taught you to salivate at the taste, sight, and smell of a hamburger—the unconditioned stimulus. Now suppose you continue to return to that same food chain enough times to recognize its golden arches and associate the sight of those arches with the taste of a juicy hamburger. Eventually the arches themselves will stimulate you to salivate the same way the hamburger did originally. Now the golden

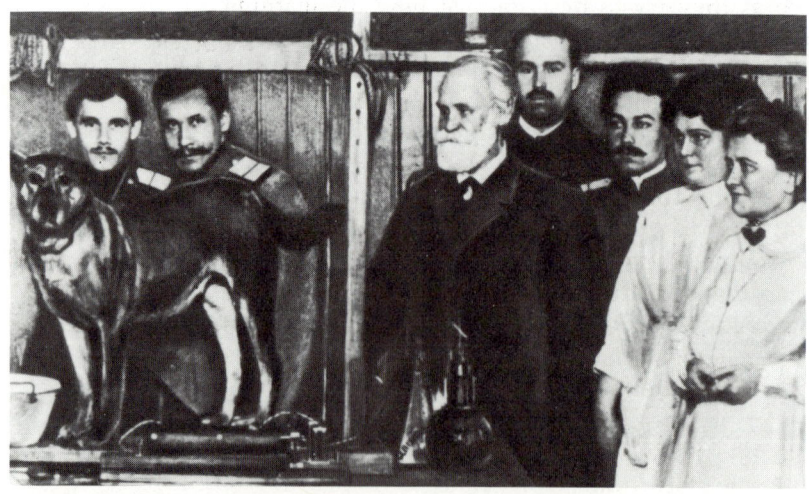

Ivan Pavlov made important discoveries concerning the extent to which we can be conditioned. (Culver Pictures)

arches have become a conditioned, or learned, stimulus. This salivation is also learned and, therefore, termed the conditioned response.

Pavlov saw the important implications of his experiment. He theorized that his dogs had been fundamentally changed. They had been conditioned, or trained, to react in new ways. The discovery so excited Pavlov that he devoted himself to its psychological implications, although he worried about his fellow physiologists' reaction. Adelaide Bry tells us of Pavlov's important decision to continue his study.

> Pavlov struggled with the question of whether to pursue this line of observation further. He knew that he would meet with disapproval from his fellow physiologists for diverting his research from the physical to the mental, psychology then being held in some dis-esteem. In the end, however, Pavlov decided to proceed.

Further Discoveries

Pavlov made a series of further discoveries as he studied the responses of his dogs to stimuli under various circumstances. For example, Adelaide Bry tells us:

> Pavlov found that an animal's response to the conditioned stimulus, if not reinforced by re-presentation of the unconditioned stimulus, tends to disappear. Thus Pavlov's dogs, which learned to salivate at the ringing of a bell, would stop salivating on the presentation of this conditioned stimulus after a time unless meat powder was periodically placed on their tongues. (2)

The phenomenon was called extinction (Case 3.1).

Think again of the hamburger and the golden arches, and the conclusion is obvious. If you must pass the golden arches regularly and have no opportunity to stop for a hamburger, your tendency to salivate will begin to disappear. The stimulus — the golden arches — loses its potential to stimulate you. However, the power of the stimulus to cause salivation after another hamburger can be renewed. Suppose, after a year of a hamburger-free existence, you stop again to indulge. The golden arches will almost immediately recover their power to stimulate digestive juices. This recovery of stimulus power is called **spontaneous recovery.**

Pavlov also studied **generalization** and **discrimination.** Bry continues:

> Generalization is the tendency of a variety of similar stimuli to induce the conditioned response. For example, a sound of a certain pitch is originally used to elicit the reflex of salivation; and then sounds of higher and lower pitch are used to accomplish the same purpose. The range of pitches at which salivation occurs is the extent of the process of generalization. (3)

The mother who hits middle C on the piano and then produces ice cream conditions her son to respond to the sound as he might to the ice

Peanuts. © 1957 United Feature Syndicate, Inc.

cream itself. Each time his mother hits middle C, the boy salivates. Now if the mother begins to experiment with other notes on the piano, the child can soon learn to respond to them similarly. Pavlov referred to such stimulus extension with the term, *generalization*.

Once the child responds to all the notes on the piano equally, the mother can then begin another process. She can train her son to discriminate. She can train him to respond only to middle C. She only needs to stop bringing out ice cream after other piano notes, while consistently producing ice cream after middle C. The child quickly learns to respond only to middle C. This process Pavlov called *stimulus discrimination*. Dogs, children, and adults can all learn to discriminate between minute differences in sound, sight, taste, and touch through such conditioning processes.

• Case 3.1

Quite often doctors come across people with conditioned responses that are no longer useful to the individuals. For example, Navy veterans of World War II learned to respond to a particular sound when called to their battle stations during battle. Even though fifteen years had elasped between the end of the war and one controlled experiment, the nervous system of the men studied still responded to the battle alarm. They became jumpy, nervous, and excited.

Terry had a similar problem with a childhood conditioned response to dogs. When he was only five years old, Terry had been bitten by a rabid dog. The fear that attack caused and the painful shots that followed left lasting psychological scars on Terry. Even the sight of the friendliest dog would begin Terry's heart pumping, his hands perspiring, and his entire body trembling.

Over the years, Terry's reactions grew more intense. Not only did the sight of dogs terrify him, but even the fear that he might suddenly be startled by a dog bothered him. He talked over his phobia with his doctor who became quite concerned with Terry's condition. The doctor even suggested that this form of tension could account for the peptic ulcer Terry had developed quite early in life. Both Terry and his doctor agreed that Terry might do well to see a psychologist.

The psychologist who talked to Terry explained that such conditioned reactions can be particularly resistant to change, but both agreed they should try. The psychologist taught Terry relaxation techniques, talked to him at length about the painful first experience with the rabid dog, and even put Terry in hypnotic trance to try to erase the conditioned response. Little by little, Terry's responses to dogs diminished, and he was soon able to tolerate remaining in the same room with them. Though he never completely overcame his fearful responses, he did become calmer and better able to live with his phobia.

Operant Conditioning

Pavlov's conditioning experiments are usually referred to as forms of classical conditioning, one way in which we learn. He felt we learn to respond one way rather than another because of the things that happen to us. Like the dogs that learned to salivate when the sound of footsteps, a piano tone, or a flashing light preceded their food, people learn to respond in certain ways because of the way we are conditioned.

A second approach to conditioning is **operant conditioning.** B. F. Skinner introduced the term to suggest another way we learn through conditioning. In operant conditioning, we are rewarded for some action we perform, because we are rewarded, we tend to repeat that action. For example, the infant who makes random sounds during infancy receives little reward until she happen to hit the sound "Mama." Once she makes that sound, the child gains an immense reward in the form of smiles, hugs, and warmth. The chance of the child repeating such a sound then increases greatly.

In classical conditioning, dogs perform with instinctive behavior. Dogs have always salivated. They simply learn to respond to new stimuli—bells instead of food. In operant conditioning, dogs learn new behavior. For example, they are rewarded for lifting a paw at the sound of the word "shake." This new behavior is then rewarded so that the dog will respond quickly and automatically to the word "shake."

B. F. Skinner tells us:

> The standard distinction between operant and reflex behavior is that one is voluntary and the other involuntary. Operant behavior is felt to be

Behaviorists believe we remain quiet in a library because we are reinforced through social approval for our silence. (Peter Vandermark)

under the control of the behaving person and has traditionally been attributed to an act of will. Reflex behavior, on the other hand, is not under comparable control and has even been attributed to invading wills, such as those of possessing spirits. Sneezing, hiccupping, and other reflex acts were once attributed to the Devil, from whom we still protect a friend who has sneezed by saying, "God bless you!" . . . When no invader is assumed, the behavior is simply called automatic. (4)

Both the classical conditioning theories based on **reflex behavior** and the operant conditioning theories based on voluntary behavior evolve from studies with animals. Many people do not like to think their behavior resembles that of dogs and rats, yet we know our learning patterns do follow the conditioning patterns we observe in animals. We, too, repeat behavior for which we are rewarded. For example, we learn to remain relatively quiet in a library because we receive social approval for such quiet. Grades are strong reinforcers for most students. Money has come to be the strongest reinforcer available to press people to perform difficult, tedious, and even dangerous actions.

Behavior Shaping

Operant conditioning produces new behavior. A bit of random behavior that is reinforced begins immediately to dominate an animal's responses. For example, a dog can be taught to press a buzzer with its nose by the use of rewards. At first, the dog is rewarded for simply straying near the buzzer. Then the reward system becomes more selective. The dog must be facing the buzzer to gain its reward. Finally, rewards only appear when the dog's nose actually rings the buzzer. This application of operant conditioning is called **behavior shaping** (Case 3.2).

Such operant conditioning of animals has reached a highly scientific level. Psychologists have helped animal trainers develop dramatic routines for marine shows featuring whales and porpoises. Among the most humorous shows developed by shaping animal behavior was called "Priscilla, the Fastidious Pig." During the course of the show, a pig ate breakfast from a table, turned on and watched television, vacuumed the carpet, picked up clothes from the floor and put them in a hamper, and even answered questions from the audience by flashing lights marked "Yes" or "No."

A most interesting aspect of behavior shaping is termed *noncontingent reinforcement*. In one experiment Skinner and his colleagues rewarded a group of hungry pigeons at some random point in time by turning on a light and, moments later, giving the pigeons a food-pellet reward. The randomness of the food rewards had an interesting effect on the pigeons. No matter what the pigeon happened to be doing when the light went on, it tended to repeat that action. If a pigeon had one leg in the air when the light and food combination occurred, then the pigeon was more apt to have its one leg in the air the next time reinforcement occurred.

Animals are frequently trained by behavior-shaping techniques. (Peter Vandermark)

The noncontingent reinforcement led pigeons to behave in a way we might call "superstitious." Like the gambler who repeats certain phrases before working the slot machine, the pigeons came to believe their behavior, like leg lifting, caused the food reward. Much of our own superstitious behavior, Skinner suggests, can be explained as a form of noncontingent reinforcement.

•Case 3.2

Behavior shaping has practical applications for everyone and can, at times, have important consequences. For example, a man named George used behavior shaping to help prolong his life. As a young man, George maintained a reasonable weight, sometimes putting on a few extra pounds. However, the mere mention of the excess weight by friends, even in a kidding fashion, was enough to press George to begin a crash diet. In his early thirties, however, George took a job that required him to stay at his desk most of the day. The work also involved a good bit of pressure. George's weight steadily began to climb, but now even his friends' remarks did not push him to reduce. Eating became a form of pressure release. He kept peanuts at his desk and watched a good deal of television at home, nibbling almost constantly through football games, comedy shows, and late-night talk shows. His weight soon reached problem proportions.

His doctor became alarmed at the weight gain and told George that his excess weight was becoming a definite health hazard. He also warned George that added weight can become very difficult to lose as a person gets older. The doctor and George talked about how eating gradually became associated with everything in George's life. George associated eating with working at his desk, passing the refrigerator, watching television, and even evening walks past the ice cream parlor.

The doctor warned George that his life style was shaped toward gaining weight. Daily associations all signaled eating. The only way for him to change this behavior was to reverse the behavior shaping by beginning to associate eating with specific times and places. At home he must think of eating only after rising, at noontime, and around six o'clock in the evening. He should only eat while seated at the dining-room table or at the office cafeteria. And in order for this diet plan to work, he must be heartless with himself.

In the beginning, the plan seemed impossible for George to follow. He felt hunger pains almost constantly. More important, his anxiety reached severe levels. In time, however, the pattern took shape as George started to think of himself as a person who never eats between meals. He also learned to stop work when his anxiety attacks began, close his eyes, lean back in his chair, and breathe easily until the anxiety passed. Once this new pattern began to develop, the weight loss that followed gave George a new feeling of accomplishment and control. In the end, he lost nearly all of the weight he gained under the pressure of his new job by reversing harmful behavior shaping.

THE COGNITIVE APPROACH

Much of our learning can be examined and explained by conditioning experiments. We need only look about us to see that classical conditioning forms an important part of our life. We might learn quite early that when our father arrives home with a small, white sack in his hand, we will soon have candy. Salivation can come to be associated with that white sack just as if it were the candy itself. Operant conditioning also plays an important role in our learning. We can learn a hug waits for us on those days when we play quietly. So that quiet play becomes more apt to occur when we can look forward to a bit of affection to reward our quite behavior.

Many psychologists believe the conditioning explanations of learning offer us valuable information. However, they also feel that to reduce all learning to a series of small stimulus and response actions and reactions is overly simplistic. One group of psychologists who believe conditioning explanations are simplistic are **cognitive psychologists.** These psychologists think of the learning process in terms of a cognitive structure.

A **cognitive structure** is the organization people use to preserve whatever they learn. Whenever we learn something complex, cognitive theorists claim, we organize our learning into patterns or maps. We group great amounts of material into arrangements that make sense to us and allow us to retrieve that information easily. Then when we are tested on our knowledge, we mentally reproduce the map and find that part of the material which seems pertinent to our problem.

Chimpanzee Insight

Wolfgang Kohler was one of the psychologists who protested most vigorously against the attempt to reduce learning to simple stimulus-response associations. To make his point most dramatically, Kohler performed a series of experiments with chimpanzees. In each experiment, the chimpanzees seemed to grasp a solution to a problem by a sudden insight into the nature of the difficulty. Such experiments led Kohler to conclude that, even in animals, **insight** into the relationship of parts formed an important basis for learning.

One of the many experiments Kohler used to prove his point involved a chimpanzee in a cage. Beyond the chimp's reach was a piece of fruit. A stick too short to reach the fruit was long enough to reach another stick that could reach the desired fruit. A long pause preceded the chimp's discovery of the solution to his problem. This pause, during which the chimp viewed the entire scene, occurred in almost every Kohler experiment. Such pauses suggest that a thinking process precedes the final insight. Once the chimp began to act again, no pauses occurred in his movement toward the solution of the problem. The chimp used the short stick to retrieve the longer stick, then the longer stick to retrieve the fruit. (5)

Such experiments as these appealed to many people, because their own experience confirmed the insight theory Kohler illustrated. We know we approach a problem by arranging the problem in our minds in an appropriate way. We search, by using images, for ways to water a garden with a hose that appears too short, to give children freedom to roam around a lawn without mishap, to arrange things in a drawer to give us more space. Once our mental image forms an adequate solution, we proceed to solve the problem without hesitation. This final image is the cognitive structure that gives us insight into the problem. One cognitive-structure solution can have many applications. For instance, our insight in arranging one drawer can apply to many drawers. Such solutions do not resemble the many small learned steps toward a solution that conditioning theory suggests. Instead, as Kohler and other cognitive psychologists claim, our experience supports the theory that insight is integral to our learning experience (Self-Quiz 3.1).

Sign Learning

Edward C. Tolman, another cognitive learning psychologist, thought learning involves **sign learning,** as well as insight. Sign learning is the process whereby we learn that one thing signals another. Even the rat running through a maze does not learn a simple series of left and right turns. Instead, it develops a map or cognitive structure of the maze. So

This rat may be making a mental map of the maze. (Peter Vandermark)

Self-Quiz 3.1 — Intuition and Insight

This test is designed to help you discover how much you rely on intuition and insight in problem solving. Indicate your answer to each statement by checking the appropriate box to the left of that statement. Please try to choose the alternative that best describes your attitude. Do not omit any of the questions.

Often	Occasionally	Seldom	
☐	☐	☐	1. I do not bring a particular plan to most problem solving. I think about several ideas until an answer emerges.
☐	☐	☐	2. I can tell when a good friend has a personal problem without being told.
☐	☐	☐	3. I trust my feelings when making major decisions in my life.
☐	☐	☐	4. The opinions of others do not dissuade me from doing what I want to do.
☐	☐	☐	5. My first impression of people is based on my feelings.
☐	☐	☐	6. I can tell when people are telling me the truth.
☐	☐	☐	7. I can understand the feelings of people who are quite different from me emotionally.
☐	☐	☐	8. I believe faith healing cures people.
☐	☐	☐	9. I do not need to find a reasonable explanation for everything that happens.
☐	☐	☐	10. I would not take a job I disliked even if it paid me a great deal.

This test cannot conclusively say whether or not you tend to be intuitive. However, a high score indicates you score with those who describe themselves as most intuitive. To total your score, give yourself 3 points for each time you checked "often" on the test, 2 points for each "occasionally," and 1 point for each "seldom." Add up the total number of points and compare that total with the following scale.

30–22   You score in the high range. You probably pay more attention to intuition than logic.

Self-Quiz 3.1 continued — Intuition and Insight

21–14   You score with most students who took this test. You seem to blend logic and intuition to the same degree as most people do.

Below 14 You seem uncommonly skeptical concerning intuition. Your approach to life might rely too heavily on concrete thinking.

---

that any time one path in the maze is blocked, the rat may refer to its cognitive map and develop an alternative route (Case 3.3).

Tolman felt that the rat, like the person, does not learn to follow, by rote, a chain of responses. Instead, the rat learns to expect one thing to follow from another. Even if the context of the learning changes dramatically, the rat can still find its way to its goal. To prove this point, Tolman took a rat, well trained in running a particular maze, and placed it in that maze after the maze was flooded with water. The rat swam to its destination without hesitation. (6)

● Case 3.3

Some of the most dramatic psychological studies of signs are the attempts to teach chimpanzees to talk. For many centuries, we believed that the ability to communicate with signs was the one clear distinction between man and animal, but early studies by psychologists brought the distinction into question. Two chimpanzees in psychological studies communicated vocally with one another as early as 1933. However, the inability of the chimps to form vocal signals left much to be desired in that and similar efforts. Then in 1971, the Gardners, both of them trained psychologists, hit on the idea of training chimpanzees in sign language. Chimps are quite facile with their fingers, so the work with a sign language seemed natural.

The Gardners began to work with Washoe, a female chimpanzee, when she was one year old. By the time Washoe was three, she used 34 signs effectively and even combined some of the signs into two-word and three-word sentences. By the age of five, Washoe used over 130 signs and combined many of them appropriately in short sentences.

No doubt remains that Washoe could generalize from one sign to another. One example cited by the Gardners was the use of the word "more." She used the same word in connection with "more tickling" and with "more food." She finally used the word in connection with writing, reading, and even swinging. Washoe enjoyed leafing through magazines and signing the familiar objects she found in pictures. She even became eager to use the sign for "What's this?" whenever faced with an unfamiliar object. Such a tendency significantly increased her vocabulary. In the end Washoe had control over 160 signs and opened up an entirely new area of study for psychologists. (7)

Latent Learning

Any time we learn to behave in a given way without actually having behaved that way, we are involved in what Tolman called **latent learning.** Usually such learning takes place at a time when you do not immediately need or want the information. For instance, if a friend tells you how to drive to a new pizza parlor, Tolman would say you have learned latently the directions to the pizza parlor. If the next day at noon you have a sudden craving for pizza, you can make your latent learning practical by referring to your friend's directions and driving to the pizza parlor.

To demonstrate that this kind of learning takes place even in rats, Tolman set up a unique experiment. Tolman ran two groups of rats through the same maze for ten days. The first group was rewarded regularly for running the maze properly. The second group only explored the maze and was given no reward for its efforts. Predictably, the first group, those rats that were rewarded, learned to run the maze quickly and made the fewest number of errors. After the ten days of conditioning ended, both groups of rats were rewarded for their efforts. Within two days, the second group was making fewer errors than the first group of rats who received rewards every day. Obviously, by exploring the maze, even the unrewarded rats learned a great deal. Yet, they revealed that learning only when the food became available at the end of the maze. (8)

"For what it's worth, Jane, I, too, found first grade a drag. But I hung in there, and now, needless to say, I'm mighty glad I did."

Controversy and Resolution

Controversy over the different learning theories has a long history. One group of behaviorists wants to explain all learning in terms of *stimulus-response* associations. Such explanations make a good deal of sense. However, the appeal of this theory applies mostly to the more rote and automatic kind of learning. Clearly, the salivation reactions that transfer from food to other stimuli, such as footsteps of the person carrying the food or "golden arches," can be explained best by stimulus and response theories.

At the other end of the learning spectrum, complex mental operations such as difficult mathematical solutions do not yield so readily to stimulus-response explanations. Such feats of memory and insight seem better explained by *cognitive* theories. The more complex operations of our minds occur through thinking in cognitive patterns that we follow to our solutions.

With the present state of our knowledge of learning, we can assume our minds have two distinct functions. In the simple mental tasks, we can visualize our minds making simple stimulus-response associations. In more complex problem solving that necessarily involves complicated patterns of thought, the cognitive processes explain our mental functions better. In the middle ground of types of learning problems, such as the rote operations of memorizing the multiplication tables or memorizing foreign language vocabulary, we probably perform a mixture of these two operations.

We may need more than one explanation for the wide variety of learning experiences in life. (Cary Wolinski/Stock, Boston)

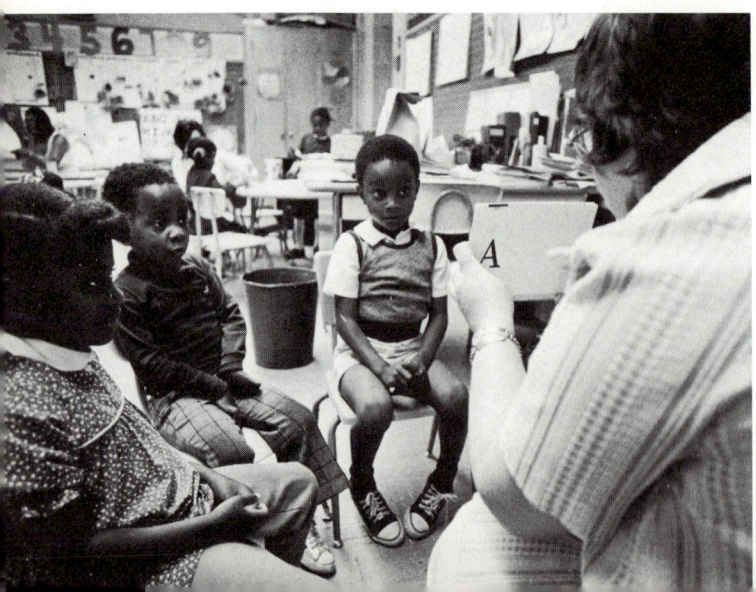

Tiger. © King Features Syndicate, Inc., 1969. World rights reserved.

THE HUMANISTIC APPROACH

The humanists do not believe that the behaviorists' minute examination of learning helps us understand the learning process. Instead, they point out, teaching and learning can be improved fundamentally without such studies. If we really want to help students learn better, we should spend more time trying to develop methods of instruction that would not force young people into the predetermined patterns the classroom so often implies. We would also do well to stop forcing students to memorize material that has little or no significance in their lives.

One failure of the educational system, humanists claim, is obvious in most classrooms — fear. We find classrooms with fearful students in every part of our country. No one needs to study the effects of fear on learning very long to see how harmful such fear quickly becomes. Yet teachers, instead of working to relieve fear, often seem oblivious to its presence. The testing and grading systems, in particular, can promote fear. Humanists believe that under such emotional strain students learn to memorize rather than learn in order to get good grades.

Blocks to Learning

A study in the Oak Park Elementary School in San Francisco confirmed what many psychologists already believe about the role of teacher expectations. A group of randomly selected students were placed in classrooms with teachers who were told these particular children showed unusual potential for intellectual growth. Eight months later the I.Q. scores of these children were compared with those of the rest of the children in the school. Nearly half of the "unusual" children gained 20 I.Q. points during the eight-month study. Only 19 percent of the children in the rest of the school gained 20 I.Q. points. Quite obviously, the teacher's expectations of the children's intelligence had a great influence on the performance of the children. (9)

The dangerous power of such teacher expectations becomes obvious when we examine the approach many instructors take to student grading. Those teachers who follow traditional grading practices tend to expect that two-thirds of their students will be assigned a C grade. Since the C grade is the norm for teachers as they prepare to teach any group of students, their expectations have great potential to lower the expectations that students have for themselves. The humanists look for ways to change the expectations teachers bring to their students. Nothing else, they claim, can have a greater impact on the learning that takes place in any given classroom.

Discovery Learning

The humanists regularly point out that the lecture-test method, dominant in so many classrooms, can be ineffective in helping students learn. The lecture-test method often produces conformity. Rather than help students explore new and interesting avenues of interest, the lecture-test method often teaches students to learn how to please the teacher, how to memorize material quickly without retaining it effectively, and how to take the easiest path through school with the best possible grades.

Humanists would like to replace the lecture-test approach with a classroom atmosphere that encourages discovery rather than memorization. They call this approach **discovery learning.**

Though Jerome Bruner is considered a cognitive psychologist, he reflects humanistic concerns when he asks teachers to adapt their teaching to allow students to discover new knowledge for themselves. If students can be encouraged to learn the elements of radio transmission, the battle strategy of the Civil War, or the corporate structure of the oil industry, they will come to enjoy the activity of learning rather than simply striving for a grade reward at the end of the semester. Such a teaching style also helps students learn general methods of studying problems rather than pressing them to memorize the specific solutions. For instance, the method discovered for researching the battle strategy involved in the Civil War can be applied to any historical question. Students who learn the principles of radio transmission by experimenting on their own will remember far more of those principles than students forced to memorize similar material for an examination (Case 3.4).

Jerome Bruner sums up his goals and the goals of most humanists:

> The emphasis in much of school learning and student examining is upon explicit formulations, upon the ability of the student to reproduce verbal or numerical formulae. It is not clear, in the absence of research, whether this emphasis is inimical to the later development of good intuitive understanding—indeed, it is even unclear what constitutes intuitive understanding. Yet we can distinguish between inarticulate genius and articulate idiocy—the first represented by the student who, by his opera-

The humanists believe that discovery learning is more effective than the traditional lecture-test method of learning. (Peter Vandermark)

tions and conclusions, reveals a deep grasp of a subject but not much ability to "say how it goes," in contrast to the student who is full of seemingly appropriate words but has no matching ability to use the ideas for which the words presumably stand. (10)

● Case 3.4

Bill taught grade-school children for over five years. He enjoyed his work at first because he liked young people and found the contact stimulating. However, as the years passed, the work became less satisfying. His early hope to make personal contact with his students seemed distant. He had more students in his classroom each year. He found most of his time taken up with disciplinary measures and paper work. He spent time collecting money for lunches, separating students who spent too much time talking with one another, and drilling students in the rote work of the multiplication tables and spelling exercises. Bill frequently thought now about leaving teaching all together.

Just as he was about to give up hope, Bill learned about a new approach to education begun in several states called the Open Classroom Approach. The idea so attracted Bill that he returned to graduate school to learn the new techniques. In school, Bill learned how to discover student interests and help them pursue those interests individually. He was shown a series of games that helped young people learn mathematics quickly and effectively. A host of classroom projects to stimulate science interests was also demonstrated. More important, Bill learned how to interest students in most every aspect of learning.

By the time he returned to the classroom, Bill knew how to test students in order to discover their weaknesses, not to categorize them. Once student weaknesses were uncovered, they could receive special supplementary help. Rather than spending his day drilling students, Bill could now spend most of his time guiding them individually. He was much happier and looked forward to continuing his career as a teacher. And just as important, Bill's students learned more than they ever previously did.

Real Teachers

Carl Rogers, a humanist, believes we cannot teach others anything of significance, but we can **facilitate** their learning processes. Thus, many of Rogers' theories emphasize the effectiveness of those teachers who allow their students the most freedom to learn on their own. To give students this freedom to learn, teachers must be warm, real people to their students.

Carl Rogers believes teachers must give their students the freedom to learn. (Nozizwe S.)

Rogers feels teachers who remain aloof from students do not give them an effective model to follow, but when students see that their teachers learn through trial-and-error with struggles, and despite frustrations, the teachers become models for effective learning.

Teachers who want to help their students become effective learners must accept their students as people. The teacher who reduces students to numbers and treats them as objects cannot encourage them to learn effectively. As we saw in the Oak Park Elementary School study, the teachers' attitudes toward students can bring out the best in them. Those students who experience concerned and encouraging teachers have trouble doing anything less than their best. Carl Rogers summarizes this humanistic approach to learning:

> Those attitudes which appear effective in promoting learning can be described. First of all is a transparent realness in the facilitator, a willingness to be a person, to be and live the feelings and thoughts of the moment. When this realness includes a prizing, a caring, a trust and respect for the learner, the climate for learning is enhanced. When it includes a sensitive and accurate listening, then indeed a freeing climate, stimulative of self-initiated learning and growth exists. The student is trusted to develop. (11)

CONCLUSION

The behavioristic, cognitive, and humanistic approaches to learning give us three important perspectives for understanding ourselves and our learning.

The behaviorists help us understand how we can become conditioned to perform actions without much reflection. Like Pavlov's dogs, we find ourselves instinctively responding to certain stimuli such as grades, money, or social approval. Other behaviorists, such as Skinner, point out that our behavior is largely shaped by rewards. We perform those actions that lead us to expect rewards.

The cognitive learning theorists take a dim view of describing learning in terms of stimulus and response alone. Cognitive psychologists think we form mental maps in our memories that organize our knowledge. Then, when we are tested on our knowledge, we refer to those mental maps and search for the necessary combination of information to give us insight into the problem.

The humanists, by contrast, spend more of their time looking at the classroom atmosphere. They feel far too many of students fail to learn because of the great fear that fills the classroom. The competitive atmosphere, say the humanists, deters most students from learning and understanding. The humanists want us to change the atmosphere so that students can spend more time exploring subjects that interest them, because only when students are free to pursue self-initiated learning can they be expected to learn effectively. To achieve this atmosphere of free inquiry, Carl Rogers insists that the teacher, or facilitator, must be a real person to students. Facilitators of learning can only grant students learning freedom when they are empathetic with student struggles and trust that the students will develop into effective learners.

SUMMARY

1. Pavlov discovered what has come to be known as classical conditioning. He conditioned his dogs by producing a sound, light, or other signal just before presenting food. The dogs soon came to salivate involuntarily at the signal as if they had actually been presented with the food. B. F. Skinner introduced the term operant conditioning for another form of conditioning that relies on rewards. When Skinner rewarded his animals for one particular form of behavior, they learned to repeat the rewarded behavior. Thus, Skinner found he could shape animal behavior.
2. The cognitive psychologists do not think complex learning can be described by Pavlov and Skinner's simple stimulus-reponse conditioning. They feel we form cognitive maps that help us preserve what we learn. Mental images organize many details. Then, when presented with problems, we scan our cognitive maps for the knowledge necessary to produce solutions. The solutions, according to many cognitive psychologists, do not grow out of many simple associations. Instead, solutions quite often come in one sudden insight into relationships of parts to the whole.
3. The humanists do not want to spend their time studying the minute details of learning behavior. It is more important, they tell us, to look at the classroom atmosphere. Most learning is now blocked because classrooms are filled with students afraid of examinations, grades, and even teachers. We must begin to eliminate this fear and help students spend more of their time making discoveries. When students discover answers on their own, they understand better, retain longer, and enjoy the learning process more. And the best way to bring discovery learning to the classroom, Carl Rogers tells us, is to make certain that teachers are real people with a profound concern for their students.

KEY TERMS

unconditioned response
unconditioned stimulus
conditioned stimulus

reflex behavior
behavior shaping
cognitive psychologists

conditioned response
classical conditioning
spontaneous recovery
generalization
discrimination
operant conditioning

cognitive structure
insight
sign learning
latent learning
discovery learning
facilitate

STUDY QUESTIONS

1. Think of one way in which you believe you have been conditioned. How would you go about changing that conditioning?
2. If behaviorists were to gain a dominant influence on mothers today, how might children change as a consequence?
3. Do you believe most of your learning occurs by the effects of reward and punishment or by insight? Explain.
4. Think of one example in your personal life where you learned something before you actually did that thing physically. Do you consider that true learning? Explain.
5. Think of one situation in which fear blocked your attempt to learn. Would you say that fear has prevented you from learning very often?
6. Do you agree with Carl Rogers that teachers cannot teach you anything of any significance? In what specific ways do you agree or disagree?

ADDITIONAL READING

Bandura, A. L. *Social Learning Theory.* Englewood Cliffs, N.J.: Prentice-Hall, 1977.

Bruner, Jerome S. *The Process of Education.* New York: Random House, 1963.

Hilgard, E. R., and Bower, G. H. *Theories of Learning.* Englewood Cliffs, N.J.: Prentice-Hall, 1975.

Holt, John. *How Children Fail.* New York: Pitman, 1964.

Hulse, S. H.; Deese, J.; and Egeth, H.: *The Psychology of Learning.* New York: McGraw-Hill, 1975.

Peterson, L. R.: *Learning.* Glenview, Ill.: Scott, Foresman, and Co., 1975.

Postman, Neil, and Weingartner, Charles. *Teaching as a Subversive Activity.* New York: Delacorte, 1969.

Rogers, Carl. *Freedom to Learn.* Columbus, Ohio: Merrill, 1969.

Skinner, B. F. *The Technology of Teaching.* New York: Appleton-Century-Crofts, 1968.

Chapter Four

Motivation and Emotion

OUTLINE

The Psychoanalytic Approach
    Extraverts and Introverts
    Homeostasis
    Psychological Balance
    Individuation

The Behavioristic Approach
    Emotional Byproducts
    Turning Adjectives into Nouns
    The Behaviorist Explanation

The Humanistic Approach
    Embarrassment
    Balancing Conflicting Emotions
    Self-Trust

Conclusion

LEARNING OBJECTIVES

After reading this chapter you should be able to:

1. Understand Jung's theories of homeostasis and individuation.
2. Discuss psychological balance and its application to extraversion and introversion.
3. Explain the behaviorists' attitude toward motivation and why they feel emotions remain byproducts rather than causes of behavior.
4. Discuss what the humanists mean by the mask and why they encourage us to reveal our feelings.
5. Understand the humanistic attitude on balancing conflicting emotions and its emphasis on trusting our feelings.

Chapter Four

Craig, a tall and angular young man, approached me at a party recently. His eyebrows were pulled together with concern. After we chatted for short time, he said, "You know, I worry a lot about spending so much time doing stupid things."

"Join the crowd," I replied.

"No, I mean it. I waste an awful lot of time." Craig looked me straight in the eye. "It seems like most of my day passes before I even think of doing something useful."

"I suspect a great many people feel that way." I hoped my voice registered the proper concern. "I know I waste a great deal of valuable time."

"I just can't understand why I don't put more of my time to good use." Craig squinted as he pulled at his ear lobe. "I mean, what makes me want to spend so much time foolishly?"

"Do you need a reason?"

"Well, I hope that if I figure out why I waste so much time I might be able to change myself." Craig smiled. "Maybe then I could start doing more reading, take a class over at that college where you teach, or I might even work up enough energy to paint the garage."

Like Craig, most of us wonder why we do the things we do. We look at others and wonder what motivates some students to become doctors. We puzzle over the unusually bright student's decision to leave school for a year to travel abroad. We wonder what motivates criminals to follow their life style. We question why one couple decides to have children while the next couple prefers to remain childless. We can wonder what motivates presidential assassins, lumberjacks, and Olympic gold medal winners.

The attempt to understand what motivates others is discouraging enough. But when, like Craig, we look at our own behavior, we become even more baffled by the seeming lack of reason behind much of our behavior. We can spend hours agonizing over our inability to talk before a group of strangers. We can wonder why we waste so much time watching television shows we do not enjoy. And what keeps us from concentrating on studies so important to our career plans? Even the reasons we think might explain our behavior are often unsatisfying. For instance, we might say that laziness keeps us in front of the television set and away from more important matters, but that answer is not complete enough to really help us understand ourselves better.

When we turn to the psychologists for help in our search for motives behind our behavior, we find each approach follows its characteristic path. The behaviorists look for objective and measurable causes. Unmeasurable feelings are inadequate causes. The tennis player, according to Skinner, develops a good game because of the hours he practices, not because he feels confident. His confident feeling, in fact, comes from the many hours he practiced. The emotion of confidence is never responsible for a good tennis game to the behaviorists.

In contrast with the behaviorists, the psychoanalysts and humanists look into our personality to search for motivation behind our behavior. Carl Jung, a friend and colleague of Sigmund Freud for many years, suggests most of our actions are motivated by an innate desire to find unity in our personality. An unexplained upset, a particularly enjoyable day, or our need to avoid a stranger can all occur because of an inner drive for unity that occurs deep within our personality. Carl Rogers, the important humanist, also sees a struggle within the personality as the basic motive for behavior. We grow angry, fearful, resentful, and lonely, Rogers tell us, all because of an inner struggle to abandon our masks and to discover our selves. We have allowed external social demands and expectations to cover up our natural tendencies to openness. All of these theories can give us insights into the motives behind our behavior.

THE PSYCHOANALYTIC APPROACH

Carl Jung, toward the middle of his life, finally broke off his professional and personal relationship with Sigmund Freud. Jung could no longer accept Freud's premise that sex played the central role in explaining our behavior. Jung saw us primarily motivated by drives more fundamental than the sex drive. Jung thought our most powerful motivating drive is to achieve a balanced personality, not to search singlemindedly for sex.

Extraverts and Introverts

We seek balance in our personality in many ways, according to Jung. One way deserves special mention—the equilibrium we constantly seek between the **introverted** and the **extraverted** parts of our personality. Our extraverted self seeks involvement in events, people, relationships, and, in general, in the world around us. When anyone habitually looks outside himself or herself for involvement, Jung describes that person as extraverted. The extravert is comfortable at social events and relaxes in unfamiliar surroundings. The extravert enjoys a good argument and hopes, through persuasion, to shape others according to his or her personal desires.

The introvert is very different from the extravert. Frieda Fordham, in her introduction to Jung's work, explains this personality:

The introvert prefers reflection to activity. (Owen Franken/Stock, Boston).

The introverted attitude is one of withdrawal; the libido [sexual energy] flows inward and is concentrated upon subjective factors, and the predominating influence is "inner necessity." When this attitude is habitual Jung speaks of an "introverted type." This type lacks confidence in relation to people and things, tends to be unsociable, and prefers reflection to activity. Each type undervalues the other, seeing the negative rather than the positive qualities of the opposite attitude, a fact which has led to endless misunderstanding and even in the course of time to the formulation of antagonistic philosophies, conflicting psychologies, and different values and ways of life. (1)

Most of us find ourselves oriented either toward the world of extraversion or introversion (Self-Quiz 4.1). Our final goal, however, is to achieve some balance between these two aspects of our personality. This balance is possible because people who appear to be extraverts, Jung says, have only been clever enough to hide their introversion in their uncon-

The extravert seeks involvement with people, relationships, and the world generally. (Frank Siteman/Stock, Boston)

Self-Quiz 4.1 — Extravert/Introvert Scale

Next to each statement place the number 1, 2, 3, 4, or 5—depending on how characteristic each statement is of you. Continue the process for each of the statements. Then total your score.

- 5 strongly characteristic of me
- 4 moderately characteristic of me
- 3 neutral
- 2 moderately uncharacteristic of me
- 1 strongly uncharacteristic of me

____ 1. I often take the lead in group conversations and am almost never ill at ease in groups.

____ 2. I am comfortable talking on the telephone and rarely became nervous in such conversations.

____ 3. The thought of a vacation at a luxury camp with a lot of friends has far more appeal than spending time developing a hobby or traveling alone.

____ 4. I would much rather spend a free evening with friends than stay home relaxing by myself.

____ 5. I come to quick, well-balanced decisions.

____ 6. I frequently become involved in heated arguments and rarely back away from a good verbal battle.

____ 7. I find it fairly easy to produce a high level of steady, productive work.

____ 8. Others probably think of me as an active, friendly, and pleasant person.

____ 9. If I would see myself as others see me, I would probably be quite pleased and even flattered.

____ 10. Variety is the spice of life.

____ TOTAL SCORE

No test can actually measure your personality traits. Extraversion and introversion are too personal to measure quantitatively. However, your score on this test, when compared with other student scores, can give you an indication of whether you tend to be outgoing or withdrawn.

41–50   Students who score in this range are unusual. They tend to be far more extraverted than the norm.

30–40   The vast majority of students taking this test score in this range. Their mixture of extraversion and introversion probably is typical of most people.

Below 30   Few students score in this range. Students in this area tend to be more introverted than the norm.

scious. Introverts also hide from part of their personality, their extraversion. We move toward our own fulfillment when we begin gradually to expose those parts of our personality we hide. Each time the naturally extraverted person takes a chance and follows intuition, he or she moves closer to the balance we all need for best expressing ourselves (Case 4.1). When the introvert takes special note of the objective world, he or she moves toward personal fulfillment.

• Case 4.1

At times we can balance our own personality through our friendships with others. At least that was what happened to Joyce and Kathy.

Joyce was one of the most intelligent students in her high school. She had a wonderful sense of humor and was very attractive. Yet against the solid background of her intelligence, sense of humor, and attractive looks, Joyce had one personality problem. She was shy. For some unexplained reason, Joyce remained locked inside the isolation of her own thoughts and feelings. She rarely shared her ideas or presence with anyone. Even at parties, she sought out some hidden corner or obscure part of the room to hide from any active participation in the good times.

For some obscure reason, during her last year at high school, Kathy befriended Joyce. Ironically, Kathy was all the things Joyce was not. Kathy was very vivacious, ordinary looking, and into everything. She was head cheerleader, a member of the honor society, and had lost a narrow election for class president. Kathy came to every party and, when things slowed down, made suggestions to increase the tempo again.

Their classmates saw the friendship between Kathy and Joyce as strange. Yet the two of them felt they were made for one another. In Jungian terms, Joyce saw in Kathy the hidden part of her own personality. And Kathy could watch Joyce to know what she lacked in her life. They became quite open with one another during that last year of high school. Kathy taught Joyce to come out of her shell a little more. Before long, using Kathy as her model, Joyce spoke up on an occasion or two and finally even became active in the social life at school. Most important, Joyce started to feel better about herself as she experienced the balance Carl Jung says we all search to discover. Joyce began to discover her self.

Kathy had parallel experience. The more she talked with Joyce and grew close to her, the more Kathy began to reflect a little more before she spoke or acted. She realized many of her actions were superficial and impulsive. Without losing any of her charm, Kathy developed a more mature approach to life. She began to see the other side of her personality and, like Joyce, allowed it to emerge. Kathy became a more satisfied, balanced person.

When the time came for the two of them to part and attend separate colleges, Joyce and Kathy were very upset because they felt they were losing a part of themselves. However, they later realized they also carried part of each other with them.

Homeostasis

Jung saw our drive for balance between the introverted and extraverted parts of our personality as only one aspect of our general need for balance. He felt the same search for balance explains many of our motives. To help explain our need for balance, Jung drew many analogies from physiology. In physiology **homeostasis** is a guiding principle. The term homeostasis refers to the body's natural tendency to maintain a balance. The body uses every possible mechanism to sustain the proper amount of salt, to control the temperature in the brain, to assure an adequate amount of sleep. In this manner, the body constantly seeks homeostasis, or equilibrium.

Cathy. Copyright, 1978, Universal Press Syndicate.

British psychoanalyst Anthony Storr explains physiological homeostasis:

> Scientists have been perfectly used to accepting the idea that the body is a self-regulating entity. Human physiology is governed by an internal system of checks and balances which ensure that any tendency to go too far in one direction is compensated by an opposing swing in the other. Thus, if the blood becomes too alkaline, mechanisms are set in operation by which the kidney excretes more alkali and retains acid, thus ensuring that the chemical composition of the blood does not stray too far from its proper mean. The endocrine system is a highly complicated arrangement of self-regulating mechanisms. For example, the pituitary secretes a hormone which stimulates the thyroid gland to produce its own hormone, thyroxine. The more thyroxine there is in the blood, the less will the pituitary produce its thyroid-stimulating hormone. In the terminology of cybernetics, this is a negative feedback, aimed at ensuring that the right amount of thyroxine is always in circulation. Sometimes the mechanisms go wrong, as in thyrotoxicosis or other diseases; but, on the whole, the physiology of man is wonderfully well arranged so that his "internal environment" keeps constant in spite of fluctuations in, and varying exchange with, the world outside." (2)

In a fashion parallel to this balancing action in the body, the mind also seeks equilibrium. The woman who avoids people for a long time, for example, will soon find herself yearning to see and to talk with friends. Loneliness pushes her back into the social world. By contrast, a man who spends too much time with others will soon develop an aversion for social groups and begin to search for some time alone. In both cases, people simply follow the mind's desire to maintain balance.

Psychological Balance

Jung saw homeostasis as a most important principle behind all the significant drives that motivate our behavior. Though we might find ourselves brave one day in the face of danger, a tendency toward balance will press us the next day to be fearful. The same principle causes us to vacillate between the extremes of happiness and sorrow. Even in a strong friendship we feel warm one day and angry the next toward the same person. Much of our behavior is caused, Jung believed, by this psychological tendency to seek balance, and the better we understand that tendency, the healthier we will be.

Jung felt the homeostasis process was so powerful that it could operate unconsciously. The young man who tries too hard to be brave in the face of financial failure, for example, can fight the natural balance his personality desires. If he presses his fear into his unconscious for too long, however, that fear can emerge in a nightmare that forces the young man to experience the fear he tried to hide. In one way or another, despite our best efforts, our mind will achieve emotional balance.

Anthony Storr gives us a good example of a dream providing psychological homeostasis:

> A young woman had a dream in which she was being pursued by a steamroller. As she reached the bottom of the garden and was about to be overwhelmed, her mother appeared on the other side of the fence and laughed with hideous glee at her predicament. The subject was extremely fond of her mother, who indeed had looked after her devotedly. As a child, the girl had suffered from a physical disability which had necessitated her having special feeding and a great deal of maternal "overprotection." This had actually kept her childish and unduly dependent upon the mother. Hence, in the dream, the mother appears in a totally different light; as a menace, a destructive person who is "steamrollering" the subjects's individuality out of existence, or at least acquiescing in her being crushed. (3)

Another interesting example of psychological homeostasis occurred recently during an experiment in driver's education. Rodger Griffeth and Ronald Rogers, psychologists at the University of Southern California, explored the effects of fear on students learning to drive. The 144 high school students in a driver education program were divided into two groups and exposed to different conditions. One group saw a 12-minute film depicting grisly car wrecks. The other group watched a simple car maintenance movie. All students then filled out mood questionnaires and were observed behind the wheel of a simulated automobile.

In Jungian terms, we might say that those exposed to the fearful movie compensated for their fear by becoming cautious, as measured by their mood questionnaire and their behavior behind the wheel. They made far fewer braking, steering, and speeding errors than the other group. The group exposed to the simple car maintenance movie made three times as many driving errors as their frightened counterparts. Student caution evolved, then, to balance the exposure to the fearful thoughts and feelings, just as Jung might have predicted. (4)

Individuation

The search for psychological balance motivates our entire personality. We finally search for a sense of unity that affects our entire self. Jung called that search the process of **individuation**. Jung developed this theory of individuation during the second half of his life. At that point, he looked back on his early career and noted how many of those years he spent establishing himself in a profession, marrying and raising a family, and, in general, fulfilling his obligations. Not until the second half of his life did Jung develop a need to explore the "spiritual" aspects of his personality. Anthony Storr tells us in his book on Jung:

> Toward the end of the First World War Jung began to emerge from his period of mental upheaval. Like other creative people emerging from a mid-life crisis, he achieved a sense of acceptance and finality. His fanta-

sies, which by then he had begun to draw and paint, altered in character. Instead of images of persons, Jung became preoccupied with abstract, circular patterns, often subdivided into four or some multiple of that number. These patterns which, as he later discovered, were similar to those used for meditation and known as mandalas in the East, seemed to symbolize his achievement of a new balance within his own psyche: a balance in which there was some reconciliation between the opposing forces which had been tearing him apart. The journey toward this new integration came to be known as the process of individuation; and the mandala patterns in which it was expressed symbolized a new center within the psyche which was neither conscious nor unconscious but partook of both. The center Jung named the Self. (5)

Drawing on his own experience and his work with others, Jung decided the more reflective personality traits must emerge later in life if a person hopes to achieve "wholeness." Business people must, once they have established themselves personally and professionally, turn to their own sense of inner value in order to gain a balanced personality. Men should be willing to accept the feminine side of their personalities. They must explore the soft and sensitive parts of their nature just as women must explore their masculine tendencies (Case 4.2). Balance must be sought by the housewife, the airline pilot, the bank teller, and the television announcer. Unity implies a development of both the spiritual and practical parts of the self.

A great deal of recent research and writing about the adult stages of life supports the Jungian concept of individuation. The more scientific studies were popularized by Gail Sheehy in her book, *Passages*. A group of Yale researchers pioneered the work on adult stages of growth. Daniel Levinson and his Yale colleagues discovered that most men grow in a period of self-expansion during their thirties. They deepen their commitments, make long-range plans, and open themselves up for new possibilities.

At the peak of their self-expansion (between the ages of 35 and 39) a new stage begins which the researchers call *Becoming One's Own Man*. No matter how accomplished, men begin to feel they lack independence at this point in life. They may want to leave constricting marriages, oppressive work conditions, or even repressive social restrictions. Most men then set a new goal for themselves. They may look to a promotion, a new marriage, some public recognition to measure their abilities. "At 38 he thinks that if he gains the deserved success, he'll be all set," say the researchers. "The answer is, he will not. He is going to have a transition whether he is affirmed (by society) or not; it is only the form that varies."

The stage will bring these men into acute awareness of their own mortality, of the loss of youth, of the reality of advancing age, and of the more feminine qualities within themselves. The research points out only too clearly how accurate Jung's original insight was. (6)

● Case 4.2

The lack of a Jungian balance in the personality was obvious in Alex. As a business man and a professional architect, few could surpass him. He won honors for his work just two years after he left college. The most prestigious firm in a large metropolitan city invited him to join as a partner at an age when most men are still learning the trade. He achieved success so quickly that he began his own firm before he was thirty years old. The awards and money came in abundance, and nothing seemed beyond his grasp. Alex only had problems when he tried to think about how he could continue, year after year, to surpass his previous accomplishments.

During his late thirties, Alex began to have troubles with his family. His teenage daughters showed signs of resentment toward him. His youngest daughter, a high school sophomore, even told him one day, "If you really loved us, you wouldn't spend all your time at work." Alex tried to explain to her the pressures he faced, his work load, and the debts he incurred. He felt his explanation a failure. His wife also grew resentful of his work. She argued that all their money seemed to drive them apart rather than closer together.

Alex did not heed the warnings, but instead he hid in his work. He worked long hours at his office and became preoccupied with his professional struggles. This steady diet of work, combined with personal and professional pressures, gave Alex a severe case of bleeding ulcers. Again, he ignored the signs of breakdown and pursued his career relentlessly. Unlike Carl Jung, he did not pay attention to his mind and body calling for a more reflective approach to the last half of his life. His drive for more and more success tried to cover an inner cry for spirituality.

Only when his wife and daughters could no longer stand the sight of his constant self-torture did the situation come to a head. A trial separation forced Alex to face his personal conflict, but it was almost too late. The crisis landed him in a hospital for medical and psychological treatment. Because he waited so long to turn from his preoccupation with work, Alex had to spend months coming to grips with his inner self. In time, he did begin to appreciate his spiritual self, and once his attitude changed, his wife and daughters returned to his side.

THE BEHAVIORISTIC APPROACH

Imagine you have just seen a young woman pound her fist into a wall. A fellow immediately asks you, "Why did she do that?" You might reply, "She hit the wall because she was angry." Our common sense seems to tell us that the motive behind such an irrational act is anger. The behaviorists, however, deny this seeming logic and tell us that emotions do not cause behavior. Emotions may accompany behavior, but they never *cause* behavior.

Suppose we look again at the example of the young woman. Something happened that left her feeling angry. Maybe she twisted her ankle, or a friend told her she was inconsiderate. It makes no difference. Some experience generated a feeling of anger in her. The signs of anger—flushed face, dilated pupils—might help you predict she would do something irrational, but the emotion of anger did not cause her violent act. Her friend's remarks or her twisted ankle motivated her action. Some people might feel the behaviorists are only engaging in a great word game or simply nitpicking. Not so, say the behaviorists. The world of psychology has perpetuated serious errors by suggesting that emotions cause behavior. B. F. Skinner explains that the *cause* for such anger is most important.

> An angry person may have a rapid pulse and a flushed face; his behavior may be strongly focused on the object of his anger and uncontrolled by other features of the environment; he may show a strong tendency to harm that object ("I could have killed him") or may actually harm him. He may feel much of the condition of his body at such a time and take it as the cause of his behavior, but it is in fact part of the effect for which a cause is sought. Both the behavior and the collateral conditions felt are to be explained. After all, why did he act and feel angry? (7)

Emotional Byproducts

The behaviorists claim that it is wrong to believe that emotions *cause* behavior. Suppose we recall the earlier section on Jung's theory of homeostasis. Jung said, for example, that the extremes of loneliness will urge us

to seek out the company of others. Too much gregariousness will, in turn, press us to look for isolation. Such statements upset behaviorists, because they insist that lonely feelings do not cause us to look for company nor does gregariousness press us to seek isolation. Emotions can never cause behavior. Whatever causes the emotion also causes the behavior.

Suppose we look at the same theory from a behaviorist's point of view. The person who spends too much time in isolation begins to have a feeling commonly called loneliness. The feeling reminds the person that he or she has not seen anyone socially for a long time, and the person, once reminded, searches out some company. The lonely feeling did not cause the person to search for a friend. Rather the lack of contact with others caused the person to find a friend and engage that friend socially. The behaviorists feel we make a serious mistake when we allow ourselves to say we look for friends because we are lonely. By so doing we overlook the more important question, "What caused the lonely feeling?"

Skinner explains the problem:

> Many supposed inner causes of behavior such as attitudes, opinions, traits of character, and philosophies, remain almost entirely **inferential** [or deduced]. That a person is pro-labor, planning to vote for a given candidate, intelligent, liberal, or pragmatic is known not from what he feels but from what he says or does. Nevertheless, terms referring to traits of character are freely used in explaining behavior. A politician continues to run for office because of "ambition," makes shady deals because of "greed," opposes measures to eliminate discrimination because of "moral callousness," holds the support of his followers because of his "leadership qualities," and so on, where no evidence of the inner causes is available except the behavior attributed to them. (8)

Turning Adjectives into Nouns

Skinner sees many problems when we attribute unobservable emotional causes to observable behavior.

> Turning from observed behavior to a fanciful inner world continues unabated. We tend to make nouns of adjectives and verbs and must then find a place for the things the nouns are said to represent. We say that a rope is strong, and before long we are speaking of its strength. We call a particular kind of strength tensile, and then explain that the rope is strong because it possesses tensile strength. The mistake is less obvious but more troublesome when matters are more complex. There is no harm in saying that a fluid possesses viscosity, or in measuring and comparing different fluids or the same fluid at different temperatures on some convenient scale. But what does viscosity mean? A sticky stuff prepared to trap birds was once made from *viscus,* Latin for mistletoe. The term came to mean "having a ropy or glutinous consistency," and viscosity "the state or quality of being ropy or glutinous." The term is useful in refer-

ring to a characteristic of a fluid, but it is nevertheless a mistake to say that a fluid flows slowly because it is viscous or possesses a high viscosity. A state or quality inferred from the behavior of a fluid begins to be taken as a cause. (9)

Psychologists who use labels in assigning motives and causes run into many problems, according to Skinner. They tend to say, for example, that the disease **schizophrenia,** which is only a label, causes a lack of contact with reality. So that when an individual makes statements such as, "I am Abraham Lincoln," many psychologists will say that schizophrenia caused the loss of reality contact. Behaviorists continue to repeat that mental constructions such as schizophrenia cannot cause behavior. The same is true of the labels **manic-depression** and **paranoia.** Such terms are descriptive only. They are all adjectives. We can talk about a person with schizophrenic tendencies, for example. But psychologists, behaviorists claim, turn them into nouns by saying, "Because this person is *a* schizophrenic, we can expect him to lose contact with his reality."

The tendency to use adjectives as nouns is particularly dangerous in therapy. Once a person is labeled a schizophrenic, a therapist will look for certain motives and behaviors (Case 4.3). And the person labeled as a schizophrenic, knowing the psychologist expects to find some irrational behavior, may behave the way the psychologist expects. As the patient begins to act in the schizophrenic ways that therapist expects, he or she can actually become worse.

One label that causes most people to distort their perceptions and make unwarranted assumptions is "mentally disturbed." For example, many people assume mentally disturbed people would be less likely than so-called normal people to help a person in need. To prove that such assumptions are often incorrect, psychologist Alexander Tolor and some associates exposed 25 college students and 25 hospitalized psychiatric patients to identical situations.

They asked all 50 subjects to agree or disagree with statements, on a written scale, such as "Every person should give some of his time for the good of his town or city." After the subjects completed the form, the examiner, before he left the room, said someone else would soon come to collect the forms. An accomplice later hobbled into the room on crutches and began to collect the forms. He then suddenly shouted in pain and fell to the floor. The subjects were watched closely to see how much assistance they would give the handicapped person.

The college students and the psychiatric patients all scored about the same on the written scale of attitudes. However, when it came to taking action, the psychiatric patients offered significantly more help to the fellow on the floor. Many possible explanations might be suggested for their different behavior, but one important fact remains. We can easily make assumptions about a person's behavior, based on a label such as "mentally disturbed", that do not hold true in reality. (10)

Case 4.3

Therapists can do serious harm when they decide people fit into categories such as "mentally disturbed." In at least one case, such a category upset a person seriously.

Alice, a middle-aged woman looked smart and attractive. Only a small touch of grey in her hair gave the impression of age. The day she talked to me she showed no sign of the ordeal she suffered earlier in her life. "Before I went into therapy, I had never even met a psychiatrist," she told me one day after we had become close friends. "So I remember feeling quite in awe of my first therapist. I assumed anything he said must be true."

"I can see how you might feel that way," I replied.

"Unfortunately, that faith in the man led me into the worst experience of my life," she told me.

"How did that happen?" I felt uneasy with my question.

"Well, once he heard me describe how I talked with my deceased mother, he began to assume there was something terribly wrong with me." Alice looked at me anxiously. "There wasn't. At least not as serious as he assumed. My mother and I were always close and I felt her presence quite strongly even though she was dead for many years."

"I know lots of people who carry on relationships after death separates them. Actually, it is quite common among lovers who experienced a great deal of intimacy during their life." I hoped my words would reassure Alice.

"I'm glad you feel that way. And I wish you were my therapist at that time." Alice smiled. "The guy I saw began to ask me about other behavior. I remember he wanted to know if I ever heard voices. And you know what? Those conversations began to worry me. Before long I found myself in turmoil over what once seemed quite normal to me."

"It sounds as if your therapist had some definite expectations of you."

"That's the way it seemed to me, also."

The therapist had, in fact, overreacted to what sounded like a sign of emotional instability. Before long he had pressed Alice, with his expectations, into a category of illness that did not fit her. And in the process, he upset her considerably.

The Behaviorist Explanation

Behaviorists believe they have a simple and accurate way of explaining motivation and emotion. In contrast to other psychologists, behaviorists believe we are motivated to perform actions by rewards and avoid actions by lack of reinforcement. Suppose we consider the student of the violin. He practices regularly and, as a result of that practice, begins to hit the correct note most of the time. Before long, he can play for hours without hitting a sour note. We say he gained a feeling, or emotion, of confidence. Many psychologists would say that the young man plays well *because* he

Behaviorists believe we perfect our skills through reinforcement. (Peter Vandermark)

has confidence in himself. The behaviorists balk. They would rather say the person, through the constant *reinforcement* of correct notes, comes to play almost flawlessly. The confident feeling is nothing more than a by-product of the cause of his near-perfect performance.

The same holds true for extinction. Suppose our violinist develops a serious arthritis condition later in life. He begins to hit the wrong note frequently. We say he becomes depressed and this emotion of depression causes him to give up the violin. Again, behaviorists would point out that the depression did not motivate him to abandon the violin. In fact, he abandoned the violin because of his arthritis or the number of wrong notes the arthritis now makes him produce. The lack of reinforcement (accurate playing) extinguished his good performances.

THE HUMANISTIC APPROACH

Carl Rogers believes that our need to discover who we are motivates most of our behavior. He points out that most of the people who come to him for therapy hide behind a **mask** (Self-Quiz 4.2). A middle-aged man, for example, might act calm and at ease in order to hide feelings of inadequacy. An adolescent boy might pretend to care only about his intellectual interests rather than admit his lack of social grace. An apathetic business woman might pretend to possess a strong interest in her profession rather than admit her boredom. All these people in their own way, hide from admitting what they truly feel inside.

> When a person comes to me, troubled by his unique combination of difficulties, I have found it most worth while to try to create a relationship with him in which he is safe and free. It is my purpose to understand the way he feels in his own inner world, to accept him as he is, to create an atmosphere of freedom in which he can move in his thinking and feeling and being, in any direction he desires. How does he use this freedom?

Momma by Mell Lazarus. Courtesy of Mell Lazarus and Field Newspaper Syndicate.

It is my experience that he uses it to become more and more himself. He begins to drop the false fronts, or the masks, or the roles, with which he has faced life. He appears to be trying to discover something more basic, something more truly himself. At first he lays aside masks which he is to some degree aware of using. (11)

Much of our behavior, Rogers suggests, is motivated by defensiveness. Most people do not want to admit that they are ashamed or embarrassed by their own lack of talent, skill, or aptitude. They put a great deal of energy into projecting an image of themselves that they think will impress others. We fool others into believing that we are calm when we are angry, that we are confident when we are anxious and uneasy, or that we are unruffled when we are terrified.

Embarrassment

Humanists believe that once people experience freedom in the therapy relationship, a new form of motivation begins to operate. They start to rebel against the mask they show other people. The young woman admits she hates smiling and pretending that she enjoys her mother's visits. She talks about wishing she had the freedom to tell her mother how difficult visits are while her own children are still young. The bank clerk talks about how hard it is to remain polite when customers grow angry and abusive. He says he would love to be able to tell such people they have no right to be rude to him.

Angry feelings emerge slowly at first. They seep through small cracks in the masks that we hide behind during our daily lives. But as angry feelings become easier to express, behavior begins to change both in and out of the therapy session. Sometimes a great deal of excitement accompanies the new ability to reveal how we really feel. Feelings that have been pent up for a long time can burst out in anger. The young woman who finally speaks up to her mother can be sharp and hostile. The bank clerk may re-

Self-Quiz 4.2   The Mask

This test contains a number of statements about personal attitudes. Read each statement and choose the alternative that best describes your attitude by checking the proper box to the left of the statement. Answer all of the statemements.

Often   *Occasionally*   *Seldom*

□ □ □   1. I keep my feelings to myself.
□ □ □   2. I consider myself more serious than most people I know.
□ □ □   3. Personal statements upset me.
□ □ □   4. I am uncomfortable when I meet people for the first time.
□ □ □   5. I would rather observe a conversation than join in.
□ □ □   6. I am most comfortable when left alone.
□ □ □   7. I am a lonely person.
□ □ □   8. I avoid letting my close friends meet.
□ □ □   9. I am tense around people.
□ □ □   10. I feel people could not like the real person I hide inside me.

This test cannot tell you to what extent you rely on a defensive mask, but it does tell you how you compare with others who took the same test. To total your score, give yourself 3 points for each time you checked "often" on the test, 2 points for each "occasionally," and 1 point for each "seldom." Add up the total number of points and compare that total with the following scale.

30–22   Few students score in this range. A score this high indicates a more than average tendency to mask your feelings.
21–14   The vast majority of students taking this test score in this range. You are probably fairly well able to set aside masks and pretense.
Below 14   Few students score this low. Scores in this range suggest an unusual amount of freedom from masks.

---

lease a barrage of angry feelings because he waited so long to express himself. Whatever form the outburst of feelings takes, the important thing is that the feelings are finally out in the open after years of hiding (Case 4.4).

Carl Rogers talks specifically about this burst of anger in the context of **encounter groups,** or **group therapy.**

> Curiously enough, the first expression of genuinely significant "here and now" feeling is apt to come out in negative attitudes toward other group members or the group leader. In one group in which members introduced themselves at some length, one woman refused, saying that she preferred to be known for what she was in the group and not in terms of her status outside. Very shortly after this, a man in the group attacked her vigorously and angrily for this stand, accusing her of failing to cooperate, of keeping herself aloof from the group, of being unreasonable. It was the first current personal feeling brought into the open in that group. (12)

● Case 4.4

Discussion of the angry explosion of hidden feelings usually reminds me of Buddy. At the time he came to see me, he could not have appeared more in charge of his life. During his last year in college, Buddy, engineering major, was on the honor roll, president of his class, and editor of the undergraduate engineering journal. On the cold and damp March day that he came to my office at the counseling center, I of course assumed he wanted to talk about what graduate school might be the best for him.

I recall my shock when Buddy said he came for counseling because his grades had plunged during his last semester in school. I did not take him seriously until he became quite specific about the number of classes he had missed, the exams he had already failed, and the weeks of assignments he had not yet completed. Once my shock subsided, we began to discuss the possible cause of his poor performance.

During the first hour that we talked, Buddy suggested a few reasons why he might be finding his last semester so difficult. He mentioned several times how disappointed his father would be over his failure. Each time those comments seemed unrelated to our discussion. Yet, whenever I pursued the confusion those remarks caused me, Buddy smiled and said he meant nothing by them. He only wanted me to know how much his father meant to him and how disappointed his father would be in his failure.

As the remarks about his father persisted, I told Buddy we had to discuss his relationship with his father. It sounded as if they had the ideal father-son relationship. At first, Buddy made his father sound like a modern-day saint. The more we talked, however, the more Buddy became nervous and uneasy; and the more uneasy he became, the more he talked. Finally, in a burst of passion, he shouted, "I hate him! I hate my father. He never cared for me. He never loved me. He only loves his money."

Buddy's remarks were angry and vengeful. He had bottled up his feelings for so long that they erupted violently. The outburst uncovered so many hidden, unresolved feelings about his father that Buddy finally needed to withdraw from school to sort things out. In time, he calmed down and talked with his father about the mixed feelings he had held inside for so long. The following fall Buddy returned to school, finished the year, entered graduate school, and began his life anew.

Balancing Conflicting Emotions

The initial outburst of pent-up emotions does eventually spend itself. People finally express most of the anger, loneliness, hurt, sadness, or frustration that have grown over the years. As that initial period ends, people discover that facing and expressing their strong emotions did not cause them or others lasting damage. All the energy they had spent trying to hide from their feelings suddenly appears unnecessary and even wrong. For the first time, powerful emotions that seemed destined to harm or destroy look friendly.

Once people discover that feelings they once considered destructive actually have no power to destroy, they look more carefully at their emotions and begin to trust the same emotions they once feared. They learn to expect their emotions to give them postitive motivation. The mother who was angry over her mother's visits comes to believe her anger was appropriate. The bank clerk realizes his upset with some of his customers made sense. Anger, before it grows out of proportion through repression, has its place in our personality along with love, joy, and happiness.

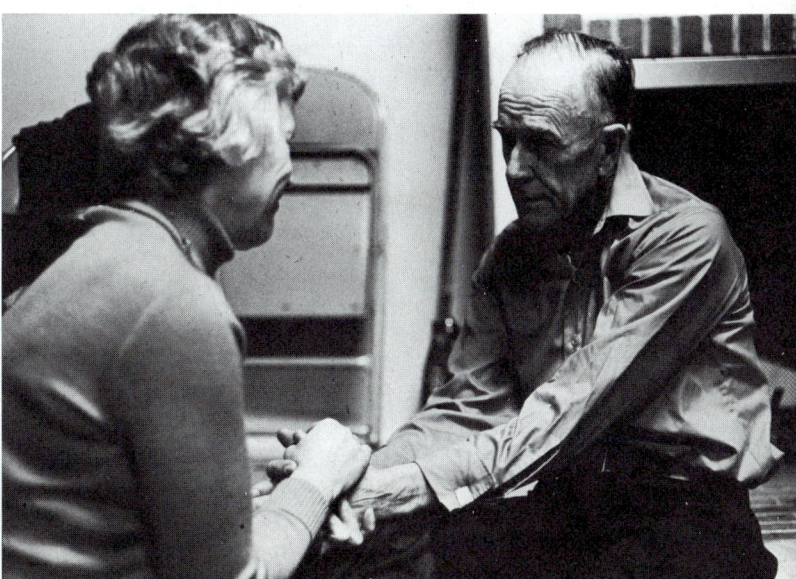

Humanists believe that expressing strong feelings of hurt or sadness can help people live more comfortably with their emotions. (Karen R. Preuss/Jeroboam)

Carl Rogers is particularly sensitive to the ability people gain, once they have expressed hidden feelings, to let conflicting emotions live side by side. In his book *On Becoming a Person* he discusses several clients, one of whom said:

> "I have thought I must feel only love for my parents, but I find that I experience both love and bitter resentment. Perhaps I can be that person who freely experiences both love and bitter resentment." For another client the learning may be: "I have thought I was only bad and worthless. Now I experience myself at times as one of much worth; at other times as one of little worth or usefulness. Perhaps I can be a person who experiences varying degrees of worth." For another: "I have held the conception that no one could really love me for myself. Now I experience the affectional warmth of another for me. Perhaps I can be a person who is lovable by others—perhaps I am such a person." For still another: "I have been brought up to feel that I must not appreciate myself—but I do. I can cry for myself, but I can enjoy myself, too. Perhaps I am a richly varied person whom I can enjoy and for whom I can feel sorry." Or, to take a last example, "I have thought that in some deep way I was bad, that the most basic elements in me must be dire and awful. I don't experience that badness, but rather a positive desire to live and let live. Perhaps I can be that person who is, at heart, positive."

●Case 4.5

Talk of expressing feelings we once thought might cause permanent harm or damage reminds me of Gayle, an effervescent young mother. I vividly remember the day she approached my lecture podium after a late afternoon class. "Remember that lecture you gave on expressing feelings?" she asked.

"I certainly do," I replied.

"Well, you may remember how much I objected to your claim that feelings could not cause lasting damage if they were expressed genuinely." Gayle smiled. "I told you I could see many people destroyed by honesty in relationships."

"Do you also remember I agreed with you that people might be seriously hurt, though not permanently damaged, by expressing their true feelings?" I asked defensively.

"I think I probably didn't pay too much attention to what you were saying." A flush betrayed Gayle's embarrassment. "I could only think of Hal, my husband, and how jealous I was of his relationship with his secretary."

"No wonder you couldn't hear me."

"I have been jealous of Hal for two years, but I was just certain if I mentioned my true feelings, he would surely leave me." Gayle pulled nervously at her blouse. "I know it's wrong to be jealous, but I can't stop those feelings."

"Did you finally tell Hal about your jealous feelings?"

"Yes, and you know what? He knew all along I was jealous. He was afraid of talking to me about those feelings for the same reason I could not mention them to him. He feared if we talked about my reaction it might damage our relationship."

"But you did finally talk about your jealousy?"

"Yes. We talked and talked. One night we talked until three in the morning. I told Hal how much I want him to be free to form other relationships, but that my jealousy also makes me want to seal him off from all other women. He said he would like to have easy relationships with lots of other people, including women. Yet he also assured me he does not want to cause me unnecessary anxiety." Gayle's lips pursed with concern.

"So did you decide you could have your jealous feelings and still be happy together?"

"We did. We decided we could not know where my jealous feelings and his need for other friends might lead us in our relationship. But we also agreed we must give all our feelings their freedom. So I hope that maybe I can be jealous of Hal and still love him completely."

Self-Trust

Once we set aside our masks and begin to experience our true feelings, we realize that our motions are complex, unpredictable, and very changeable. Sadness can shift to happiness within moments. A person who seems so close one day can be the object of anger the next. More important, feelings do not always fall into nice, neat categories of sadness, loneliness, or happiness. Loneliness can have an edge of sadness and, simultaneously, overtones of happiness. Complex feelings can be difficult to untangle and define.

As we explore our feelings, we see that they can be valid guides for helping us decide what to do. People who have discovered the value of their feelings look to their feelings more and more often to determine which way they should move when decisions become difficult. The young man who turns to engineering rather than business because it feels right has learned to trust his feelings. A young woman might go to business school rather than starting a family right after college because her emotions keep directing her that way. Many people follow their feelings to help them make appropriate decisions.

Carl Rogers believes that this growing sense of self-trust is very important for our happiness.

> Still another way of describing this pattern which I see in each client is to say that increasingly he trusts and values the process which is himself. Watching my clients, I have come to a much better understanding of creative people. El Greco, for example, must have realized as he looked at some of his early work that "good artists do not paint like that." But somehow he trusted his own experiencing of life, the process of himself, sufficiently that he could go on expressing his own unique perceptions. It was as though he could say, "Good artists do not paint like this, but I

Rogers cited Hemingway as an example of a man who followed an internal set of directions. (John Bryson)

paint like this." Or to move to another field, Ernest Hemingway was surely aware that "good writers do not write like this." But fortunately he moved toward being Hemingway, being himself, rather than toward someone else's conception of a good writer. Einstein seems to have been unusually oblivious to the fact that good physicists did not think his kind of thoughts. Rather than drawing back because of his inadequate academic preparation in physics, he simply moved toward being Einstein, toward thinking his own thoughts, toward being as truly and deeply himself as he could. This is not a phenomenon which occurs only in the artist or the genius. Time and again in my clients, I have seen simple people become significant and creative in their own spheres, as they have developed more trust of the processes going on within themselves, and have dared to feel their own feelings, live by values which they discover within, and express themselves in their own unique ways. (14)

CONCLUSION

When we ask behaviorists to explain the motives behind our actions, they talk about different things than the psychoanalysts and the humanists do. The behaviorists believe the causes of our actions can be observed and measured, as they talk about motives in immediate and concrete terms. They discuss tennis players, pianists, and painters, and their theories on motivation apply to everyone. The pianist wants to play well because of the rewards she receives for playing well. The child wants to be reflective because his parents rewarded reflective behavior early in his life. Our motives are the result of reinforcement; that is, we would rather do this thing instead of that because of the rewards we received for such actions in the past.

After thinking about behavioristic theories of rewards and reinforcement, the psychoanalytic and humanistic theories can seem unnecessarily complicated at first. Why analyze our personality and its dynamics to understand our motives? Yet, we know their explanations are important, too. In Jungian terms, we experience the odd fluctuations our personality can take at times. We know our motive for seeking out others can result from a lonely feeling that comes out from isolation—we want companionship because of too much solitude. An excessive interest in material goods can press us to look for more spiritual values. Our inner motives, then, certainly come partly from our personal search for balance in our life.

Carl Rogers and many other humanists see many motives arising out of our frustrated drive for open expression of our feelings. Social demands and personal expectations press us to hide behind masks. The more we hide from our embarrassing feelings, however, the more our need for openness grows. All our actions can become dominated by this motive to be honest and open. We can then explain many of our motives, even those apparently unrelated to the need for openness, by our need to stop hiding behind the social masks we wear.

We are once more left with several insightful explanations of our behavior. Yet, no one insight seems sufficient to explain all our motives and emotions. If we take parts of each theory and begin to develop our own theory of motivation, we can begin to understand why we do the things we do.

SUMMARY

1. Carl Jung thought an innate quest for personal unity is behind most of our drives and motives. He saw us constantly striving to maintain a balance among the many forces that pull at our personality. This internal search for harmony presses us to seek friends during periods of loneliness and urges us to find solitude when our social life begins to overwhelm us. This psychological need for equilibrium, or homeostasis, explains most of our needs, drives, and desires.
2. B. F. Skinner and many other behaviorists think theories that use emotions to explain behavior are useless. It may seem that anger causes a person to slam a fist into a wall, but actually anger merely may accompany the action. For Skinner, the anger cannot cause a fist-slamming incident. To discover the cause of the blow, we must find out what caused the anger in the first place.
3. Carl Rogers, like Carl Jung, looks at the inner workings of our personality to understand our motives. He feels that we hide behind masks that protect us from other people. Because we are embarrassed by our true feelings, we spend time and energy pretending and hiding. Much behavior can be explained by this need to hide. However, we can, either in or out of therapy, discover our true feelings and begin to live by

them. The feelings that we once considered angry and destructive can come to be trustworthy guides for action and give us an entirely new set of motives in our lives.

KEY TERMS

extraverts
introverts
homeostasis
individuation
inferential
schizophrenia

manic-depression
paranoia
mask
encounter groups
group therapy

STUDY QUESTIONS

1. Recall some occasion on which you were experiencing the extremes of fear, loneliness, or another emotion. Did it seem, as Jung suggests, that your mind almost automatically adjusted to bring you to a more balanced state?
2. Do you consider yourself more of an extravert or an introvert? Why?
3. How would Jung probably react to the behaviorists' attitudes toward motivation and emotion?
4. Think of three friends. How often have you seen each of them wearing a mask? When you noticed their pretense, did you respond by putting on a mask of your own?
5. Do you think of your feelings and emotions as a reasonable guide for your life?

ADDITIONAL READING

Abraham, K. Korman. *The Psychology of Motivation.* Englewood Cliffs, N. J.: Prentice-Hall, 1974.
Bolles, R. C. *Theory of Motivation.* New York: Harper and Row, 1975.
Fordham, Frieda. *An Introduction to Jung's Psychology.* Baltimore: Penguin, 1953.
Glickman, S. E., and Milner, P. M. (Eds.) *The Neurological Basis of Motivation.* New York: Van Nostrand Reinhold, 1969.
Hall, Calvin S., and Nordby, Vernon J. *A Primer of Jungian Psychology.* New York: New American Library, 1973.
Rogers, Carl R. *On Becoming a Person.* Boston: Houghton Mifflin, 1961.
———. *Carl Rogers on Encounter Groups.* New York: Harper & Row, 1970.
Skinner, B. F. *About Behaviorism.* New York: Vintage, 1974.
Storr, A. *C. G. Jung.* New York: Viking, 1973.
Zuckerman, M., and Spielberger, C. D. (Eds.) *Emotions and Anxiety: New Concepts, Methods, and Applications.* Hilsdale, N. J.: Lawrence Erlbaum, 1976.

Chapter Five

Anxiety and Stress

OUTLINE

The Psychoanalytic Approach
The Anxiety Experience
Reality Anxiety
Neurotic Anxiety
Moral Anxiety

The Behavioristic Approach
Sinfulness
Generalization
Thoughts and Anxieties

The Humanistic Approach
The Roots of Anxiety
The Meaning of Life
Facing Anxiety

Conclusion

LEARNING OBJECTIVES

After reading this chapter you should be able to:

1. Explain Freud's distinction between reality anxiety, neurotic anxiety, and moral anxiety.
2. Distinguish between the three types of neurotic anxiety.
3. Compare and contrast the psychoanalytic and the behavioristic theories of anxiety.
4. Discuss how generalization creates phobias.
5. Explain how the humanists view anxiety.
6. Discuss how humanists would have us use anxiety to understand ourselves better.

Chapter Five

"I guess I'm just afraid," a law student named Sandy told a group therapy session a few years ago.

"Afraid? Afraid of what?" Bill, a middle-aged college professor, asked.

"That's just it," Sandy replied, looking Bill straight in the eye. "I don't know what I'm afraid of."

"I don't understand." Bill pursed his lips with concern. "How can you be afraid and not know what you fear?"

"My worst fears are my fears of the unknown," Noel, a nurse from a nearby hospital, interrupted. "As long as I can identify what I fear, I can deal with it. Last month, for example, I knew my boss would call me down for spending too much time on my lunch hour. That upset me and I worried about it, but I didn't lose any sleep over it." Noel smoothed out the sleeve on his white uniform. "But two nights ago I suddenly got scared that I would never find anyone who would love me enough to want to marry me. Now I know that's crazy. I have lots of good women friends. But you know? I can't get that fear out of my mind."

"Now I think I understand," Bill interrupted. A look of recognition smoothed out his face. "I've had fears like that."

"You're nice. I mean, I really connect with your pain."

"For the last two nights," Noel continued. "I have not had more than three hours sleep. And it's ironic. My greatest fear lies in not knowing what my real fear is."

Most of us have experienced that fear of the unknown Noel talked about. We call it anxiety. In fact, anxiety and modern life have become almost synonymous. Almost any discussion of war, environmental pollution, or cancer-causing chemicals seems to link the words "anxiety" and "modern life." History points out, however, that all generations thought anxiety was peculiar to their special time and place. Psychologists suggest that anxiety is not peculiar to our age, although our particular anxieties, such as our fear of an atomic holocaust, may be unique. According to the psychologists we will discuss, anxiety is part of being human.

We have good reason for many modern anxieties. (Jim McHugh/Sygma)

Psychologists have different ways of looking at anxiety. The psychoanalysts look inside the personality to find the root of anxiety. They hope we can rid ourselves of unnecessary pain by better understanding what causes our inner conflict. The behaviorists, by contrast, see anxiety as a natural reaction to punishment. They believe that we learn to extend fears which are natural and appropriate in one situation to other, inappropriate situations. We might, for example, learn to extend our early fear of parental punishment to other authority figures, such as police officers. The humanists see anxiety in much the same way as the psychoanalysts do—as a sign of an inner personality conflict. They deviate from the psychoanalytic viewpoint, however, by looking more carefully at anxiety as a symptom of an inner struggle for health. Just as a fever is a symptom of a disease, anxiety, for humanists, is a warning of an important struggle deep within our personality.

THE PSYCHOANALYTIC APPROACH

A brief look at the Freudian model of the personality makes it easier for us to understand the role of **anxiety** in our lives. First of all, Freud spoke of the id, the source of all instinctive impulses, operating according to the pleasure principle. That is, it demands immediate satisfaction of all instinctive drives regardless of the consequences. The ego, by contrast, acts as a moderator for the id's impulsiveness, observing the world and adjusting the id's drives according to a reality principle. The resulting conflict between the id and the ego, as we will see, can be a source of much anxiety. The third part of Freud's personality scheme is the superego. The superego, according to Freud, develops as a result of our contact with parents and their moral codes. They set up rules for us to follow that persist long after we leave their protective custody. The anxiety that results from the conflict between the id and the superego we commonly describe as **guilt.** Here is an example of how the three parts of the personality interact. If we are afraid to shoplift some attractive item because we fear being caught, we are responding to our ego and its reality principle. But if we are afraid of moral punishment for stealing, we are responding to our superego's rules.

● Case 5.1

At times, parental restrictions can place an enormous burden on a child. When the child grows up, the moral restraints of the superego can become overwhelming.

Such early parental restrictions had a physical as well as an emotional effect on Dorthy. In fact, everyone who met Dorthy a few years ago was struck by her gaunt look. She looked emaciated and sad. The reason for her appearance was based on a painful childhood. Dorthy's father had victimized her with his religious fervor by constantly berating her for her "sins." Dorthy's sins were usually nothing more than incidents that upset him personally.

More than anything else, Dorthy's father feared financial ruin. He made a modest income and constantly feared it would not maintain the family. His fear of poverty made every purchase a reason for anxiety. Even the smallest new item would create tension in the house. Rather than admit his anxieties, however, Dorthy's father made spending money seem sinful.

No wonder Dorthy was haunted by guilt feelings most of her life. Money gradually took on overtones of evil. She found it extremely difficult, even in later life, to spend money. Therapy helped Dorthy a great deal. She can now regulate her life quite effectively. However, she will probably never completely rid herself of moral anxiety. Even her most casual purchases can bring her anxiety and guilt. However, each day finds her better able to cope with such problems.

The Anxiety Experience

Freud had a concrete understanding of anxiety. Calvin Hall probably spelled out the Freudian meaning of anxiety better than anyone else.

> Anxiety is a painful experience which is produced by excitations in the internal organs of the body. These excitations result from internal or external stimulation and are governed by the autonomic nervous system. For example, when a person encounters a dangerous situation his heart beats faster, he breathes more rapidly, his mouth becomes dry, and the palms of his hands sweat. (1)

When Sigmund Freud talked about anxiety, he was thinking of fear. In fact, he used the term anxiety only because he thought our common understanding of the term fear would be misleading. Whenever we speak of fear in our daily speech, we think of fearing *something.* We talk about our fear of muggers, communists, and even politicians. Freud realized such fears can and do exist and discussed the real fears we must contend with in the objective world. However, he also knew that all fears do not originate in the real world. A great many of our most significant fears have no clear and concrete basis.

A great many people suffer from **phobias,** for example. Phobias are intense, often irrational fears. The fear of heights is a good illustration. Just the thought of climbing up on a tall ladder leaves some people paralyzed, but if you ask them why heights terrify them so, they cannot answer. Some people with this phobia will talk about fearing that an uncontrollable urge will overcome them to throw themselves from the ladder. Others will mention an unidentified fear of falling. In either case, the result is the same: they become panic stricken because of some indefinite fear.

Obviously, this girl's fear is rooted in her objective world. Freud believed, however, that many of our fears are irrational. (Peter Vandermark)

Reality Anxiety

Freud talked a great deal about **reality anxiety,** anxiety that comes from objective fears. Whenever we perceive a real danger in the external world, we fear that danger. Even the fear of darkness, which some people might think of as an unreasonable fear, Freud considered a reality fear. For example, the fear of darkness could well have been passed down from one generation to another. Surely, most people in history have lived with the constant fear of the very real dangers darkness hid.

Calvin Hall tells us in his book, *A Primer of Freudian Psychology:*

> Reality anxiety is a painful emotional experience resulting from a perception of danger in the external world. A danger is any condition of the environment which threatens to harm the person. The perception of danger and the arousal of anxiety may be innate in the sense that one inherits a tendency to become afraid in the presence of certain objects or environmental conditions, or it may be acquired during the person's lifetime. For example, fear of darkness could be inborn because past generations of men were constantly being endangered during the night before

they had the means of making light, or it could be learned because one is more likely to have fear-arousing experiences during the night than during the day. Or it is possible that heredity and experience are co-producers of fear of darkness. Heredity might make a person susceptible to the fear while experience might transform the susceptibility into an actuality. (2)

Neurotic Anxiety

In spite of Freud's recognition of reality anxiety, he focused most of his attention on **neurotic anxiety.** For Freud, the neurotic anxieties become aroused whenever the instinctive drive from the id, the source of the pleasure principle, struggles with the ego and its reality principle.

The classic example, for Freud, always seemed to involve sex or aggression. The primitive sexual instinct that begins in the unconscious element of the id begins to emerge into the unconscious. Rather than admit this sexual drive exists, people begin to worry and fret about other concerns. These other concerns or fears that prevent a person from recognizing the sexual drive we call anxieties.

Freud divided the general category of neurotic anxiety into three separate parts. He describes the division here.

> We then turned to neurotic anxiety and pointed out that we observe it under three conditions. We find it first as a freely floating, general apprehensiveness, ready to attach itself temporarily, in the form of what is known as "expectant anxiety," to any possibility that may freshly arise—as happens, for instance, in a typical anxiety neurosis. Secondly, we find it firmly attached to certain ideas in the so-called "phobias," in which it is still possible to recognize a relation to external danger but in which we must judge the fear exaggerated out of all proportion. Thirdly and lastly, we find anxiety in hysteria and other forms of severe neurosis, where it either accompanies symptoms or emerges independently as an attack or more persistent state, but always without any visible basis in an external danger. We then asked ourselves two questions: "What are people afraid of in neurotic anxiety?" and "How are we to bring it into relation with realistic anxiety felt in the face of external dangers?" (3)

Freud's first category of neurotic anxiety is a free-flowing type of *general apprehensiveness*. Most of us know people who have a vague fear of some unknown force or danger. Often we say such people are afraid of their own shadows. We could also say they fear their own ids. They have a generalized fear of the impulses hidden deep within their personalities.

Freud's second form of neurotic anxiety is an intense and irrational fear called a *phobia* (Self-Quiz 5.1). We talked earlier about the fear-of-heights phobia. People can also have the same intense fear reaction to crowds, knives, birds, water, and a host of other common experiences and objects (Case 5.2). Again, Freud linked such fears to the id. The feared object in a phobia is often actually the id's repressed desire or a symbol of the desire.

The Psychoanalytic Approach 111

Animal Crackers. Reprinted by permission of the Chicago Tribune-New York News Syndicate, Inc.

As an example of a phobia, Calvin Hall tells the story of a young woman who was deathly afraid of touching anything made of rubber.

> She did not know why she had this fear; she only knew that she had had it as long as she could remember. Analysis brought out the following facts. When she was a little girl, her father had brought home two balloons, one for her and one for her younger sister. In a fit of temper she broke her sister's balloon, for which she was severely punished by the father. Moreover, she had to give her sister her balloon. Upon further analysis it was learned that she had been very jealous of her younger sister, so much so that she secretly wished her sister might die and leave her the sole object of her father's devotion. The breaking of her sister's balloon signified a destructive act against her sister. The ensuing punishment and her own guilt feelings became associated with the rubber balloon. Whenever she came into contact with rubber, the old fear of the wish to destroy her sister made her shrink away. (4)

The third and last form of neurotic anxiety Freud talked about might be described as *panic reactions*. They occur when a person breaks out into some impulsive behavior. Such behavior can have violent consequences, such as murder, but is usually much less dramatic. We might see someone

Self-Quiz 5.1 — Phobias

This test contains a number of statements regarding phobic reactions. Read each statement and choose the alternative that best describes your attitude by checking the proper box to the left of the statement.

Often	Occasionally	Rarely	
☐	☐	☐	I have an unreasonable fear of high places or open spaces.
☐	☐	☐	The thought of being in a closed space such as an elevator or a tunnel upsets me.
☐	☐	☐	I become a bit panicky in crowds.
☐	☐	☐	Even pictures of snakes, worms, or spiders unsettle me.
☐	☐	☐	I become upset by the thought of a long trip.
☐	☐	☐	Other things besides those mentioned cause me mild panic.

To total your score, give yourself 3 points for each time you checked "often" on the test, 2 points for each "occasionally," and 1 point for each "rarely." This test does not easily adapt to any definite conclusions. However, it might be informative to know how your score compares with those students who already took this test. The vast majority of students scored between 6 and 12 points. Higher scores suggest that you suffer more from phobic reactions than the norm; lower scores indicate that you are unusually free of phobic reactions.

---

who has appeared calm and stable for many years suddenly begin to scream and shout for no apparent reason. Or a friend might make an uncharacteristically insulting remark, shoplift for the first time, or have a sudden burst of offensive language. In each case, the panic reaction reveals an impulsive form of behavior. The ego loses control of the id's drive; an impulse, usually under the control of the ego, breaks free.

Terminally ill patients often engage in neurotic behavior. Panic reactions over their fear of impending death often make them unreasonable and difficult to cope with. Some terminal patients, once they learn of their condition, refuse all efforts to make them comfortable, cut off communication with loved ones, and even talk of suicide. Psychiatrist David Spiegel treats the clear signs of neurotic anxiety among terminal patients. Group therapy sessions help the patients cope with their fear of dying.

To help his patients avoid unreasonable anxiety, Dr. Spiegel asks the group members to prepare lists of their principal attributes and then meditate on the loss of these attributes—one by one. Once they face such losses, they are able to look at the self that remains. A hiker was shocked to realize she would still be the same person after she could no longer climb mountains. Others could accept themselves as valuable even after they lost the ability to care for their children.

As their faculties diminish, the group members seem to grow in their ability to make difficult decisions. As members die, Spiegel presses living members to look at their own anxiety and anger at death's victory. Each time they face such emotions, the members of the group can see their death as more real and less frightening.

The results of surveys taken among Spiegel's patients and a similar group of terminal patients without such support show that the experience provides significant help. The therapy-group members expressed their feelings more spontaneously and denied their condition less often. They seemed better able to look realistically at death. "Many members," Spiegel says, "have become less like passive victims of the disease process and more like experts on living." (5)

• Case 5.2

I have a phobic reaction to birds. As far back as I can remember, the sight of a bird in flight in my general direction could cause me to panic. My heart begins to beat faster. My palms sweat. My breath comes in short gasps. If the bird comes upon me suddenly from behind, my panic increases significantly. Though I have never fainted in my life, a large black bird, obviously protecting a nearby nest, once nearly caused me enough panic to pass out. The bird swooped silently on me from behind and screamed into my ear at the last possible moment. My heart did not stop pounding violently for nearly fifteen minutes.

Over the years I have tried to analyze my fear of birds. I have looked carefully at Freud's explanation of such phobic responses, and I feel the symbol represented by the bird must mean something. However, no matter how far back I search in my memory or how many associations I make between my fear of birds and my life, I cannot find any significant connection. Freud would probably tell me that I so fear recalling the incident which created my phobia that I have selectively forgotten it. I cannot say, but I know that, after years of pondering my phobia, I have not unraveled its mystery.

My phobia does generalize to other animals. I feel uneasy around snakes, even when they are sealed behind glass at the zoo. A similar uneasiness extends to horses, cows, and even domestic dogs. But something about birds, probably because I feel so powerless to control their flight, causes me the most anxiety. I suppose I could enter analysis and spend years and several thousand dollars to discover the cause of my phobia. Personally, I would rather try to avoid birds and save the money.

Moral Anxiety

Freud called the third type of anxiety that people can experience **moral anxiety.** Calvin Hall analyzes this category:

> Moral anxiety, which is experienced as feelings of guilt or shame in the ego, is aroused by a perception of danger from the conscience. The conscience as the interalized agent of parental authority threatens to punish the person for doing something or thinking something which transgresses the perfectionistic aims of the ego-ideal that have been laid down in their personality by the parents. The original fear from which moral anxiety is derived is an objective one; it is fear of the punitive parents. As is the case with neurotic anxiety, the source of moral anxiety lies within the personality structure, and as with neurotic anxiety the person cannot escape from feelings of guilt by running away from them. (6)

Moral anxiety, then, evolves when the superego, or conscience, is in conflict with the ego. We feel morally anxious when we violate the rules we learned from our parents. Naturally, those people whose parents passed on a strict code of ethics will suffer more pain from their consciences than those who learned a more flexible attitude. The amount of moral pain that a person suffers does not depend on how much or how little immoral behavior that person performs. Rather, the amount of moral pain depends on how rigid the parental code of ideals was. The person living according to a strict standard suffers more pain just thinking about immoral behavior than the person with a lax standard of ethics suffers by actually the same immoral behavior.

Moral anxiety, like neurotic anxiety, warns us when id impulses threaten the ego. In both cases, the anxiety experienced does not relate to any concrete form of external danger. The danger is actually the pain the conscience causes the person. That anxiety can become so painful and troubling that the person will do anything to secure some relief. Guilt feelings become so unbearable, at times, that guilty people will actually do something to invite punishment and thereby feel the same kind of relief they experienced when their parents punished them. Some people even commit crimes out of a sense of guilt. They are easily caught and punished because they want to be caught, punished, and thus freed of their guilt feelings.

A recent study of accident victims done by Ronnie Janoff Bulman and Camille Wortman suggests moral anxiety operates in the aftermath of freak accidents. These two psychologists inverviewed twenty-three men and six women paralyzed in shootings, falls, and other accidents. Their study points out that these victims often put more blame on themselves than the "objective" evident warranted.

At some point after their accidents, Bulman and Wortman tell us, all of the victims asked themselves, "Why me?" In over one-third of the cases, the answer involved God. Such responses usually suggested God had his reasons. "God wanted me to learn my lesson. I wouldn't listen . . . . So he made me listen," one paralytic suggested.

As might be anticipated by the Freudian theory of moral anxiety, the best-adjusted victims were those who saw their accident as following logically from freely chosen activities. The successful copers did not need to punish themselves with personal guilt feelings. (7)

THE BEHAVIORISTIC APPROACH

The behaviorists do not identify anxiety with some inner conflict within our personality as the psychoanalysts do. Rather, they think of anxiety as a perfectly natural reaction to **punishment**. The body simply resists, with all its reserve, painful circumstances. B. F. Skinner explains the behaviorist view of what he calls **aversive stimuli** and anxiety:

> Aversive stimuli, which generate a host of bodily conditions felt or introspectively observed, are the stimuli which function as reinforcers when they are reduced or terminated. They have different effects when related to behavior in other ways. In respondent conditioning, if a previously neutral stimulus, such as a bell, is frequently followed after an interval by a noxious stimulus, such as an electric shock, the bell comes to elicit reactions, primarily in the autonomic nervous system, which are felt as anxiety. The bell has become a conditioned aversive stimulus, which may then have the effect of changing the probability of any positively reinforced behavior in progress. Thus, a person engaged in a lively conversation may begin to speak less energetically or more erratically or may stop speaking altogether at the approach of someone who has treated him aversively. On the other hand, his negatively reinforced behavior may be strengthened, and he may act more compulsively or aggressively or move to escape. His behavior does not change because he feels anxious; it changes because of the aversive contingencies which generate the condition felt as anxiety. The change in feeling and the change in behavior have a common cause. (8)

Rather than work on anxieties directly, the behaviorists insist we look for reasons behind those anxieties, the aversive stimuli that produce the anxious feelings. Identifying the source of the anxiety can sometimes be quite difficult. Pat Stich, a behaviorist therapist, had difficulty discovering the sources of anxieties faced by young children about to undergo surgery. In trying to help children about to have surgery at the University of California at San Francisco's Moffit Hospital, she finally turned to an ingenious use of puppets. Her therapists help children awaiting surgery wheel a puppet into a play operating room, put a miniature oxygen mask over its face, and after the imaginary operation help puppet nurses return the toy patient to a recovery room.

This bit of play gives children an actual character to which they can relate. During the course of the puppet play, children can ask questions like: "Why can't the puppet have breakfast before surgery?" or, "Are you sure the puppet will wake up again after the operation?" Many anxieties previously hidden away emerge during these performances, as the children faced their anxieties about hunger, death, and pain and worked them out.

No rigid scientific tests have proven this play therapy effective. The children and parents exposed to the plays have been favorably impressed, however. Children who return to the hospital for follow-up surgery inevitably request the puppet shows each time. Stitch claims, "The child can get into the character of the puppet, put it on his hand and relate to its problems." Such identification seems to help children who fear some hidden dangers lurk for them once they enter surgery. The variety of questions that the plays provoke from children also suggests how anxieties can be systematically relieved by finding their roots. (9)

In this case, the children experienced surgery as an aversive stimulus, a kind of punishment. When they came into contact with the pre-operative conditions, they began to experience anxiety. The play with puppets gave them a chance to overcome their anxiety and thus reduce the power of the aversive stimuli.

Sinfulness

Freud described a complex personality structure built on the interaction of the id, ego, and superego. Behaviorists do not believe this complicated scheme is valuable to an understanding of anxiety. They also see no use in distinguishing between moral anxiety and neurotic anxiety as psychoanalysts do. Skinner only points out that the anxiety a person feels depends on the punishing agent. Punishment with a religious context will have moral overtones, Skinner says, and lets it go at that.

> What a person feels when he is in a situation in which he has been punished or when he has engaged in previously punished behavior depends upon the type of punishment, and this often depends in turn upon the punishing agent or institution. If he has been punished by his peers, he is said to feel shame; if he has been punished by a religious agency, he is said to feel a sense of sin; and if he has been punished by a governmental agency, he is said to feel guilt. If he acts to avoid further punishment, he may moderate the condition felt as shame, sin, or guilt, but he does not act because of his feelings or because his feelings are then changed; he acts because of the punishing contingencies to which he has been exposed. (10)

A woman may feel good about herself if she spends her leisure time reading her Bible for example. Therefore, most evenings she devotes some time to her Bible. Such a constructive use of time can even have the force of a religious conviction. A thunderstorm, on a given night, can distract the person enough to make her disrupt this schedule. The disruption in itself can create a sense of moral anxiety. Her fear of thunderstorms can also provoke her, because of previous religious associations and subsequent punishments, to cower in the corner of her room. The cowering can also trigger feelings of sinfulness. By this time, the young woman feels intensely sinful. However, the thunderstorm did not make her feel sinful. She only feels sinful because she stopped reading her Bible and began cowering in a corner. Both of those actions were the immediate cause of her sinful feelings.

Generalization

If a dog learns to salivate when someone strikes middle C on the piano, that dog is in a position to generalize its response. We can teach the dog to salivate when sounds of higher and lower pitch are produced. That tendency for a variety of similar stimuli to induce the conditioned response is termed **generalization.**

The process of generalization is particularly important in understanding the behaviorists' explanation of the phobic response. Behaviorists believe that as a person's anxiety in one situation generalizes to occur in another similar situation, the phobic reaction sets in.

The classic example of the story of little Albert will help us understand the phobic reaction as a behaviorist might see it. This version of the story is from Adelaide Bry who in turn quotes from the original study.

> Albert B., "was reared almost from birth in a hospital environment; his mother was a wet nurse in the Harriet Lane Home for Invalid Children. Albert's life was normal: he was healthy from birth and one of the best developed youngsters ever brought to the hospital, weighing twenty-one pounds at nine months of age. He was on the whole stolid and unemotional."
>
> Watson and Rayner ran stolid, unemotional Albert through a series of tests designed to elicit fear reactions. Specifically, Albert was successively confronted with "a white rat, a rabbit, a dog, a monkey, with masks with and without hair, cotton, wool, burning newspapers, etc. . . . . At no time did this infant ever show fear in any situation." Finally the authors introduced a loud gong. The child soon broke into a fit of crying.
>
> So classic conditioning was undertaken with the objective of inducing a fear reaction with the previously harmless white rat, by pairing the stimulus of the animal with the stimulus of the gong. After about three and half months of such conditioning sessions, not only did Albert show fear of the white rat, but the reaction had generalized so that a Santa Claus mask, a fur coat, a dog, and a rabbit caused him to whimper or cry. (12)

This cruel experiment showed how the fear reaction little Albert felt for the white rat soon generalized to include masks, dogs, and rabbits. Such generalizations, to one degree or another, afflict many people. A friend of mine who had an early traumatic experience with a vicious dog soon generalized that fear to all dogs, including obviously mild and harmless ones. Even more dramatic, he even learned, in time, to generalize his fear to pictures of dogs.

The generalization of anxiety can also extend to what behaviorists call *higher-order conditioning*. In higher-order conditioning the symbol of the fear that originally sparked the anxiety becomes cued to a new symbol. In Albert's case the white rat that gave him so much trouble could have been signaled, for example, by a flashing light. Then the flashing light would remind Albert of the white rat, which originally induced the anxiety caused by the gong. Naturally, the further the symbol is removed from the experience, the less its power. However, there is no doubt that the flashing light, even though twice removed from the anxiety experience, could also produce a good deal of turmoil (Case 5.3).

• Case 5.3

A little girl named Anne experienced the generalization of a phobia. Even after she had forgotten the source of her fear, Anne's anxieties continued to increase. The phobia started with an experience that occurred before Anne's fifth birthday. That was the day her doctor decided Anne needed to have a delicate heart operation. Her parents and the doctors decided not to tell Anne about the critical nature of the surgery. They only told her she was going to have a "small" operation. As is normally the case, Anne sensed from the tone of such explanations that more was involved than the words indicated. Consequently, she reached a state of nervous exhaustion by the time the operation day arrived. The doctors became particularly worried about Anne's ability to endure major surgery. However, they decided to operate anyway and, fortunately, Anne survived the operation.

Though her heart grew strong, something else was wrong with Anne. She emerged from that operation with a terrible fear of hospitals. Even the word hospital finally caused Anne to panic. One day Anne did not realize she was close to a hospital until she spotted a nurse's white uniform. The uniform signaled to Anne that she was near a hospital, and her nervous anxiety came on quickly. That frightening incident generalized her fear of hospitals to include any white uniform. In time, the word white also caused Anne serious anxiety.

Over the years, Anne's phobia became worse and continued to generalize. She would endure the serious and even dangerous symptoms of colds and flu without any support from drugs rather than contact a doctor. Her phobia extended beyond white to certain metals that reminded her of surgical instruments. There seemed no end to her problem until her parents, nearly desperate by the time Anne entered high school, brought her to a psychiatrist. Only a great deal of therapy helped Anne begin to understand her phobia, and she finally started to find some relief from the anxiety that had kept her imprisoned for so many years.

Thoughts and Anxieties

This discussion of anxiety that has been learned will be incomplete unless we talk about the role of *thoughts* in anxiety, because we all know that our fears and anxieties extend beyond our actual experience of the source of the fear. As long as Albert retained his phobia for the white rat, for example, he undoubtedly also reacted anxiously even to the thought of a white rat.

We can understand why many people forget the source of their anxieties. If even the thought of the original pain causes pain, we will undoubtedly try to avoid all such thoughts. For instance, most of us try our best not to think about the dentist and the pain that often accompanies our visits. Only when the visit is immediate and we can no longer avoid such thoughts, do we allow them to emerge.

Our ability to link words to situations and thus stimulate thoughts about the situations makes anxiety a persistent part of our lives. Such words as "speed kills" can be linked to auto accidents. The same words can then stimulate thoughts of auto accidents, which remind us of the fearful reality of death that such accidents imply. The same can be said of many words and phrases that are a part of our lives. Many people use phrases such as "I told you so" to punish others for real or imagined pain. The use of such trigger words stimulates anxiety in ourselves or others and makes it possible to extend anxiety into every corner of our lives.

THE HUMANISTIC APPROACH

Psychological theories usually describe anxiety in a completely negative context. The Freudian explanation of anxiety with the ego, id, and superego in constant conflict leaves us with the feeling that anxiety is something to be avoided at all costs. The behaviorists also believe anxiety should be avoided and eliminated. Humanists, on the other hand, admit that anxiety is generally associated with pain, but they also point out that anxiety is an important part of life. They believe we should be able to discover how to use this fact of life constructively.

One recent study points out just how much a part of life anxiety is. Canadian researcher Peter Waxer discovered that people "leak" the truth about their state of depression by a series of nonverbal cues. Waxer taught even uninformed observers to diagnose accurately a state of depression by watching a person's tilt of the head or movement of the body. Following this study, Waxer discovered the same "leaks" can be detected in people afflicted with anxiety.

In his anxiety study, Waxer showed silent one-minute video-tape segments of 20 psychiatric patients to 46 psychology majors. The students were asked to rate the patients' anxiety levels on a scale of 1 to 10 and then indicate which of the ten body areas revealed the anxiety level.

Rollo May believes that loneliness is integral to modern life and a basic cause of our anxiety. (© Joel Gordon)

The students were fairly successful in rating the patients' anxiety levels when their assessments were compared with anxiety tests the patients had taken at the time the videotapes were made. Various parts of the body were cited as revealing anxiety levels. The students talked about "jittery" or "clinging" hands, "shifting" eyes, a "tight" or "twitching" mouth, and a "stiff" torso. The study clearly supports the humanistic claim that anxiety is an intimate part of life. The students were able to read the patients' messages of anxiety very well, probably because everyone is used to reading this kind of communication every day. Anxiety, then, is a significant part of our communication with one another even when we are not aware of that communication. (13)

Rollo May is the one humanist (some would call him an existentialist) most often associated with the study of anxiety. Besides insisting on anxiety as a persistent and important part of life, he freely acknowledges its pain. However, rather than thinking solely in terms of eliminating anxiety, May considers the function of anxiety and how we might learn more about ourselves by better understanding our anxiety. He explains in his book, *Man's Search for Himself*.

> Indeed, the phrase "age of anxiety" is almost a platitude already. We have become so inured to living in a state of quasi-anxiety that our real danger is the temptation to hide our eyes in ostrich fashion. We shall live amid upheavals, clashes, wars and rumors of wars for two or three decades to come, and the challenge to the person of "imagination and understanding" is that he face these upheavals openly, and see if, by courage and insight, he can use his anxiety constructively. (14)

The Roots of Anxiety

To help us understand the context in which our anxiety takes root, Rollo May discusses two problems basic to people today. He first talks about the **hollow people** or empty people. Hollow people know what they "should" feel and what they "ought to" want to do, but have no idea how they do feel and what they really want to do. Emptiness and boredom are significant parts of these people's lives. They follow the latest fashion, learn the latest gossip, become active in ways their friends and neighbors tell them are important. Yet through it all, they never feel truly alive. And every time they look for a reason for their empty feeling, they find nothing. This feeling of emptiness is a major source of our anxiety.

The other problem in our lives that creates anxiety for us is **loneliness.** People today feel lonely, unimportant, and isolated. To combat this loneliness we spend a great deal of time hoping to be invited to the right parties, to be involved with the correct group, or to be a part of the proper activities. We yearn for such activity because we desperately fear being alone. Ironically, though being in activities with other people may help keep us from being alone, it often only intensifies our loneliness. Rollo May explains his humanistic theory of emptiness and loneliness:

Rollo May believes that emptiness and boredom are important problems for many people today. (Antonio Mendoza/The Picture Cube)

It may sound surprising when I say, on the basis of my own clinical practice as well as that of my psychological and psychiatric colleagues, that the chief problem of people in the middle decade of the twentieth century is emptiness. By that I mean not only that many people do not know what they want; they often do not have any clear idea of what they feel. When they talk about lack of autonomy, or lament their inability to make decisions — difficulties which are present in all decades — it soon becomes evident that their underlying problem is that they have no definite experience of their own desires or wants. Thus they feel swayed this way and that, with painful feelings of powerlessness, because they feel vacuous, empty. The complaint which leads them to come for help may be, for example, that their love relationships always break up or that they cannot go through with marriage plans or are dissatisfied with a marriage partner. But they do not talk long before they make it clear that they expect the marriage partner, real or hoped-for, to fill some lack, some vacancy within themselves; and they are anxious and angry because he or she doesn't. (15)

James J. Lynch, a psychiatrist at the University of Maryland School for Medicine, supports May's contention that loneliness is a central problem for people today. He concludes that many people die of loneliness and has some impressive statistics to support his point. The medical records may suggest that heart attacks, cancer, or lung disease cause death. However, Dr. Lynch claims that having no one to love actually causes us to smoke, drink, or brood ourselves into the grave.

A look at the National Health Census reveals that death rates for people who live alone are significantly higher than for couples. No matter how the statistics are broken down, by race or sex, those living alone die first. The death rates for white bachelors under 65 from heart disease and cancer are double the rate for married men. Most startling, the death rates from motor vehicle accidents and cirrhosis of the liver are four and seven times the rates for those who are married.

Lynch suggests lonely people often can escape isolation only by getting sick. The single people in hospitals stay, on the average, twice as long as those married. Lynch further points to studies that show how people in deep comas show improved heart rates when their hands are held. With such an impressive array of evidence, Lynch concludes that loneliness is indeed a central problem for people today. (16)

The Meaning of Life

Rollo May makes the same basic distinction between normal (reality) anxiety and neurotic anxiety that Freud made. In normal anxiety we are energized to take care of ourselves in a threatening situation. The threat is visible, and we use our extra energy to escape its consequences. In neurotic anxiety, the threat cannot be discovered easily. Through his study, however, May has defined neurotic anxiety as "the human being's basic reaction to a danger to his existence, or to some value he identifies with his existence." It is the most significant kind of anxiety in humanistic philosophy.

May suggests that as long as our dangers are real, they cannot cause us permanent damage. The person in a fight may be hurt, even permanently scarred, but he struggles with a force he can identify. The same is true for students who need a grade-point average to enter medical school; their anxiety is concrete. However, when we have been snubbed by a friend, even inadvertently, we face a more formidable kind of anxiety. We cannot define the pain we feel, and we can find our dreams filled with nightmares symbolizing our fear of the snub and its meaning. Our waking hours become dominated by a search for the "meaning" behind a snub that might only have been part of our imagination. The doubt and uncertainty that follow become anxiety that goes beyond the actual snub. This kind of anxiety can question the very meaning of our lives (Case 5.4). May explains:

> It is the quality of an experience which makes it anxiety rather than the quantity. One may feel only a slight gnawing away in one's stomach when a supposed friend passes one on the street and does not speak, but though the threat is not intense, the fact that the gnawing continues, and that one is confused and searches around for an "explanation" of why the friend snubbed one, shows the threat is to something basic in us. In its full-blown intensity, anxiety is the most painful emotion to which the human animal is heir. "Present dangers are less than future imaginings," as Shakespeare put it; and people have been known to leap out of a lifeboat and drown rather than face the agony of continual doubt and uncertainty, never knowing whether they will be rescued or not. (18)

● Case 5.4

At times, the realistic anxiety over such things as good grades can take on the qualities of neurotic anxiety, but the grade anxiety in such a case is only a substitute for a deeper need and anxiety.

For Ben, the decision to study medicine and maintain the necessary high grade point average caused him great anxiety when he reached college.

While he was in high school, he had easily stayed at the top of his class. In his valedictory address, Ben told the audience that "success was available to all those who worked to achieve it." Ben began to wonder about his words the minute he discovered the stiff competition that waited for him in college. His first examination in an introductory chemistry class was a disaster. He always thought a "C" grade was reserved for those who did not study, but Ben had studied harder than he had for any high school class and still received a "C."

Ben became more and more preoccupied with grades. He never measured time in terms of weeks and months, but as the distance from one examination to another. He talked about seeing a movie after his physics final, visiting his parents before the history test, and getting more sleep once his English term paper was finished. By his junior year, Ben regularly had fearful dreams about examinations. In one dream he found himself unable to take a test because his pen would not work. None of his classmates were willing to lend him one, and his teacher became angry because his requests for a pen looked like attempts to cheat. He woke up from that dream anxious and perspiring.

When Ben began to develop ulcers during his senior year, he went to the student infirmary where the doctor ran a complete examination on Ben. Nothing physical could account for the ulcers. The doctor suggested Ben's next stop might be at the student counseling center. Therapy helped Ben understand his drive for grades. It seems his competitiveness with his father had always driven Ben to excel. His father, a successful industrialist, had let Ben know he expected excellence. Ben's medical career and his preoccupation with grades were really ways Ben thought he could prove himself as a person to his father, not stimulating goals arising from his own enthusiasm.

Ben finally began to study architecture. In that field, he did not have the same need to strive for a high grade point average. Without the constant pressure for achievement, Ben began to achieve higher grades. More important, Ben became deeply involved in learning the skills of architecture, and only secondarily interested in collecting high grades.

Facing Anxiety

Rollo May and many other humanists see our neurotic anxiety as painful and undesirable. However, they also point out that our anxieties, no matter how extreme, are only symptoms of our problems (Case 5.5). Like the fever that signals the disease which threatens our body, anxiety indicates problems that challenge the roots of meaning in our lives. Thus, if we can find what is at the root of our anxiety, we can face the problem and try to solve it. The pain of anxiety can then disappear. Rollo May discusses the importance of actively exploring the source of our anxiety:

Momma by Mell Lazarus. Courtesy of Mell Lazarus and Field Newspaper Syndicate.

[Just as bodily fever is] a symptom of the battle between the bodily powers and the infecting germs, so anxiety is evidence of a battle between our strength as a self on one side and a danger which threatens to wipe out our existence as a self on the other. The more the threat wins, the more then our awareness of ourselves is surrendered, curtailed, hemmed in. But the greater our self-strength—that is, the greater our capacity to preserve our awareness of ourselves and the objective world around us—the less we will be overcome by the threat. There is still hope for a tuberculous patient so long as he has fever; but in the final stages of the disease, when the body has "given up" as it were, the fever leaves and soon the patient dies. Just so, the only thing which would signify the loss of hope for getting through our present difficulties as individuals and as a nation, would be a resigning into apathy, and a failure to feel and face our anxiety constructively (Self-Quiz 5.2). (19)

When Rollo May looks at the roots of our neurotic anxiety, he sees our loss of a sense of self. Because we are lonely and empty, we look at others to discover what we "ought to" think and feel. In the process, we become more and more distant from our own sense of self. When we turn outward for our identity we lose the sense of personal security, and this loss can lead to neurotic anxiety. If we are ever to cope with modern anxieties, Rollo May tells us, we must begin to find ourselves by discovering our *own* attitudes, feelings, and values. We must turn away from others and look to ourselves if we hope to discover security in an insecure world.

• Case 5.5

Anxiety can often distract us from the source of our problem. A relaxation exercise such as yoga can sometimes put us in the right frame of mind to focus on our conflicts more clearly.

Connie came from a very wealthy family and had every material thing she could wish for. She attracted friends with her pleasant manner and never reminded anyone of her family name or fortune in any way.

Toward the end of her junior year, Connie began to develop anxiety attacks. For some unknown reason, she would suddenly feel her heart pound, her head ache, and her breath come in short gasps. At first, the attacks only lasted a few minutes at a time, but the length of the attacks grew until one lasted almost an hour. Fortunately, about that time Connie met a friend, Tim, who encouraged her to join a yoga class he attended. Tim felt yoga could help Connie find the cause of her anxiety. Connie had no idea how yoga might help her relieve her anxiety attacks, but felt she had nothing to lose by trying.

Connie was pleased by how quickly the yoga exercises helped her relax. The stretches and pulls associated with yoga showed how tense she kept her body and helped give her immediate relief from her physical symptoms. But it was the meditation exercises that brought Connie to the root of her anxiety. When she let her mind freely wander, Connie noticed it most often returned to

Self-Quiz 5.2 — Anxiety Scale

Next to each statement place the number 1, 2, 3, 4, or 5—depending on how characteristic each statement is of you. Continue the process for each of the statements. Then total your score.

5 strongly characteristic of me
4 moderately characteristic of me
3 neutral
2 moderately uncharacteristic of me
1 strongly uncharacteristic of me

____ 1. If I overhear two people talking about a person whom they describe as moody and hard to get along with, I am apt to feel they were talking about me.
____ 2. Occasionally I can be easy with members of the opposite sex, but normally I find such relationships difficult.
____ 3. I think the old saying "spare the rod and spoil the child" is completely false.
____ 4. I often think the future looks black.
____ 5. I often find myself in need of a good cry.
____ 6. I tend to wake up quite early in the morning.
____ 7. I commonly feel that life demands too much effort.
____ 8. My appetite is rarely strong.
____ 9. I tend to tire quite easily.
____ 10. I am a worrier.

I regularly use:

____ 11. Aspirin or tranquilizers.
____ 12. Sleeping pills.
____ 13. Herbal tonics or medicine.
____ 14. Alcohol.

____ TOTAL SCORE

41–50   Students who score in this high range are probably fairly anxious.
25–40   This is the score range of the vast majority of students taking the test. You probably have an average amount of tension in your life.
Below 25   Scores this low suggest an unusually low degree of tension.

---

thoughts of her mother, especially when she turned to yoga in the midst of an anxiety attack. She discovered she felt both love and anger toward her mother and realized that, deep inside, she had never felt loved by her mother.

In time, Connie talked with her mother about her feelings. Their relationship never completely resolved itself, but it did improve. And most important, Connie experienced the anxiety attacks much less frequently.

Meditation can help people relax and explore the roots of their anxiety. (Peter Vandermark)

CONCLUSION

Our three viewpoints give us three important clues to understanding our anxiety. Freud pointed out the clear distinction between reality anxiety and neurotic anxiety. Yet it often is nearly impossible, especially when we look at our own emotions, to know if our anxieties have real or imaginary causes. We might honestly think we were upset by a casual remark because of its content, when instead we are in a turmoil over something having little to do with the remark. However, just asking ourselves the question, "Is this anxiety reasonable or not?" helps us understand ourselves and our fears better.

The behaviorists give us practical advice on understanding how we learn to be anxious at inappropriate times and places. We know from their explanation and our experience that fears do generalize. A fear of snakes can become a fear of other animals. A fear of our father can extend to all authority figures.

Finally, the humanists have their own valuable approach. They urge us to look at our anxieties as a sign of inner turmoil. Rather than searching for some easy way to erase the anxiety, they want us to face and explore its roots. When we look at the situations that cause us anxiety, Rollo May tells us, we will discover a common theme. In each case, our anxieties emerge from an emptiness and loneliness within ourselves that comes from our tendency to look to others for our identity. Because we fear relying on ourselves for inner strength, we grow uneasy about the roots of our very existence. Once we have faced the reasons for our anxiety, we can begin to feel better.

SUMMARY

1. Freud believed that conflicts between the id, ego, and superego account for our neurotic and moral anxiety. He broke neurotic anxiety into three separate categories—a free-floating form of apprehensiveness, phobias, and panic reactions. Our moral anxiety we learn from our parents. Its strength depends on the rigidity of the moral standards they passed on to us.
2. Behaviorists, by contrast, think of anxiety as nothing more than a natural reaction to aversive stimuli, or punishment. Anxiety reaction can generalize so that it occurs at times and places that seem quite inappropriate. Our fear of a dangerous dog, for example, can generalize to include all dogs, even mild and harmless ones.
3. The humanists admit that our anxieties can cause us pain and, to that extent, are sympathetic with our desires to rid ourselves of them. However, they also see value in anxiety. Our anxiety can reveal to us the threats we experience in the world. By paying close attention to those threats that upset us and by challenging them, we can help ourselves lead a more healthy and happy life.

KEY TERMS

anxiety
guilt
phobia
reality anxiety
neurotic anxiety
moral anxiety

punishment
aversive stimuli
generalization
hollow people
loneliness

STUDY QUESTIONS

1. Think of an extremely anxious moment you faced during the past year. Would you label it reality, neurotic, or moral anxiety? Why?
2. If you have a phobia, try to imagine how that phobia began. Does your explanation tend to agree with the sort of explanation Freud might give?
3. Do you believe your own phobias or fears could be overcome by a psychologist applying a series of rewards to your behavior? Explain.

4. Imagine what Freud might say about the behaviorists' theory that phobias are nothing more than learned behavior. What part of the theory might Freud find appealing?
5. Has any anxiety experience ever helped you understand yourself better? In what ways?
6. If your own anxieties began to grow out of control, and you sought the advice or help of a psychologist, would you likely talk to a psychoanalyst, a behaviorist, or a humanist? Why?

ADDITIONAL READING

Beck, A. T. *Depression: Clinical, Experimental and Theoretical Aspects.* New York: Hoeber Medical Division, Harper & Row, 1967.

Brenner, C. *An Elementary Textbook of Psychoanalysis.* New York: Doubleday, 1957.

Bry, Adelaide *A Primer of Behavioral Psychology.* New York: Mentor, 1975.

Davison, G. C., and Neale, J. M. *Abnormal Psychology: An Experimental Clinical Approach.* New York: John Wiley and Sons, 1974.

Freud, Sigmund *New Introductory Lectures on Psychoanalysis.* New York: Norton, 1933.

Hall, Calvin *A Primer of Freudian Psychology.* New York: Mentor, 1954.

Horney, Karen *The Neurotic Personality in Our Time.* New York: Norton, 1937.

May, Rollo *Man's Search for Himself.* New York: Signet, 1953.

May, Rollo *The Meaning of Anxiety.* New York: Ronald, 1950.

Skinner, B. F. *Science and Human Behavior.* New York: Macmillan, 1953.

Chapter Six

Conflict, Anger, and Aggression

OUTLINE

The Psychoanalytic Approach
    The Death Instinct
    Our Destructive Nature
    The Inevitability of Human Aggression

The Behavioristic Approach
    Frustration and Aggression
    Social Learning
    Obedience to Authority

The Humanistic Approach
    Anger and Violence
    Healthy Aggression
    The Fair Fight

Conclusion

LEARNING OBJECTIVES

After reading this chapter you should be able to:

1. Discuss Freud's concept of the death instinct.
2. Explain how Freud linked the death instinct to aggressive behavior.
3. Understand how behaviorists link frustration and aggression.
4. Discuss the social-learning explanation of aggressive behavior.
5. Explain how humanists link anger and violence.
6. Understand how the humanists would use aggression to help people live healthier lives.

Chapter Six

"I wish there were some way I could control my temper better," Ken, a middle-aged accountant told me in a therapy session recently. "Sometimes I become so angry I fear I might get violent."

"Tell me about a time when you thought you might become violent," I asked.

"One thing that happened last week still bothers me." Ken's face tightened with strain. "This friend of mine at the office was out sick for a week. During that time, I covered all his work for him. When he got back, everything was up to date. I broke my back doing two jobs for a week, and do you know, he never even thanked me."

"Did you tell him how angry you were?"

"Are you kidding?" Ken's mouth opened in surprise. "I wouldn't give him the satisfaction."

"But you're the one suffering. You might be in this turmoil for several more days, even weeks. If you ever hope to relieve yourself of all this emotion, you better tell him how you feel."

"I know." Ken looked down at the carpet as his voice softened. "Each day I become more upset. No matter what the guy says to me, I resent it."

"So why don't you tell him you expected some word of thanks after all the work you did for him?" I paused to choose my words carefully. "At least tell him how angry you are."

"No. I could never tell him I was angry. It's just too hard for me. I suppose it's the way I was raised. My parents never spoke an angry word in their lives. I could see they often got angry, but they would always smile and cover their feelings." Ken's face colored with embarrassment. "I guess I learned their lesson too well."

All of us experience aggression. We know what it is to become angry with others. We may, like Ken, hold our angry feelings inside and try not to let others know how upset they make us. Or we may, at the other extreme, shout and scream when our anger overwhelms us. In either case, according to the psychoanalytic school of thought, our experience is innate. Freud believed that aggression was instinctive and, therefore, inevitable in our lives.

The behaviorists look at aggression and anger in a different manner. Because they focus their attention on visible and measurable signs of behavior, they seek a cause for aggression that they can see and measure.

One group of behaviorists thinks frustration causes aggression. For instance, when we break off a key in a lock because of our haste, we react in anger. That frustration, then, stimulates aggression in a simple cause and effect relationship. Another group of behaviorists, the social-learning theorists, points out the major role imitation plays in stimulating aggression. The child who watches television violence, for example, will learn to react aggressively through imitation.

The humanists take a careful look at aggression and analyze it characteristically by pointing out how important it is for us to express our assertive tendencies. The inclination for us to repress an assertive impulse only bottles up our feelings and makes us aggressive. We must speak the angry word, they say, and assert ourselves openly and honestly. Then we will not only avoid the danger of letting emotions build to a dangerous level, but we will also enhance our self-esteem.

THE PSYCHOANALYTIC APPROACH

Freud did not pretend to know how many instincts we possess. He assumed there is a separate instinct for each bodily need. That is, the hunger instinct depends upon our need for food, while our thirst instinct depends upon our need for water. The list is long, and Freud thought the list would be better drawn up by a physiologist than by a psychologist.

However, Freud did make one important conclusion concerning the instincts. He assumed that, no matter how many instincts we actually possess, they can all be separated into one of two categories: **death instincts** or **life instincts.** Instincts such as hunger, thirst, and sex are for survival and can be classified as life instincts, while our destructive tendencies, which will be our interest in this chapter, come under the classification of death instincts (Case 6.1). Freud explains his theory of the two instincts:

> I have lately developed a view of the instincts which I shall here hold to and take as the basis of further discussions. According to this view we have to distinguish two classes of instincts, one of which, Eros or the sexual instincts, is by far the more conspicuous and accessible to study. It comprises not merely the uninhibited sexual instinct proper and the impulses of a sublimated or aim-inhibited nature derived from it, but also the self-preservative instinct . . . . The second class of instincts was not so easy to define; in the end we came to recognize sadism as its representative. As a result of theoretical considerations, supported by biology, we assumed the existence of a death-instinct, the task of which is to lead organic matter back into the inorganic state. (1)

The Death Instinct

Freud's theories about the death instinct grew, in part, out of his speculation concerning the evolution of matter. Freud thought that all living matter contained an instinct for death, the return to its inorganic state. Even during the earliest point in evolution, when cosmic forces brought inorganic matter to life, death instincts quickly returned that matter to its original inorganic form. This was true, Freud believed, for even the most primitive forms of life. For Freud, then, all life was unstable, waiting to return to its natural, original inorganic state, or death. In fact, Freud concluded that death was the natural aim for the life force: "The goal of all life is death."

As evolution proceeded more elaborate forms of energy created longer periods of life. Those life periods increased until their forms finally were able to reproduce themselves, and a continuity of life was assured. However, no single living element could expect to live forever. Death, then, is the destiny of each individual life form, and life is no more than a path to death.

● Case 6.1

Discussion of the death instinct makes me think of Marsha. Nothing ever seemed to work right in that young woman's life. I cannot recall seeing Marsha smile or even attempt to smile.

If life was painful for Marsha, she had good reason for that pain. She never knew her parents. As an illegitimate child, she entered a foster home within days after her birth. From that point on, Marsha lived in a series of such homes. She never knew anyone long enough to form an intimate relationship.

When I first met Marsha, she was in the hospital recovering from a fall down a flight of stairs. In that fall she broke her right arm and wrist. I soon found out, however, that such "accidents" were part of Marsha's life. Her hospital record showed that she had "accidently" swallowed household ammonia, been involved in five automobile accidents, taken three serious falls, and nearly died from an overdose of sleeping tablets. And these incidents all occurred within the course of five years.

Marsha's unhappiness and her constant accidents point out how the death instinct can affect people when they lack the emotional reserve to deal with that instinct.

Our Destructive Nature

The brutal nature of the First World War convinced Freud that the death instinct played a central role in our personality. He became so convinced of our innate aggression that he gave the death instinct the same primary position in our personality that he once reserved for the sexual instincts alone.

One part of our death instinct is directed against ourselves. We systematically destroy ourselves, Freud said. In some ways, many of our colds, diseases, and even some forms of paralysis are nothing more than manifestations of our self-destructive instincts. These destructive forces can be so subtle as to escape our detection, but become more and more obvious

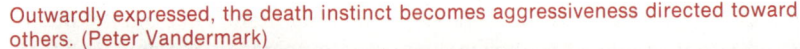

Freud believed the death instinct plays a central role in our personality. (© D. McCullin/Magnum)

as our inner aggressive drive grows. In suicide, for instance, our self-destructiveness is obvious.

When we turn our death instinct outward it becomes aggressiveness and hatred directed toward others (Case 6.2). We aim small and large bursts of anger at others so that we can release our pent-up instinctive drive. Freud offered little hope that we would ever find freedom from our drive toward more and more aggression, because for him aggression is not

Outwardly expressed, the death instinct becomes aggressiveness directed toward others. (Peter Vandermark)

a reaction to stimuli, but rather an impulse imbedded in the roots of our personality (Self-Quiz 6.1). Erich Fromm, a prominent neo-Freudian, explains the two directions of the death instinct:

> The death instinct is directed against the organism itself and thus is a self-destructive drive, or it is directed outward, and in this case tends to others rather than oneself. When blended with sexuality, the death instinct is transformed into harmless impulses expressed in sadism or masochism. Even though Freud suggested at various times that the power of the death instinct can be reduced, the basic assumption remained; man was under the sway of an impulse to destroy either himself or others, and he could do little to escape this tragic alternative. It follows that, from the position of the death instinct, aggression was not essentially a reaction to stimuli but a constantly flowing impulse rooted in the constitution of the human organism. (2)

At times we seem surrounded by evidence that Freud was correct in defining a death instinct that can express itself in violence. A most gruesome example of this destructiveness is child abuse. David Kaplun, a social worker, and Robert Reich, a psychiatrist, recount some upsetting details from their study of the 112 child homicides that occurred in New York City during the years 1968 and 1969. First of all, that rate of about one child homicide per week would be four times as large, they suggest, if we counted the "accidents" that have obvious homicidal overtones.

The fact that fathers, mothers, or lovers accounted for over two-thirds of these murders gives Freud's theory a foundation in grim reality. The same mothers who fret over battered children and worry that they get proper treatment and healthy meals in the hospital quite often had put those children there in the first place. And even when children die from such violent assaults, mothers continue to abuse their remaining children in over 30 percent of the cases studied. (3)

● Case 6.2

The death instinct can take many forms. In Ned, that force took the form of anger and aggression. Many people smiled when they met Ned at the post office where he worked. They commented on his controlled manner. Some people wondered why the post office needed him when he did his job as automatically as the coin-operated stamp dispenser next to his window. Still, he was dependable, and people appreciated his prompt attention to their needs.

His wife knew another side to Ned's controlled nature. She saw the look in his eyes when their three-year-old daughter made too much noise or disturbed Ned during one of his depressions. Something violent seemed to tremble within Ned. Whenever that turmoil began to stir, Ned tensed his entire body as if he were resisting an evil force deep within his personality.

One evening his little girl began to cry for no apparent reason, and Ned strode angrily toward her. Only when his wife jumped between Ned and the child did he regain control of himself. He leaned on a nearby wall and began to pound it. His blows finally struck with such force that he stained the white wall red with blood from his hand. Ned's wife left him that night. She feared for herself and her little girl. She said, "Ned is driven by an inner force that seems intent on destroying him."

The separation from his family woke Ned up. He sought help immediately. His psychiatrist, a strict Freudian, had no trouble relating to the dark force that haunted Ned. Yet, their struggle to explore that force and bring it under control continues to this day.

The Inevitability of Human Aggression

Freud thought of **aggression** as fundamental to our nature. Hall and Lindzey explain Freud's theory of aggression:

> An important derivative of the death instincts is the aggressive drive. Aggressiveness is self-destruction turned outward against substitute objects. A person fights with other people and is destructive because his death wish is blocked by the forces of the life instincts and by other obstacles in his personality which counteract the death instincts. It took the Great War of 1914–1918 to convince Freud that aggression was as sovereign a motive as sex. (4)

Our hatred and aggression toward one another both individually and as nations springs from the most innate part of our being. We are our aggression. We can no more stop being aggressive toward one another than we can stop breathing, eating, or living. Peace on earth may be a fine, idealistic dream, but to Freud peace lies outside the reach of our psychological grasp. As long as we live we will continue to be aggressive and try to destroy one another.

Toward the end of Freud's life, historical events confirmed his view concerning our innately destructive nature. As the Nazis overran Europe in 1938, they destroyed as many of Freud's books as they could confiscate. As a German-Jew, Freud undoubtedly knew what his fate would be if he did not escape. He did escape Vienna in 1938 when close friends intervened on his behalf, but his theories on aggression and the death instinct were never to change.

THE BEHAVIORISTIC APPROACH

Once again, the behaviorists reject any explanation of behavior that asks us to look inside the personality. Freud's observations concerning the death instinct, therefore, have little or no appeal to the behaviorists. They would rather look at the behavior they can observe and measure to explain any given response. Thus, in their study of aggression, they look for an observable cause.

Self-Quiz 6.1 — Aggression Scale

This test contains statements about aggression that you may or may not find self-descriptive. Mark the box to the left of the statements to indicate how often you think you might engage in the behavior described by each statement. Choose the best alternative, and do not omit any of the questions.

Often   Occasionally   Seldom

☐ ☐ ☐ 1. I do things that worry people.
☐ ☐ ☐ 2. I get upset when things go wrong.
☐ ☐ ☐ 3. I like to bring up subjects that upset people.
☐ ☐ ☐ 4. I get annoyed by inconsiderate people.
☐ ☐ ☐ 5. I get angry when someone takes advantage of me.
☐ ☐ ☐ 6. I ask questions of people I know they cannot answer.
☐ ☐ ☐ 7. I say things that hurt people's feelings.
☐ ☐ ☐ 8. Other people's mistakes annoy me.
☐ ☐ ☐ 9. My remarks make others feel guilty.
☐ ☐ ☐ 10. I get angry when people upset my plans.

This test cannot tell you how aggressive you are, but it does tell you how you compare with others who took the same test. To total your score, give yourself 3 points for each time you checked "often" on the test, 2 points for each "occasionally," and 1 point for each "seldom." Add up the number of points and compare that total with the following scale.

24–30   Few students scored in this range. This score indicates you have the honesty to admit your aggression.
14–24   Most students who took this test score in this range. These scores suggest that you manage to keep your anger within the range most people find acceptable.
Below 14   You release much less hostility than most of the students who took this test.

Frustration and Aggression

Many behaviorists point to **frustration** as the basic cause of anger (Case 6.3). Most of us know from our own experience that aggression can follow frustrating episodes. We know what it means to wait anxiously, day after day, for an important letter to arrive. Each day of expectation brings new emotional intensity until finally, if that letter brings bad news, our frustration becomes intense. We then need to express our angry feelings in one aggressive way or another.

There are several forms of frustration. A physical frustration might occur when the car will not start on some cold morning. Social frustration results when we discover we do not qualify for a scholarship. And personal frustration might be failure on an important examination. Frustration in all its forms can generate anger and aggression.

Psychologist John Dollard, in his book *Frustration and Aggression*, emphasizes the central role that frustration plays in aggressive behavior:

> Aggression is always a consequence of frustration. More specifically the proposition is that the occurrence of aggressive behavior always presupposes the existence of frustration and, contrariwise, that the existence of frustration always leads to some form of aggression. From the point of view of daily observation, it does not seem unreasonable to assume that aggressive behavior of the usually recognized varieties is always traceable to and produced by some form of frustration. But it is by no means so immediately evident that, whenever frustration occurs, aggression of some kind and in some degree will inevitably result. In many adults and even children, frustration may be followed so promptly by an apparent acceptance of the situation and readjustment thereto that one looks in vain for the relatively gross criteria ordinarily thought of as characterizing aggressive action. It must be kept in mind, however, that one of the earliest lessons human beings learn as a result of social living is to suppress and restrain their overtly aggressive reactions. This does not mean, however, that such reaction tendencies are thereby annihilated; rather it has been found that, although these reactions may be temporarily com-

"Thank you for not smoking."

Frustration takes many forms in our daily life. (Peter Vandermark)

pressed, delayed, disguised, displaced, or otherwise deflected from their immediate and logical goal, they are not destroyed. (5)

Frustration, then, according to most behaviorists, is always followed by feelings of aggression, even though the aggressive behavior may be suppressed.

Studies of people and animals placed in frustrating conditions tell us a great deal about our reactions to frustration. For example, each time people or animals are frustrated in an attempt to reach some goal, they tend to repeat their effort, with even more vigor. Children strain harder to free themselves the longer they fight constricting playpens. Adults pump the gas pedal with more vigor while trying to start a reluctant car. Even laboratory rats press levers harder when expected food does not appear. In other words, frustration increases the strength of the need that caused the behavior originally.

A corollary to this first principle suggests that the vigor of responses is also related to the distance a person is from the frustrated goal. The student who fails an examination by one point, the person whose car is ticketed just as she arrives to replenish the parking meter, and the commuter who misses his bus by seconds all feel the frustration of their effort most intensely. The **near-miss** raises our expectations of reaching our goal, and the resulting frustration is all the greater.

The final point about frustration and aggression that fits closely into this discussion concerns habitual responses. When a person's car starts regularly for three years, its first breakdown causes more frustration and aggression than if breakdowns occurred periodically. A failed examination in a class in which a person regularly scores high grades is more painful than failing in courses where that person always feels less secure. Our

The closer we come to achieving a goal, the more frustrating the loss. (Peter Vandermark)

near-miss of a bus can cause more aggression if the person has not missed that bus in over three years. Again, the explanation of such intense feelings might lie in our raised expectations. Whatever the reason, however, failure of an habitual response causes us great frustration.

● Case 6.3

Frustration can become so central in a relationship that it breeds anger and aggression. At least that is what happened to Mary and her parents.

Mary's parents had hoped to send Mary to the university when she graduated from high school, but some financial difficulty changed their plans. So they asked Mary if she would mind attending the local community college for two years and live at home so they could get together enough money to send her to the university for her last two years. Though Mary had counted on leaving home and attending the university, she understood the situation and agreed to delay her trip to the university.

Problems began almost immediately after Mary entered the community college. Many of her friends at the college were away from home, with no parental restrictions. Mary's parents, unable to appreciate the difference in social attitudes between college students and themselves, reacted badly to her late hours and unaccounted absences. Mary found that her desires to be with friends were regularly frustrated by her parents' demands that she not stay out beyond a certain hour. Resentment and hostility crept into her relationship with her parents. The more upset they became with her behavior the more she became frustrated and angry.

Mary came to identify her parents with any frustration she faced at college. Whether she became angry because she flunked an examination or upset because of a fight with her boyfriend, her parents were the target for her frustration and subsequent aggression.

Finally, the pressures from home became too great. She found a job and made arrangements with a friend to share an apartment. Her parents thought her move an unnecessary waste of money, but they, too, felt the pressure of the situation and agreed to the arrangement. The change in their relationship was dramatic. Without the need to account for her time, Mary relaxed and enjoyed her studies and her social life. Once away from her parents and their constant concern, she could also enjoy her visits home much more. By removing the source of the frustration in their relationship, they also removed much of the aggression.

Social Learning

Some behaviorists, while they accept the fact that frustration can cause aggression, feel frustration does not cause all aggression. The **social-learning** psychologists, for instance, point to the fact that children (and adults) can learn aggression through **imitation,** the process of watching and learning a behavior. Imitation learning, especially for children, can

Some psychological studies suggest that television violence does create aggression in children. (Peter Vandermark)

cause aggressive behavior. Albert Bandura is one social-learning theorist who stresses imitation.

> Imitation plays an important role in the acquisition of deviant, as well as of conforming, behavior. New responses may be learned or the characteristics of existing response hierarchies may be changed as a function of observing the behavior of others and its response consequences without the observer's performing any overt or observable responses himself or receiving any direct reinforcement during the acquisition period. In some cases the amount of the learning shown by the observer can, in fact, be as great as that shown by the performer. (6)

In a novel experiment that helped prove his point, Bandura and his colleagues divided 96 children at Stanford University Nursery School into four groups. The average age of the children was a little over four years. The first group watched live models performing aggressive acts on a Bobo doll. The second group watched a film in which the same adults performed the same aggressive acts on the doll. The third group watched a cartoon character become aggressive toward the Bobo doll. The fourth group had no exposure at all to aggressive models.

After the experiment, all the children were brought into a room with many different kinds of toys. They were observed and scored by researchers according to how much or how little aggression they showed with the toys. The results indicated that those children exposed to either live or filmed aggression had significantly more aggressive play than their counterparts who did not observe aggressive models. The results clearly suggest that aggression can be taught by modeling and imitation. (7)

Obedience to Authority

The most frightening experiment performed by the social-learning theorists concerns our response to authority. It suggests that we all will, if the conditions are right, commit extremely aggressive acts on others out of response to authority. The experiment has particularly frightening overtones when we reflect again on the Nazi brutality toward the Jewish people during the Second World War. Those shocked at the inhumanity of such actions might wonder if they, too, could respond similarly if commanded by strong authority figures.

In the famous experiment, called the Milgram experiment, subjects were told they would act as teachers for a study of the effects of punishment on learning. The "teacher" was told to give electrical shocks to "students" in another room whenever the student answered incorrectly. And with each error, they were to increase the shock level. The teacher could see the student strapped into something that looked like an electrical chair. The simulated shock apparatus was marked with descriptions ranging from *slight shock (15 volts)* to *dangerous: severe shock (450 volts)*. The students were actually experimental collaborators who made prearranged mistakes and acted out reactions to the shocks. As the teachers increased the voltage, the collaborators faked more and more intense screams of pain.

Of the forty "teacher" subjects in the experiment, all went to 300 volts (extreme intensity shock) and 26, or 65 percent, went all the way to 450 volts (danger: severe shock). The conclusion of the Milgram experiment was that we will respond to command more than we would like to admit (Case 6.4). (8)

● Case 6.4

Discussion of obedience to authority reminds me of a talk I had with a colleague about his experience in World War II. We just finished chatting about the Milgram experiment and its implications when Chuck said, "You know, I was shocked when I heard about what the Nazis did to the Jews. The movies alone were enough to make me sick. My first reaction was to think that no force on earh could make me be a part of such cruelty."

"Your first reaction?" I asked.

"Yeah. At the time I thought no one would ever force me to slaughter innocent people." Chuck looked away. "Then later I thought about my reaction a little more."

"Did that later thinking change your mind?"

"You bet it did." Chuck looked at me directly. "You know, I never even made corporal in the army. I did nothing but take orders. And my friends who decided to disobey or even hesitated to follow orders often found themselves in the brig. That was no picnic. The brig was hard time. I did everything I could to avoid the place."

"So if someone had commanded you to march a group of people to an oven, you might have done it?" I hoped my voice sounded sympathetic.

"I'm not proud to say so." Chuck lowered his eyes. "But I think I would have."

THE HUMANISTIC APPROACH

Carl Rogers and many other humanists believe we suffer when we fail to express our genuine feelings openly and honestly. The more we hide behind masks and fail to let others know our emotional reactions, the more apt we are to let those reactions cause us pain.

> I have little sympathy with the rather prevalent concept that man is basically irrational, and that his impulses, if not controlled, will lead to destruction of others and self. Man's behavior is exquisitely rational, moving with subtle and ordered complexity toward the goals his organism is endeavoring to achieve. The tragedy for most of us is that our defenses keep us from being aware of this rationality, so that consciously we are

Martin Luther King approached violence with nonviolence. (Bob Adelman 1979/Magnum)

moving in one direction, while organismically we are moving in another. But in the person who is living the process of the good life, there would be a decreasing number of such barriers, and he would be increasingly a participant in the rationality of his organism. The only control of impulse which would exist, or which would prove necessary, is the natural and internal balancing of one need against another, and the discovery of behaviors which follow the vector most closely approximating the satisfaction of all needs. The experience of extreme satisfaction of one need (for aggression, or sex, etc.) in such a way as to do violence to the satisfaction of other needs (for companionship, tender relationship, etc.) — would be greatly decreased. He would participate in the vastly complex self-regulatory activities of his organism — the psychological as well as physiological thermostatic controls — in such a fashion as to live in increasing harmony with himself and with others. (9)

Most people do hide their feelings, however, and of the many emotions we might suffer from if repressed, anger is high on the list. Ironically, anger and aggression also seem the most likely emotions to be repressed. We live in a culture in which anger and the expression of aggression rarely occur openly. We fume silently while the supermarket checker gossips with a customer rather than moving the line. We bite our lips rather than let a friend know we hate his habit of saying, "You know." We smile rather than tell a colleague her work is not up to par. Telling someone directly that we are angry seems difficult, because we have learned from our culture that such expression is wrong.

Our tendency to hide angry and aggressive feelings begins quite early. Childhood training includes punishment for angry outbursts. Most of us heard our parents retort "Don't you dare get angry with me." We were taught directly and indirectly that anger was not all right.

Anger and Violence

Humanists worry about bottled-up hostility. They do not believe direct displays of anger are unhealthy; instead, they feel that repressed anger becomes volatile and unstable. The person who finds herself jarred by a friend's insensitive remark can clear up hurt feelings with that friend by simply saying, "I became really upset by your remark." The matter can be talked through, and strained feelings have a chance to return to normal. If the same person represses the upset and allows her **self-esteem** to be damaged, then anger begins to grow and become explosive. If the remark creates further feelings of impotence, the troubled person can lose sleep, remain preoccupied, and even grow bitter over the same experience that could so easily have been dealt with directly.

The humanist's concern goes even deeper. Some repressed anger can grow and eventually become violent. If the tendency to repress angry feelings becomes strong and habitual, the person creates internal pressure. One angry feeling reinforces another, and the bottled-up anger soon reaches dangerous proportions. Humanists not only believe that the repression of anger does not prevent **violence,** but also that repressed anger *causes* most serious violence.

Rollo May explains the humanist view of violence and self-esteem:

> In its typical and simple form, violence is an eruption of pent-up passion. When a person . . . is continuously burdened with feelings of impotence which corrode any remaining self-esteem, violence is the predictable end result. Violence is an explosion of the drive to destroy that which is interpreted as the barrier to one's self-esteem, movement, and growth. This desire to destroy may so completely take over the person that any object that gets in the way is destroyed. Hence the person strikes out blindly, often destroying those for whom he cares and even himself in the process. (10)

Ezra Stotland is a social psychologist from the University of Washington who also links emotional violence with the need to protect self-esteem. He feels the brutal prison riot at Attica in the early 1970s confirmed his theory. The prison guards there, he suggests, saw their dignity challenged regularly and had no adequate way to release their hostile reactions. Thus, anger and hatred grew to explosive proportions before a prison riot gave them the chance to release their pent-up hostility.

In the months preceding the uprising, the prison guards witnessed many prison reforms that undermined their authority. Under the cloak of those reforms, the inmates became increasingly belligerent and demanding. They taunted the guards who had no adequate way to express their own resentment. On the day of the uprising, even when a few guards were taken hostage, official resistance came slowly. The guards' self-esteem faded further and their explosive feelings built. The pressure only grew worse when, in less than two hours, 42 hostages were taken and the guards lost complete control of the situation.

To further frustrate and anger the guards, prisoners were given new power in negotiations designed to save the hostages. The prisoners further agitated the guards' violent feelings by using the negotiations as an opportunity to denounce the guards publicly. By the time the guards were finally given the signal to charge the prisoners, their pent-up violence and brutality erupted. The guards restored their sense of self-esteem by violently releasing their emotions. In some cases, guards used personal weapons on prisoners, and the McKay Commission, when it officially investigated the incident, reported guard brutality continued long after they contained the threat. Stotland suggests, however, that such violent outburst could easily have been predicted by an observation of the guards' growing anger and loss of self-esteem. (11)

Healthy Aggression

Most humanists suggest that we should do more than simply avoid the suppression of feelings—we should encourage **assertiveness,** and parents should teach their children to be assertive (Self-Quiz 6.2). It is better, say the humanists, for children to take charge of their lives and make mistakes rather than go timidly through life fearful of challenges. And the angry outburst from a child who feels frustrated with her inability to tie her shoes, carry a heavy suitcase, or reach the top shelf in the bookcase is appropriate. Those children given parental permission to release tensions appropriate to the failures that learning entails will be less likely to develop into the type of adults who bottle up their anger (Case 6.5).

Anthony Storr, the distinguished British psychologist, agrees with this attitude.

Momma by Mell Lazarus. Courtesy of Mell Lazarus and Field Newspaper Syndicate.

Self-Quiz 6.2 — Assertiveness Scale

Next to each statement place the number 1, 2, 3, 4, or 5—depending on how characteristic each statement is of you. Continue the process for each of the statements. Then total your score.

   5 strongly characteristic of me
   4 moderately characteristic of me
   3 neutral
   2 moderately uncharacteristic of me
   1 strongly uncharacteristic of me

_____ 1. If someone breaks in line ahead of me, I ask them to please go to the end of the line.

_____ 2. If seats were free in the back of a crowded bus, I would push through the crowd to the empty seats.

_____ 3. If a car cuts me off on the highway, I will step on the gas and challenge that car.

_____ 4. If I find I have been overcharged at a store, I will return and demand my proper change.

_____ 5. Even though doing so is not part of my duties, I will point out mistakes to fellow workers.

_____ 6. I let friends know immediately when they upset or embarrass me.

_____ 7. I let my parents know when they make sweeping generalizations that upset me.

_____ 8. When I see someone attractive at a party, I take it upon myself to strike up a conversation with that person.

_____ 9. I go out of my way to meet and impress important or influential people.

_____ TOTAL SCORE

32–45   Most students do not achieve a score this high. You have an unusually high degree of assertiveness.

18–32   The vast majority of students taking this test score in this range. Consequently, your level of assertiveness seems healthy.

Below 18   People scoring this low probably lack assertiveness in their lives.

There is the need to cling to the mother to be sure of her affection and support. But there is also a drive to explore and master the environment, to act independently. It is easy to see this in a child of three or four. "Let me do it" is a recurrent entreaty in small children; and wise mothers encourage their children to do as much as possible for themselves, however tiresome it may be to wait patiently while the child takes minutes to tie a knot which the adult can tie in seconds. (12)

People can also learn an assertive attitude in adulthood, in an assertiveness workshop or on their own. As many of the workshops point out, we unnecessarily fear saying, "No." Many times we honestly want to tell a friend we would rather not attend the movies on this particular night, but spoil our evening anyway because we fear that word no. With a little assertiveness and confidence, we could have more honest, stable friendships.

Women have traditionally had difficulty being assertive because of their cultured and parental training from childhood. Thus, they are more apt than men to attend assertiveness training workshops to learn how to take command of their lives and to change deep-seated attitudes.

Women's tendency to let men take charge is sometimes manifested in subtle ways. Two Purdue University psychologists, Richard Borden and Gordon Homleid, isolated one way when they observed 199 male-female couples walking across the Purdue campus holding hands. The psychologists stopped the couples and asked each partner whether they were left-handed or right-handed. In nearly 62 percent of the cases, females were walking on the side of the male's dominant hand while her dominant hand was free. The same tendency was present between couples who were entwined more intimately. Nearly two-thirds of this group "were arranged so that the female's dominant hand was left dangling at her side while she was touched by the male's dominant hand."

Some people might suggest this dominant-hand tendency occurs because males are accustomed to having their female friends on their right while driving a car. The facts of the study suggest otherwise, however, because 22 of the 32 left-handed men observed walked with women on their left side. This study indicates that men "strong-arm" women in very subtle ways. (13)

● Case 6.5

Once a child learns to fear assertiveness, the quality can be difficult to recapture, but can be done with a great deal of time and patience. And just such an effort was necessary for a child named Susan. The first day I met little Susan I knew she lacked confidence. She had none of the vitality and inquisitiveness most four-year-old children seem to come by naturally. She hid behind a chair while her mother and I talked about Susan's reserved nature. Once her mother left, Susan revealed no new aggressiveness. Even though she was surrounded by every imaginable toy, she only sat motionless. Not until the end of the first therapy session did Susan even make a move toward any of the toys, and then she walked over and tightly gripped a doll.

The second therapy session Susan and I shared went much the same. Once Susan found her doll, she sat almost motionless. However, toward the end of that day, she did speak a few words with me. She wanted to know if I had a little girl. When I told her I did not, she asked, "Would you take me home with you?"

It nearly broke my heart to tell her I could not. But Susan showed no outward emotion over my refusal.

Our further sessions together followed the same pattern. Susan became a little more assertive each time. My talks with her mother helped me see how desperately Susan needed to be given freedom to make choices and face up to mistakes. Her mother watched over Susan relentlessly, fearful the child would harm herself. I worked nearly as hard with Susan's mother as I did with Susan. In time, however, her mother saw that Susan needed to grow in her own way and follow her own direction. By that time, Susan had become quite assertive in our therapy sessions. She played a great deal with mother and child dolls. She told me how the mother doll would not let the little girl doll do anything on her own, how much the little girl wanted to play freely with her friends, and how angry the little girl grew toward her mother. Such talks helped Susan become free with herself and, now that her mother responded, grow more and more assertive toward life.

The Fair Fight

Assertiveness is important to most relationships; and the more intimate the relationship, the more important honest assertiveness becomes. Of course, simple shouting and uncontrolled angry outbursts cannot help any relationship grow. Blaming is a particularly destructive form of assertion to a friendship, because when we blame a friend or lover for our feelings, we engage in a kind of attack. "You make me angry," is a form of blame and attacks a partner directly.

We can express genuine feelings without making those feelings the object of blame. Instead of saying, "You make me angry," we can say, "When you don't keep your promises, I become angry." The second version does not place blame—it simply states a fact. Certain behaviors seem to trigger unpleasant emotions. The unkept appointment that stimulates anger is a good example. An honest expression of that anger opens up a

Animal Crackers. Reprinted by permission of the Chicago Tribune-New York News Syndicate, Inc.

relationship, because partners see one another better after they understand how their behavior affects a partner. Then they can take steps to make their friendship smoother and more intimate.

A good fight that avoids blame can be an important element in any relationship, particularly any love relationship. Such **fair fights** clear the air and bring lovers closer together, but they do not come easily to most of us. Either we play the blame-game or we repress our anger for fear we will offend our friend. But people who have learned to express anger openly in their relationships not only grow closer to their partners, they live happier and healthier lives.

Because so many couples lack skill in fair fighting, psychologist George Bach began workshops to train partners in the art. Bach tells us that

> when our trainees fight according to our flexible system of rules, they find that the natural tensions and frustrations of two people living together can be greatly reduced. Since they live with fewer lies and inhibitions and have discarded outmoded notions of etiquette, these couples are free to grow emotionally, to become more productive and more creative, as individuals in their own right and also as pairs. (14)

CONCLUSION

Once again, our look at the three viewpoints has given us much to think about. Even though Freud's theory about the death instinct may seem extreme to some, he leaves us with valuable insights. When we look at the world of war, highway slaughter, and violent movies, we can wonder if an instinct for aggression is not fundamental to our nature. At times our tendency toward destructiveness seems even more basic in our nature than our instinct for love, peace, and harmony.

If we turn from Freud's large perspective of human nature and look at our individual acts of aggression, the behaviorists make some good points. For instance, frustration does seem to precede many angry acts. The missed bus, the examination failure, and the broken date seem to generate frustration and anger. And we do learn aggression, as the social-learning theorists claim, by watching others. When children watch a parent express anger, they have a model for healthy way to free themselves from angry feelings.

Finally, the humanists add their unique vantage point to our discussion. Since anger is a genuine feeling, we are not surprised that humanists consider its expression important. The humanists feel we must express our anger as it occurs or risk letting it grow under the pressure of repression and become destructive. More important, the humanists also think our self-esteem is linked to our ability to assert ourselves. Assertiveness, then, is important for our emotional stability.

SUMMARY

1. Freud believed each of us possesses an instinct for death. We can turn that instinct against ourselves in the form of diseases, ulcers, and even suicide. Or we can direct the instinct against others as anger and aggression. In either case, Freud's belief in the death instinct made him pessimistic about the world's chances for peace.
2. Many behaviorists explain our aggression by pointing to its link with frustration. They have discovered that we are most frustrated the closer we are to our goal and the more habitual the response that is frustrated, the more our frustration will lead to aggression. Another group of behaviorists, the social-learning theorists, feel that not all aggression emerges from frustration. They point out that imitation is also a primary cause of aggression.
3. Because humanists consider all emotions healthy, they look carefully at our assertive impulses. Characteristically, they point out that our assertiveness, rather than causing violence, can lead to violence if we leave it unexpressed for too long. We must, if we are to remain healthy emotionally, learn to assert ourselves and take time to help our children learn to express their assertive needs.

KEY TERMS

life instincts
death instincts
aggression
frustration
near-miss
social learning

imitation
self-esteem
violence
assertiveness
fair fights

STUDY QUESTIONS

1. Does Freud's belief that we have an instinct for death make sense to you? Explain.
2. Would you say that you learned your aggressive tendencies or were you born with them? Explain your answer.
3. Think of an example in your life where frustration led to aggression. Do you believe your own anger can have other causes? Name one other explanation for your anger.
4. If we learn aggression by watching and imitating others, behaviorists might say we do so because we receive rewards for such imitation. What might some of these rewards be?

5. Think of a recent time when you bottled up your anger instead of expressing it. Did your suppression have any unhappy consequences? Explain.
6. Do you believe you would lead a happier life if you expressed your angry feelings? Discuss.

ADDITIONAL READING

Bach, G. R., and Wyden, P. *The Intimate Enemy.* New York: Avon, 1970.

Bandura, A. *Aggression: A Social Learning Analysis.* Englewood Cliffs, N.J.: Prentice-Hall, 1973.

Berkowitz, Leonard. *The Roots of Aggression.* New York: Atherton Press, 1969.

Delgado, J. *Physical Control of the Mind: Toward a Psychocivilized Society.* New York: Harper & Row, 1969.

Dollard, J., et al. *Frustration and Aggression.* New Haven: Yale, 1939.

Freud, S. *The Ego and the Id.* New York: Norton, 1920.

Fromm, E. *The Anatomy of Human Destructiveness.* New York: Fawcett, 1973.

Storr, A. *Human Aggression.* New York: Bantam, 1968.

Wertheimer, M. (Ed.) *Confrontation: Psychology and the Problems of Today.* Glenview, Ill.: Scott, Foresman, 1969.

Chapter Seven

Psychotherapy

OUTLINE

The Psychoanalytic Approach
The Talking Cure
Dream Interpretation
Freudian Slips
Transference

The Behavioristic Approach
Social Learning
Assertiveness Training
Learned Helplessness

The Humanistic Approach
Effective Concern
Trust
Emotional Maturity

Conclusion

LEARNING OBJECTIVES

After reading this chapter you should be able to:

1. Discuss Freud's method of free association.
2. Explain how dream interpretation and transference form a part of the free-association technique.
3. Distinguish between desensitization and social-learning approaches to phobias.
4. Understand how assertiveness training helps people lead more productive lives.
5. Discuss why Rogers believes a therapist should care about his client.
6. Explain how trust between the therapist and the client helps a client achieve emotional maturity.

Chapter Seven

Pat, a young woman in one of my late afternoon classes, approached me while I searched about in the library stacks. She looked quite distracted and spoke urgently. "I hate to disturb you," she told me, "but I need your advice."

"Certainly," I replied, motioning to a nearby table and chairs.

"Lately I find myself becoming more and more depressed." Pat rubbed her finger along the edge of the table. "I can't think of any reason why I go through those spells, but they do begin to worry me."

"Have you thought about going to someone to talk?" I asked.

"I tried talking to my husband, but he doesn't seem to understand. He tries. He really does." The tone in Pat's voice rose sharply. "But he doesn't know what to do."

"How about seeing a professional?" I brought the subject up as gently as possible.

"A psychiatrist? I don't need to see a psychiatrist. I'm not crazy." Pat's voice became so shrill that two students at a nearby table looked over.

"You don't need to be crazy to see a counselor," I replied in hushed tones. "Many well-balanced people seek help from therapists every day because they find themselves under strain."

"Do you think talking to a counselor about my depression would help?" Pat now returned to rubbing her finger along the edge of the table.

"I have no idea if you would find relief by talking to a therapist." I paused to collect my thoughts. "However, I think you would be foolish not to give it a try."

Though we claim to be enlightened about therapy, most people, like Pat, still are afraid of it. For some reason, we assume any person who enters therapy must be crazy. Rather than seeing therapy as a process that helps people become better able to enjoy life, we look upon it as a sign of insanity. Our attitudes continue to change for the better, however. Many students now talk more openly about their experiences in therapy. Their freedom encourages others who could benefit from that experience to seek help.

Of course, there are many methods of therapy. Each therapist has a different personal approach to helping people adjust to tension. Most therapists, however, do choose one of several general paths. We will consider three of the most popular approaches. First of all, we will discuss the psychoanalytic method of Sigmund Freud. Freud relied heavily on the free-association technique, encouraging his patients to talk freely about anything that came into their minds. During such unstructured talk, Freud helped them search their unconscious for the source of the problem buried there. The principal aid Freud used in his probing of the unconscious was dream interpretation. Freud claimed that the symbols in any dream can lead a skilled interpreter back to the source of a person's pain.

The behaviorists do not search troubled people's personalities and past problems in order to help them. For behaviorists, personality is behavior and behavior is personality. If you want to change the personality, you simply change the behavior. To change behavior, the behaviorists use many techniques. One popular technique is desensitization. If a person has a snake phobia, for example, behaviorists find that gradual exposure to snakes or even the image of snakes helps a person gradually erase the unreasonable fear of snakes. We will also discuss, in this chapter, other approaches behaviorists take to change behavior patterns.

More important than probing the personality or altering behavior directly, say the humanists, is the attitude therapists bring to therapy. People have the best chance of finding their own way out of their emotional turmoil if the therapist forms a personal bond with them by creating a safe atmosphere for intimate communication. Once a bond of trust develops, people in therapy can begin to explore their pain themselves. People, no matter how troubled, are in the best position to find their own way out of their pain.

THE PSYCHOANALYTIC APPROACH

The first psychologists studied only conscious phenomena. They ignored dream experiences, for example. Though dreams had interested ancient philosophers and contemporary poets, the psychologists did not venture into such territory. And if the early psychologists would not look at dreams, they certainly did not even want to discuss hypnosis and amnesia. The few psychologists who did choose to look into such phenomena were viewed with suspicion by the established medical and scientific community.

Freud's decision to study the hypnotic trance, then, was risky. Yet his fascination with the work of Charcot, a French psychologist, led him to study with him in 1885. While in France, Freud saw Charcot produce and remove hysterical symptoms, such as paralysis, through the use of hypnosis. In 1889 Freud attended Berheim's hypnosis experiments in Nancy, France. Bernheim made subjects produce several hallucinations in trance they could not recall on awakening.

These experiments with hypnosis convinced Freud that each person possesses an **unconscious** where all memories are stored, memories that we are unaware of on a conscious level, but which influence much of our behavior. Freud began to believe that we can be pushed, pulled, and even mentally tortured by the forces of the unconscious completely unknown to us (Case 7.1; Self-Quiz 7.1). Calvin Hall believes that these ideas occupied Freud for many years.

> From our present vantage point it now appears that what Freud was trying to accomplish during the thirty years between 1890 and 1920, when the unconscious mind reigned as the sovereign concept in his psychological system, was to discover those determining forces in the personality that are not directly known to the observer. For example, man is not directly aware of the process of digestion as it takes place, but the science of physiology can tell him what happens during digestion. This knowledge does not enable him to perceive (be directly aware of) his own digestive processes as they are occurring; nevertheless he knows (understands) what is taking place. In a similar manner, one is not aware of unconscious mental processes, but psychology can teach him about what is going on below the level of awareness. (1)

• Case 7.1

My own work with hypnosis makes my very interested in these early days of Freud's life when he used hypnosis. I am still baffled by many of the things that happen to people in hypnotic trance. In particular, I recall a young man named Daryl. Daryl said he wanted to see if he could enter a deep trance. When I asked him if there was any particular reason why he wanted to explore trance, he told me he was only curious. However, he then said, "Oh, you might ask me, if I get into trance, why I get these headaches." He explained he had always been subject to severe headaches. About once a month, he would have a headache so severe he could not function normally.

Daryl turned out to be an excellent subject. He went almost immediately into deep trance. We talked for a little, and then I asked his question about why he had such severe headaches. Without hesitation, as if he had been waiting a long time to talk about it, he told me how much he hated his father. His angry tones grew harsh and shrill as he talked about the terrible pain his father's attitude had caused him. The headaches, he told me in trance, only occurred because he could not admit, even to himself, how he felt toward his father. Whenever his attitude toward his father began to emerge, Daryl distracted himself with the headaches.

When I lifted Daryl from trance, we talked about what a good subject he was, how he reacted under trance, and how refreshed he felt afterwards. I finally told him he had talked about the cause of his headaches. His reaction seemed strained, so I proceeded cautiously. When I finally asked him if he remembered talking about his father, he said he did not and quickly changed the subject. I decided I had better not pursue the matter any further with him, and we soon parted. But before he left, Daryl said, "I think you cured my headaches." His statement stunned me, but I only told him I hoped that was true. I did not see Daryl again for nearly three months. At that time he made a special point of coming to see me to thank me for ending his headaches which he felt certain were gone forever. We never mentioned his relationship with his father.

I cannot be certain, but I assume Daryl's ability to talk about his conflicts with his father ended his headaches. I still wonder whether or not he did remember our conversation. In the end, I can only be happy that I helped him free himself of his pain.

The Talking Cure

Freud believed we are often tortured mentally by memories we press into our unconscious. The small child who sees her mother brutally beaten by her father at an early age can push the memory of the incident into the depths of her unconscious. Such a hidden memory does not lie dormant in the unconscious, however, but seethes there causing the girl mental grief for many years, possibly even for the rest of her life.

Freud felt that if we could help people recall unconscious memories, we could also relieve them of the terrible pain they create. Because he developed his theory by watching demonstrations of **hypnosis,** Freud first chose to delve into the unconscious with this method. By recalling forgotten memories under hypnosis, patient after patient found relief from their psychological pain. In some cases, even physical paralysis was cured. Many other symptoms also vanished when Freud helped people explore their unconscious, even though results were often unpredictable.

Freud's authoritarian manner, however, made it difficult for him to use hypnosis. Although he claimed people resisted hypnosis, his patients were probably resisting Freud and his authoritarian manner. Calvin Hall explains Freud's shift from hypnosis to a new method:

> When Freud began the practice of medicine it was natural, in view of his scientific background, that he should specialize in the treatment of nervous disorders. This branch of medicine was in a backward state. There

Sigmund Freud's (1856–1939) psychoanalytic technique has helped many people free themselves of painful memories that they had pressed into their unconscious. (The Bettmann Archive, Inc.)

Self-Quiz 7.1 — The Unconscious

This test contains a number of statements about the unconscious. Choose the alternative that best describes your attitude by checking the appropriate box to the left of the statement. Answer all of the statements.

Often *Occasionally* *Seldom*

Often	Occasionally	Seldom	
☐	☐	☐	1. I get the feeling when I visit a new place that I've been there before.
☐	☐	☐	2. I mistake strangers for people I want to see.
☐	☐	☐	3. I develop strong dislikes for people without any apparent reason.
☐	☐	☐	4. When I must avoid a taboo subject like death, while visiting a sick friend in a hospital, I am constantly aware of the topic.
☐	☐	☐	5. My dreams are quite vivid.
☐	☐	☐	6. The images in my dreams are too confused to classify.
☐	☐	☐	7. I lose confidence in myself for no apparent reason.
☐	☐	☐	8. I avoid people I don't like.
☐	☐	☐	9. I follow instincts that warn me to avoid certain people and places.

No test can give an accurate measure of how much the unconscious intrudes into your conscious. However, you can see how you compare with other students who took this test. Give yourself 3 points for each time you checked "often" on the test, 2 points for each "occasionally," and 1 point for each "seldom." Then total your score and compare that total with the following scale.

23–27   Few students score in this high range. Such a high score indicates your unconscious is quite active in your life.
14–22   The unconscious intrudes in your life about the same as it does for other students taking the test.
Below 14   With a score this low, it seems your unconscious rarely intrudes in your life.

was not a great deal that could be done for people suffering from aberrations of the mind. Jean Charcot, in France, was having some success with hypnosis, particularly in the treatment of hysteria. Freud spent a year in Paris (1885–86) learning Charcot's method of treatment. However, Freud was not satisfied with hypnosis because he felt that its effects were only temporary and did not get at the seat of the trouble. From another Viennese physician, Joseph Breuer, he learned of the benefits of the cathartic or "talking-out-your-problems" form of therapy. The patient talked while the physician listened. (2)

In any event, Freud discovered he could work better with people by using a method he called **free association.** The free-association method allowed people to talk about anything that came to mind concerning their pain, with their minds freely associating between one incident and another. Their talk seemed to ramble from one train of thought to another because nothing was too trivial for consideration. Freud would only enter into the free-association process if patients needed help to continue the flow. This lengthy psychoanalytic process, under the direction of a skilled analyst such as Freud, finally led back to the same kind of painful memories that hypnosis originally revealed.

Dream Interpretation

As he continued his study of the unconscious, Freud discovered the importance of his patients' dreams. He tells us:

> It was discovered one day that the pathological symptoms of certain neurotic patients have a sense. On this discovery the psycho-analytic method of treatment was founded. It happened in the course of this treatment that patients, instead of bringing forward their symptoms, brought forward dreams. A suspicion thus arose that the dreams too had a sense. (3)

To help patients more quickly probe their unconscious through the free-association technique, Freud developed his method of **dream interpretation** (Case 7.2). Freud soon came to believe that dreams are direct messages from the unconscious, calling them "the royal road to the unconscious." But, in order to keep repressed thoughts out of the conscious mind, we disguise our dreams with **symbols** that represent the painful memories. Part of the work of the analyst is to help the patient unravel these dreams and their symbols to eventually lead back to the repressed memories.

In a recurring dream one patient had during analysis, a man appeared with only one eye in the middle of a faceless head. In a later dream, the same eye appeared in the middle of a reflecting pool. The dream continued to recur in several variations of this same theme. Finally, the reflecting pool became a head mirror doctors use to examine patient's throats. The eye in the middle of the mirror was only the doctor's eye peering through the hole in the mirror. Such obscure symbols blocked the patient's memory of an incident with a family physician that had that bizarre sexual overtones. Only the careful unraveling of such symbols helped the analyst and patient find the painful memory that had been repressed many years earlier.

Quite obviously, Freud felt that dreams can help the disturbed individual. They provide insight during periods of stress and help people begin to bring focus to their lives in their most troubled times. Edward F. Foulks, an associate professor of psychiatry and anthropology at the University of Pennsylvania in Philadelphia, believes a parallel phenomenon occurs in society also.

Historically, schizophrenics and their visions have helped societies in times of crisis. Schizophrenic visions have acted like dreams in giving societies a means of centering their energies during periods of cultural and social disorganization. In times of sudden crisis, such as a natural disaster or a disease epidemic, the normal ways society copes with change can become inadequate. Foulks believes that visions from schizophrenic people, during such periods, may

> provide a mystical, affective focus bringing people together in ritual and communal behavior which in turn provides the social ordering necessary for more mundane, concrete group adaptations to the prevailing problems of society.

One of Foulks' examples is the case of Handsome Lake, a Seneca Indian in the mid-eighteenth century, who helped his tribe adapt to the changes forced on them by the arrival of the white people. Drinking white man's alcohol had disrupted the strong family ties of the Seneca. Handsome Lake hallucinated angel messengers who ordered him to establish a new order without alcohol. In this new society, the angels told him in his "dream," men instead of women would work in the fields. The Seneca society followed the hallucination in the same way Freud's patients followed their dream messages in therapy. So complete was the Seneca's cultural restructuring that even when tempted and prodded by the white men, the Indians would no longer drink. Instead, they injected new health into a society that had appeared to be near collapse. (4)

● Case 7.2

In therapy, dreams can bring new understanding to patients. A fifty-year-old woman named Janice found her dreams very helpful.

Janice's dream occurred soon after her husband retired and began pressing Janice to retire from her job and "begin living the life of leisure." As Janice faced the prospect of spending all day with her husband, she became upset. She wanted to believe she loved her husband. Yet, she grew more and more troubled at the thought of the two of them with so much time to themselves.

Janice became so confused over her attitude that she went to a therapist. She told the therapist she loved her husband, but the thought of spending all day with him upset her. The therapist felt her anxiety had much deeper roots. However, he did not confront Janice but rather let her talk out her conflict. The more she talked the more Janice revealed to herself and to the therapist the depths of her anger.

Janice continued to resist the conclusion that she did not love her husband until one night she had a vivid dream filled with obvious symbolism. In the dream, her husband hung from the edge of a cliff. He pleaded with Janice to reach down and help him return to solid ground. Janice looked at him and watched his fingertips turn white as he clung to the edge of a jagged rock. She thought of helping him. Instead, she stepped on his fingers with the full weight of her body until he could no longer stand the pain and fell to the floor of the canyon below. Janice woke up screaming.

The dream pressed Janice's therapy into new directions. She now admitted to the therapist and herself that she did not love her husband. With this block to her thinking removed, Janice was free to explore the possibility of leaving him and beginning a life of her own.

Freudian Slips

Another Freudian technique that helps uncover repressed material is sometimes called the error, or **Freudian slip** (Self-Quiz 7.2). Such slips tell us according to Freud, what our unconscious actually wants to say. Some of the more humorous slips that occurred during the early days of radio have been collected into a series of records. Most interesting, in

The Wizard of Id by permission of Johnny Hart and Field Newspaper Enterprises Inc.

Self-Quiz 7.2 — Freudian Slips

This test contains a number of statements related to the Freudian slip. Mark the statements below depending on how often or seldom they apply to you by checking the appropriate box to the left of the statement.

Often	Occasionally	Seldom	
☐	☐	☐	1. The same type of person always attracts me.
☐	☐	☐	2. Crowds make me fearful.
☐	☐	☐	3. I have called someone close to me by the wrong name.
☐	☐	☐	4. I dislike people who represent authority.
☐	☐	☐	5. I find myself driving my car in the opposite direction from the way I intended to go.
☐	☐	☐	6. My dreams make little sense when I try to interpret them.
☐	☐	☐	7. I forget to sign letters.
☐	☐	☐	8. I dislike the same type of person.
☐	☐	☐	9. I forget dental appointments.
☐	☐	☐	10. I forget the day of the month when writing checks.

This test can give you a general idea of how likely you are to use the Freudian slip. To total your score, give yourself 3 points for each time you checked "often" on the test, 2 points for each "occasionally," and 1 point for each "seldom." Add up the total number of points and compare that total with the scale below.

22–30   You are more prone to the Freudian slip than the average person taking this test.
13–22   You make the Freudian slip about as often as others taking the test.
Below 13   You appear to be unaware of the unconscious messages in your life.

---

view of Freudian theory, many of these radio slips have sexual overtones. One announcer speaks of Sunshine bread for those who want "the breast in bed—uh, the best in bread." A politician tells an audience he wants them all to know about his "pubic record—that is, my public record."

From *Non-Being and Somethingness: Selections from the Comic Strip "Inside Woody Allen,"* by Woody Allen, drawn by Stuart Hample. Copyright © 1978 by IWA Enterprises and Hackenbush Productions, Inc. Reprinted by permission of Random House, Inc.

Transference

At some point in analysis, patients express deep feelings toward their therapist that were originally intended for parents, brothers or sisters but never expressed. This important part of the analytic process is **transference**. By the time these feelings of love, hate, and even eroticism evolve, they have intense emotional overtones. The skilled analyst then works directly with the feelings so that the patient will have an opportunity to understand the hidden emotion. The emotional relationship, transferred to the analyst, whether it happens to be love or hate, continues until the patient finally understands the emotions that were originally intended for his or her parents, brothers, or sisters, and is able to cope with them effectively.

Analysis takes the patient through transference, dream interpretation, Freudian slips, and free association to material buried deep within the unconscious. Painful childhood memories free themselves in the process. The technique might be compared to peeling an onion. One layer of material at a time must be removed until the analyst has helped the individual probe down into the depths of the unconscious. In successful analysis, the unconscious material is revealed and the troubling memories no longer cause pain.

THE BEHAVIORISTIC APPROACH

Not surprisingly, behaviorists have little use for Freud's elaborate approach to therapy. They are not interested in repressed memories, dream analysis, or free association. Since personality is, for the behaviorists, nothing more than behavior, we change undesirable personalities by changing behavior. Much better, say the behaviorists, to concentrate our energy on learning to exercise the behavior that makes us feel good and eliminate the behavior that upsets us.

Learning, then, is a key element in the behavioral theory of psychology. We learn to respond, for various reasons, to certain circumstances with behavior that causes us anxiety. Yet we can learn to extinguish the anxiety-producing behavior and put in its place behavior that gives us pleasure.

An important learning method that helps people reduce anxieties is called **desensitization.** Joseph Wolpe, a noted behaviorist, explains this method:

> The desensitization method consists of presenting to the imagination of the deeply relaxed patient the feeblest item in a list of anxiety-evoking stimuli repeatedly, until no more anxiety is evoked. The next item on the list is presented, and so on, until eventually, even the strongest of the anxiety-evoking stimuli fails to evoke any stir of anxiety in the patient. It has consistently been found that at every stage a stimulus that evokes no anxiety when imagined in a state of relaxation will also evoke no anxiety when encountered in reality. (5)

Another example of desensitization is the anxiety that a person faces when forced to speak in front of a group. The therapist and patient want to desensitize the patient to the fear of public speaking. In this method, the person rates all the anxiety provoking aspects of speaking before an audience on a scale. The least provoking situation might be talking with one person casually in a living room. The most anxiety could result when the same person is forced to speak before hundreds in an auditorium. As part of the treatment, the patient enters a state of deep relaxation. Once deeply relaxed, the patient is asked to visualize the conversation with a

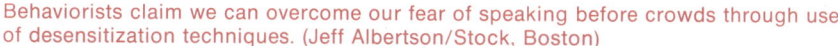

Behaviorists claim we can overcome our fear of speaking before crowds through use of desensitization techniques. (Jeff Albertson/Stock, Boston)

person in a living room until that image no longer produces anxiety. The process continues until the person has moved along the personal scale of anxiety producing images to the thought of speaking in front of hundreds of people. The treatment is successful when the person can actually speak (without relaxation techniques) to a large crowd without suffering.

In 1975 Stephen Brand, a high school student, performed a unique desensitization experiment with himself that was published in *Adolescence* magazine. Following behavioral techniques, Brand set out to change his behavior during his stressful senior year. First of all, he labeled what he thought were relevant behaviors and noted them on index cards every time they occurred. He kept careful track of his "Cogent thoughts," "Urges to take care of business," "Mental muddles," and "Excessive angers."

A teacher provoked a good bit of anger at one point during that year. Brand noted on his three-by-five card every time he felt "Excessive anger" with that teacher. Only six days of counting erased the anger. He desensitized himself by paying closer attention to the teacher's actual behavior and how it affected him. Each noted experience brought him better understanding of his reaction until no reaction of any consequence remained.

Brand says his charts allowed him to clarify his thinking about himself and his life. Once he saw his life in perspective, he decreased many of the anxieties that had plagued him. He claimed his system helped him to "pass beyond observation to management of my own behavior. I have a ready system of feedback on what I do . . . [thus] change can become something you make, rather than something that happens to you." (6)

Social Learning

Bandura and Walters, the well-known social-learning theorists, emphasized the importance of **imitation** in learning. Hall and Lindzey discuss this important contribution to behaviorism:

> In common with most other learning-theory approaches to personality the social learning theory of Bandura and Walters is based on the premise that most human behavior is acquired and that principles of learning are sufficient to account for the development of that behavior. However, previous learning theories have . . . failed sufficiently to take into account the social context in which this behavior is acquired and the fact that much important learning takes place vicariously—an individual observing the behavior of another and learning to imitate that behavior or in some way model himself after the other person. (7)

Bandura has amassed an impressive number of experiments to support the role of imitation in learning. Their theories can help people troubled by various problems. One study that stands out in my mind was concerned with snake phobia. Bandura and his colleagues assembled 48 people with snake phobia and separated them into three groups. The first group followed the desensitization technique described in the previous section. The second group watched films of adults and children playing with snakes. The last group looked out a window and watched a man approach a snake, touch it, and finally let it crawl around his neck. The observers in this third group were asked, whenever they were ready, to try to imitate this behavior. The results showed that the people in all three groups lost some of their fear. But those in the third group who watched and imitated lost their fear more quickly and more completely. (8)

An experiment performed at the University of California also lends credence to the social-learning theories on imitation. Lawrence Harper and Karen Sanders decided to look at the eating behavior of 80 children

Behaviorists believe imitation is a key element in learning. (Los Alamos Scientific Laboratory, right; © Frank Siteman 1979, below)

between the ages of four months and four years. A female experimenter visited the homes of the children with a food they had never seen before—a blue tortilla filled with ham and cheese. Mothers, in each case, assured the experimenter the child was completely unfamiliar with the food.

Half the children were offered the food without any preliminaries. The rest were only offered the food after they saw an adult taste the food first. The results showed that children were more likely to taste the food if they first saw an adult taste it. Most of the youngsters even asked for some of the food as they saw it eaten, before they were offered any.

Whether or not the visitor liked the food had no influence on the children—only the mothers' enjoyment was important. The experiment confirmed what parents have known for years—children eat more readily once they see their parents eating. The experiment confirmed for Albert Bandura and other learning theorists that imitation has a strong influence on changing behavior. (9)

Assertiveness Training

Assertiveness training, many behaviorists tell us, is really nothing more than a specialized approach to behavioral training. According to those who advocate such training, many people fail to lead healthy and happy lives because they do not assert themselves as much as they ought to (Case 7.3). Often a vicious circle captures us. We do not tell others about our needs—our need for praise, for affection, for recognition—and then we grow resentful because these needs remain unfulfilled.

David Knox, a counseling psychologist, believes that therapists can help their patients by emphasizing assertion.

> Anxiety is often a result of the unwillingness and/or inability to assert one's self. People who are often intimidated unreasonably do not assert themselves. This results in frustration, anxiety, guilt, and disappointment. The therapist, acting on the assumption that every person has worth and dignity and should be related to as a human being, will often train his clients to assert themselves and to insist on their legitimate rights as persons. (10)

To break the circle of resentment that results from nonassertion, assertiveness therapists often use a technique similar to desensitization. Trainees are encouraged to set specific goals for themselves, usually graduated from easy to difficult. Each goal is directed at making life more rewarding and fulfilling. For example, a person might decide to express one simple feeling as a first goal. A student might express a need for friendship by asking her roommate to join her on a walk after dinner. Such a small assertion of needs could then lead step-by-step to asserting greater needs. Such a technique might sound simplistic when first encountered, but many have conquered serious problems through just such an ap-

Cathy, by Cathy Guisewite. Copyright, 1978. Universal Press Syndicate.

proach. Assertiveness training has helped people reach such goals as meeting new friends, improving failing marriages, overcoming sexual difficulties, and correcting bad habits.

• Case 7.3

A lack of assertiveness keeps many people trapped in routines they find dull and boring. Joanne found herself bound by just such constrictions once her children were in school.

Joanne could never finish all the housework that seemed to go on relentlessly, but she needed stimulation rather than more activity. Even with the constant activity of laundry, shopping, or vacuuming, she felt bored. Her tasks were all mindless and lacked challenge, but when she complained to her husband, he only said he wished he could find a little boredom in his job.

A neighbor invited Joanne to join her at an assertiveness class given evenings at the local high school. Even one night away from the routine had an appeal Joanne thought would be refreshing. The class became far more than one night away from the routine, however. The teacher, a dynamic young woman, challenged all the students in the class to fix goals for themselves. Joanne, at first, had no idea she even had any goals. However, after she listened to other students gradually determine their goals, Joanne realized how much she wanted to return to college. The more she talked about it and thought about it the more convinced she became that she must start college at least on a parttime basis.

The thought of approaching her husband, an extremely emotional man, paralyzed her. Fortunately, the class also explored several techniques for self-assertion in difficult situations. The technique Joanne thought most appropriate for dealing with her husband's emotional outbursts the teacher called **simple assertion**. Joanne simply made the statement one night that she intended to sign up for two classes at the local college the following semester. Her husband became quite upset and objected violently to her decision. Joanne, as she had been taught, waited patiently for him to end his tirade. She then stated once more that she planned to take classes the following semester. No matter what arguments, threats, or objections her husband produced, Joanne simply returned calmly to a statement of her decision.

After the initial outburst of emotion subsided, Joanne and her husband talked about her need for stimulation. In a calmer moment, the decision seemed correct even to her husband. Her return to college gave Joanne new excitement, and now, thanks to lessons in self-assertion, Joanne has a college degree and, more important, a lot more self-esteem.

Learned Helplessness

We develop the need to assert ourselves at some time early in life. We were not born with the tendency to keep feelings to ourselves. As children, we spontaneously asked for what we wanted. Sometime during our childhood, however, we learned to suppress our needs, as parents, relatives, friends, and peers trained us to hide our desires. Without necessarily being conscious of what they were doing, others taught us the negative emotions of guilt, fear, and anxiety in order to control our childish demands.

Those early experiences with repressed demands were powerful for most of us because they occurred at such an impressionable age. Now,

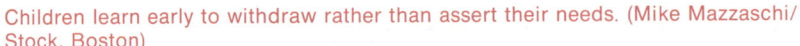

Children learn early to withdraw rather than assert their needs. (Mike Mazzaschi/Stock, Boston)

"Of course you have strengths, dear. It's just that you don't communicate them."

many years later, we still withdraw when we encounter problems rather than face them directly. A need for affection arises, for example, and rather than asking for affection we sometimes flee from our desire and withdraw from the person most likely to meet our need. Another person might grow angry and aggressive when encountering the person who could fulfill that desire for friendship. In whatever way we choose, we follow the immature approach we learned in childhood of withdrawing from the need we want satisfied.

Assertiveness training helps us discover techniques for asking that our needs be met. Workshops train people to ask for their "rights" and assert their opinions. Trainees also learn how to speak up in conflicts with others, make their wishes known, and gain confidence in themselves.

THE HUMANISTIC APPROACH

Carl Rogers, the well-known humanist, places the emphasis of his therapeutic method on the person seeking help rather than on the therapist. Rogers says that we all have an instinctive drive to become healthy and happy, although outside factors may temporarily prevent our spontaneous desire for health from emerging. However, the primary forces in the personality press us, no matter how troubled, to grow in positive ways. This positive force for happiness exists in everyone, Rogers tells us, from the temporarily upset to the deeply troubled. The humanist therapist approaches a client in ways that help or **facilitate** (a favorite word for Carl

Rogers) the natural growth tendencies in the person. Counselors, or therapists, help a troubled person best when they *like* the person coming for help. Effective counselors, therefore, like people. Rogers explains the importance of liking and **acceptance**:

> I find that the more acceptance and liking I feel toward [the client] the more I will be creating a relationship which he can use. By acceptance I mean a warm regard for him as a person of unconditional self-worth—of value no matter what his condition, his behavior, or his feelings. It means a respect and liking for him as a separate person, a willingness for him to possess his own feelings in his own way. It means an acceptance of and regard for his attitudes of the moment, no matter how negative or positive, no matter how much they may contradict other attitudes he has held in the past. This acceptance of each fluctuating aspect of this person makes it for him a relationship of warmth and safety, and the safety of being liked and prized as a person seems a highly important element in a helping relationship. (11)

A recent study supports Carl Rogers' emphasis on the importance of therapists liking their patients. Iradj Siassi, a psychiatrist, and Stanley Messer, a psychologist, examined the relationship between therapists and those patients who come from lower social and economic classes. Their study showed that therapists are reluctant to engage in any long-range therapy with poor clients.

The high dropout rate among patients from lower classes is usually attributed to the fact that they are typically inarticulate, unwilling to work for distant goals, and unable to profit from introspection. However, Siassi and Messer produce some impressive evidence to suggest that the therapists may have the major share of responsibility for the dropouts.

The therapists in the study, Siassi believes, held stereotyped attitudes toward the poor and had trouble identifying with the powerlessness, aggressiveness, and impulsiveness of many poor clients. Rather than risk identifying with such personality factors, the therapists used techniques that kept the lower-class patients at a distance—particularly drug treatments.

Simply put, the study suggests that therapists avoid the lower-class patients because they do not like them. Even if therapists did put forth solid effort to help their poorer clients, Rogers would probably say that their attempts would be in vain because they do not like those patients. (12)

Effective Concern

Therapists can develop a fondness for their clients in many ways. One important way is to take the time to try to understand just how the troubled person feels (Case 7.4). The effective counselor will never be satisfied with a client's statement that he or she feels unhappy, sad, or depressed.

Good therapists want to explore those feelings. They want to know just how this person experiences his or her sadness, for example. The causes of the sadness need exploration, also. As these aspects of a person's emotion begin to take shape, effective therapists find themselves drawing closer to the person in need of help.

Counselors also draw close to clients by remaining honest and open in the therapy relationship. They do not maintain an "I-am-the-doctor-and-you-are-the-patient" attitude. Instead, they freely express their own feelings with clients. If a story a client tells causes them sadness, for example, they do not hesitate to share that feeling. They also reveal feelings, when appropriate, of joy, disappointment, concern, and even affection.

Counselors must work hard to achieve this closeness. Carl Rogers explains how easy it is to become distant:

> I feel quite strongly that one of the important reasons for the professionalization of every field is that it helps to keep [a distance between persons]. In the clinical areas we develop elaborate diagnostic formulations, seeing the person as an object. In teaching and in administration we develop all kinds of evaluative procedures, so that again the person is perceived as an object. In these ways, I believe, we can keep ourselves from experiencing the caring which would exist if we recognized the relationship as one between two persons. (13)

• Case 7.4

Ralph always comes to mind when I discuss how important it is for therapists to like their patients. I recall how disturbed he looked the day he came to my office last spring.

"I just decided therapy has no value at all," he told me.

"How's that?" I asked, leaning back in my chair.

"I've been going to see this guy for almost three months and he hasn't helped me a bit." Ralph's eyebrows pulled together in anger.

"What makes you think you haven't been helped?" I noticed the strain in Ralph's face.

"I went to the guy because I have so much anxiety in my life. Almost everything makes me anxious." Ralph rubbed his hand nervously back and forth across his jeans. "Now I feel more anxiety than I did before I went to see the guy. Even when we talk casually with one another I become anxious."

"Do you have any idea why the talks with your therapist make you anxious?" I let my swivel chair pull me forward.

"Sure. The guy doesn't like me. I mean, he asks me a question and then never listens to my answers. He sometimes asks me the same question two or three times during the same hour." Ralph looked out the window. "But there's more to it. I guess I don't like him either. I know I would never choose him for a friend."

"So why did you choose him for a therapist?" My tone seemed sharp, even to me.

"Because he's a psychiatrist." Ralph looked surprised by my question. "He's supposed to be able to help me."

Ralph and I talked for some time about the need for trust in a therapy relationship. Rather than give up on therapy, I suggested, he might do better to give up this one particular therapist. He seemed stunned when I told him that the first criterion, for me, in determining whether or not a therapist is effective, is to decide if the therapist cares about people. The more we talked, however, the more he understood my point. The next time Ralph selected his therapist with more care and found someone who helped him relieve his anxieties.

Trust

When a client finds a facilitative therapist, Rogers tells us, he or she will know it. When the therapist likes the client, the client will feel that warmth and respond to it. And once the client tests the relationship to make certain the bond is genuine, he or she will begin to feel a freedom to open up and talk about problems as if the therapist were a close friend.

This openness does not happen immediately. Like any growing relationship, the freedom to express the embarrassing and painful feelings comes slowly. But in time, the troubled person reveals himself or herself to the therapist, and **trust** grows within the relationship. Trust is another key word for Carl Rogers. He regards it as the element in a therapeutic relationship that makes growth possible. When trust is present, the client can look honestly at himself or herself and reveal that self to the therapist. Without trust, the communication becomes filled with partial truths and guarded statements.

Emotional Maturity

One of the most important steps in human growth, according to Rogers, is when people start to listen to their own feelings about right and wrong. He explains:

> One of the basic things which I was a long time in realizing, and which I am still learning, is that when an activity feels as though it is valuable or worth doing, it *is* worth doing. Put another way, I have learned that my total organismic sensing of a situation is more trustworthy than my intellect. (14)

Once healthy, trusting relationships form between clients and therapists, clients reveal themselves in most intimate ways. The first part of the clients' self to emerge is usually an admission that they hide behind masks. They admit, with some pain, that their life contains a great deal of pretense. They smile when they would rather shout. They pretend to be in command when they feel helpless and useless. They act competent though they feel inadequate.

As the therapy continues, clients begin to discard their masks. They also abandon their desires to please others before themselves and grow less likely to live according to the rules of parents, friends, or society. Instead, they begin to explore for themselves which directions will bring the most self-fulfillment.

This process of exploration soon reveals that personal feelings and inclinations can provide a suitable guide for life. If a client feels she would rather leave school now and take a job, she finds that such feelings give her good counsel. And, in the end, the entire process leads her back to herself, when she discovers herself as someone who has value. She can like and trust herself. She has achieved **emotional maturity**.

This entire process, Rogers is quick to point out, is a natural one that occurs *within* the person. The woman's own instinctive drive for health found a chance to emerge. The therapist only cleared the way by providing a warm friendship in which the client could begin to discover himself or herself. The trust, implicit in the relationship, allowed that growth, but the client made it all happen.

CONCLUSION

The three approaches to therapy discussed in this chapter reflect the three attitudes or philosophies we have followed throughout the book. The psychoanalysts look into the personality to uncover the forces that cause anxiety and grief. To probe the unconscious, Freud used a variety of techniques. His interest in hypnosis led him to use free-association techniques that helped the unconscious reveal itself in the conscious. Only by looking beneath the surface of the personality, Freud claimed, could we see the roots of any disturbance.

Behaviorists, by contrast, look directly at outward behavior to help people cope with their anxieties. To conquer phobias, for example, some behaviorists gradually bring people into contact with the source of these phobias, while teaching them relaxation. Behaviorists believe that self-assertion can help people reach a variety of personal goals. Self-assertion, too, is learned by gradual behavioral changes.

Humanists think people overcome their fears and inadequacies by talking through their problems with someone who acts as a friend. When an effective therapist meets people seeking help in a person-to-person relationship, a bond of trust grows between them. With that basis of confidence, troubled people can gradually reveal the source of their conflicts. Carl Rogers claims that once people possess the freedom and safety of a trusting relationship, they will find their own personal solutions to the problems that plague them.

SUMMARY

1. Early in his career, Freud became convinced that the unconscious contained the source of our psychological problems. To explore the unconscious he used hypnosis and then developed the technique of free association. The technique relied heavily on the interpretation of dreams and errors, or slips of the tongue, to help the analyst discover the roots of maladies. But it was transference, the emotion that develops between the patient and doctor, that helps patients discover and understand aggravating feelings that cause emotional turmoil.
2. Behaviorists avoid explorations into the personality. Instead, they try to teach troubled patients to learn new behaviors that do not cause them so much pain. In desensitization, phobic people learn to react in new ways to the source of their phobia. Imitation helps others learn new reaction patterns. Recently, assertiveness training has helped many people learn to take better care of themselves in personal relationships.
3. Carl Rogers believes the people coming to therapy for help have within themselves all the potential necessary to grow in positive ways. The therapist simply helps such people by befriending them. In the warmth of a trusting relationship, clients grow free to explore their most embarrassing feelings with the therapist. Slowly, the clients begin to emerge from behind the masks that have hidden their personality as they learn to trust the feelings that were once hidden. And once the emotions emerge as trustworthy guides, troubled clients are well on their way to health.

KEY TERMS

unconscious
hypnosis
free association
dream interpretation
symbols
Freudian slip
transference
learning

desensitization
imitation
assertiveness training
simple assertion
facilitate
acceptance
trust
emotional maturity

STUDY QUESTIONS

1. Freud said that our little slips of the tongue often reveal the truth we try to hide. Can you think of an instance when that was true in your life?
2. Freud said our dreams often reveal our hidden wishes to us. Can you think of any dream you have had in which that was true?

3. Do you believe, if you suffered from a severe fear of snakes, you could overcome that fear by using the desensitization process explained in this chapter? Explain your answer.
4. Think of a time when you wished you had been able to say "no" to someone when you felt imposed upon. Why did you fail to say no? Do you believe with training you could learn to say no in a similar circumstance?
5. If you were to enter therapy, would you want to choose a therapist you could also consider a friend? Mention any disadvantage of such a relationship that could interfere with your therapy.
6. Name at least three important ways in which trust is critical in a therapy relationship.

ADDITIONAL READING

Ayllon, T., and Arzin, N. *The Token Economy: A Motivational System for Therapy and Rehabilitation.* New York: Appleton-Century-Crofts, 1968.

Barton, Anthony, *Three Worlds of Therapy.* Palo Alto, Calif.: National Press, 1975.

Chesler, Phyllis. *Women and Madness.* New York: Doubleday, 1972.

Evans, Richard I. *Carl Rogers: The Man and His Ideas.* New York: Dutton, 1975.

Fensterheim, Herbert, and Baer, Jean. *Don't Say Yes When You Want to Say No.* New York: McKay, 1975.

Freud, Sigmund. *Therapy and Technique.* New York: Collier, 1963.

Lieberman, M. A., Yalon, I. D., and Miles, M. *Encounter Groups: First Facts.* New York: Basic Books, 1973.

Rogers, Carl. *Client-Centered Therapy.* Boston: Houghton Mifflin, 1951.

Waelder, R. *Basic Theory of Psychoanalysis.* New York: International Universities Press, 1960.

Wollheim, Richard. *Sigmund Freud.* New York: Viking, 1971.

Wolpe, Joseph, and Lazarus, Arnold A. *Behavior Therapy Techniques: A Guide to the Treatment of Neurosis.* New York: Pergamon, 1967.

Chapter Eight

Attitudes and Values

OUTLINE

The Psychoanalytic Approach
The Archetypes
The Shadow
Anima and Animus

The Behavioristic Approach
Manipulating Propinquity
First Impressions
Shared Values

The Humanistic Approach
Self-Actualization and Values
Psychology Implies Values
The Highest Values

Conclusion

LEARNING OBJECTIVES

After reading this chapter you should be able to:

1. Understand the origin of Jungian archetypes and their place in the unconscious.
2. Discuss the shadow and anima/animus archetypes and their influence on our attitudes and values.
3. Explain propinquity and its effect on our attitudes toward others.
4. Discuss how our first impression of peoples affects our attitudes toward them.
5. Explain why psychologists feel they should avoid value judgments in their study of people.
6. Understand how Maslow tried to base the study of values on scientific evidence.

Chapter Eight

An early morning psychology class came alive when a young man in the back of the room wanted to know why some people become so prejudiced in their thinking. An extremely tall young woman felt that people are either born with prejudice or they are not. A black basketball player stated flatly that all white people are prejudiced. After these comments, I stated that I thought everyone was prejudiced against one group or another.

A moment of quiet followed my remark. Then the black ball player said, "I know I hate cops."

"Why would you say you hate cops?" I asked, relieved that someone understood my point.

"Because I don't want to know those guys as people." His voice grew sharp. "I just want to know them as cops. I want to think of cops as nothing more than badges and uniforms. If I knew them as people, I might like one of them. And I don't want to like cops."

"That's what I mean." I smiled at his clear definition of prejudice. "We all have prejudice."

"And I can't stand athletes," the tall young woman said, looking at the basketball player. "They are conceited and have nothing to be conceited about. None of them have any brains."

"I guess I ought to admit I'm prejudiced against blacks." A young man with blond hair and sensitive blue eyes talked now. "I am not happy about my prejudice, but it's there. My family had a great deal of prejudice against all minorities. For years I didn't understand what they were saying. Then, when I did understand and tried to change my attitude, it was difficult. No matter how many black people I befriend, a small part of me reacts against them as a race."

The class opened up after that remark. One by one the students admitted that their reactions against one group or another were stereotyped. No one understood why they had become so biased and prejudiced, but all admitted they were. Of course, we should not be surprised that these students did not understand the causes of their prejudice, because even the great thinkers of the psychological world have struggled with the problem and found no simple explanation.

One great psychoanalytic thinker, Carl Jung, looked at the unconscious mind to try to understand prejudice. At first he thought the nature of the unconscious was much the same as Sigmund Freud had described it.

However, the more Jung studied, the more he discovered. Beneath the personal unconscious Freud described, Jung saw a collective unconscious where we store memory traces inherited from our ancestors. These emotion-filled traces still have an impact on our attitudes and values, Jung told us. The fact that our ancestors all had mothers and reacted to those mothers in a particular way, for example, means we have an image of mother even before we encounter our own mother. And this memory trace, because it is so universal, also is strongly idealistic, which can create problems for us when we relate to our own mother.

Behavioral research also helps us understand our attitudes and values. For example, we discover that we like people in direct proportion to our proximity to them, whether we are talking about how close we live to people in the neighborhood or how near we stand to them at a cocktail party. Our attitudes toward others is also affected by the first impression they make upon us. Their height, weight, skin color, and other physical characteristics directly affect our attitudes. And finally, we like best those people who share our values and shy away from those who take exception to our beliefs.

Abraham Maslow, a humanist, deplored the general tendency of psychologists to avoid questions of morals and values in their study. He felt any theory unable to condemn the Nazi extermination of the Jews during World War II, for example, could not be honest. And Maslow also thought that, regardless of the past inability of humanists to avoid subjectivity in studies of values, times had changed. Maslow's study of extremely well-balanced people led him to conclude that their value system could stand as an objective model for the rest of us.

THE PSYCHOANALYTIC APPROACH

Carl Jung, a friend and colleague of Freud for many years, broke with the founder of the psychoanalytic school largely because of Freud's sexual theories. Another important difference between the two men, however, concerned Jung's belief in the **collective unconscious.** Jung saw the unconscious existing at two levels. The upper level of the unconscious Jung assumed existed much the way Freud described it. Jung labeled this level the **personal unconscious.** But underneath the personal unconscious another conscious level existed that Jung called the collective unconscious.

We all have a collective unconscious, Jung said, where we store latent memories we inherit from our ancestors. Experiences our forebearers repeated or saw repeated throughout the evolutionary process were passed on to us as part of our birthright, stored in our unconscious. Throughout history, for example, humans experienced danger in the dark. We inherited that fear of the dark even before we personally experienced anything frightening in the dark. Another example is the fear of snakes.

This fear predates our experience with the possible dangers that snakes might pose. According to Jung, many of our attitudes and values are present within us at birth. They live in a state of potential existence in our collective unconscious, waiting for some life experience to reveal them to us.

Hall and Norby, Jungian scholars, describe the nature of the collective unconscious:

> The collective unconscious is a reservoir of latent images, usually called primordial images by Jung. Primordial means "first" or "original"; therefore a primordial image refers to the earliest development of the psyche. Man inherits these images from his ancestral past, a past that includes all of his human ancestors as well as his prehuman or animal ancestors. These racial images are not inherited in the sense that a person consciously remembers or has images that his ancestors had. Rather they are predispositions of potentialities for experiencing and responding to the world in the same ways that his ancestors did. Consider, for example, man's fear of snakes or of the dark. He does not have to learn these fears through experiences with snakes or the dark, although such experiences may reinforce or reaffirm his predispositions. We inherit predispositions to fear snakes and the dark because our primitive ancestors experienced these fears for countless generations. They became engraved upon the brain. (1)

The Archetypes

In Jung's collective unconscious, then, a host of images exist in potential form. For example, generation upon generation of humans have seen the sun rise and set as a regular part of their experience. For most of human

Jung believed that archetypes are passed on from one generation to another. (Susan Meiselas/Magnum)

Momma by Mell Lazarus. Courtesy of Mell Lazarus and Field Newspaper Syndicate.

history, people knew this pattern was critical to their existence, and they invested a great deal of emotion in hoping this ritual would continue. Out of such hope, sun gods were worshipped, and religious rituals grew to elaborate proportions to honor them. This emotion-packed memory trace of the sun rising and setting exists at the moment of birth, according to Jung.

Each of the emotion-filled memory traces that lives in our collective unconscious Jung calls the **archetype.** The most important thing about archetypes in this discussion is how they affect our attitudes and values. The archetype of mother, for example, predates our experience of our own mother. Many of our attitudes toward our mother, or toward ourself as a mother, arise from this image we have of mother. Because we already have a strong inclination about the function of a mother at birth, we respond immediately to the natural life-giving attention our real mother extends toward us. Later in life, however, our image of mother can remain too fixed. Many people come to expect too much of themselves or their mothers because the emotional archetype of mother is powerful (Case 8.1). Calvin Hall explains how the mother archetype ideally works:

> An archetype is a universal thought form (idea) which contains a large element of emotion. This thought form creates images or visions that correspond in normal waking life to some aspect of the conscious situation. For example, the archetypes of the mother produces an image of a mother figure which is then identified with the actual mother. In other words, the baby inherits a preformed conception of a generic mother which determines in part how the baby will perceive his mother. The baby's perception is also influenced by the nature of the mother and by the infant's experiences with her. Thus, the baby's experience is the joint product of an inner predisposition to perceive the world in a certain manner and the actual nature of that world. The two determinants usually fit together compatibly because the archetype itself is a product of racial experiences with the world, and these experiences are much the same as those that any individual living in any age and in any part of the world will have. That is to say, the nature of mothers—what they do—has remained pretty much the same throughout the history of the race, so that the mother archetype which the baby inherits is congruent with the actual mother with whom the baby interacts. (2)

● Case 8.1

Often, when I talk to students about their emotional conflicts, I think of the archetypes. So many times, those archetypes appear at the root of their turmoil.

I particularly remember the day I almost passed Jan without recognizing her as I walked across campus to the library. Her shoulders hunched forward uncharacteristically as she sat eating her lunch on the lawn near the auditorium. I stopped, sat down on the grass, and chatted for a few minutes. Jan tried to follow the conversation, but soon her troubles erupted. "I just can't stand my mother," she told me.

"A lot of students have trouble relating to their parents," I replied sympathetically.

"I know. I know. What is it? You're a psychologist. Why do we all have such trouble getting along with our parents?"

"I have no answer to the generation gap question," I replied, leaning away from her question. "I think maybe parents and children must, in the end, accept the distance between them." I paused. "However, I do think some things can be done to ease the strain."

"What's that? Tell me. I would be willing to do anything to get along better with my folks."

"It just strikes me that students often seem to expect their parents to understand them before they make any effort to understand their parents."

"I'm not sure I understand."

"Have you any idea how your parents feel about themselves? Do you know what makes your mother happier than anything else in the world? Do you know your father's greatest fear?' "

"I don't." Jan looked down at a blade of grass as she pulled it out of the lawn. "But I don't know how I could, either. I just can't go up and say, 'What makes you happy, Mom?''

"Maybe you can and maybe you can't. I don't see why you couldn't spend one conversation asking your mother nothing but questions. Ask her what makes her happy, lonely, sad, or content. Ask her about her life, her experiences, and her disappointments. I'll bet you would learn a great deal about your mom and even wind up enjoying yourself."

Jan did take my suggestion. She spent one entire hour asking her mother questions. Her mother got so involved and excited, she could hardly stop talking. That one conversation did not eliminate all of Jan's stereotype thinking about her mother. But it did begin a new friendship between herself and her mother.

The Shadow

As part of our evolutionary inheritance, we all possess an archetype of animal instincts. These animal impulses have a tendency to frighten us, particularly when we exist in a repressed society. Jung called this archetype of our animal tendencies the **shadow.** The name was well chosen,

Tumbleweeds. © 1966 United Feature Syndicate, Inc.

because we tend to keep this shadow side of our personality hidden. We fear the power of our spontaneous animal impulses if we expressed them fully.

Often we give the repressed desires that the shadow represents some personification outside of ourselves and then condemn that person. For example, psychoanalysts tell us that white people who have trouble accepting their hidden desires often project them on blacks, and then condemn the black people for possessing the white people's own projected desires. Blacks in this country, especially where discrimination is most rigid, have much projected on them. They are accused of sexual excesses, innate ignorance, and violent tendencies. What the accusers do not realize is that when they accuse blacks of such excesses, they are revealing their own latent desires. Frieda Fordham, a friend and colleague of Carl Jung, explains the nature of the shadow:

> Jung calls that other side of ourselves the shadow. That shadow is the inferior being in ourselves, the one who wants to do all the things that we do not allow ourselves to do, who is everything that we are not, the Mr. Hyde to our Dr. Jekyll. We have an inkling of this foreign personality when, after being possessed by an emotion or overcome with rage, we excuse ourselves by saying, "I was not myself," or "I really don't know what came over me." What "came over" was in fact the shadow, the primitive, uncontrolled, and animal part of ourselves. The shadow also personifies itself when we particularly dislike someone. If it is an unreasonable dislike, we should suspect that we are actually disliking a quality of our own which we find in the other person. (3)

Projection of the shadow as bias against blacks invades every corner of our lives. According to psychologist Raymond E. Rainville, it even intrudes into the sportscasting of professional football. Rainville has a unique perspective for making his judgment—he is blind. Yet, when listening to the announcers of the NFL football games, Rainville can tell the color of a player's skin from the way the announcers talk about him.

To document his claim Rainville, along with graduate student Edward McCormick, made audio tapes of twelve NFL games televised by the three major networks. They paired up statements about black and white players with similar performances at the same position. Then they played the tapes before judges who characterized the announcers' comments.

Many white people project their own fears onto black people. © John Marmaras/Woodfin Camp & Associates)

White sportscasters often reveal their hidden prejudice against blacks in many subtle ways. (Pamela Schuyler/Stock, Boston)

Black players lost in all categories. White announcers, the judges discovered, apparently begin with the assumption that blacks are inferior to whites and broadcast the game in a way that supports this belief. They even interjected remarks about previous failures by black players that had nothing to do with the game. White, by contrast, received more praise for physical and mental attributes and also got more special focus and sympathy. Speculation about the game also hurts blacks. A black making a long run or catching a touchdown pass was most often seen as lucky. Whites performing similar feats were credited with skill, strength, and initiative. (4)

The strong social prohibition against racism in the public media makes any direct statement of prejudice impossible. Yet, as Jung points out, the repressed feelings will emerge. Especially in the world of professional sports, where blacks have achieved great success, Jung would not be surprised to hear that remarks by white announcers were full of hidden prejudice.

Anima and Animus

The last archetype we will consider in this section helps us account for our attitudes toward our sexual selves. Jung's archetype theories predated our present understanding of **bisexuality.** Yet his theory explains well the fact now accepted by most psychologists and social thinkers—we are physiologically, intellectually, and psychologically a blend of male and female characteristics. Hall and Lindzey explain:

> It is fairly well recognized and accepted that man is essentially a bisexual animal. On a physiological level, the male secrétes both male and female sex hormones, as does the female. On the psychological level, masculine and feminine characteristics are found in both sexes. **Homosexuality** is just one of the conditions, but perhaps the most striking one, that has given rise to the conception of human bisexuality. (5)

Every man, Jung tells us, possesses a female archetype. Because of his experience throughout the evolution of life, an emotion-laden archetype of woman lies in each male's collective unconscious. That archetype, called the **anima,** helps males understand women. A similar archetype in women, called the **animus,** performs a parallel function for them. Unfortunately, like the other archetypes, this archetype can not only help men understand women, for example, but it can also lead men to idealize women. Much of the tension between men and women, Jung suggests, originates in an archetype that has remained too idealistic. No woman can live up to the anima ideal, nor can any man achieve the ideal of any woman's animus.

A researcher at the University of Cincinnati suggests that the male anima is very much alive today. Roger A. Woudenberg administered a "personal opinion survey" to 350 young, white college men, 104 from a southern state university and the rest from institutions in the midwest. The long list of questions included items designed to reveal sexual guilt, depersonalization of sex, control of sexual expression, adherence to traditional roles, and the dichotomization of women as nonsexual and good or sexual and bad.

The strongest correlation found in the study was between stereotypical attitudes toward women and constricted, depersonalized attitudes toward sex. Jung might say that when the depersonalized anima, or female ideal, controls a young man's thoughts, he must respond by remaining impersonal in his sexual attitudes also. A Jungian dynamic seems to take place in the minds of these men. They feel threatened by female sexuality, so they try to control its expression. To gain control, in their minds, they label female sexuality as bad and withdraw from it by removing themselves emotionally. This withdrawal further depersonalizes the woman and increases their sense of control. The woman remains a person who falls short of the idealized anima. She cannot live up to the male ideal anima, and is condemned by the male. This condemnation relieves him of the burden of intimacy. (6)

The anima not only exists to help men understand women. It is also an important part of their personalities. Those characteristics considered female throughout the history of evolution—sensitivity, warmth, and understanding—are also an important part of each man's personality. The same holds true for women and their animus. The animus possesses characteristics of courage, strength, stamina, and other attributes normally assigned to the male. According to Jung, both men and women must allow their bisexuality to emerge. Only men who let themselves be sensitive and warm can achieve balance in their personalities (Case 8.2). And only women who show their strength and stamina can also free themselves to grow psychologically. Otherwise, the repressed part of the personality can produce distortions. Men, for example, who hide from their feminine characteristics are most apt to become preoccupied with fear of homosexuals. Clearly, men most anxious to crack jokes about "queers" and vigorously assert their male virtues have the greatest insecurity concerning their own masculinity. They are afraid that they cannot both express their female characteristics *and* maintain their masculinity.

Repressed attitudes toward homosexuality reveal themselves in several ways. One myth that shows a clear prejudice is the conclusion that homosexuals are "sick." And possibly more than any other group, the social scientists have contributed to this myth's persistence. The bulk of studies done to prove that homosexuals are pathological have been conducted with homosexuals who were already either in therapy or in some behavioral difficulty, not with socially well-adjusted homosexuals.

Thomas Clark, a psychologist, attempted to set the record straight. To do so he selected 140 college-educated non-patient males with varying

Jung believed that both men and women must allow their bisexuality to emerge. (© Leonard Freed/Magnum, below; Abigail Heyman/Magnum, right)

degrees of sexual preference. The men functioned normally in various professional capacities, and none were in therapy due to homosexual difficulties.

Clark rated the men with Kinsey's Heterosexual-Homosexual Rating Scale to separate the men into groups of 20 to represent each of the seven levels of the scale. To eliminate any other differences interfering with the results, the groups were arranged to match one another in socioeconomic background. The group was then tested on the Tennessee Self-Concept Scale, which measures psychopathology.

No significant difference could be found between the homosexual group and the heterosexual group either in overall scores or in individual measures. The increase in homosexuality did not indicate any increase in pathology. The study shows that homosexuality, rather than being a sickness, is "a deviation in sexual patterns and object choice which is within the normal range psychologically." (7)

● Case 8.2

Not everyone can accept the true balance in their personalities between the male and female characteristics. Hank was such a person. No one ever looked more like a truck driver. His large frame filled most doorways, and most people felt overwhelmed the first time they met him. Hank always thought truck driving was hard work, and he enjoyed it. The work seemed to appeal to his masculine sense—he felt powerful whenever he thought about controlling such a large piece of machinery.

Problems emerged in Hank's life three years after he married Ivy. About that time Ivy began to complain Hank did not satisfy her sexually. Nothing could have embarrassed Hank more, because his virility seemed at stake. Ivy tried to tell Hank her needs lay elsewhere. She missed the tenderness and sensitivity she always found with her family. Hank could not listen or understand what she said. In Hank's life, sex had never had anything to do with sensitivity and tenderness. As he attempted to please Ivy, his approach to lovemaking became more aggressive and rough. Ivy became progressively more and more cool to his advances until she became completely frigid.

Ivy tried one final time to communicate with Hank. She found a marriage counselor with a warm and sympathetic nature. He seemed to understand her dilemma instinctively. She expressed herself well and, in time, felt at ease with her turmoil. Once she developed a good rapport with her counselor, she invited Hank to come to therapy with her. Only with great reluctance did he agree. The session was a disaster. Hank insulted the counselor and even left the session before the hour ended. His only comment to Ivy afterwards was, "I suppose you expect me to act like that pansy." At that moment, Ivy became convinced her struggle was hopeless. She separated from Hank before the end of the month, and their divorce became final a year later.

THE BEHAVIORISTIC APPROACH

Social psychologists have done a great deal of behavioral research to learn more about our attitudes and values. Rather than looking into the personality to understand how values and attitudes form, these researchers study behavior itself. What attracts people to one another? What drives them apart? An interesting conclusion reached by the behavioral psychologists is that **propinquity**—how physically near individuals are to each other—has a great impact on the likelihood that those people will get to know one another. The closer two people are situated physically to each other the more apt they will become close personally.

The principle of propinquity and its effects have a significant amount of supporting research. Studies show that the closer two people live to one another the more likely they will marry. Within housing tracts studied, the families living on the same street were much more likely to know one another socially than people who lived around the corner from one another. In apartment buildings, people on the same floor were significantly more apt to form friendships than people living on different floors. Study after study could be cited to show that the closer two people are to one another physically the more apt they are to become close personally. (8, 9, 10)

Manipulating Propinquity

Social scientists decided to carry the study of propinquity one step further. They wanted, first of all, to know if the physical arrangement of people within the same room can alter the chance for friendship. One study showes that the principle holds here, too. Within classrooms and offices the closer two people are physically the more apt they are to form a friendship. Two people seated opposite one another at a table talk more than two people seated on the same side of the table. No matter how closely the study looked at the effects of proximity, the principle continued to hold. (11)

Social scientists then looked at their knowledge of propinquity and began to think in new directions. Could a direct manipulation of the proximity of people to one another affect the social atmosphere between them (Case 8.3)? They discovered it could. Architects could affect the social pattern of a planned community by careful designing the sidewalk paths. Teachers using seating charts can affect interaction in classrooms by arranging students according to prearranged plans. (12, 13)

Then, social scientists were ready to ask the most important question

Social scientists have discovered that they can change attitudes by manipulating propinquity. (Peeter Vilms/Jeroboam)

that surrounds the principle of propinquity—can propinquity manipulation help end racial segregation? The busing of school children still has emotional overtones so explosive that careful scientific study is still almost impossible. However, at least one study did draw some conclusions in a comparison between black and white interaction in segregated and nonsegregated building units. Clearly, the whites in the nonsegregated units responded more favorably to blacks. Both blacks and whites in the nonsegregated units had more friendly contacts with one another and had more positive feelings toward one another than those in the segregated units. The psychologists concluded that the princple of propinquity might be strong enough to heal some of the friction between the races. (14)

● Case 8.3

Peg knew nothing about social psychology and even less about the theory of propinquity. Yet, with the help of a friend, she used those principles to help herself enjoy life more. Though she had not yet reached thirty, she had begun to act and to look like the stereotypical middle-aged housewife. For one thing, she let herself become about twenty pounds overweight. But most of all, she let her life grow predictable. At first, Peg did not see her life falling into a rut. Only when her best friend, Dee, said, "Peg, you act like an old woman," did Peg realize the embarrassing truth of that statement.

Peg and Dee had a long talk. Only because she was such a good friend could Dee tell Peg how matronly she had become. When Peg saw clearly how true Dee's observations were, she asked Dee what she could do. Dee gave good advice. "Change your routine. Try taking a different route when you pick up the kids after school. Shop at a supermarket you've never been to before. The next time you and Harris go out to dinner, insist on going to a new restaurant. But above all, meet some new people. Don't neglect us old friends, but find some new ones, too."

The advice seemed a little too simple to have any effect. Yet, Peg had no more than begun to change her routine when she brightened up considerably. Just seeing new people gave her a new burst of energy, and before long she began to meet new friends. A woman at the supermarket asked her if she understood unit pricing, the conversation became a nice chat, and eventually developed into a friendship. As part of this new enthusiasm, she and Harris joined a square dancing group, and the contacts there have only begun to blossom. To an amazing extent, the contact with a new group of people brought Peg a fresh attitude toward life.

First Impressions

Another interesting discovery made by behavioral scientists concerns observable characteristics of people that act as cues to attract others. We all know how strong our **first impression** can be of another person without

Tumbleweeds. © 1966 United Feature Syndicate, Inc.

ever having met that person before, but how are such impressions formed? Presumably, the impression is a carry-over from experiences with other people. Attraction to one person with certain characteristics simply carries over to another person with the same characteristics. Behaviorists refer to this process as **generalization.**

An interesting study that supports this theory concerns eye glasses. Eleven graduate students appeared before two groups of undergraduates. Before one group the graduate students wore eye glasses and before the other group they wore no glasses. The graduate students, strangers to those judging them, were rated more intelligent, more industrious, and less inclined toward humor when they wore glasses as opposed to when they did not. The results suggest the student judges responded with stereotyped thinking. (15)

The conclusions reached with regard to stereotyped thinking toward glasses has obvious implications in race relations. Much more powerful than our automatic reaction to eye glasses is our response to skin color, religion, or nationality (Self-Quiz 8.1).

When most people think of prejudice, they think of white prejudice against blacks. Yet bigotry works both ways. To make the point clearly, Mark J. Jones of Westminster College at Salt Lake City, Utah, and a colleague, Wilma Oliver, a counselor at Salt Lake City's Planned Parenthood Center, developed a study of black male attitudes.

Jones and Oliver asked 100 black men aged 16 to 22 to join them in a study of prejudice. The men were Utah University students from mostly lower-class to middle-class backgrounds and from various parts of the country. These men were instructed to write out five common stereotypes or generalizations about whites.

Sixty-five percent of these black men said that whites think of themselves as superior to nonwhites. Forty percent of the group said whites have a "strange" body odor which many attributed to the smell of white people's hair when wet. About 36 percent said whites have small genitals, 35 percent wrote whites engage in "abnormal" sexual practices such as

Self-Quiz 8.1 — Tolerance

This test contains a number of statements regarding your ability to tolerate others. Read the alternative that best describes your attitude by checking the proper box to the left of the statement. Answer all of the statements.

Often	*Occasionally*	*Rarely*	
☐	☐	☐	1. I cannot forgive someone who has seriously hurt me.
☐	☐	☐	2. I become furious with people who distract me when I try to concentrate.
☐	☐	☐	3. I become angry at and envious of people who have good luck.
☐	☐	☐	4. I try to persuade others of my point of view.
☐	☐	☐	5. I believe people are responsible for their actions and must take the consequences.
☐	☐	☐	6. The personal habits of my friends annoy me.
☐	☐	☐	7. I become angry when people question authority.
☐	☐	☐	8. Fussy old people annoy me.
☐	☐	☐	9. People who think morality is relative upset me.
☐	☐	☐	10. People who disagree with me make me angry.

This test cannot tell you how tolerant you are or are not, but it does tell you how you compare with others who took the same test. To total your score, give yourself 3 points for each time you checked "often" on the test, 2 points for each "occasionally," and 1 point for each "seldom." Add up the total number of points and compare that total with the following scale.

22–30   Your score ranks among the highest achieved by those taking this test. It suggests you might be intolerant.
15–22   Your score ranks with the vast majority of students taking the test. You have about the normal amount of tolerance found in society generally.
Below 15   Your score is in the range of those who seem highly tolerant.

oral sex, and 32 percent thought that whites are sexually inadequate. A much smaller group made some interesting comments also. They felt whites teach their children prejudice, that they are physically weaker than blacks, and finally that whites are the "devil incarnate." (16)

Shared Values

The studies of attitudes and values published by social scientists seem almost limitless. I could not possibly even allude to them all. Before we leave the subject of attitudes and value studies, however, I believe one last point is important. It seems that we choose as friends those people who support our attitudes and beliefs. A host of studies show that friends and spouses tend to hold the same attitudes and values, ranging from communism to birth control.

A question immediately arises, of course. Do people choose their friends because they share similar values, or does the friendship between two people lead them to agree on certain values? An interesting approach to this question begins by gathering people in an informal atmosphere after determining their individual value systems. Then we can watch and see which people relate best with one another. In one study a group of people, after being identified with a value system according to the Allport-Vernon Scale of Values, were assembled informally and observed. The result of the study showed that those who shared similar values tended to form friendships more often than those who had dissimilar values. (17) Other approaches have been utilized over the years. The results always draw the same conclusion. We are attracted to those people who share our values and avoid those who challenge our values.

THE HUMANISTIC APPROACH

Scientists tend to retreat from any consideration of values. This attitude began with the physical scientists, who felt their study of nature's laws was hampered by questions of right and wrong. So they decided to set aside all value judgments and simply study the way the physical world operates. Many scientific discoveries, such as Copernicus' revelation that the earth rotated around the sun and was not itself the center of the universe, deeply offended the religious establishments of their day. However, such discoveries also confirmed the scientists in their belief that value decisions should be separated from scientific study.

This scientific history and tradition followed the social scientist into the study of psychology. Psychologists should study behavior, and people ought to look elsewhere for insight into morality. Religion, God, and the Bible normally help people find their values. Let that arrangement continue, the psychologists suggested. But Abraham Maslow, the great humanistic psychologist, felt that moral values mean nothing unless they can be confirmed scientifically. And the most important part of his life's work was his attempt to show in a scientific way that a value system is an inherent part of our human nature (Case 8.4).

> Humanists for thousands of years have attempted to construct a naturalistic, psychological value system that could be derived from man's own nature without the necessity of recourse to authority outside the human being himself. . . . it is my belief that certain developments in the science and art of psychology, in the last few decades, make it possible for us for the first time to feel confident that this age-old hope may be fulfilled if only we work hard enough. We know how to criticize the old theories; we know, even though dimly, the shape of the theories to come, and most of all, we know where to look and what to do in order to fill in the gaps in knowledge, that will permit us to answer the age-old questions, "What is the good life? What is the good man? How can people be taught to desire and prefer the good life? How ought children to be brought up to be sound adults? etc." That is, we think that a scientific ethic may be possible, and we think we know how to go about constructing it. (18)

● Case 8.4

Maslow does not believe that we have complete freedom to choose any value system. He thinks values are an innate part of our nature that is difficult to ignore or fight. If Maslow knew James, he might use him as an example of a person who could not escape a personal value system.

James lived the life of the successful business man. He owned a five-bedroom house in the suburbs, two automobiles, a motor home, a swimming pool, and the other luxuries of the affluent. James did not care that he lived in debt. As long as his earning potential remained high, so did his expectations. The more money he made, the more money he needed to fulfill his expanding material desires.

In time, the pressure of the suburban life style began to tell on James. Success in the business world meant a constant round of high pressure decisions. Each day placed him in more and more precarious positions. He did not see how he could retreat from his high life, but he did not think that he could maintain the pressure of his high executive position. The first sign of a break came in his health. Ulcers, nervous exhaustion, and finally a heart attack brought home the dangers of his life style.

Fortunately, James knew himself well enough to know he had to retreat from the pressures of affluent living. Though the move was difficult, James and his family sold everything they owned, moved to another city, and started over again. James took a job as an auto mechanic at a local garage, something he had always wanted to do. More important for his psychological health, his family began leading a simple life. They found more time to be together and enjoy one another. Instead of expensive socializing, they lingered over family picnics in the woods. The nervous exhaustion subsided and, in time, James' ulcer cleared up completely.

James said of his high pressured life, once he gained some perspective on it, "It was as if I were violating some inner sense of value. My strain to make money seemed to damage an intimate part of myself. Now that I have more time with my family I can honestly say I feel restored. And my restoration is more than physical. I feel as if I also remembered to pay attention to my own inner needs."

Self-Actualization and Values

The key to Abraham Maslow's attempts to find an innate value system is found in his study of self-actualized people. Maslow became upset, early in his work, with the emphasis psychologists place on abnormally disturbed people because too many conclusions concerning balanced people were made from studies of the emotionally unbalanced. He decided he would take a new approach by studying extremely well-balanced people in society. Maslow separated out for his study those people who had an unusual amount of security, trust, and stability in their psychological makeup. These people, whom he spent his life studying, he called **self-actualized**.

Self-actualized people gave Maslow a basis for drawing conclusions concerning values. Self-actualized people, it turned out, held many values in common. Not only did the values of these extremely healthy people tend to follow definite patterns, but those values remained the same regardless of the cultural environment in which they were studied (Self-Quiz 8.2).

A study that impressed Abraham Maslow and had implications for his theories was performed by W. F. Dove and reported in the *American Naturalist*. Dr. Dove gathered a large group of chickens and exposed them to many possible foods. Each chicken was allowed to select a personal diet according to instinct. It soon became evident that some of the chickens were good choosers. Those chickens became stronger, larger, and more dominant than the poor choosers. Once the difference between the good choosers and poor choosers became obvious, the poor choosers were forced, by Dove, to follow the diet of the good choosers. At that point, the poor choosers also began to become stronger, bigger, healthier, and more dominant, even though they never reached the high level of the good choosers. This experiment suggests that good choosers among chickens can better select what is good for the poor choosers than the poor choosers can for themselves. (19)

Maslow believed that conclusions for humans could be drawn from this experiment.

> I propose that we explore the consequences of observing whatever our best specimens choose, and then assuming these are the highest values

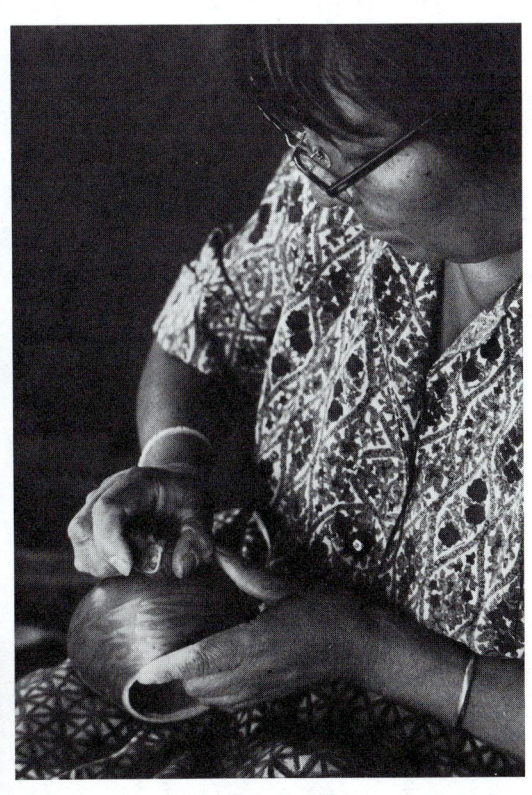

Abraham Maslow found that self-actualized people possess a high degree of creativity. (Jean-Claude Lejeune/Stock, Boston, top; Los Alamos Scientific Laboratory, left; Shirley Zeiberg/Taurus, above)

Self-Quiz 8.2 — Creativity

Creativity is an important aspect of the self-actualized person. Read each statement and choose the alternative that best describes your attitude by checking the proper box to the left of the statement. Answer all of the statements.

Often *Occasionally* *Seldom*

☐ ☐ ☐ 1. I am eager to have new experiences.
☐ ☐ ☐ 2. I usually question things others take for granted.
☐ ☐ ☐ 3. Once I find a topic that interests me I pursue it relentlessly.
☐ ☐ ☐ 4. I can almost never follow instructions exactly but always seem to improvise.
☐ ☐ ☐ 5. An unusual ending to a movie leaves me pondering it until I work out a plausible explanation.
☐ ☐ ☐ 6. I like change and excitement in my life.
☐ ☐ ☐ 7. Changes in my life make me excited about the new possibilities that open to me.
☐ ☐ ☐ 8. On special occasions I like to do something new and different.
☐ ☐ ☐ 9. I pursue things that make me happy even though my activities might bring disapproval from friends.
☐ ☐ ☐ 10. I have a great fear of boredom.

This test does not claim to tell you how creative you might be. It rather tells you how your score on questions relating to the characteristics of creative people compares with others. To total your score, give yourself 3 points for each time you checked "often" on the test, 2 points for each "occasionally," and 1 point for each "seldom." Add up the total number of points and compare that total with the following scale.

27–30   You have scored in the high range with a minority of students who took this test. Your score seems to indicate you have many characteristics common to highly creative people.

18–27   Your score indicates you have the same level of creativity as most of the students taking this test.

Below 18   You scored with those who fell to the bottom of the test range. Such scores do not mean you have no creativity. They only indicate you seem to lack the adventurous spirit common to most creative people.

for all mankind. That is, let us see what happens when we playfully treat them as biological assays, more sensitive versions of ourselves, more quickly conscious of what is good for us than we are ourselves. This is an assumption that, given enough time, we would eventually choose what they choose quickly. Or that we would sooner or later see the wisdom of their choices, and then make the same choices. Or that they perceive sharply and clearly where we perceive dimly. (20)

Psychology Implies Values

The behavioristic idea that values have no scientific basis upset Maslow. He thought that determining whether or not behavior was moral actually lay at the heart of all psychological studies. Maslow felt scientists who avoid the problem of right and wrong also refuse to come to grips with the most important question psychology must face. "The casting out of values by psychology," Maslow tells us, "not only weakens it, and prevents it from reaching its full growth, but also abandons mankind to supernaturalism or to ethical relativism." (21)

Ethical relativism, the refusal to consider the question of good and evil, puts men like Adolf Hitler beyond the consideration of psychological study. Worse yet, such men could be considered healthy in a purely relativistic psychology. Hitler did, after all, conduct his march across Europe

Abraham Maslow believes that men such as Adolf Hitler should be included in the study of psychology. (The Bettmann Archive, Inc.)

and his systematic extermination of the Jews in an efficient and well-organized manner. From the point of view adapted by most behaviorists Hitler would not be considered emotionally unstable. The idea that psychology could put itself in a position unable to declare the acts of men like Hitler evil appalled Maslow. Frank Goble, a Maslow scholar, declares:

> A man like Adolf Eichmann cannot be explained by a behavioristic, relativistic theory of behavior. As far as Eichmann was concerned, everything was fine; he did a good job; he was most efficient. This exemplifies the very danger of value-free science. Without ethical ends, a society must expect men like Eichmann and Hitler, and atom bombs, and the like. In Maslow's words, "Instead of cultural relativity, I am implying that there are basic, underlying, human standards that are cross-cultural—which transcend cultures and which are broadly human. Without these standards we simply would have no criterion for criticizing, let us say, the well-adjusted Nazi in Nazi Germany." (22)

The Highest Values

Most studies on values seek the opinions of many people. The results often yield little in the way of positive results because of the size of the sample and also because most people's value systems are obscured by cultural pressures and self-centered tendencies. The self-actualized people Abraham Maslow interviewed were, by their very nature, less influenced by the ordinary cultural pressures than most. Their aspirations transcended selfish drives. And because there are so few self-actualized people, his study of their values did not become diffuse.

A few of the values the self-actualized people in Maslow's studies prized most were: truth, beauty, wholeness, aliveness, uniqueness, perfection, justice, order, simplicity, richness, playfulness, and self-sufficiency. Most important to realize, self-actualized people considered an attack on any of these values the same as a personal attack. The values are so important to them that any retreat from the values could lead them to physical illness. Such illnesses led Maslow to believe that the decision to choose values can be explained at the biological level. We choose a value system in much the same way we choose healthy food or proper rest, because to neglect a healthy set of values is to neglect our own best interests.

> It is certainly true that mankind, throughout history has looked for guiding values, for principles of right and wrong. But he has tended to look outside of himself, outside of mankind to a god, to some sort of sacred book perhaps, or to a ruling class. What I am doing is to explore the theory that you can find the values by which mankind must live, and for which man has always sought, by digging into the best people in depth. I believe, in other words, that I can find ultimate values which are right for mankind by observing the best of mankind. If under the best conditions and in the best specimens I simply stand aside and describe in a scientific

way what these human values are, I find values that are the old values of truth, goodness, and beauty, and some additional ones as well—for instance, gaiety, justice, and joy. (23)

CONCLUSION

Once again our three vantage points give us three approaches to understanding our topic. We can look at our attitudes and values in three distinct ways. The psychoanalytic approach of Carl Jung asks us to believe that our attitudes and values are affected by the centuries of human development that preceded us. The archetypes formed gradually with the passing of the ages, so that we cannot look at any situation in a way that is separate from our cultural heritage. Everything we think about or react to is colored by the entire history of the human race.

Behavioral scientists give us another way of considering our attitudes and values. They watch how we react and tell us some facts about our behavior. For example, we are more likely to befriend those people who live close to us than those who live at a distance. Our first impression of someone has a great impact on how much we will like or dislike that person. And finally, we tend to form friendships with those people who share common beliefs and values with us.

Finally, Abraham Maslow feels our values should be considered scientifically. Studies of values undertaken by social scientists in the past were subjective. Maslow's look at values in the self-actualized person avoids such subjectivity. And Maslow goes on to say that the study of values is vital to the field of psychology. If we ignore values, it is impossible to distinguish between the efficient and self-contained efforts of an Adolf Hitler and a psychologically healthy individual working for the advancement of society.

SUMMARY

1. Besides the personal unconscious, Carl Jung saw that each person possessed a collective unconscious. In this collective unconscious, we store memory traces of events important in the lives of our ancestors. The regular rising and setting of the sun, for example, was so important in our evolutionary history that men created sun gods to express some of the emotion they felt toward the sun. We inherit these latent memories in such a way that they have an impact on our attitudes and values. The male image of woman, for example, predisposes him to respond to his mother immediately at birth. When the idealistic image becomes too dominant, however, it can cause conflicts in his relationship with women later in life.

2. Behaviorists watch people and note their behavior. They notice, for example, that the closer two people are to one another physically the more likely they are to become friends. They also tell us that external characteristics such as weight, height, and skin color, affect our attitudes toward people. In one study, even the presence or absence of glasses made a difference in the attitudes of observers. Finally, it would appear we protect our value system by forming friendships with those people who share our attitudes and shunning those with different values.
3. Abraham Maslow felt psychology sidestepped its obligation when it failed to consider values. He admitted many of the past attempts to study values were often filled with subjectivity. But Maslow felt such problems could be avoided if we studied only those people with the soundest psychological balance. By studying the self-actualized person, Maslow narrowed down the range of values considered worth cultivating. Those values, Maslow tells us, turned out to be the traditional values of truth, beauty, honesty, and goodness.

KEY TERMS

collective unconscious
personal unconscious
archetype
shadow
bisexuality
homosexuality
anima
animus
propinquity
first impression
generalization
self-actualized
ethical relativism

STUDY QUESTIONS

1. Think of some motion picture images that had a significant impact on you. Did any of them satisfy Jung's concept of an archetype?
2. Describe some part of yourself that you would rather keep hidden from others. Is your hidden self similar to Jung's shadow archetype?
3. Have those people you drew closest to over the years always lived near you? Does your own experience seem to verify the theory of propinquity? Discuss any exceptions.
4. Have your first impressions often prejudiced your view of others? Discuss how you might avoid this tendency in the future.
5. How well do you believe psychologists are able to understand people they study if they avoid any value judgments? Explain.

ADDITIONAL READING

Allport, Gordon W. *The Nature of Prejudice.* Garden City, New York: Doubleday, 1958.

Bem, D. *Beliefs, Attitudes and Human Affairs.* Belmont, Calif.: Brooks-Cole, 1970.

Fordham, Frieda. *An Introduction to Jung's Psychology.* New York: Pelican, 1953.

Kelman, H. C. *A Time to Speak: On Human Values and Social Research.* San Francisco, Jossey-Bass, 1968.

Maslow, Abraham H. *Religion, Values and Peak Experiences.* Columbus, Ohio: Ohio State, 1964.

———. *Toward a Psychology of Being.* New York: Van Nostrand, 1968.

Middlebrook, P. N. *Social Psychology and Modern Life.* New York: Knopf, 1974.

Rokeach, M. *The Open and Closed Mind.* New York: Basic Books, 1960.

Zimbardo, P., and Ebbesen, E. *Influencing Attitudes and Changing Behavior.* Reading, Mass.: Addison-Wesley, 1977.

Chapter Nine

Communication

OUTLINE

The Psychoanalytic Approach
Repression
Projection
Reaction Formation

The Behavioristic Approach
The Space Between Us
Touch Talk

The Humanistic Approach
Congruence
Passing Judgments
Listening

Conclusion

LEARNING OBJECTIVES

After reading this chapter you should be able to:

1. Describe three of Freud's defense mechanisms.
2. Point out how the defense mechanisms examined in the chapter interrupt communication.
3. Explain how body language affects communication.
4. Discuss the space we maintain between ourselves and other people.
5. Explain what Rogers means by congruence.
6. Discuss how Rogers would have us overcome our tendency to evaluate other people.

Chapter Nine

The day before I began to write this chapter I found myself looking for an example of poor communication. I wanted to begin this study with an example that would not only point out how we fail to communicate effectively, but also show that poor communication can be dangerous to ourselves and others. The answer came while I idly fingered some brightly colored volumes at a local bookstore. Near me, a little boy pestered his mother. She tried to ignore him, but the four-year-old would not be denied. He began to push a stray wooden chair about the store so that the scraping sound of wood on linoleum penetrated the store. The young mother glared at her little boy and snapped, "Don't push that chair around. Remember what the man told you." The child, quite obviously stunned by the threat, paused a moment to feel its impact. He then began to cry for a time while his mother continued to ignore him.

When he lost his mother's attention again, he returned to pushing the chair. The mother escalated her threats. "If you continue to push that chair, the big bird will come and take you away." Fear filled the child's face. His panic became so severe he could not cry for a minute. He was completely distracted with fear. His tears led him to an exaggerated need to push the chair. His mother's final retort was the most cruel of all. She looked at her son, grabbed him by the arm, and snapped, "I don't want you any more." This time nothing could contain the child's screams. So his mother gathered him up and fled from the store.

Few of us engage in this sort of psychological cruelty or even see it demonstrated. However, knowing that it does occur helps us avoid the involuntary cruelty our communication can impose on others. For without ever intending to hurt other people, or leave them confused, or ignore them completely, our attempts to communicate can have such effects even on our best friends. We all know what it means to leave a conversation, even the most superficial, and find ourselves depressed, angry, or confused. By looking at some of the dynamics behind our communication, however, we can better understand what causes pain for ourselves and others and avoid such experiences.

A look at the personality dynamics behind our communication can help us understand ourselves. Freud had some useful insights into the ways we distort reality. For example, we try to hide from ourselves and from others those experiences that cause us pain. Freud said we might repress

Communication can be a tool of cruelty when we are unaware of its powers on others.
(Peter Vandermark)

thoughts about a painful incident, a feeling of inadequacy, or even our family background in order to make life easier for ourselves. Unfortunately, by distorting and falsifying reality with a defense mechanism such as repression, effective communication with other people becomes almost impossible.

Whenever we attempt to hide our true feelings from others or ourselves, the message we try to disguise will emerge involuntarily. Behaviorists believe that our bodies will give away the truth we are trying to hide. The science of body language explores our unconscious communication. A woman who claims to love her husband but clenches her fist for emphasis when she talks about him reveals her hidden anger. The young man who tries to appear calm displays his anxiety by a constant nervous twitch of his foot. These and many other messages from our bodies can both help and hinder our communication.

Finally, Carl Rogers, the humanist, points to congruence as the single most important aspect of communication. If our words do not match our feelings, we hinder clear communication. The person who tries to disguise his anger toward a friend with words of friendship gives a double message. By contrast, people with friendships so sound that they can express angry moments without fear of losing the friendship have a better chance to draw closer to those with whom they would like to be intimate.

THE PSYCHOANALYTIC APPROACH

Most of our failures to communicate develop because we do not listen accurately to one another. We fail to really hear what a friend says to us, or we assume a spouse wants to embarrass us with a statement that is only a point of information. We grow angry over a statement made by a daughter when, in reality, our anger should be directed at our employer. Such distortions of reality are common for most of us, and we simply accept them as part of life. However, Sigmund Freud thought carefully about such common experiences and developed theories concerning them.

The tendency we all have to distort reality, Freud realized, can operate consciously or unconsciously. That is, we might know at the time we shout at our daughter that she does not deserve our anger. At other times we can be completely convinced she is the source of our anger even though we are actually angry with someone else. The more Freud considered reality distortion the more distinct versions of the tendency he found.

Freud called our many ways of distorting or falsifying reality the **defense mechanisms.** He felt that we use such mechanisms to prevent ourselves from suffering anxiety. At times, facing reality may make us too uncomfortable. For example, a young woman I once knew saw her parents engage in a bitter relationship while she was quite young. That memory became so painful that she put all thoughts of her father out of her mind once her parents divorced one another. And for nine years, until she entered therapy, she completely forgot that her father ever existed. The defense mechanism of forgetting helped her avoid experiencing the anxieties connected with her memory of her father.

Freud defined a series of defense mechanisms. In this chapter we will focus on those mechanisms that are most damaging to effective communication: repression, rejection, and reaction formation.

Repression

Calvin Hall describes the defense mechanism of **repression:**

> Repression may prevent a person from seeing something that is in plain view or distort that which he does see, or falsify the information coming in through the sense organs, in order to protect the ego from apprehending an object that is dangerous or that is associated with a danger that would arouse anxiety. Similarly, repression operates upon memories that are associated with a traumatic experience. The associated memories may be perfectly harmless in themselves, but by recalling them the person runs the risk of remembering the traumatic experience as well. Therefore a whole complex of memories may fall under the influence of repression. Dangerous ideas may also be repressed. In every case, whether it be a perception, a memory, or an idea that is repressed, the purpose is to abolish objective, neurotic, or moralistic anxiety by denying or falsifying the existence of the external or internal threat to the ego's safety. (1)

The problem that repression can cause in a conversation, or any other form of communication, cannot be overestimated. A young student can become so embarrassed by her parent's poverty that she can momentarily forget where she lives or what her family owns. In a conversation, she may unconsciously answer questions vaguely, change the subject abruptly, and even express two completely contradictory statements in order to avoid any reference to her family (Case 9.1).

● Case 9.1

The young student I mentioned in the text example was named Suzy. She looked happy enough to those who met her briefly, but her closer friends recognized how rigid her posture was and how she held her lips together tightly as if she feared revealing something personal.

Suzy, as I already mentioned, felt deeply embarrassed by her family's poverty. Her father earned a decent enough salary as a mailman, but it was inadequate for a family of six children. Suzy tried to cover the poverty she faced at home in every way possible. Whenever the subject of her family came up, Suzy pretended not to hear what was said. She changed the subject, answered questions with a question, or simply stared into space. At first her tendency to avoid questions about her family was deliberate. Gradually, however, she lost control over her defense. She began to lose track of conversations at critical times without even knowing she did so.

Fortunately for Suzy, her good friend, Val, worried about the conversation blocks. She saw Suzy change the subject, stare off into space, and make contradictory statements. However, Val had no idea what lay behind Suzy's difficulties with communication. Finally, when Val could stand it no longer, she asked Suzy about her defensiveness. Suzy did not understand Val's question, but Val did not drop the subject. As a good friend, she promised Suzy she would point out the times when Suzy acted defensively. Because Val persisted in her determination to show Suzy how the defensiveness came between them, Suzy finally did recognize her attitude and admitted her feelings of inadequacy to Val. The admission, rather than drawing them apart, brought them closer together than ever. And because Val insisted on clear communication, Suzy began to accept her family's struggle and became less anxious because of her hard look at reality.

Projection

A second defense mechanism that impairs good communication Freud called **projection.** We project on others when we accuse them of possessing qualities we hate in ourselves. Men often blame their desire to have extramarital affairs on the women who "lead them on," because they fear looking honestly at their own desire to have sex outside their marriage. So they blame the woman who "seduced" them. In extreme cases, a man

Momma by Mell Lazarus. Courtesy of Mell Lazarus and Field Newspaper Syndicate.

who hates himself for his sexual desires can turn that hatred against his lover, but has no idea that his hatred should really be directed at himself. He releases a great deal of emotion that would otherwise remain bottled inside himself, even though the emotion is incorrectly focused. Calvin Hall explains the nature of this defense mechanism:

> The essential feature of projection is that the subject of the feeling, which is the person himself, is changed. It may take the form of exchanging the subject for the object. "I hate you" is converted into "You hate me." Or it may take the form of substituting one subject for another subject while the object remains the same. "I am punishing myself" is changed into "He is punishing me." A person who is afraid of his own aggressive and sexual impulses obtains some relief for his anxiety by attributing aggressiveness and sexuality to other people. They are the ones who are aggressive and sexual, not he. Likewise, a person who is afraid of his own conscience consoles himself with the thought that other people are responsible for bothering him, and that is not his conscience. (2)

Obviously, our tendency to project our feelings onto other people makes effective communication difficult if not impossible. We can be totally convinced our anger, for example, arises from a dispute with a supermarket clerk, while someone else can look more objectively at the facts and know that our anger is arising from our frustration with school or work. Such misplaced aggression obviously makes good communication impossible (Self-Quiz 9.1).

Another aspect of this communication difficulty arises when an individual projects emotions or attitudes on society in general. A student projects his own guilt feelings concerning examination cheating by claiming, "Everyone does it." Our conviction that others cheat, hate life, or are unhappy may come not from an objective examination of the facts, but rather from internal feelings of guilt, unhappiness, or disappointment in ourselves. And such projections continue to interrupt effective communication until they are confronted and disssolved.

Self-Quiz 9.1 — Revealing Feelings

One way most people differ from one another is in the amount of feelings they reveal. Some people control their feelings so completely that they cannot be read emotionally. Others have "rubber faces" and immediately display their feelings. The following test is designed to help you discover how much or how little you reveal your feelings compared to other students who have taken this test.

Next to each statement place the number 1, 2, 3, 4, or 5—depending on how characteristic each statement is of you. Continue the process for each of the statements. Then total your score.

5 strongly characteristic of me
4 moderately characteristic of me
3 neutral
2 moderately uncharacteristic of me
1 strongly uncharacteristic of me

____ 1. If a movie or television drama grips me, I cry quite easily.
____ 2. Whenever I am late for a party, I find the hostess and apologize immediately.
____ 3. Any important event in my life means I must call friends and share the news.
____ 4. In a fight with someone close to me I shout and argue.
____ 5. A criticism makes me not only defend myself, but also think of ways to get back at the detractor.
____ 6. A newlywed couple embracing passionately in public makes me envious of them.
____ 7. If I am in physical pain and a friend appears, I groan and swear.
____ 8. If someone tells a joke I think in poor taste, I let that person know my feelings immediately.

____ TOTAL SCORE

31–40 Few people who took this test score so high. Your score appears to indicate you let your feelings flow freely.
17–30 Most people score in this range. You seem to express your feelings in the range acceptable to most people.
Below 17 Your low score suggests you hide your true feelings quite frequently.

Reaction Formation

One more defense mechanism Freud discussed has important ramifications for communication. The mechanism has the awkward title of **reaction formation.** Simply stated a reaction formation is the ability to prevent the expression of one emotion by exaggerating an opposite feeling. A young man may cover his angry feelings toward his parents by generating false feelings of love. A business woman who begins to feel love for a colleague may hide those feelings by expressing anger. A mother who feels like being cruel toward her children at times may disguise those feelings with feigned kindnesses.

The most zealous crusaders against drinking, sexuality, and gambling are quite often attempting to hide their needs for sensuality when they preach against it. You might know a teacher who imposes severe penalties for cheating on examinations. Perhaps that teacher is attempting to control personal desires to cheat in some way.

Ruth Monroe, a Freudian scholar, has explored this defense mechanism.

> A great many people show something of the reaction-formation pattern. Generally orderly, thrifty, gentle, or whatever to a fault, these people are likely to display sporadic evidences of the opposite characteristics, either in situations so unimportant as to fall outside the area of our control, or when we are caught off guard, or when pressures mount beyond possibility of control. I remember an unusually tender, sensitive man deep in an intellectual discussion when our cat rubbed against his legs in an unexpected friendliness. He gave the animal a vicious kick, out of all proportion to the element of surprise and quite different from his usual gentle manner. This man was by no means a hypocrite. It is very possible, nonetheless, that his general life pattern is in the nature of a reaction formation against strong hostilities and fears which remain strong precisely because they so rarely are permitted to emerge at all and which therefore cannot be integrated with the bulk of his conscious experience. (3)

The implications of this form of defense mechanism in communication seem obvious. Any of us who has ever talked with a person who pretends to like us can vouch for how little contact we then make with that person. People who feign friendship are usually so obvious in their attempts to cover their true feelings that we instinctively distrust everything they tell us. The same comment could be made for every form of pretense in conversations. Any time the words people speak fail to match the emotions the person is revealing in other ways, the communcation breaks down.

THE BEHAVIORISTIC APPROACH

After looking at Freud's defense mechanisms, students may wonder, "How can I tell when someone hides behind such mechanisms?" I suppose the final answer has to be, "You can't." However, people often give clues to the meanings they are trying to hide. Those clues come in the form of **body language.** When we try to hide our true feelings from others, our bodies unconsciously give off messages from our unconscious. A nervous twitch, a trembling hand, a rigid body posture can all reveal the feelings we try to conceal. Not only do we reveal hidden messages, we

Our bodies often generate unconscious messages. (Susan Lapides, above; Nick Passmore/Stock, Boston, left)

also can read the unconscious communication of others by closely watching their bodies (Case 9.2).

Though a great deal of popularization of body language has taken place during the past few years, the study has scientific foundations. Technically, the study of body language is called **kinesics.** Studies of the subject are appearing in scientific journals more and more regularly, all of them advocating reading the body to discover hidden messages. A businessman can shake hands with a client he claims he is happy to see, but then he unconsciously wipes his hand on his trousers to indicate his hidden distaste for the man. A woman can claim, in a marriage counselor's office, that she has to look to her husband for all her needs and is forever submissive. She then crosses her legs and sits up straight in her chair. Her husband instantly crosses his legs and sits in the same erect posture. That moment of body language says more than all the woman's words could ever tell us.

Behaviorists consider body language an important tool, but body language is not only interesting to behaviorists. The humanists and psychoanalysts also see strong implications for their work. However, we will consider kinesics under the topic of behaviorism because of the work's obvious behavioral orientation.

• Case 9.2

My most vivid encounter with body language occurred a number of years ago. At that time, a slender young man named Art came to see me for therapy. By anyone's standards, Art looked fragile. His clothes always seemed to hang on him. But more than anything else, Art's long slender fingers expressed his delicate look, and I found it difficult to take my eyes off them.

Art took a great deal of time in our first few sessions to tell me about his wife and their relationship. The more he discussed her, the more animated he became. Only when I tried to turn the discussion back to him did he become subdued. At that point, his words came slowly, almost painfully. Yet Art was quite convincing when he suggested he had nothing to say about himself—he wanted to concentrate on his wife and their relationship.

Art nearly convinced me that the problem he needed to discuss did surround his relationship with his wife. However, the last time I asked him if he did not want to talk about himself I noted an involuntary sign of body language from the same delicate fingers that had earlier distracted me. He reached up and squeezed his nose as if to say, "I can't stand my own smell." Then I had something concrete to refer to. His involuntary gesture embarrassed Art. As we discussed the move, Art became more and more self-conscious. He could not take his long and delicate fingers away from his nose. Nor did he any longer try to deny, even to himself, that his problems began with himself.

That awkward bit of body language proved to be the turning point in Art's therapy. Up to that moment he did believe his relationship with his wife lay at the heart of his problems. Now that the focus shifted to a more personal perspective, however, Art began to make swift progress in therapy.

The Space Between Us

The study of kinesics suggests that an invisible boundary exists around each person. We allow people to draw only so close to us before we become nervous and anxious. The physical distance we keep from other

"Jules is a great believer in touching."

people is not inflexible and constant, however—it varies according to several factors. One of the many factors is our relationship to the person who draws near us. For example, a spouse, an intimate friend, or lover have access to our intimate space. A stranger, an employer, or a teacher we might have to keep at a distance.

The need we have to protect ourselves publicly extends beyond physical closeness. It also includes more symbolic contact. For example, we must follow a predetermined ritual in our eye contact with others. We cannot let our eyes rest too long on a stranger, for example, but lovers aggressively seek eye contact.

One common example of our need to keep a ritualized distance between ourselves and others occurs when we pass strangers on the sidewalk. At a distance of about eight feet, we are allowed to exchange glances with a stranger, but then we must let our eyes slide away from this contact. One last glance is permitted at an intimate distance of about two feet. To look at an approaching stranger at any distance between eight and two feet would be quite awkward for us and the stranger.

Julius Fast describes a study done on crowd size and **personal space** in his book *Body Language*.

> The need for personal space and the resistance to the invasion of personal space is so strong a thing that even in a crowd each member will demand a given amount of space. This very fact led a journalist named Herbert Jacobs to attempt to apply it to crowd size. Since estimation of crowd size tends to vary according to whether the observer is for the crowd or against it, the size of political rallies, peace rallies and demonstrations are inflated by the marchers and deflated by the authorities.
>
> Jacobs, by studying aerial photographs of crowds where he could actually count heads, concluded that people in dense crowds need six to eight square feet each, while people in loose crowds require an average of ten square feet. Crowd size, Jacobs finally concluded, could be gauged by the formula, length times width divided by a correction factor that took density of the crowd into account. This gave the actual number of people in any gathering. (4)

The power of eye contact was recently studied by psychologist Carol Werner and Lee Hanchett of the University of Utah. In their experiment they tried to determine if eye contact between the driver of a car and a hitchhiker cut down the hiker's waiting time. They asked two male students to hitchhike on equally crowded streets at the same time of day. When the hikers made eye contact with drivers they cut down the average amount of time they waited for a ride from 12.4 minutes to 4 minutes.

To make certain the difference in time resulted from the eye contact, Werner and Hanchett introduced other variables into the experiment. The most noticeable variation was the color of the hitchhiker's jacket. Even when the young men were dressed in bright red jackets, the results were the same. The eye contact provided the only crucial difference.

Even in a crowd, people demand a certain amount of space. (Peter Vandermark)

The researchers suggest that their findings are consistent with the studies concerning people in need of help. Those who need help are more likely to get it when there are fewer witnesses. The more witnesses, the more spread out the responsibility is and the less obligation any one person feels to help. The eye contact in the hitchhiking experiment apparently produces an intimacy between hiker and driver that creates a similar feeling of responsibility not otherwise felt. (5)

Touch Talk

As children, most of us expressed ourselves spontaneously through touch. We had no inhibitions about embracing our parents, relatives, and friends. We thought nothing of jumping on the lap of a friendly relative and snuggling there for as long as that person's patience lasted. As time went on, however, we became more and more aware of the social taboos against touch. At some point in time, our need for an embrace was met with an expression such as "You're a big boy (or girl) now." And, depend-

Touch is a natural part of a child's life and can help adults achieve emotional and even physical health. (Frank Siteman, left; Arthur Grace/Stock, Boston, above)

ing on the rigidity or flexibility of our family life, we learned to become aloof and distant from the world of touch (Case 9.3).

In many cases our fear of touch and intimacy can become so rigid that it affects our bodies. A man who is constantly unhappy can develop a frown as part of his facial set. Another person with restrained sexual attitudes can actually throw her lower back alignment askew. An aggressive person who thrusts his head forward can make that posture permanent. I have known people who smile so constantly to cover their true feelings that their expression cannot be changed, even in times of extreme sadness (Self-Quiz 9.2).

By contrast, those unafraid of touch, either physical or emotional, have a spontaneity about them. Their freedom to make contact with other people makes them at ease in most personal relationships. For this reason, many psychologists believe that touch helps people achieve emotional and even physical health. As a result, many group therapies are aided by physical contacts between the group members.

• Case 9.3

By paying attention to body language, we can gain fresh insights into what other people are communicating. Some of those insights may do nothing more than amuse us, but others can have a rather profound impact on our lives. In his book *Body Language* Julius Fast tells us of a rather important breakthrough two people gained by using body language.

"A friend of mine told me recently that in his own family he was having some very serious problems between his seventeen-year-old daughter and his fourteen-year-old son. 'They've gotten to the stage where they can't be in the same room without exploding. Everything he does is wrong in her eyes, and she's always at him.'

"At my suggestion he tried a nonverbal game with the two of them and told them to do whatever they wanted, but not to use words.

" 'For a few moments,' he told me later. 'they were at a loss. Without words she couldn't scold him, and it seemed as if she didn't know what else to do, what other way to relate to him. Then he came over to where she was sitting and grinned at her, and all at once she caught him, pulled him down on her lap and actually cuddled him to the amazement of the rest of the family.'

"What came out of this in a discussion later was that the entire family agreed that by her actions she had seemed to be mothering him. She did indeed feel like a mother to him, and her constant scolding was less in the nature of criticism and more in the nature of possessive mother-love. Her body language action of cuddling made her aware of this and opened his eyes as well. Afterward, my friend reported, while they continued their bickering, it was hardly as serious as before and underlying it on both parts was a new warmth and understanding." (6)

Self-Quiz 9.2 — Your Body

Most people wonder what their bodies says about them. This test may help you answer that question. Read each statement and choose the alternative that best describes your attitude by checking the proper box to the left of the statement. Answer all of the statements.

Often	Occasionally	Seldom	
☐	☐	☐	1. When I am standing, I fold my arms over my chest.
☐	☐	☐	2. When I am sitting, I cross my knees.
☐	☐	☐	3. I keep my eyes wide open and never let them slip closed during the day.
☐	☐	☐	4. I let my head hang down.
☐	☐	☐	5. When I talk to someone, I like to intertwine my fingers.
☐	☐	☐	6. I stoop rather than stand straight.

To find out how you compare with others who took this test, give yourself 3 points for each time you checked "often" on the test, 2 points for each "occasionally," and 1 point for each "seldom." Add up the total number of points and compare that total with the following scale.

16–18 Few students scored this high. You appear to constrict your body language.

 9–15 Most people taking the test saw themselves in the same way you did. Apparently, you have about the same amount of openness to people as they have to you.

 6–8   You appear to have more spontaneous body movements than most students who took this test.

THE HUMANISTIC APPROACH

Our look at the defense mechanisms of Sigmund Freud helped us see that we are not always perfectly aware of our emotions. We may become quite angry without even realizing the extent of that anger. Freud used several theories to explain why a gap may arise between our feelings and our awareness of those feelings. Carl Rogers, a humanist, suggests we might better spend our time examining the gap itself rather than its cause. He calls the gap **incongruence** and gives an example here:

> To pick an easily recognizable example [of incongruence] take the man who becomes angrily involved in a group discussion. His face flushes, his tone communicates anger, he shakes his finger at his opponent. Yet when a friend says, "Well, let's not get angry about this," he replies, with evident sincerity and surprise, "I'm not angry! I don't have any feeling about this at all! I was just pointing out the logical facts." The other men in the group break out in laughter at this statement. (7)

Rogers does not focus on the personality mechanisms working behind this kind of experience. Rather, he concentrates on the separation (incongruence) between the words this man consciously utters and his actual emotions that he is unaware of. His words tell us something factual. His emotional tone says, "I am angry at you."

I should quickly point out that this example is not the only form of incongruence. Rogers explains another:

> Mrs. Brown, who has been stifling yawns and looking at her watch for hours, says to her hostess on departing, "I enjoyed this evening so much. It was a delightful party." Here the incongruence is not between experience and awareness. Mrs. Brown is well aware that she is bored. The incongruence is between awareness and communication. Thus it might be noted that when there is an incongruence between experience and awareness, it is usually spoken of as defensiveness, or denial to awareness. When the incongruence is between awareness and communication it is usually thought of as falseness or deceit. (8)

Failures to express congruence, if sustained over long periods of time, can result in serious blocks to emotional stability. How do therapists deal with incongruence in people whose anger becomes so repressed that they cannot seem to release it? Lewis Brodsky, a psychiatrist in charge of the Crisis Intervention of Sinai Hospital in Detroit, found an answer for one of his patients the day when he missed an appointment with that patient.

The patient was hospitalized and was so depressed that he was beginning to display suicidal tendencies. A critical element in this patient's depression was unexpressed hostility. When Brodsky missed the appointment, he did not apologize. Instead, he simply told the patient the truth—that he had forgotten the appointment entirely. The patient flew into a rage.

"Telling him that I had forgotten the appointment justified his anger with me, and this justification allowed him to express the angry feelings that he had been unable to acknowledge," Brodsky explained. "For the first time he became aware that he had such feelings. In a relatively short time we were gaining much access to the anger, guilt and ambivalence in his relationship with his mother. At a followup two years later he was symptom-free."

Since that experience, Brodsky has been more willing to jar his patients with some hard feelings he has had toward them. Letting patients experience some of his own hostile feelings toward them lets them contact their own emotions. The result of letting patients experience a moment of congruence has begun the healing process for many. (9)

Congruence

Congruence, of course, is the opposite of incongruence. Yet it is important to highlight the fact that congruence occurs when we have an accurate awareness of our emotions. A student grows angry with a teacher over an unjust test, realizes his anger, and communicates it effectively. A young woman decides she feels rushed into a marriage and explains her uneasiness clear to her fiancé. A grandmother becomes overwhelmed by her love for her grandchildren and lets that love flow freely. The blending of *feeling* emotions, being *aware* of those emotions, and being able to *communicate* the emotions is what Rogers calls congruence.

Rogers makes an important point concerning the experience of congruence in communication.

> I believe all of us tend to recognize congruence or incongruence in individuals with whom we deal. With some individuals we realize that in most areas this person not only consciously means exactly what he says, but that his deepest feelings also match what he is expressing, whether it is anger or competitiveness or affection or cooperativeness. We feel that "we know exactly where he stands." With another individual we recognize that what he is saying is almost certainly a front, a facade. We wonder what he really feels. We wonder if he knows what he feels. We tend to be wary and cautious with such an individual. (10)

Being able to communicate the emotions we feel is what Rogers calls congruence. (Susan Lapides)

The implications of a congruent approach to communication can be significant. The more we bring to our communication with other people a congruence between our thoughts and feelings, the better they will understand us. That is, when we do not try to hide anything from the people with whom we would like to communicate, we engage in clear communication. We do not have to defend ourselves from possible attacks. We need not steer conversations to avoid certain topics. When we bring ourselves to a conversation without any **facade,** or disguise, we can put most of our energy into understanding and being understood (Case 9.4).

● Case 9.4

Carl Rogers' theory of congruence is important for me because of the many incongruent experiences that occurred early in my own life. My conversations always seemed to show an implicit lack of honesty with my feelings. If a friend upset me with some remark, for example, I would do my best to cover my reaction. In much the same way, I disguised my strong positive feelings of love and friendship. Those feelings embarrassed me so much that I tried to express my warmth with gifts, special favors, and personal contact, but even the thought of saying, "You are one of the best friends I have ever had," left me weak and speechless.

Later in my life, many important things occurred as I met significant people, joined therapy groups, and found love. Many good experiences helped me find the courage to reveal my true feelings. I also began to tell friends about my uneasiness when they irritated me and abandoned the need to smile constantly, instead letting people see the variety of my moods. Friends heard directly about my affection for them.

My life grew more pleasant. I no longer needed to waste energy protecting myself from showing feelings. I could pay closer attention to other people and what they tried to tell me. I watched my own moods change and flow. I found that telling a friend about an irritation could clear the air between us and bring us closer together. Most important, I learned about the special feeling connected with those moments when I told friends how much I loved them.

Passing Judgments

Carl Rogers writes again and again about one major block to communication: he feels we most often break off our contact with others because of our compulsive tendency to judge and evaluate. As usual, Rogers supplies us with vivid examples of his message. In a talk he gave at Northwestern University on communication, he said:

> As you leave the meeting tonight, one of the statements you are likely to hear is, "I didn't like that man's talk." Now what do you respond? Almost invariably your reply will be either approval or disapproval of the attitude expressed. Either you respond, "I didn't either. I thought it was

terrible," or else you tend to reply, "Oh, I thought it was really good." In other words, your primary reaction is to evaluate what has just been said to you, to evaluate it from your point of view, your own frame of reference. (11)

The example is so common as to be embarrassing. We have all been in such situations. The moment someone communicates something to us we tend to look at the statement only from our own point of view. It seems we must evaluate, judge, approve, or disapprove most everything that others say to us. Some hidden force keeps us from realizing the statement came from another person who, more often than not, did not seek our judgement.

Quite often, the process continues. Our reply, "Oh, I don't know. I sort of liked the talk," can trigger a similar reaction from the individual who made the original statement. He replies, maintaining his own point of view, "If you paid close attention to the early part of the speech, you could see the man contradict himself." In no time, the early statement of fact becomes filled with emotion. And emotions only escalate this communication problem because our tendency to evaluate one another is heightened any time feelings and emotions are deeply involved. The more our feelings intervene, then, the more likely we are to experience obstacles in our communication with other people. The two people in the discussion will likely exchange two different ideas, two distinct judgments, or two opposite feelings. Most of us observe this best when we stand outside an emotional discussion. We see that the argument involves two people talking about two distinctly different things. And any tendency, Carl Rogers writes, "to react to any emotionally meaningful statement by forming an evaluation of it from our own point of view is the major barrier to interpersonal communication." (12)

Listening

Rogers suggests an important way to combat this deep-seated tendency we have to evaluate and judge one another constantly — **listening.** He asks us to begin, maybe in just one conversation at first, to listen carefully to the person talking. Even if that person makes a statement we do not believe to be true ("I did not like that man's talk."), we should listen with understanding. Without approving or disapproving, we should try to understand why the fellow did not like the talk. We might ask questions, search for clarification, or express confusion. However, our goal would be to understand rather than evaluate, judge, or approve.

Many people feel they listen quite well to other people and do not disturb conversations with judgments. For those people who are willing to test their ability to listen with understanding, Rogers suggests a small experiment.

The Lockhorns. © King Features Syndicate, Inc., 1978. World rights reserved.

The next time you get into an argument with your wife, or your friend, or with a small group of friends, just stop the discussion for a moment and for an experiment institute this rule. "Each person can speak up for himself only after he has first restated the ideas and feelings of the previous speaker accurately, and to that speaker's satisfaction." You see what this would mean. It would simply mean that before presenting your own point of view, it would be necessary for you to really achieve the other speaker's frame of reference—to understand his thoughts and feelings so well that you could summarize them for him. Sounds simple, doesn't it? But if you try it you will discover it is one of the most difficult things you have ever tried to do. However, once you have been able to see the other's point of view, your own comments will have to be drastically revised. You will also find the emotion going out of the discussion, the differences being reduced, and those differences which remain being of a rational and understandable sort. (13)

• Case 9.5

My first attempts to listen in the manner that Rogers suggests were most exciting. I remember thinking that an entirely new world was beginning to open up to me—the world of other people. I started to see how others thought and how they came to conclusions quite different from my own. Careful listening gave me insight into the complexity of thoughts and emotions. I discovered that the difference between myself and others would never be dissolved by logic alone. The separation proved to be more fundamental than that. Instead, a fascination emerged that opened me to people in a way I never even knew existed before.

The more I attempted to understand people from their points of view, however, the more the process frightened me. As I explored other ways of thinking,

I also discovered I could be changed by these people with attitudes and values quite different from my own. The fear of having lifelong values changed left me uneasy, but still I persisted in the exciting experiment of attempting to understand people. In the exciting process, many of my most cherished values were altered, but I believe my new attitudes and values give me more happiness.

CONCLUSION

Our three vantage points give us three ways of looking at communication. The psychoanalytic approach emphasizes a personality mechanism that blocks our attempts to communicate—we repress certain thoughts and feelings because they become too frightening for us to face. As we avoid certain parts of reality in this way, even our most casual approach to communication can quickly become distorted. The same sort of problem arises when we project our feelings on others or when we distort an angry feeling, for example, and try to convert it into a pleasant emotion. In the process, we make effective communication almost impossible.

The behaviorists use the scientific study of body language to attempt to read the messages hidden away in our unconscious. By watching a clenched fist, a nervous twitch, a furrowed brow, or a hunched shoulder, we can discover the truth people are trying to hide from conversations.

The humanists, led by Carl Rogers, focus their attention on trying to make communication clear. Rogers is aware of the defense mechanisms Freud described, the behaviorists' body language studies, as well as the other signs of communication breakdown. He feels the most significant factor behind all inadequate communication, however, is our tendency to judge one another. Even the simplest statement will provoke us to agree to disagree. Rogers believes that if we spent more time trying to understand one another through good listening and less time evaluating each other, we would communicate much more effectively.

SUMMARY

1. Freud believed defense mechanisms operate in the unconscious to distort, deny, and falsify reality. Such falsification makes effective communication impossible. For example, when we repress our memories of past events, we block out a part of the real world necessary for good communication. The same falsification occurs when we project our feelings about ourselves onto others or try to disguise our feelings by covering them with false emotions.
2. We can all, with attention, read one another's body language and guess at the true feelings that are hidden by a facade of spoken language.

Body language also tells us how much we like or dislike other people by revealing how closely we let them approach us. We give an intimate friend, for example, much closer access to our personal space than we would permit to a stranger.
3. Carl Rogers emphasized the concept of congruence in his approach to communication. He believed our incongruence—the discrepancy between words and feelings—causes most breakdowns in communication. He particularly worried about our constant tendency to evaluate one another. That inclination to quickly agree or disagree with what someone says distracts us from our efforts to understand. If we would reply to others only after we completely understood their comments from their points of view, our communication would improve immensely.

KEY TERMS

defense mechanisms
repression
projection
reaction formation
body language
kinesics

personal space
incongruence
congruence
facade
listening

STUDY QUESTIONS

1. Have you ever become angry with another person only to realize that you were really upset with yourself? How might you avoid that tendency in the future?
2. Which of the Freudian defense mechanisms interferes most with your communication? Explain why you chose that mechanism by citing specific examples.
3. Many people claim they can communicate better in person than they can on the phone. Is that true for you? In what specific ways do people's body language help you understand their communication?
4. Do you allow people you care about to draw closer to you physically than those who you know only superficially? Explain the difference.
5. Do you believe others will know when your emotions are out of line with the words you speak? How much will this lack of congruence affect your communication?
6. Does a tendency to evaluate others stand between you and friendship with others? How might you overcome such tendencies?

ADDITIONAL READING

Birdwhistell, Ray L. *Kinesics and Context.* Philadelphia: University of Pennsylvania, 1970.
Brown, R. A. *First Language: The Early Stages.* Cambridge, Mass.: Harvard, 1973.
Chomsky, N. *Language and Mind.* New York: Harcourt Brace Jovanovich, 1968.
Darnell, Donald K., and Brockriede, W. *Persons Communicating.* Englewood Cliffs, N.J.: Prentice-Hall, 1976.
Fast, Julius. *Body Language.* New York: Pocket, 1970.
Hinde, R. A. *Non-Verbal Communication.* New York: Cambridge, 1972.
Monroe, Ruth L. *Schools of Psychoanalytic Thought.* New York: Holt, 1955.
Rogers, Carl R. *On Becoming a Person.* Boston: Houghton Mifflin, 1961.
Slobin, D. I. *Psycholinguistics.* Glenview, Ill.: Scott, Foresman, 1971.

Chapter Ten

The Individual and the Group

OUTLINE

The Psychoanalytic Approach
Karen Horney
Harry Stack Sullivan
Erik Erikson

The Behavioristic Approach
Leadership Styles
Group Pressure
The Risky Shift

The Humanistic Approach
The Encounter Group
Feeling Expression
Encounter-Group Dangers

Conclusion

LEARNING OBJECTIVES

After reading this chapter you should be able to:

1. State an important distinction between Freud and the neo-Freudians.
2. Distinguish between the theories of Karen Horney, Harry Stack Sullivan, and Erik Erikson.
3. Explain how group interaction can help or hurt individual attempts to complete tasks.
4. Discuss the effect of several different leadership styles.
5. Explain Carl Rogers' attitude toward encounter groups.
6. Discuss the potential dangers in an encounter group.

Chapter Ten

Every Wednesday noon, when the weather is decent, our college invites someone to perform for the students as they eat their lunch on the lawn. Some music groups make conversation impossible, but the day I spotted Daphne on the grass, a folk singer made a pleasant background for conversation. Daphne interrupted her chat with a young man to wave me over.

"Jim and I have just been talking about something," she smiled, pulling awkwardly on the sleeve of her blue sweater. "We wondered why it is that we change so much when we enter different groups."

"It seems as if you become a new person in various situations?" I smiled, remembering how often this question arises.

"Yeah. If I'm by myself, I think about certain kinds of things, like my future, my health, and," Daphne's cheeks flushed slightly, "about my love life. When I'm with a friend, I talk about other things entirely."

"You aren't the only one," I began.

"But the biggest difference," Daphne interrupted, "happens when I get with a group of people. Sometimes I think I'm a new person altogether."

"That's about right," I replied. "People do change a great deal when they enter a group. For all our desire to be individuals, we take on new values, react in uncharacteristic ways, even refuse to believe the evidence before our eyes."

"You mean we don't see as well in a group?" Daphne and Jim laughed.

"I know that sounds funny. But it's true. The pressure of a group may make us deny our senses."

My statement interested Daphne and Jim and we began to chat about group pressures and conformity. I talked about the many ways our personality can be shaped temporarily and even permanently by our interaction with others.

Most of us are curious about our reactions to groups. Many psychologists with a similar fascination about the interaction between the individual and the group study this behavior carefully. The psychoanalysts, however, never look closely at the dynamics of a group as such. Their interest, particularly for the neo-Freudians, centers on the effect society generally has on our personality. These neo-Freudians do not believe, as Freud stated, that our personality is fixed by the age of five. Instead, they believe that we continue to change as our interactions with others become

Peanuts, by Charles Schulz. © 1959 United Feature Syndicate, Inc.

more complex and more demanding. As a reaction to the insecurities we develop at birth, we may, according to Karen Horney, relate to others in certain neurotic ways. Harry Stack Sullivan believed we conform to the expectations of others in determining our own attitude toward ourselves. That is, if others like us we think of ourselves as good, but if others dislike us our self-image becomes negative. Erik Erikson, finally, thinks our search for identity during adolescence is a search for a self that lies somewhere between what we think of ourselves and what others think of us.

Social scientists regularly study group behavior. Like the psychoanalysts, they consider the effect of social relationships on the individual personality, but they also look at the inner dynamics that occur within groups. They suggest that groups work better than individuals when it comes to solving problems that have one correct answer, such as mathematical problems. However, they also tell us that creativity tends to be stifled in group situations. Groups also develop distinct personalities depending on the style of leadership that guides them. And, finally, groups exert tremendous pressure on us to conform, even to the point of causing us to deny our senses.

The humanists have come to be identified with encounter groups. Group experiences are effective for many people who want to learn to express their feelings more spontaneously. Effective group leaders give their groups a maximum amount of freedom to express their feelings. This expression of feeling—anger, concern, anxiety—evolves quite slowly;

but once a group does begin to express their feelings in an atmosphere of freedom, they draw close to one another in the process. Many people, after attending encounter groups, report a greater internal freedom with their feelings. Of course, encounter groups can also have negative results, particularly if the leader lacks training or is unstable emotionally. A bad experience in an encounter group can leave a participant less stable emotionally.

THE PSYCHOANALYTIC APPROACH

Sigmund Freud emphasized the childhood experience in personality development to the exclusion of events that occur later in life. He saw the adult personality determined by the age of five. Freud's emphasis on these early stages of development was so exclusive that it became a principal point of departure from his theories for them. Several major figures in the history of psychology who agree with Freud on such matters as unconscious motivation, the defense mechanisms, and the importance of early childhood have broken with him over his insistence that childhood experiences alone determine the adult personality.

The neo-Freudians believe that childhood is significant in personality development. However, they see the later influence of groups outside the family contributing to our development, also. The influence of our culture and environment, as reflected in the social groups we encounter, helps or hinders the growth that began in earliest childhood.

Neo-Freudians believe that the personality continues to develop beyond the age of five, often through the influence of groups outside the family. (© Susan Lapides 1979, above; © 1976 Joel Gordon, right)

As we grow and mature, the neo-Freudians claim, we seek out groups beyond our immediate family. These groups—educational groups, social groups, religious groups—have a great influence on us. They can change us for the better by helping us grow and gain new freedom. They can also hinder our growth by restrictions and demands for conformity. Our interaction with groups, whether helpful or hindering, does have an effect on us.

Karen Horney, a famous neo-Freudian told us:

> We have to take a definite step beyond Freud, a step which is possible, though, only on the basis of Freud's revealing discoveries. For although in one respect he is far ahead of our own time, in another—in his overemphasis on the biological origin of mental characteristics—Freud has remained rooted in its scientific orientations. He has assumed that the instinctual drives or object relationships that are frequent in our culture are biologically determined "human nature" or arise out of unalterable situations.
>
> Freud's disregard of cultural factors not only leads to false generalizations, but to a large extent blocks an understanding of the real forces which motivate our attitudes and actions. (1)

Karen Horney

Karen Horney (1885–1952) was one of the most prominent neo-Freudians to break with Freud over his theories on the influence of social and cultural factors. Horney's emphasis on the cultural and group factors influencing our personality led her to examine cultural norms carefully. Her study convinced her that we are considered normal or abnormal psychologically according to the extent to which we conform to cultural and **group norms.** For example, the same behavior that would place an American in a mental hospital might well be considered a sign of divinity among Peruvian Indians. Her close look at our culture also pressed her to conclude that society's industrialization and competitive living create anxieties not present in less competitive cultures.

Horney did not agree with Freud's explanation of our personality development in terms of sexual drives. She thought our motivation comes instead from our need for security. The child who experiences an abundance of love early in life achieves a sense of security. Children who do not receive enough affection develop an adult anxiety toward life and constantly search for security (Self-Quiz 10.1).

> If a child is fortunate enough to have, for example, a loving grandmother, an understanding teacher, some good friends, his experience with them may prevent him from expecting nothing but bad from everybody. But the more difficult are his experiences in the family, the more will a child be inclined to develop not only a reaction of hatred toward the parents and other children but a distrustful or spiteful attitude toward everyone.

Self-Quiz 10.1 — Status/Security Need

All of us want status with others. This security need is perfectly normal—our only concern should arise when we allow that desire to dominate us. Next to each statement place the number 1, 2, 3, 4, or 5—depending on how characteristic each statement is of you. Continue the process for each of the statements. Then total your score.

- 5 strongly characteristic of me
- 4 moderately characteristic of me
- 3 neutral
- 2 moderately uncharacteristic of me
- 1 strongly uncharacteristic of me

____ 1. I would rather be content than admired.
____ 2. I believe my success ultimately depends on *what* I know rather than *whom* I know.
____ 3. I would rather be rich than famous.
____ 4. I have no special desire to meet famous people.
____ 5. The turmoil famous people suffer would bother me a great deal.
____ 6. Gossip columns bore me.
____ 7. I would rather gain understanding of myself than achieve self-confidence.
____ 8. I would not attend any particular school no matter how prestigious if I thought I would not receive a good education there.
____ 9. I have no interest in the private lives of famous people.
____ 10. I would rather have friends than admirers.

____ TOTAL SCORE

No test can tell you how much you turn to others for status and security. Such a trait remains too personal to quantitatively measure. However, your score on this test, when compared with other student scores, can give you an indication of your tendency to seek the approval of others.

- 44–50 You score with those few students who indicate a high degree of contentment. You apparently do not often look outside yourself for status and security.
- 30–43 You score with the majority of students who took this test. Like most people, you look to others for identification and approval.
- 10–29 You score with a minority of students who have a great need for the approval of others. You, more than most, seem to look to others for your status.

The more a child is isolated and deterred from making other experiences of his own, the more such a development will be fostered. And finally, the more a child covers up his grudge against his own family, as for instance by conforming with his parents' attitudes, the more he projects his anxiety to the outside world and thus becomes convinced that the "world" in general is dangerous and frightening. (2)

The child who is deprived of security early in life may neurotically search for that security in adult social groups. One way a person who was deprived of security as a child might react to the anxiety that results is to become dependent on other people. Such people forever seek to be dominated by others in order to become dependent on them. The henpecked husband is a stereotype of the dependent personality. Other people looking for security try to dominate others, as power and authority become their answer to insecurity. And the third way Horney sees people neurotically search for security is by turning away from others. These people withdraw from groups and society altogether, usually slipping into a world of fantasy or isolation.

Karen Horney's belief that the child who receives an adequate amount of affection will feel secure as an adult is supported by a recent study. Martin L. Hoffman, a University of Michigan psychologist, found that children develop **altruism** (concern for others) most often when they have good parental models. Hoffman studied 80 fifth-graders at a suburban school in Detroit. The children were rated on their altruistic tendencies by their classmates. Each child suggested who among the group would be most likely to be concerned for others. The parents of each of the 80 children were then interviewed separately.

Children with altruistic attitudes often have parents with the same tendencies. (Peter Vandermark)

Hoffman discovered that those parents who valued altruism highly most often fostered altruistic concerns in their children. Parents of altruistic children also were affectionate and used victim-centered disciplinary techniques. Such discipline encourages children to empathize with the feelings of others and apologize and try to repair any damage to another's trouble. The study clearly points out that children who receive affection learn altruism, a form of security, just as Karen Horney might have predicted. (3)

Harry Stack Sullivan

Harry Stack Sullivan (1892–1949) also falls into the category of neo-Freudian theorist. Like Horney, he followed Freud and agreed with many of Freud's insights. He could not, however, accept Freud's theory of childhood sexuality. Instead, he thought our search for personal security is our primary drive. Sullivan thought that we discover the security we yearn for by finding out who we are.

Our contact with social and cultural groups becomes important because we turn to others for knowledge about ourselves. When we lack our own sense of identity, we ask those around us to tell us who we are. We tend to interpret every word, action, or gesture from other people as a sign of our worth or value. If a friend extends herself on our behalf, we tend to think of ourselves as a **good-me.** The gift given, the word of praise, the thoughtful gesture all let us say to ourselves, "I might be all right." This dependence on social groups for our sense of identity also extends to the **bad-me.** When others ignore us, criticize us, or reject us, we think there is something wrong with us. Our personality can be permanently altered by negative responses if they come regularly enough and with enough impact (Case 10.1). In the extreme stages of the bad-me experience, people can turn with disgust and anxiety to a **not-me** self-concept. They simply refuse to recognize themselves at all and break off from reality.

Most of us can recognize ourselves in Sullivan's theory. We look to others for our own identity. We become overly inflated by the praise of others, while a word of criticism can last days, weeks, even permanently. We would rather not ever be so dependent on the opinions of others, but we know we are.

● Case 10.1

At times, the distinction between how we look upon ourselves and how others see us can be striking. This distinction often arises because significant people distort the self-image of impressionable children. At least that happened to Pam, a young woman I met early in my work as a therapist.

Pam had classical beauty, and a first look at this young woman would leave most people envious. Yet, inside Pam, there was little to envy. Rather than seeing her natural beauty, Pam could only see ugliness. Whenever she looked in the mirror, Pam was blind to the beauty that struck everyone else.

Her father convinced Pam quite early in life she lacked any attractive qualities. His comments to her, when he became angry, were cruel. He would say, "You had better grab the first man who comes along. He may be your last chance." Pam could not look inside her father's confused mind and see that his words only reflected his own bitterness and anguish. The one way he could relieve himself of some pain was by directing his anger at others, particularly Pam.

For Pam the attacks seemed personal. She believed her father's descriptions of her. She came to know herself as ugly. No comments about her beauty by others could penetrate the image her father planted early in her life. She became, in her own eyes, ugly, cruel, and disgusting. She believed her father's prediction that no man would ever love her. When Errol fell in love with Pam, he found it almost impossible to convince Pam of his sincerity. His struggle to prove to Pam he cared for her and that he thought she was attractive seemed endless. Pam did finally grow to believe Errol enough to marry him, and over the years his love gradually began to change her image of herself. Today, Pam accepts Errol's love completely, but she still wonders, at times, if he sees her as she truly is.

Erik Erikson

Erik Erikson (b. 1902) is the last neo-Freudian we will discuss in this section. He also emphasizes the role of social groups in the formation of the personality. Erikson took Freud's stages of personality development, elaborated on them and extended them to cover all of life—to the eighth stage of old age. He sees each stage as a conflict that a person must resolve before moving on to the next stage. In the oral stage, or breast-feeding stage, the child faces a crisis of trust versus mistrust. Once that crisis is resolved, the anal stage poses a crisis in autonomy versus shame. Such crises, for Erikson, continued right into old age.

Erikson thinks that the study of ego identity offers us the principal clue to personality development, and he considers the security of **personal identity** to be the basis for a healthy personality. This stage occurs during adolescence, long after Freud claimed the personality was set for life. The critical identity struggle all adolescents face is between who they think they are and who others think they are. The young woman must decide she wants to become a surgeon despite pressure from others to press her to become a nurse. The young man must choose to leave school and be on his own rather than fulfill the expectations of those who insist he finish college. The crisis is resolved only when we decide to take full responsibility for our own life. Often the clearest sign of taking such responsibility comes when a young person accepts his or her parents. Rather than anxiously wishing to change one's parents, young people accept their parents for who they are once they resolve their identity crisis. Erikson explains the crucial adolescent stage in *Identity: Youth and Crisis:*

Erikson believed the search for identity to be the principal task of adolescence. (Paul S. Conklin)

Adolescence is the last stage of childhood. The adolescent process, however, is conclusively complete only when the individual has subordinated his childhood identifications to a new kind of identification, achieved in absorbing sociability and in competitive apprenticeship with and among his age mates. These new identifications are no longer characterized by the playfulness of childhood and the experimental zest of youth: with dire urgency they force the young individual into choices and decisions which will, with increasing immediacy, lead to commitments "for life." The task to be performed here by the young person and by his society is formidable. It necessitates, in different individuals and in different societies, great variations in the duration, intensity, and ritualization of adolescence. Societies offer, as individuals require, more or less sanctioned intermediary periods between childhood and adulthood, often characterized by a combination of prolonged immaturity and provoked precocity. (4)

THE BEHAVIORISTIC APPROACH

The neo-Freudians are interested in the effects of society and social groups on individuals. They do not spend much time on any analysis of **group dynamics** as such. Today, however, social scientists regularly study the inner dynamics of groups. They would like to understand why individuals behave so differently in a group setting than with one other person. You may have noticed how a friend determined to speak out on a given issue at a club meeting, for example, became silent once that meeting began. It often seems as if we take on a new personality once we join with others in some common effort.

A basic discovery psychologists made about groups is that groups can solve certain types of problems more quickly than individuals. As early as 1935, J. F. Dashiell reported a study in the *Handbook of Social Psychology* that showed students working in a group completed more problems than they did working individually. (5) Many other studies confirm this basic concept. The reason usually cited for the result seems reasonable. People working in a group can reject one another's false suggestions and correct each other's mistakes. In problem-solving activities, groups make fewer false starts and solve problems in less time.

The collective effort is not equally suited for all work, however. The efficiency of such an approach appears limited to problems that have correct solutions. When creative rather than analytical thinking is involved, groups fall short of individual efforts. Using an interesting technique to study the effects of creative thinking, psychologists asked a group of research scientists and advertising men to "brainstorm" some complicated questions that demanded creative answers. The subjects were told to think of as many ideas as possible and to generate the wildest ideas possible. Each of the subjects worked on ideas in groups of four and also individually. The subjects produced more and better ideas when they were working alone than they did when working in a group. Evidently, the group atmosphere suppressed the flow of ideas by inhibiting some individuals from expressing their creativity. (6)

Leadership Styles

In an experiment that is now a classic in the field, a group of psychologists looked at leadership styles. To see how a leader's approach would affect the behavior of group members, Kurt Lewin and his associates divided 15 ten-year-old boys into three groups. Each five-member group experienced, in seven-week periods, leaders trained in each of three different styles of leadership—authoritarian, democratic, and laissez-faire (permissive).

The **authoritarian leader** completely dominated the group assigned to him. He decided all group activities, determined who would work with whom, dictated how the activities would be performed, and remained aloof from the group as much as possible. The group members in the authoritarian group became most unhappy with their situation, demanded more attention from their leader, and became most dependent on the leader. However, that same group accomplished the most work.

The **democratic leader** encouraged his group to make group decisions. The members decided who would work at what activities and with which members. The leader did little of the actual work though he did participate in the group actively and help provide a warm atmosphere. This democratic style led to high scores on such measures as friendliness among the members, work-minded conversation, and eliciting group-centered suggestions.

The **laissez-faire,** or "do as you will," **leader** entered the group atmosphere as little as possible. He only answered questions when directly

Tumbleweeds. © 1975 United Feature Syndicate, Inc.

asked. In short, he left the entire group in the hands of the boys. This leadership style created a friendliness among the boys, but provoked a great need for stimulated help from the leader.

The boys became more dependent under the authoritarian leader and simultaneously displayed less individuality. The atmosphere was submissive as well as unhappy. As the experiment progressed, the boys became more hostile toward each other, their leader, and even toward outsiders who entered the group.

The democratic group was the happiest. Though they produced less work than the authoritarian group, they worked more efficiently and with more interest. A friendly spirit prevailed that produced a great deal of sharing among members. They regulated themselves and preferred not to be given instructions by the leader.

And finally, though the laissez-faire group offered its members more freedom, initiative was low. A distinct lack of interaction existed between the members and the leader. As a result the group produced less work, and their work was judged the poorest in the study (Self-Quiz 10.2). (7)

Group Pressure

The pressure to conform to group standards is an important part of our lives. As children we conform principally to our parents and their norms for our behavior. As we grow older we begin to conform more to our friends' expectations. Conformity is a constant part of our lives as we move from home, to school, to work. Most of us reluctantly admit we respond to the norms others set for us. We know the style of our clothes, the brand name of products we buy, and even the television we watch are influenced by pressure from others. We consciously conform to these pressures to maintain our status with others.

An important experiment by Mazafer Sherif in the 1930s pointed out that our inner need to conform can even affect our visual perception. A group of experimental subjects were placed in a completely dark room. At

Self-Quiz 10.2 — Leadership

Two qualities are generally recognized as important for good leadership. One is an innate tendency to press for your own way and achieve your goals. The other, usually learned through experience, is a more subtle awareness of others and a desire to help them understand your motives and come to desire your goals. These two aspects of effective leadership are measured separately in the following tests. Read each statement and choose the alternative that best describes your attitude by checking the proper box to the left of the statement.

TEST A

Often	Occasionally	Seldom	
☐	☐	☐	1. I am an aggressive person and want to get things done at all costs.
☐	☐	☐	2. I enjoy responsibility.
☐	☐	☐	3. In social gatherings, I love to be the center of attention in a large group of people.
☐	☐	☐	4. I do not believe manners make the person.
☐	☐	☐	5. Firmness is the most important quality in any leader as far as I am concerned.
☐	☐	☐	6. I feel confident in my attempts to convince people over the phone.
☐	☐	☐	7. I raise my voice in my efforts to convince some people.
☐	☐	☐	8. I cannot stand to take "no" for an answer.
☐	☐	☐	9. I will press others to accomplish things even when they do not like my aggressiveness.

TEST B

Often	Occasionally	Seldom	
☐	☐	☐	1. I would describe myself as quiet and withdrawn, though I know how to achieve my goals.

☐	☐	☐	2. In social groups I do little talking but manage to steer conversations toward topics I enjoy.
☐	☐	☐	3. If I had to give someone bad news, I would do so in a way that would be least embarrassing to that person.
☐	☐	☐	4. I believe a firm handshake denotes a strong personality.
☐	☐	☐	5. I do not believe that committees are necessarily the best way to solve problems.
☐	☐	☐	6. If invited to give an after-dinner talk, I would use the opportunity to present some new ideas.
☐	☐	☐	7. I work hard to achieve my goals and compromise only when necessary.
☐	☐	☐	8. I usually do not have to work too hard to get my way in things.
☐	☐	☐	9. People generally seem to respect me.

Score the tests separately. Give yourself 3 points for each time you checked "often," 2 points for each "occasionally," and 1 point for each "seldom." Your score on Test A suggests how much aggressiveness you might have as a leader. Test B indicates your more subtle qualities of leadership. Ideally, you would have a balance between these two scores. The descriptions below, however, refer to your total score.

44–54   You have indicated strong leadership qualities by your answers. If your score on Test A dominates, however, your leadership might be too pushy and could make you disliked as a person. For effective leadership, search for a balance between the two qualities measured.

32–43   Your score lies within the range indicated by most people. You probably have the necessary qualities for leadership but have not brought them into play. A high Test A score could mean you dominate people too much for leadership. A high Test B score might suggest you are not aggressive enough for strong leadership.

18–31   Your low score, in comparison with others who took this test, suggests you lack the temperament for leadership.

248 The Individual and the Group

one end of the room, a small pinpoint of light was turned on. Since the light had no context, it appeared to move. This movement is called the **autokinetic illusion.** The people in the room were asked to indicate how much the light moved. When the guesses were made privately, the movement was estimated at anywhere from a few inches to several feet. But when the guesses were made public, they merged toward a common range of numbers—that is, a group norm evolved.

Even stronger power of group pressures was revealed in a further elaboration of the same experiment. A male participant made private guesses about the movement of light in the darkened room. His average guess hovered around 4 inches. The subject was then placed in the same room with a group of three experimental confederates, employed to see how much they could influence the young man's decision. They estimated the light movement to be about 15 inches. Under such pressure, the experimental subject changed his estimate from 4 to 14 inches. (8)

This tendency to follow the group rather than the evidence of our own eyes suggested another experiment to Solomon Asch in the 1950s. This time the task performed was much easier. The participants were asked to match the length of lines. One line of, say, 8 inches was drawn next to three lines of say 6, 8, and 10 inches. Each subject was asked which of the

Group pressure can even dictate the clothing we wear. (Peter Vandermark)

"All those in favor of passing the added cost along to the consumer signify by saying 'Aye.'"

three lines matched the first line in length. The task was so simple that almost no one missed the obvious match.

Then each subject was placed in a group with seven experimental confederates. All the confederates deliberately selected the same incorrect match between lines. The subject then had the choice of sticking to his initial choice or going along with the group decision. About one-third of the participants exposed to this experiment conformed fairly consistently with the incorrect majority decision. About one-fourth followed their independent judgment and always chose the correct answer. The rest conformed at some times and not at others. This experiment made even more clear the point that Sherif explored nearly twenty years earlier — groups have an amazing degree of control over the individual (Case 10.2). (9)

● Case 10.2

Though our experiences cannot have the scientific validity of a controlled experiment, we can see how much we influence one another by recalling certain episodes in our lives. Norm experienced group influence after he was recently elected a member of the city council.

Norm fought a hard campaign and won on the promise that he would make the city a better place to raise a family. His promise made him quite sensitive to the series of attacks that occurred at a local park. Norm was particularly concerned about the number of muggings that were provoked by the use of alcohol.

The park attacks were on his mind when Norm noticed the council was scheduled to consider granting a liquor license to a market across the street from the park. Because the issue was so important to him, Norm approached over half of the council members on his own time. He explained how strongly he felt about keeping the park safe for families to enjoy. Each member he discussed the issue with agreed with Norm that the liquor store posed a potential hazard to the park atmosphere.

When Norm told the entire council about his opposition to the liquor store, several members thought his objections foolish. "If people want to bring liquor to the park," one veteran member suggested, "they'll do it. After all, there's already a store not more than two blocks from the park." Norm expected support from some of the members he approached on his own. In the group atmosphere, however, they all hung back and did not respond. Those opposing Norm took the initiative in the debate, and before long, Norm himself discovered his own attitude changing. He started to think his stand was irrational. In the end, Norm was the only person to vote against granting the liquor license. And even he wondered if he was only being stubborn.

The Risky Shift

Another phenomenon occurring in groups seems to defy common sense at first glance. We would expect group decisions to follow a conservative line, because consensus would seem to press people to discard extreme positions. Experience proves, however, that this does not always happen. Once in a group, people often feel free of individual responsibility for the decision and therefore more willing to take a chance. This **risky shift,** as psychologists often call it, results in a group opting for stances they might never take as individuals.

The risky shift loses a great deal of its power, however, when the risk affects the individuals in the group personally. That is, if the individuals were deciding how much of their own money to invest in a group decision, the chances of the risky shift would be minimized. An interesting experiment by Maryla Zaleska explored this phenomenon. She formed two groups and asked each group to bet money on the outcome of an event. The members of one group stood to gain or lose personally on the result of the bet. The second group was only wagering for fun. As she predicted, the high-stakes group (those personally involved in the results) bet far more conservatively than the low-stakes group. Caution ruled those personally involved in the outcome. (10)

THE HUMANISTIC APPROACH

The neo-Freudians suggest several reasons why we might not express our true feelings in many situations. Their explanations may or may not be accurate. However, few people need proof that they do often fail to express their genuine feelings. We all find it difficult at times to tell even our closest friends how much we care about them. We often repress our anger rather than suffer embarrassment. When others tell us of their affection or displeasure with us, we can become uneasy. Though some people have a greater need to hide from their feelings than others, most of us admit that we tend to disguise our true feelings.

Our failure to express our feelings is, for many psychologists, a basic cause of anxiety. Humanist psychologists look for various ways people can open up and be honest about their emotions. One technique for helping people reveal their feelings is the **encounter group.** The encounter group encourages people to spend time talking to one another about feelings that they commonly do not express to others. When the encounter experience helps people, it does so, according to its proponents, by helping the participants gain confidence in themselves in a safe and secure atmosphere. Such an atmosphere encourages them to speak to others about things that they have held back and suffered with internally. Rather than continuing to suppress feelings that cause emotional pressure, the members reveal their turmoil and thereby ease their burden.

Carl Rogers, a leading proponent of the encounter group, defined it as usually consisting of

> ten to fifteen persons and a facilitator, or leader. It is relatively unstructured, providing a climate of maximum freedom for personal expression, exploration of feelings, and interpersonal communication. Emphasis is upon the interactions among the group members, in an atmosphere that encourages each one to drop defenses and facades and thus to relate directly and openly to other members of the group — the basic encounter. Individuals come to know themselves and each other more fully than is possible in the usual social or working relationships; the climate of openness, risk-taking, and honesty generates trust, which enables the person to recognize and change self-defeating attitudes, test out and adopt more innovative and constructive behaviors, and subsequently to relate more adequately and effectively to others in everyday life. (11)

The Encounter Group

The encounter group has had, over the years, many different images. Discussion in this chapter will accent the basic encounter as described by Carl Rogers. Fortunately, Rogers has written a great deal about these groups and describes several aspects of them in his book *Carl Rogers on Encounter Groups.* Possibly the most revealing description occurs in the chapter in which he suggests the process that groups seem to follow spontaneously when they meet in an atmosphere of freedom.

Members of any group, when first getting together in an unstructured atmosphere, do a good bit of what Rogers calls milling around. The members chat aimlessly about the weather, current events — usually remaining on a superficial level. This superficial level, Rogers suggests, sustains itself because the individuals want to maintain the same public face they show to others outside of the group. They would rather not speak personally about areas that might cause them embarrassment. If someone does speak too personally during this early stage in a group, the other members chastise that member. They seem to fear any statement that might bring them into a personal discussion.

Despite the need to remain distant from the members of the group, the superficial talk soon becomes strained and tiresome. At that point, a few people speak of past emotions. Some will mention anger between themselves and others that occurred years before. Other members talk about the bitterness they still feel toward a spouse, a relative, a parent. The feelings are real, but they are distant and less dangerous to discuss. Finally, after even the discussion of past feelings becomes too remote, an immediate here-and-now feeling emerges in the group. Some person speaks directly to another person with feeling. Interestingly, this first feeling is almost always an angry one. A group member expresses hostility to the group leader or to another group member; for instance, "I wish someone would take charge here and not let us continue to go on aimlessly like this." Rogers offers some reasons for the anger in the first here-and-now expressions.

> Why are negatively toned expressions the first current feelings to be expressed? Some speculative answers might be the following. This is one of the best ways to test the freedom and trustworthiness of the group. Is it really a place where I can be and express myself, positively and negatively? Is this really a safe place, or will I be punished? Another quite different reason is that deeply positive feelings are much more difficult and dangerous to express than negative ones. If I say I love you, I am vulnerable and open to the most awful rejection. If I say I hate you, I am at best liable to attack, against which I can defend. Whatever the reasons, such negatively toned feelings tend to be the first "here and now" material to appear. (12)

Feeling Expression

After the group has experienced freedom during the aloof, superficial stage, discussed remote feelings, and finally broken through to genuine emotion, a most interesting thing happens next. The members begin to open up to one another in a direct, personal way. The expression of genuine feelings helps a sense of trust to grow in the group. Expression of both negative and positive feelings is permitted to all participants. Housewives talk of their discontent; students reveal their anger toward parents; business people talk of affairs never before revealed. And rather than becoming jarred by such revelations, the group members draw together to support, encourage, and care about one another.

About this time in the group process, feeling expression becomes the norm. Individuals begin to accept themselves in ways they never before

The encounter group can help people grow closer together. (Karen R. Preuss/Jeroboam)

thought possible. They decide that what they had previously thought of as limitations are really important parts of their personality. Those who resist the openness that pervades the group find their pretense increasingly difficult to maintain as members lose patience with them. Those who want to continue their membership in the group must strive for honesty and openness.

Rogers writes about one member who came to accept herself in new ways through an encounter workshop. This woman wrote to Rogers and told him about her father's death and her long and difficult trip to join her mother.

> A trip that seemed interminable with its confusing connections, my own bewilderment and deep sorrow, lack of sleep, and serious concern over mother's ill-health in the future. All I knew through the five days I spent there was that I wanted to be just the way I felt—that I wanted no "anesthetic," no conventional screen between myself and my feelings, and that the only way I could achieve this was by fully accepting the experience, by yielding to shock and grief. This feeling of acceptance and yielding has remained with me ever since. Quite frankly, I think the workshop had a great deal to do with my willingness to accept his experience. (13)

Many members of encounter groups come to accept themselves in similar ways. The intensity of the experience draws the members extremely close to one another near the end of the workshops. The expression of positive feelings becomes the norm as the experience reaches its final stages (Case 10.3).

● Case 10.3

The encounter-group experience not only generates rich feelings between its members, but those emotions often carry over into life beyond the experience. That was true for Gina. Her experience within the encounter group she attended affected her deeply at the time, but the more important implications, for Gina, occurred outside the group.

On her own, Gina might never have attended an encounter group. Only because her friend Mary wanted to attend so badly and needed someone "to hang on to," did Gina go along. The experience struck Gina as rather strange at first: a group of eleven people sitting in a small room for three hours at a time talking about nothing in particular. But Gina took it in stride until one middle-aged man got angry during the evening session of the first day they were all together. "Are we all going to sit here talking about nothing?" he shouted at the group. "Or are we going to get down to business?" The anger upset Gina. She had no idea what "getting down to business" meant, and she did not like being shouted at by a stranger. The anger upset her so much, however, that she decided not to say anything for fear the man might turn on her.

Gina thought of not returning to the group the next morning. She disliked emotional displays, and the first day's experience nearly wore her out. Still, something drew her, almost beyond her power to resist, back into the group experience, the next day. When Gina entered the room, she could hardly believe she was in the same group. The atmosphere was warm and friendly. Even the man who had become so angry the day before had a friendly expression. From that point on a good feeling prevailed. The people in the group began talking to one another personally. They talked about things Gina had never heard discussed before. She became closer and closer to the members. Their honesty opened her to herself. Toward the middle of the experience, a woman talked about how little her daughter appreciated her and her pain because her daughter seemed so aloof and indifferent. Gina identified with the woman completely and felt strong emotions during the woman's story.

During the break for lunch, Gina wanted to be by herself. She slowly came to realize how distant her relationship with her mother had always been. She had never before seen it so clearly because she and her mother used the word "love" so often. It never struck her that little emotion ever seemed a part of that expression. When she returned to the group, Gina told the other members about her feelings. They sympathized with her and encouraged her to talk with her mother. Gina did not know if she had the courage. She ended the encounter experience on that note. The members wanted her to talk with her mother eventually, but only when she felt prepared.

After the group ended, Gina began to talk more freely with her mother. Her mother seemed open to the new relationship. As the weeks went by, the two of them became closer. Finally, after about three months of preparation, Gina expressed her disappointment that she and her mother never seemed to experience real emotion when they expressed their love for one another. The words would not flow easily and her emotion dominated her as Gina finally told her mother how much love she felt. This time, when Gina's mother used the word "love" she could not control her emotion.

Encounter-Group Dangers

Encounter groups can also be dangerous experiences, particularly if the wrong person leads the encounter. Studies have shown that the leaders most apt to cause stress for members have hostile or charismatic personalities. Such leaders often press people to do and say things against their will in order to achieve a good emotional show. But if emotions are not revealed in an atmosphere of freedom, serious turmoil can result. People who find themselves in a group that creates psychological pressures would do well to leave the experience immediately.

Inexperienced, and especially untrained, leaders often promote immature value systems for the group to follow. The most common false value suggests that whatever one feels is right. Some people use this as an excuse to release a great deal of hostility and damage in group experiences and excuse their excesses by declaring their feelings were honest.

Skeptics also point out the danger of assuming new behaviors within a group for a weekend and then facing real-life situations at home that do not allow such openness. Most people outside of the group will not tolerate the behavior fostered in an encounter group. A final objection that is often raised against the encounter experience is the lack of follow-up. A person who opens up emotionally in the group may find it difficult to find stability after the experience ends. Such people are rarely given any direction in which to turn in such cases and are left to fend for themselves. (14)

CONCLUSION

The neo-Freudians react against Freud's certitude that a person's personality is set by the age of five. The neo-Freudians rather insist that our personalities continue to change for the rest of our lives. Our interactions with friends, relatives, neighbors, teachers, employers, and other social contacts alter our personalities. And depending on how much we look to others for approval or disapproval, other people can have a tremendous influence.

Most of the social scientists, who study behavior in a more objective manner, do not work from a theory of personality. Instead, they approach behavior from an experimental viewpoint. They place people in social situations to see how groups affect individual behavior. They discover, for example, that groups help one another a great deal when they attempt to solve problems with one correct answer. However, groups tend to stifle their members when creative solutions are sought. The results of their studies form the basis upon which social scientists search for some understanding of the individual in the group.

Humanists and groups have become almost synonymous to many people. An abundance of group experiences have evolved from the humanistic movement. Most of these groups have the expression of feeling as their goal. The humanists believe, for the most part, that we fall short of our potential because we suppress our feelings. So the encounter group, particularly as practiced by Carl Rogers, attempts to free group members to become more open and honest with one another.

SUMMARY

1. Sigmund Freud believed we have a permanent personality set by the age of five. Many of his followers, particularly the neo-Freudians, have taken issue with this belief. Karen Horney, for example, thought that our personalities continue to develop for the rest of our lives. But children who do not receive adequate love during infancy will turn to other people as adults in unhealthy ways. Harry Stack Sullivan felt that we all too often expect others to determine our self-value. If others respond positively to us, we think of ourselves as valuable; otherwise, we consider ourselves worthless. Finally, Erikson thinks the critical point in personality development occurs at adolescence when young people decide how much their identity will be determined by their own personality and how much by other people.
2. Social scientists study the behavior of people in groups to determine their theory of personality. Their studies point out that groups work well with one another on problems with a single answer, but stifle creativity. Leaders, these psychologists have discovered, can affect the

atmosphere of the group simply by adopting various leadership approaches. A host of experiments on group pressure have shown us how much we are influenced by groups. We even deny the obvious evidence of our senses when groups press us to conform.
3. The humanistic movement has become known for the various group experiences it fosters. The humanists work with people in meditation groups, relaxation groups, sensory-awareness groups, and gestalt groups. The encounter group forms the basis for much of this activity. Encounter groups, according to Carl Rogers, help people express their feelings to one another. When properly conducted, the encounter group helps people become more personally involved in their own lives.

KEY TERMS

group norms	group dynamics
search for security	authoritarian leader
altruism	democratic leader
good-me	laissez-faire leader
bad-me	autokinetic illusion
not-me	risky shift
personal identity	encounter group

STUDY QUESTIONS

1. Does the neo-Freudian emphasis on the social role in personality development appeal to you more than Freud's early childhood development theory? Explain how much you feel society has affected your personality development.
2. Would you say the most important changes in your life occurred before or after puberty? Give specific reasons for your choice.
3. Explain the specific tasks you would rather perform by yourself and those tasks that you would rather perform with a group.
4. What sort of leader would you be if put in charge of a group? With what kinds of groups would you be most effective or ineffective?
5. How might a good encounter-group experience help you? Be specific.
6. What would be your principal fear in joining an encounter group? Explain.

ADDITIONAL READING

Asch, Solomon. *Social Psychology*. Englewood Cliffs, N.J.: Prentice-Hall, 1952.
Erikson, Erik H. *Identity: Youth and Crisis*. New York: Norton, 1968.

Horney, Karen. *The Neurotic Personality of Our Time.* New York: Norton, 1937.

Lakin, M. *Interpersonal Encounter: Theory and Research in Sensitivity Training.* New York: McGraw-Hill, 1972.

Lewin, K. *Field Theory in Social Science.* Dorwin Cartwright (Ed.) New York: Harper and Row, 1951.

Lieberman, M. A.; Yalom., I. D.; and Miles, M. B. *Encounter Groups: First Facts.* New York: Basic, 1973.

Napier, R. W., and Gerchenfeld, M. K. *Groups: Theory and Experience.* Boston: Houghton Mifflin, 1973.

Rogers, Carl R. *Carl Rogers on Encounter Groups.* New York: Harper and Row, 1970.

Sullivan, Harry Stack. *The Interpersonal Theory of Psychiatry.* New York: Norton, 1953.

Yalom, I. D. *The Theory and Practice of Group Psychotherapy.* New York: Basic Books, 1971.

Chapter Eleven

Love and Friendship

OUTLINE

The Psychoanalytic Approach
    Learning an Art
    Practicing an Art
    The Art of Loving

The Behavioristic Approach
    Plain People
    Love Is the Answer
    Hard to Get

The Humanistic Approach
    The Sounds of Silence
    The Risk of Loving
    Peace

Conclusion

LEARNING OBJECTIVES

After reading this chapter you should be able to:

1. Understand how love can be considered an art form.
2. Discuss the personal traits necessary to practice the art of loving.
3. Discuss some of the ways we react to attractive and plain people.
4. Explain how psychologists attempt to study the concept of love in spite of the many definitions.
5. Understand how remaining in the present moment makes us aware of unexpressed feeling.
6. Discuss how risks can become an important part of any loving relationship.

Chapter Eleven

Tom was about the last student in my personal and social adjustment class I thought would ever ask me about love and friendship. He was easily the best-looking fellow in the class, and his manner suggested that he fought off friends, both male and female, most of the time so that he could have some time to himself. Yet, here he was lingering after class to ask me about friendship.

"I would like to know how to get along with people," he said. "I had hoped we would learn more about that in this class."

"We will talk about friendship more directly a little later in the class," I replied, still stunned by his need for pointers in the art of friendship. "But maybe you and I could talk about the topic now."

"I just don't hit it off too well with people," Tom said, sitting on top of a nearby student desk. "As soon as I start talking to people, especially women, I get nervous and self-conscious. That's discouraging. I mean I look around at other students, and they seem to become friends without any trouble."

"One thing I can tell you right away," I said, "is that no real friendship can develop without a lot of work. Relationships take discipline, concentration, and risk."

"Yeah?" Tom's eyebrows pulled together with surprise. "It sure doesn't look like that to me."

"That's part of the problem with love and friendship. It looks so easy from the outside. We figure love just ought to happen to us. But it's never like that. A friendship takes a great deal of work."

Most of us share Tom's feelings that friendship should simply happen. Even though we struggle through one relationship after another, we somehow think the next one will go smoothly and effortlessly. Yet, a look at the psychological theories in this chapter suggests that love is difficult work.

Eric Fromm, a neo-Freudian, expressed the conviction of many psychologists when he pointed out that love is an art that must be practiced with commitment. People who want to become skilled in the art of loving must dedicate themselves to learning it as they would to any other art form. Like learning to play the piano or a good game of tennis, learning to love requires concentration, discipline, and focus on the goal. Any effort short of total dedication will leave us inept at love and friendship.

The behaviorists do not theorize about love. Instead, they measure our reactions to **interpersonal** situations. They find, for example, that most people claim to be relatively uninterested in physical beauty as a criterion for friendship. Yet, the behaviorists show us that our behavior shows that beauty *does* attract. The behaviorists also suggest that less attractive people like to associate with attractive friends, and that this association impresses other people. One psychologist in this field even made some progress in cutting through the many definitions of love to produce a scale which attempts to measure loving and liking.

Finally, the humanists consistently focus on emotions. In the case of love and friendship, a great many humanists accent the importance of existing in the present moment when encountering a friend or lover. When we free ourselves from distracting thoughts about the past and future we become aware of what we really want to say to friends and lovers. Expression of feelings of love and friendship can be risky, but it is the key to bringing love to fruition.

THE PSYCHOANALYTIC APPROACH

Erich Fromm (b. 1900), a prominent neo-Freudian, writes cogently about love. In a refreshingly clear style, he penetrates to the core of the questions that surround love by asking whether love is an art or a feeling. Most of us would do well to ask ourselves that question. Do we think of love as something that requires knowledge and takes effort? Or do we think love simply happens to us? Fromm wrote an answer to that question in *The Art of Loving*.

Most people, no matter how they might answer Fromm's question about love, act as if there is nothing to learn about love. They feel they can make themselves lovable by becoming rich and powerful, physically attractive, or by learning social graces. They search for ways to attract others to them rather than learning how to actively love another person. The emphasis in love for most people, Fromm says, shifts from the faculty of loving to a search for the object loved. We spend our time looking for the right person and hope for that magic moment when love will happen to us.

An important "error leading to the assumption that there is nothing to be learned about love" Fromm says,

> lies in the confusion between the initial experience of "falling" in love, and the permanent state of being in love, or as we might better say, of **"standing" in love.** If two people who have been strangers, as all of us are, suddenly let the wall between them break down, and feel close, feel one, this moment of oneness is one of the most exhilarating, most exciting experiences in life. It is all the more wonderful and miraculous for persons who have been shut off, isolated, without love. This miracle of sudden intimacy is often facilitated if it is combined with, or initiated by,

"I suppose, Muriel, that, in my own curious way, I've always loved you."

sexual attraction and consummation. However, this type of love is, by its very nature not lasting. The two persons become well acquainted, their intimacy loses more and more its miraculous character, until their antagonism, their disappointments, their mutual boredom kill whatever is left of the initial excitement. (1)

Learning an Art

No one learns an art, Erich Fromm tells us, without mastering the theory and the practice of that art. The statement holds true for the art of medicine, the art of tennis, and the art of the piano. We must first of all take time to understand intellectually the art that we intend to master. In medicine, we must know the parts of the body, how they function, and how to improve their function. The rules of tennis and the physical principles upon which the game is played must be intellectually mastered. The study of the piano demands that we understand the theory underlying music composition.

    The intellectual control of the theory behind the art leads to the practice necessary to master that art. Practice blends our theoretical and practical knowledge. Few of us are surprised that anyone who hopes to master the art of medicine, or music, or tennis must be dedicated to the practice of those arts. No other concern should interfere. Fromm believes that learning to play tennis, learning to love, and learning to make money all require this kind of dedication because they are all art forms.

> And, maybe, here lies the answer to the question of why people in our culture try so rarely to learn the art of loving, in spite of their obvious failures: in spite of the deep-seated craving for love, almost everything else is considered to be more important than love: success, prestige, money, power—almost all our energy is used for the learning of how to achieve these aims, and almost none to learn the art of loving.
>
> Could it be that only those things are considered worthy of being learned with which one can earn money or prestige, and that love, which 'only' profits the soul, but is profitless in the modern sense, is a luxury we have no right to spend money on? (2)

Practicing an Art

We become skilled in any art, Fromm says, when we practice with **discipline.** People do not master an art if they exercise that art only when they are in the mood. They might win the admiration of friends with their skill or have moments of pleasure, but they will never become masters of the piano, of tennis, or of love without dedicated practice. This kind of dedication to an art is difficult in our culture today, because outside of the eight-hour work day our leisure-time culture breeds laziness. Partly as a reaction against the industrialization of our times, most people are very self-indulgent. This tendency to shun discipline when work is over puts most art beyond the reach of the average person, particularly the art of loving.

A second quality we must develop in the perfection of any art is **concentration.** No one needs proof that mastering the piano or the tennis game yields only to concentrated practice. Yet, concentration is as rare in our culture as discipline. Possibly no other culture breeds people so anxious to eat, smoke, drink, watch television, read a newspaper, and carry on a conversation simultaneously. Few people can sit still with themselves for any length of time without doing anything. Even fewer can put their full attention to developing one skill.

Almost equal with the need for discipline and concentration in developing an art is the need for **patience.** Every art develops slowly, but only patient people can see the slow steps of progress moving toward perfection. Most people become discouraged with their ineptitude and abandon their efforts, but patient people will see their efforts bear fruit.

And finally, Erich Fromm emphasizes the importance of concern, or desire, in learning an art.

> A condition of learning any art is a supreme concern with the mastery of the art. If the art is not something of supreme importance, the apprentice

Erich Fromm insists that love is an art that must be practiced diligently, with patience and concern. (Terry McKoy)

will never learn it. He will remain, at best, a good dilettante, but he will never become a master. This condition is as necessary for the art of loving as for any other art. It seems, though, as if the proportion between masters and dilettantes is more heavily weighted in favor of the dilettantes in the art of loving than is the case with other arts. (3) (Case 11.1)

Case 11.1

Discussion about practicing the art of loving leaves some students confused. They think they know how to practice that art, but, the specifics of the practice can baffle them, because effective practice in love, more than most arts, is quite individual. However, the experience of Debra, a young woman I had in therapy some years ago, might help show how a person can practice the art of loving.

More than anyone I had ever met, Debra wanted to learn how to love. Yet she was almost as inept at loving as she was earnest about wanting to learn that art. In her case, we centered her efforts on listening. She practiced the art of listening to people. Listening to what other people said to her—their opinions, their observations, their beliefs—had been almost impossible for Debra. She was always interrupting friends with her own interpretations of what they told her. It took a great deal of discipline and concentration for her to listen to another person without passing judgments.

To aid herself in learning to listen to others, Debra began practicing other forms of listening. She practiced sitting quietly and listening to music. Even that simple activity proved impossible for her at first. Her impulse to be doing "something useful" nearly always overwhelmed her. The same impulse to do something useful made her efforts to sit and be quiet by herself almost futile. In time, however, Debra could concentrate longer and longer on music, herself, and others.

Little by little, Debra came to appreciate the people who surrounded her as well as herself. She found she really did not care to be around some people she once thought of as friends, but she also drew closer to people who before had appeared to share nothing with her. More than anything else, Debra started to see others as unique individuals, quite different from herself. She began to appreciate herself and others more and more for their attractive uniqueness. Her concentrated practice of careful listening made other people seek her as a friend. Debra still practices avidly. Her growth in love validates, in my mind, the effectiveness of the principles Erich Fromm so beautifully stated in his book, *The Art of Loving*.

The Art of Loving

Those of us who want to practice the **art of loving** must, according to Fromm, learn to see the world objectively. All of us see ourselves and the world around us from a subjective point of view. We are particularly

"Go along now. We'll resume our talk when you get back."

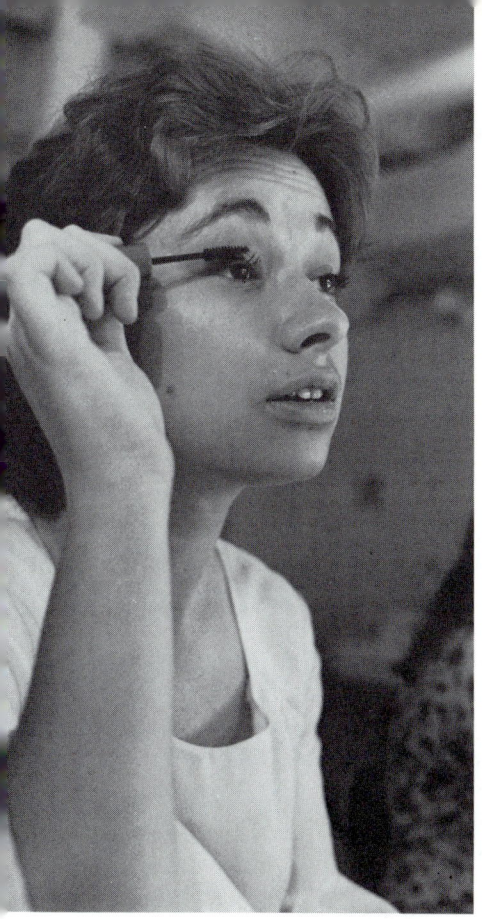

Many people believe that they must maintain another person's image of themselves if they are to be loved. (© Frank Siteman, left; © Eric A. Roth/Picture Cube, above)

subjective when we attempt to love other people: we see them as we would like them to be. Parents see offspring as the attractive, behaved, and obedient children they want them to be. Lovers see one another, not objectively, but rather as the image they always had of their eventual lover. Only with practice, Fromm tells us, can we begin to see through our own image of the person we want to love and look at the person we do love (Self-Quiz 11.1).

Practice in loving demands faith. We must believe in our love in order to perfect it. So long as we think another person loves us because of the person's image of us, and vice versa, we cannot really love and be loved. If a man thinks a woman loves him because of his ability to dominate her, he has no faith in her love. He must be willing to expose his "weaker" side to her and see their love survive in spite of the exposure. Or, a woman who thinks she is loved only because she is physically attractive must allow her lover to see her other qualities and stop emphasizing her appearance.

Fromm concludes:

> To love means to commit oneself without guarantee, to give oneself completely in the hope that our love will produce love in the loved person. Love is an act of faith, and whoever is of little faith is also of little love.

Self-Quiz 11.1 — Seeing Others Objectively

This test is designed to help you discover how objectively you see other people. Next to each statement place the number 1, 2, 3, 4, or 5—depending on how characteristic each statement is of you. Continue the process for each of the statements. Then total your score.

5 strongly characteristic of me
4 moderately characteristic of me
3 neutral
2 moderately uncharacteristic of me
1 strongly uncharacteristic of me

____ 1. I never know if I will be attracted to people just by looking at them.
____ 2. When I buy gifts for friends, I buy something they will like whether I like the gift or not.
____ 3. When friends' behavior surprises me, I take an immediate interest in their unusual behavior and ask them about it.
____ 4. People I know intimately change a great deal during the course of our relationship.
____ 5. No matter how much I have heard about people before I meet them, I do not pass judgment on them based on that hearsay.
____ 6. I like to read about people who are different from myself.
____ 7. I sometimes find myself fascinated by people I dislike.
____ 8. I am not easily persuaded by even the best salesperson.
____ 9. I fall in love gradually and, consequently, my affections last for a long time.
____ 10. People do take advantage of me, but I don't mind so long as they do not overdo it.
____ 11. My friends are quite unlike me.

____ TOTAL SCORE

40–55 You score with those students who appear to be most open toward other people, seeing them relatively objectively.
26–39 You score with most students who took this test. This means you see other people about as well as they see you.
11–25 You score with those who appear to be least open toward other people.

Can one say more about the practice of faith? Someone else might; if I were a poet or a preacher, I might try. But since I am not either of these, I cannot even try to say more about the practice of faith, but am sure that anyone who is really concerned can learn to have faith as a child learns to walk. (4)

THE BEHAVIORISTIC APPROACH

The behaviorists, as usual, shun any theory that does not emerge from controlled studies of behavior. In their attempts to study love relationships, then, the behaviorists establish experiments to help us understand this behavior. An obvious question, of interest to most of us, that can be answered by careful observation is: Do physically attractive people have a definite advantage in love and friendship relationships? The social psychologists' early attempts to answer this question were thwarted because most people, when asked if physical attractiveness were their top priority in selecting a companion, said no. They claimed they looked for characteristics such as intelligence, sincerity, and friendliness first. Physical attraction, they said, ranked quite low on their scale of priorities. Future studies, however, told a different story. Apparently what people *say* about physical attraction and how they *act* toward physically attractive people are not the same. (5)

The study most often cited to point out the discrepancy between how people say they react toward physically attractive people and how they actually respond was performed at the University of Minnesota. Social psychologists told university freshmen that they were going to a computer dance. In fact, the computer did not match the couples at the dance. Instead they were matched randomly. The ruse gave the social psychologists a chance to rate each person who attended the dance on their physical attractiveness. Then, during an intermission, each person was asked, on a questionnaire, how well they liked their dates. A strong correlation developed between physical attraction, as rated by the psychologists, and the desire of dance participants to see a partner again. Those who had attractive dates liked them best and most wanted to see them again. (6)

Plain People

The studies about attractive people naturally leads us to ask about plain people. What do the social psychologists say about people who lack physical attractiveness? One study searched for a relationship between attractiveness and dating frequency. Among the 60 females studied in a college dormitory setting, dating was least frequent among those who were rated less attractive physically. The same did not hold true for the dormitory men who were studied. Apparently no relationship exists between physical attractiveness and dating frequency for men. (7)

A similar study had some interesting aspects. It seems that attractive people were most often rejected by members of their own sex. Whether out of jealousy or because they became self-centered over their good looks, attractive people received the most rejections by members of their own sex. Moderately attractive people were most accepted. Plain people were neither accepted or rejected, they were just ignored. Most people had no reaction to the people described as plain. (8)

Plain people tend to withdraw into themselves or, to raise their self-esteem, attach themselves to attractive people. Men and women both seem to think they enhance their own attractiveness when they are seen with an attractive partner. Researchers in one study attempted to assess whether people enhance personal attractiveness by associating with handsome people. Psychologists Sigall and Landy asked college students to assess their impressions of a young man who was accompanied by a young woman. In some cases, the woman was made to look attractive; at other times she looked disheveled. Sometimes the young man's partner was described as a girl friend; at other times she was introduced as someone unrelated to him. The results of the study pointed out clearly that the man gained stature in the eyes of the student judges when they thought he had an attractive girl friend. Clearly, our tendency to think we will be more attractive when associated with someone attractive is realistic (Case 11.2). (9)

● Case 11.2

When they read the piece of research about people who try to enhance their own prestige by associating with attractive people, some students become disturbed. "Is there anything wrong with that?" an overweight young woman asked me recently. The answer is *no*. My own experience, in fact, suggests that the tendency for attractive and plain people to become friends gives both partners much that is valuable. Possibly more than any other friendship, the relationship between Carol and Lenore pointed up how two different people can complement one another.

Few people understood the relationship. Carol had a trim figure and an effervescent personality. She was always in a crowd of friends and admirers. Lenore, by contrast, looked and dressed like an old women. Her plain looks kept most young men away, and even female classmates kept their distance. Yet Carol found some strong attraction to Lenore that even she could not explain. The two of them were almost always together.

The effect of their friendship on Lenore could not be measured. She felt a great deal of self-confidence grow from her relationship with Carol. Lenore was proud someone as popular and talented as Carol would choose her for a friend. Another important effect of their friendship for Lenore was her opportunity to see the private side of Carol. She got to know that part of Carol that doubted herself and found out how much life frightened Carol. Carol even admitted she used her effervescent exterior to hide many insecurities and that she formed the friendship with Lenore because she envied Lenore's apparent calm and peaceful manner.

Lenore's relationship with Carol, then, was more than a simple social crutch. It also helped Lenore, little by little, to realize her own potential as an important and needed person.

Love Is the Answer

No one will be surprised to hear that a primary difficulty psychologists face in their attempts to study love is the multitude of definitions available. No two definitions match, and more important many definitions of love seem to be describing totally different feelings and experiences. When Eric Segal said, "Love is never having to say you're sorry," he had something quite different in mind from the writer Samuel Daniel who said, "Love is a sickness full of woes." In view of the many definitions, behaviorists have had some obvious difficulty attempting to measure the behavior we call love.

Dr. Zick Rubin, a psychologist, did some pioneering work in this area of confused definitions. He took the many definitions and reduced them to a series of statements that summarized the various meanings. The statements were copied and passed out to nearly 200 students who were asked to place the name of their boyfriend/girlfriend or platonic friend next to each statement. This process allowed Rubin to separate those statements about love that referred to liking from those that referred to loving.

The final scale established two measures—a measure of liking and a measure of loving. Three components emerged on the love scale: attachment, caring, and intimacy. A statement that would indicate caring might

be, "If I were lonely, my first thoughts would be to seek _____ out." "I would do almost anything for _____," is a typical caring statement. An intimacy statement is, "I feel that I can confide in _____ about virtually everything." In contrast to these love statements, the liking statements measured such things as adjustment, maturity, good judgment, and intelligence. (10)

Rubin warns us to be careful in using his **love scale**. Because it is still relatively untested, the scale should not be taken too literally. It may be that the scale measures infatuation rather than love—most of the statements would typically be expressed by young lovers rather than those in a lifetime relationship. Still, the work introduces to psychology an area previous investigators thought they might never penetrate. We can hope that future refinements will bring us an even a better understanding of this most important emotion.

Hard to Get

Much has been written and discussed about women and the **hard-to-get** game. Traditional wisdom says that unless women make themselves into a prize of sorts they will never attract men. This conventional approach to friendship and love is questionable, especially in this day of sexual liberation.

To gain some perspective on the question, a team of psychologists asked a large group of college men why they preferred women who were "hard to get." The men's preference for hard-to-get women, they said, was based on the feeling that such women were actually more valuable, had more choices of partners because of their looks, and because the men thought they could gain prestige by a relationship with them. More available women were perceived as desperate for a man, anxious for marriage, and generally undesirable.

The study only gave the team of social psychologists some of their answers however. They decided to look beneath the answers to see if the male behavior matched the male comments. The team recruited a group of male students at the University of Wisconsin and told them they would be part of a computer-dating experiment. They were asked to fill out questionnaires and come the following day to the counseling center. The next day they were given the folders of women who had presumably studied the men's questionnaires and responded to them. The folders were actually filled out by the counselors and carefully arranged to make the women appear easy-to-get in one case, hard-to-get in another case, and selectively hard-to-get in a third case. The results proved interesting. The most elusive and least elusive women had little appeal for the men, while far and away the most desirable women were the ones who described themselves as hard-to-get as far as everyone except the student rating her was concerned. When males thought they could be attractive to someone who was quite discriminating, they became most interested. (11)

THE HUMANISTIC APPROACH

Most of us spend most of our lives worrying about the future and fretting about the past. We project ourselves into the future to worry about what career choice is right for us, whether or not we have the ability to obtain a certain degree, or meeting someone who cares about us. When we look backward, we worry that we may have offended someone close to us, that we did not pay enough attention to our work, or that we have wasted too much of our lives. Not only can such projections forward and backward cause us excess worry, they also remove us from the concerns and joys of the present moment.

In contrast with past and future the present moment has fewer anxieties and is the one place where we can live life most intensely. A great many humanists believe we should try to live in the present. Fritz Perls was one such humanist.

> The formula of anxiety is very simple: anxiety is the gap between the now and the then. If you are **in the now,** you can't be anxious, because the excitement flows immediately into ongoing spontaneous activity. If you are in the now, you are creative, you are inventive. If you have your senses ready, if you have your eyes and ears open, like every small child, you find a solution. (12)

Living spontaneously "in the now" can reduce anxiety about the past and future and enhance a love relationship. (© Joel Gordon)

I believe that life in the now not only reduces anxiety, but also is the beginning of love (Case 11.3). *The Risk of Loving*, by my wife and me, is based on that premise.

> The most memorable times in our life are those rare moments when our whole being centers on the here and now. The experiences we value most are those when the immediate present dominates our thought, gestures and words. Memories of these moments remain close to consciousness; it takes no effort to recall them; they become a permanent part of our life. (13)

● Case 11.3

For a person who has never tried to stay in the here and now without being distracted by the future and past, the thought can seem quite foolish. "Of course, I can keep my thoughts in the present," is the first reaction of many. The ability to actually do that is difficult, however. At least it was for Dianne, a middle-aged mother of four, who lived on the edge of anxiety most of her day. As part of her therapy, I asked Dianne to practice an exercise that helped bring her out of her anxious thoughts about the future and past. This exercise has helped many people transform anxiety into excitement.

I asked Dianne to practice an exercise every evening, even though at first she could only sustain the practice for about five minutes. On her evening walk, she was to repeat to herself silently just what she was doing, seeing, and thinking. As she walked down the street through her middle-class neighborhood, she would first notice the neatly clipped bushes her neighbors maintained. As she did, she would say to herself, "I am looking at the lovely green brushes across the street." A distracting thought like, "I wonder how long I can sustain this kind of thing?" would pop into her mind. She soon learned to respond to such distractions by saying, "I was just distracted by a fear that I could not keep this mental dialogue going very long." She would then return to other observations that kept her in contact with the immediate moment.

This apparently senseless exercise began to affect Dianne after only a few weeks of practice. She could then feel herself becoming less anxious as soon as she began her evening walks. In time, the walks served as a relief from her anxious days. As the relief became more obvious, Dianne was able to stay longer and longer in the present moment. Her love of the anxious-free moments let her introduce the exercise into the rest of her day. Her waits in doctor's offices, in lines at the drug store, for class to begin, all became valuable periods for bringing herself into the present moment. She even found, in time, that when she could concentrate on the work at hand study periods were no longer anxious. More important, her interaction with friends gained more vitality when she stayed with them in the present moment and did not let her thoughts stray so easily. And like so many other people I have worked with over the years, Dianne found, in her ability to stay with the present moment, the beginnings of her search for love.

The Sounds of Silence

Though life in the present moment removes us from anxiety, it also makes us intensely aware of what we are thinking and feeling. The young man who lives in the present moment will see how much he wants to leave home and strike out on his own. The mother of a small child might discover there are times when she becomes intensely angry at her infant. The business executive who looks carefully at the present moment may see how much he or she would like to leave the pressure of work for a simpler life.

Lovers who risk entering the present moment begin to hear the **sounds of silence.** They hear inner voices speak words that were never expressed. One young lover realizes she never told her friend how intensely she needs his love. A middle-aged lover never expressed his occasional longing for freedom from the restrictions of his relationship. A young man without love realizes, in the honesty of the here and now, that he never expressed his loneliness to anyone. Again, from *Risk of Loving:*

> This silence—the lack of expression where expression should be—creates a void in our life. We actually experience an emptiness. Something we honestly wanted to experience we did not experience. We somehow could not allow ourselves to say the things we longed to say. (14)

More important, the unexpressed words and feelings tell us where we fail to experience the fulfillment of our love. Any time we leave unexpressed any deeply felt emotions we also fall short of making honest contact with those we love. Naturally, we do communicate those deeply felt emotions in one way or another. Our hidden feelings may seep out in our tone of voice, an inadvertent frown, or an involuntary lack of eye contact. Others may interpret our body language in a myriad of ways, but unfortunately, they will never know about the secret parts of ourselves unless we take the risk of communicating those secrets—the risk of loving.

The Risk of Loving

The attempt to live in the now projects any person in search for love toward a risk of being hurt. A mother may be too embarrassed to risk expressing her deep affection for an adolescent son who might rebuff her. A brother may resist showing the weakness of a warm feeling for his sister. And, of course, lovers may find it awkward to verbally express the depth of their love for one another. It is easy to put off the exposure of feelings that might lead to pain.

> We think we cannot afford to make any sort of personal statement which might commit ourselves. We stay aloof and wait for the other person to speak first. If we were to take the first risk in making ourselves vulnerable, we could be hurt. We decide to wait until some other time before

Often, brothers and sisters face risks when they express affection toward one another. (Peter Vandermark)

taking any chance of speaking personally. After all, this particular occasion is really not the best for the kind of personal conversation we anticipate. We should probably wait until some other time before risking any exposure of our true feelings. 15)

Yet, when love feelings are strong enough to persist, the occasional angry feeling, the awkward feeling, and the embarrassing feeling all have the power to help those we love know us better. As long as we hide true feelings, we block any true flow of expression. Only when we risk expressing those feelings we would rather keep to ourselves can we grow closer to those we love (Self-Quiz 11.2).

Peace

Any time we take the risk of expressing feeling to a loved one, we also show that special person a part of ourselves. If our hidden feeling is a bit of anger we free ourselves to show, we let a loved one know we are a person who can be angry at times. The sensitive word, the moody irritation, the awkward warmth are all part of our true self.

Each time we show someone close to us the truth about ourselves, we can relax a little more in that person's presence. Our freedom to be angry helps us feel comfortable expressing anger instead of spending energy pretending to be in control. We let go of that pretense and capture a bit more peace in our lives. Each time we can reveal an embarrassing fear, an awkward feeling of tenderness, a frustrated need to be alone, we let go of more pretense. Those risky expressions give us a little more chance to be at ease and bring us a step closer to peace with our self and other people.

Self-Quiz 11.2 — Interpersonal Risks

This test contains a number of statements about personal attitudes. Read each statement and choose the alternative that best describes your attitude by checking the proper box to the left of the statement. Answer all of the statements.

Often	Occasionally	Seldom	
☐	☐	☐	1. I have a great fear of intimacy.
☐	☐	☐	2. I manipulate people to gain their attention.
☐	☐	☐	3. Personal expression of feeling makes me intensely emotional.
☐	☐	☐	4. My friends will let me have my own way.
☐	☐	☐	5. I bear a grudge against former friends.
☐	☐	☐	6. I need immense support from my friends.
☐	☐	☐	7. My feelings embarrass me.
☐	☐	☐	8. I would rather lie to friends than embarrass them.

This test cannot tell you to what extent you fail to take interpersonal risks, but does tell you how you compare with others who took the same test. To total your score, give yourself 3 points for each time you checked "often" on the test, 2 points for each "occasionally," and 1 point for each "seldom." Add up the total number of points and compare that total with the following scale.

19–24 The percentage of students scoring in this range was small. A score this high might indicate an inability to take risks in relationships.
12–18 The vast majority of students taking the test score in this range. Since your score matches theirs, you probably have a sensitivity for feeling expression.
8–11 You score with those students who are most free with their feelings.

As we risk allowing another person to see us as we are, we also begin to accept other people in their uniqueness. We gradually give up our search for the perfect person who exists only in our mind and begin look at the person before us. By letting go of our need to relate only to those who fit our image of a friend, a daughter, or a lover, we gain more peace. We spend our time and energy trying to understand those we love rather than forcing them to conform to an image that exists only in our mind.

> In the peace which comes to us in the presence of this [particular] person we realize that we need not speak of him as perfect or imperfect, good or bad. Trying to squeeze this real person into categories shows itself a foolish enterprise. We are not asked to pass a verdict. We cannot judge this mystery. And when we discover that we need not appraise, even if just for now, a heavy daily tension relaxes. For a while at least, traits which we have always measured and judged wanting become nothing more than elements of the beautiful mystery which is the person before us. (16)

CONCLUSION

Our three perspectives in this chapter have given us three distinct ways of looking at love and friendship. Erich Fromm, a neo-Freudian, impressed on us the importance of considering love as an art. If we think of love as a feeling alone, we become victim to the whims of our emotions. If we think of love as an art and practice that art seriously, we can become more skilled in our relationships. However, Fromm warns us, we must practice the art of love as we would practice any other art—with discipline, concentration, and dedication.

The behaviorists study our need to form relationships through scientifically controlled experiments, which tell them just how we react toward one another. For example, they discovered a good bit about our attraction to handsome people. Though we say that physical beauty stands low on our list of priorities in an interpersonal relationship, we actually want to be with attractive people and actively seek out their friendship. Behaviorists are performing studies that are beginning to tell us just how we act and react in interpersonal relationships.

Finally, many humanists believe that the here and now is more important than the past and future. They tell us that we can escape most of our painful anxieties by learning to live in the immediate moment. It strikes me that the move into the here and now can also be the beginning of love. When we truly listen to ourselves, we become aware of the many things we fail to express to one another. When we express risky reelings, in the name of love and friendship, we are on the long path to intimacy.

SUMMARY

1. Erich Fromm pointed out that most people do not think they can learn anything new about love. Yet, loving is an art that requires the same practice as any other art. Those who develop the discipline, the concentration, and the patience necessary for the art of loving will begin to

see themselves and others more accurately. Such an objective view of any relationship brings it to perfection.
2. The behaviorists search for their answers in the rigors of scientific studies. They discovered that most people claim physical attractiveness is not a priority with them in their search for a companion. Yet, studies show that we do look for the attractive person to relate with interpersonally, partly because we like the status we gain when accompanied by someone attractive. Finally, behaviorists just now have begun to deal with the many conflicting definitions of love. By working with these definitions, one social psychologist developed a love scale that may help us understand the mutual attractions that produce love and liking.
3. Most humanists value life in the present moment because it helps us escape from unnecessary anxieties. That experience of the immediate also, I believe, makes us aware of many thoughts and feelings we so often leave unexpressed. Once we become aware of such feelings, we can risk expressing them to those we love. In turn, an open expression of feeling, when prudent, can make us more at ease with others and more at peace with ourselves.

KEY TERMS

interpersonal
standing in love
discipline
concentration
patience

art of loving
love scale
hard-to-get
in the now
sounds of silence

STUDY QUESTIONS

1. To the extent that love is an art form, how might you practice that art? What specifically might you do to bring yourself closer to other people?
2. Think of several friends. List them mentally in terms of how close you feel to them. Does their physical appearance affect how you feel toward them?
3. Name as many different ways the word love can be used as you can think of.
4. Can you think of how you might use worries about the future or regrets about the past to avoid some immediate thoughts and feelings? Be specific.
5. Think of a time when an expression of love meant taking a chance. Does love always imply risking? Discuss.

ADDITIONAL READING

Berscheid, E., and Walster, E. *Interpersonal Attraction.* Reading, Mass.: Addison-Wesley, 1969.

Fromm, Erich. *The Art of Loving.* New York: Bantam, 1956.

Pepitone, A. *Attraction and Hostility.* New York: Atherton Press, 1964.

Rogers, Carl R. *Becoming Partners: Marriage and Its Alternatives.* New York: Delacorte, 1972.

Rubin, Zick. *Liking and Loving: An Invitation to Social Psychology.* New York: Holt, Rinehart, and Winston, 1973.

Shaver, K. G.: *An Introduction to Attribution Processes.* Cambridge, Mass.: Winthrop, 1975.

Shostrom, Everett L., and Kavanaugh, James. *Between Man and Woman: The Dynamics of Interpersonal Relationships.* Los Angeles: Nash, 1971.

Simons, J., and Reidy, J. *The Risk of Loving.* New York: Seabury, 1973.

Winch, Robert F. *Mate Selection.* New York: Harper & Row, 1958.

Chapter Twelve

Sex

OUTLINE

The Psychoanalytic Approach
    Sex Roles
    Sexual Conflict
    Homosexuality

The Behavioristic Approach
    The Kinsey Studies
    The Kinsey Results
    Masters and Johnson
    The Masters and Johnson Results

The Humanistic Approach
    Sex Without Love
    The New Puritanism
    Eros

Conclusion

LEARNING OBJECTIVES

After reading this chapter you should be able to:

1. Explain how Jung's theory of archetypes explains sex roles and sexual conflict.
2. Discuss Jung's attitude toward homosexuality.
3. Explain the significance of the Kinsey studies.
4. Understand the purpose of the Masters and Johnson studies.
5. Understand what Rollo May means by the new puritanism.
6. Explain why May believes we should return to a more passionate form of love.

Chapter Twelve

Daphne and I talked about a great many things the day she came to see me in my office. Her hand nervously rubbed the arm of her chair as she attempted to work up courage to come to the point. Then, without warning, she opened up the topic that troubled her.

"I'm just not very happy sexually," she said as she lowered her voice and leaned forward in her chair. "Even though I love my husband very much, I just never look forward to having sex with him."

"I can tell you that you are not alone," I replied. "I talk to lots of people, male and female, who lack any sexual excitement in their lives."

"But that shouldn't happen to Dave and me." Daphne sat upright in her chair. "We have really modern attitudes toward sex. We read about sex constantly. Neither of us are embarrassed about discussing our sexual attitudes. I mean, there is no reason whatsoever for us to be having troubles sexually."

Though Daphne could not see the connection immediately, part of her problem sexually was her preoccupation with the flood of recent literature on sexual mechanics. In fact, the modern preoccupation with sexuality has led Rollo May, a humanist, to conclude that our society has managed to lose the passion sex once held for people by studying it too closely. We have become aloof and indifferent by reading the latest how-to book, searching for the latest position, and striving for the perfect orgasm. We can only recapture passion, May says, if we give up control and yield to spontaneity.

The behaviorists have conducted scientific studies in the area of sexuality, which have helped us understand our behavior. Of all the studies produced, however, two stand out as most significant. The early work of Alfred C. Kinsey has helped us look past our fear of discussing sex to see that we are, as a nation, far more active sexually than any of us might have guessed. The other important study that has had an impact on us nationally was conducted by Masters and Johnson. These two clinicians observed over six hundred people reach orgasm. Out of their studies came a host of clinical data that dispelled a countless number of myths about orgasm.

We will begin this chapter with a look at the work of Carl Jung. His interests centered on our personality. He saw in each person a combination of psychologically male and female attitudes. The healthy person, according to Jung, maintains a balance between masculine and feminine traits. If we fight this balance, we can only harm ourselves psychologically.

THE PSYCHOANALYTIC APPROACH

After he separated from Sigmund Freud, Carl Jung developed his own psychoanalytic theories. Prominent among these theories was Jung's belief in the archetypes, discussed in chapter nine. However, to refresh your memory, the archetypes are image traces we possess at birth. These memory traces that we inherit from our ancestors predispose us to understand events in the world around us. Since the image of "mother" is a significant part of our history, for example, we come into the world with a latent image of mother. And when this latent image of mother contacts the real person of our own mother we instinctively know how to respond to her.

In this chapter, we are most interested in Jung's sexual archetypes. He noticed that biologically we are all, male and female, composed of masculine and feminine sex hormones. Jung carried this biological fact one step further in noting that we are also composed of masculine and femine psychological attitudes. The male carries around within himself a female archetype that Jung called the **anima.** The feminine personality is balanced by a masculine archetype that Jung called the **animus.** Hall and Nordby, Jungian scholars, explain Jung's concept of the **persona.**

> Jung called the persona the "outward face" of the psyche, because it is that face which the world sees. The "inward face" he called the anima in males and the animus in females. The anima archetype is the feminine side of the male psyche; the animus archetype is the masculine side of the female psyche. Every person has qualities of the opposite sex, not only in the biological sense that man and woman secrete both male and female sex hormones but also in a psychological sense of attitudes and feelings. (1)

Like all the other archetypes, the memory trace of women in the psyche of men developed over the centuries because of the constant contact between males and females. The same holds true for women. Their contact with men helped them develop characteristics of the opposite sex and also produce appropriate responses. Jung believed that these archetypes help men and women understand each other.

Sex Roles

In this generation, we see both men and women attempting to break away from the **sex roles** that have constricted them for so long. Women are growing more and more career oriented. The women's movement ac-

More than ever before, men and women are attempting to break sex-role stereotypes. © 1976 Joel Gordon, above; © 1979 Susan Lapides, right)

counts for some of the change, but an even larger shift in social attitudes seems to underlie the movement itself. Men seem more interested in the growth and development of their families. They also seem much more willing to share household tasks once considered "women's work" only. As a friend of mine recently said, "We can measure the true impact of sex-role changes by counting the number of men who clean the toilet bowl."

Jung would surely have been pleased to see our social progress toward dropping sex-role rigidity. For not only did he see the male's willingness to perform traditionally feminine tasks as something worthwhile, he also felt that such flexibility is critical to every man's mental health. He also believed that the woman who shows courage and strength when appropriate gives her personality psychological balance.

Hall and Nordby explain the importance of the balance.

> If the personality is to be well adjusted and harmoniously balanced, the feminine side of a man's personality and the masculine side of a woman's personality must be allowed to express themselves in consciousness and behavior. If a man exhibits only masculine traits, his feminine traits remain unconscious and therefore these traits remain undeveloped and primitive. This gives the unconscious a quality of weakness and impressionability. That is why the most virile-appearing and virile-acting man is often weak and submissive inside. A woman who exhibits excessive

femininity in her external life would have the unconscious qualities of stubbornness or willfulness, qualities that are often present in man's outer behavior. (2)

The fact that we have made some strides in casting off sex roles does not mean we have overcome the tendency altogether. In fact, some research done by Deanna Kuhn, Sharon Nash, and Laura Brucken suggests that sex stereotyping still begins as early as two years.

These researchers worked with 72 middle-class nursery school students. The youngsters were introduced to two cardboard dolls named Lisa and Michael. To determine the degree to which these children had already developed sexual stereotypes, they were asked what the dolls, Lisa and Michael, might say or do.

The results among these two- and three-year-old children showed definite sex-role orientations. They said they thought girls, but not boys, like to help Mom, to talk a lot, and say, "I need help." The boys characterized girls as slow, with a tendency to cry and complain, "You hurt my feelings." The girls saw themselves as liking to play inside, look nice, and give kisses. The children all saw boys as likely to help father, build things, and say, "I can hit you." This research clearly supports Carl Jung's belief that males and females even as young as two hide from their anima or animus. However, Jung himself might have been surprised to see how strong the tendency has already become at such an early age. (3)

Sexual Conflict

"Every man carries within him the eternal image of the woman," Carl Jung tells us, "not the image of this or that particular woman, but a definite feminine image.

> This image is fundamentally unconscious, an hereditary factor of primordial origin engraved in the living organic system of the man, an imprint or archetype of all the ancestral experiences of the female, a deposit, as it were, of all the impressions ever made by woman. . . . Since this image is unconscious, it is always unconsciously projected upon the person of the beloved, and is one of the chief reasons for passionate attraction or aversion. (4)

For Jung, the battle of the sexes is rooted in the sexual archetype. For the man, the archetype of woman that he inherits at birth unconsciously establishes a standard against which he will judge all women. To the extent that one particular woman responds to his archetype, he becomes attracted, even passionately, to that woman. Those women who violate his archetype give men a feeling of strong aversion.

The same attraction and repulsion exists in women. They search for those men who fit their archetype. And more than simply causing immediate attractions and repulsions, the archetypes also make trouble in sex-

"Because, Edgar, in all these fifty-odd years you've never once asked me to do anything kinky!"

ual relationships that become intimate. As long as men and women live together, they will continue to find fresh discrepancies between their image of lover and their actual lover. And since the archetype remains unconscious, men and women must forever struggle with the gap that exists between the image and the reality.

Jung told us that we grow to the extent that we can accept our archetype. Men who can allow themselves to become warm, sensitive, and delicate will become more at ease with themselves. They will also see their sexual partner in real terms, understand her better, and grow closer to that person rather than demand that she fulfill some archetypical image. The same holds true for women. To the extent that they can accept the strong, tough, and courageous parts of their personality, they can better accept themselves and their lovers (Case 12.1).

● Case 12.1

The woman who hides from her animus is trying to suppress part of herself. No matter how much the society around her tells her that women should be weak and submissive, every woman possesses the traits of courage and strength. Women who hide from their strength usually repress their aggressive tendencies, but once aggressiveness is pushed into the unconscious it can emerge in subtle and uncontrolled ways.

In this context I remember Grace, a sensitive young woman with a warm and engaging personality. Grace appeared to be the sort of woman who would attract men without any trouble. She possessed a flair for conversation and enjoyed intimacy, both emotional and physical. Yet, Grace could not seem to sustain a relationship. By the time she was thirty, Grace had been married and divorced three times.

When she came to me for therapy, Grace felt that she was on the verge of despair. For several sessions she talked compulsively about her bad luck with men. I listened patiently because I felt she needed to release a great deal of suppressed emotion. In time, however, I discovered that Grace seemed almost incapable of dialogue. By a series of interruptions, silent pauses, and uninterrupted monologues, Grace managed to control our conversation. I even had to try several times before I could finally stop her talk long enough to tell her how completely she dominated the conversation. She finally did hear me, however, and the shock of the message upset her considerably.

Once Grace did hear my evaluation, she began to see how she controlled not only our conversation, but also the men in her life. Her parents had taught her that women can only be attractive to men if they appear weak and submissive. That lesson was so important to Grace that she completely repressed her aggressiveness behind her attempts to become feminine. In Jungian terms, she hid her animus. But the animus cannot be totally repressed. In one way or another, it seeps out into the conscious world. Therefore, although Grace was not consciously aware of her strength and did not exercise it, it slipped out unconsciously in distorted forms. Her domination of our conversation was only one sign of the animus' refusal to be restrained.

Grace and I worked together to help her accept herself as a combination of weaknesses and strengths. She gradually came to experience her aggressiveness and let others know she could take charge in situations. Her friends liked the aggressive part of Grace when it was more open. Many men found the new strength in Grace quite attractive. This time, however, Grace took much more time before she chose to marry again. But her fourth marriage was her final one. On her tenth wedding anniversary, she wrote and told me she had never been happier and never more herself.

Homosexuality

Hall and Nordby believe that the animus and anima are often underdeveloped in people in our culture.

> One reason for this difference is that Western civilization seems to place a high value on conformity and to disparage feminity in men and masculinity in women. The disparagement begins in childhood when "sissies" and "tomboys" are ridiculed. Boys are expected to conform to a culturally specified masculine role and girls to a feminine role. Thus, the persona takes precedence over and stifles the anima or animus. (5)

Jung warned us about such suppression of the archetype. Men who become overly concerned with projecting a masculine image can grow intensely fearful of their own feminine tendencies. Such a fear can make them bigoted toward homosexuals and, at times, lose control over themselves when their masculinity is challenged. The same holds true of women who press themselves too hard to appear feminine. They bury their masculine characteristics in their unconscious where it can become unruly and hostile. Women who control their masculinity too much often have violent personalities hidden beneath a calm and helpless-appearing exterior. Women who hide from their animus, as we already disussed, also tend to dominate men in subtle and disguised ways.

Homosexuality, for Jung, is no more than an unusual balance between the anima or animus and the personality. That is, most people in his society did not find emotional fulfillment in the choice of a same-sex partner. However, where homosexuality gave people stability, Jung thought the homosexual choice was appropriate. What Jung feared was the person who, under the pressure of social constraint, buried his true sexual feelings in his unconscious. Then the hidden anima could explode in distorted forms of homosexuality. Or any young woman, for example, placed under extreme pressure to avoid revealing masculine traits could relieve her pent-up feelings by turning to a homosexual life style. Under such distorting pressures, homosexuality can become destructive, but where the same-sex choice emerges naturally, Jung considered it healthy and fulfilling.

The Jungian attitude toward homosexuality is supported by the work of Elaine Crovitz, a medical psychologist who helps screen applicants for sex-change operations at Duke University. She finds it ironic that in this

Jung believed the homosexual life style could be appropriate for people with an unusual balance between the anima or animus and their personality. (Joel Gordon)

day, when a person's sex is supposed to make less and less difference, more people than ever are applying for sex-change operations. She and the other screening personnel at Duke have come to believe that many people applying to have the sex operation are not genuine **transsexuals.** Instead, they are often troubled persons looking for a medical solution to their problems.

True transsexuals do exist, however. Crovitz and her colleagues see the medical transsexual as a person who wound up in the wrong body physically. Most of them try to conform to their bodies' demands, but find it impossible. Sex is not the primary source of their anguish. Instead, they need the mental assurance of having a body that complements their mind.

Once people pass the rigid psychological screening at Duke's clinic, they are given hormones of the opposite sex and asked to live one and a half years as a member of the opposite sex. "That's really the critical test," says Crovitz, "that allows us to see if they can adapt. At the end, the surgery is a confirmation of a change that has already occurred on a psychological basis."

Jung told us that the balance we maintain between male and female traits can be unhealthy. We can bury our anima/animus and create serious psychological problems. A good number of people with such problems show up at the Duke University clinic. On the other hand, what would be a healthy balance for many people between the masculine and feminine parts of the personality can oppose other people's physical make-up. The result can be homosexuality, bisexuality, or even transvestitism. The Duke University clinic, then, performs a great service by helping those who find themselves psychologically out of phase with their bodies. (6)

THE BEHAVIORISTIC APPROACH

Some of the most important research ever undertaken by scientific psychologists was reported in the field of sexual behavior. The first two studies, performed by Alfred C. Kinsey and his colleagues, revealed our sexual behavior to us. The studies helped us look behind the secrecy that surrounded sexual behavior patterns to see how people perform sexually. The other significant study, produced by the sexologist team of Masters and Johnson, looked at the sexual act itself. They concentrated their efforts on the physiological responses that occur during **orgasm,** the physical climax of sexual excitement.

The Kinsey Studies

Before the Kinsey studies (the first was in 1948), the vast majority of people were inhibited enough to make studies of normal sexual behavior lim-

From *Non-Being and Somethingness: Selections from the Comic Strip* Inside Woody Allen, by Woody Allen, drawn by Stuart Hample. Copyright © 1978 by IWA Enterprises and Hackenbush Productions, Inc. Reprinted by permission of Random House, Inc.

ited and unconvincing. Possibly only the Kinsey study, with its massive research, could have had power enough to overcome the sexual taboo that then existed. Before publishing his two reports, the first one on males and the second one on females, Kinsey and his coworkers worked for 30 years on their interviews. They talked to over 18,000 people about their sexual experiences. The talks covered 521 topics.

When the first of the studies was released in 1948, a storm of controversy emerged. Kinsey was attacked as immoral, unethical, and irreligious. A great wave of disbelief swept the country at first. Few imagined that sexual behavior could possibly match the picture Kinsey painted. A great many people did not want to believe the moral overtones the study suggested to them. Kinsey's studies were also attacked as inaccurate. Critics were quick to show that the sample studied, no matter how large, did not represent a cross-section of the country, that Kinsey could only interview those willing to talk about sexual matters with strangers, and that questionable interviewing techniques were employed in the study. Yet the study has withstood the test of time. Subsequent studies have shown Kinsey's work to have a high degree of accuracy. And even today, decades later, the study is the best one produced to help us understand the sexual behavior of our society.

The Kinsey Results

No summary of Kinsey's work is possible. The incredible amount of data overwhelms anyone who even flips through the pages of his two studies. However, a few noteworthy pieces of his research might be mentioned to give you the flavor of the work. The range of the work covered six major forms of sexual outlet: masturbation, spontaneous nocturnal orgasm, heterosexual petting, heterosexual coitus, homosexual relationships, and animal contacts. These forms of sexual contact were cross-indexed against the socioeconomic status of subjects, religious affiliation, religious devotedness, and educational background. Ironically, some of the most interesting findings occurred when Kinsey compared people with different educational backgrounds—grade school, high school, and college educations.

The data concerning **masturbation** (self-stimulation of the genitals) surprised and shocked many. Kinsey reported that over 95 percent of all males studied had masturbated. Less than 60 percent of the women interviewed had engaged in masturbation. Education had little effect on the frequency of male masturbation. However, women with a grade school education reported masturbation 34 percent of the time. That percentage rose to 59 percent for those with a high school education and 63 percent for college-educated women.

Kinsey defined heterosexual **petting** as any deliberate sexual arousal that does not lead to **coitus** (sexual intercourse). The most interesting aspect of this study concerned petting to orgasm—the contrast with the results on masturbation are striking. For women, 39 percent reported petting to orgasm and no difference of any significance occurred with education. The results for men were quite different. Their experience of petting to orgasm grew as educational background increased, with 61 percent of the college group, 32 percent of the high school group, and 16 percent of the grade school group reporting this behavior.

Premarital sexual intercourse declined as the education of the men studied grew. That is, the men with a college background had fewer premarital sexual experiences. For women, the results went in the other direction. The more education a woman experienced, the more likely she was to have premarital sex. Finally in the area of homosexual activity, Kinsey discovered that by age 45, 37 percent of the males and 13 percent of the females had some homosexual experience leading to orgasm. These few pages do not attempt to mention even a small percentage of the Kinsey results, only an idea of the sort of data he collected. I believe from this sample you can see why the study aroused so much emotion in a sexually restrictive society (Case 12.2). (7, 8)

● Case 12.2

I suppose no one will ever be able to measure accurately the impact of the Kinsey studies. We can say, however, that before those studies our society was dominated by myths about sexuality. Kinsey did not put to rest all the myths and half-truths, but he did expose many of them. The fact that our society was far more active sexually than anyone supposed relieved a great many people of guilt feelings and self-doubts, and no one can thank Kinsey enough for that.

A friend of mine, who worked parttime in a home for adolescent boys, told me about the impact of the report on those young men. "You could feel the atmosphere lighten as soon as the report was released," he told me one day.

"Those kids, most of them in the turmoil of their adolescence, seemed to take a new lease on life." Most of them masturbated compulsively, and a great many had engaged in homosexual acts of one kind or another. Yet none had had the freedom to talk to one another about their actions or their guilt feelings. The statistics in the Kinsey report provided the openness they needed. They could look at the numbers of people involved sexually in the same ways they were and relax a great deal from the stress they had endured from feeling they were abnormal. Undoubtedly, millions of others in all walks of life experienced the same relief.

Masters and Johnson

Another significant study in the area of human sexuality was carried out by Masters and Johnson. Their study, unlike the Kinsey studies, concerned the physiology of the sexual response. They were interested in measuring the sexual responses of men and women in the laboratory setting. They worked with 382 female and 312 male volunteers. Once again, the study could never be reproduced in these few pages, but I will attempt to convey the flavor of their research and findings. (9)

Masters and Johnson spent time with each subject gathering background data. Their interest did not focus on the data itself, but the data gave them an understanding of their subjects and helped them establish a sense of trust. They then observed the men and women masturbating, engaging in artificial intercourse, and engaging in natural intercourse. Their method included direct observation, physiological recordings, and questions before, during, and after the sexual act. Masters and Johnson, according to their own estimates, observed over 10,000 complete cycles of sexual response.

The social attitudes that greeted Masters and Johnson's work were much more permissive than those that Kinsey encountered. However, this study also met a storm of protest. The same charges of immoral, irreligious, and unethical behavior greeted their work. The critics pointed to the obvious flaw of studying an essentially private act in a laboratory setting. They also suggested that the subjects did not represent the population generally. In spite of such criticisms, however, the study clearly tells us more about the sexual response than anything so far produced.

The Masters and Johnson Results

The Masters and Johnson studies showed that the same basic pattern of sexual arousal occurs in both men and women. They also discovered that the method of sexual arousal has little effect on this basic physiological response. After their extensive study, they concluded that the cycle of sexual response can be divided into four arbitrary phases: excitement, plateau, orgasm, and resolution. This cycle is fundamentally the same for

Self-Quiz 12.1 — Sexual Contentment

Next to each statement place the number 1, 2, 3, 4, or 5 — depending on how characteristic each statement is of you. Continue the process for each of the statements. Then total your score.

- 5 strongly characteristic of me
- 4 moderately characteristic of me
- 3 neutral
- 2 moderately uncharacteristic of me
- 1 strongly uncharacteristic of me

____ 1. I am satisfied with my sex life.
____ 2. I do not feel sexually deprived.
____ 3. Sex contacts have never been a problem for me.
____ 4. My sexual behavior does not cause me unhappiness.
____ 5. My love life is wonderful.
____ 6. My religious beliefs do not conflict with my sexual attitudes.
____ 7. I believe my sexual activities are about average.
____ 8. The topic of sex in a conversation does not bother me.
____ 9. I enjoy thinking about sex.
____ 10. I would rather not change anything about my sex life.

____ TOTAL SCORE

41–50 Few students scored this high on the test. Your score would indicate that you are unusually contented with your sexual life.

20–40 Your score ranks with the vast majority of those students who took this test. You can assume that you have a stable attitude toward sex, even though you might find ways to improve your feelings of satisfaction.

10–19 Your score ranks with those who scored the lowest on this test. Clearly, you seem dissatisfied with your love life.

---

men and women, although a clearly defined refractory period occurs in the male cycle. The same period does not occur in the female cycle.

The *excitement* phase for both men and women develops in the same way no matter what form of sexual stimulation is used. No clear distinction could be made between masturbation and intercourse, for example. If this stimulation continues, a second stage they refer to as the *plateau* stage evolves. Sexual tension becomes more intense. Once the stage is entered by the male, he can no longer constrain the inevitability of ejaculation.

The *orgasm* phase of the sexual cycle is pretty much the same for males no matter how it is reached. However, female orgasm can vary greatly depending on the experience. Female orgasm can follow the male cycle almost exactly or vary greatly from it. At times, women can have a multitude of micro-orgasms rather than one intense orgasm. Sometimes these small orgasms are so small that they are not even recognized as orgasms. However, the various responses do not change Masters and Johnson's answer to the questions often asked about the difference between clitoral and vaginal orgasms. The researchers conclude all female orgasms are clitoral.

Masters and Johnson have given us a great deal of knowledge concerning the human sexual response. More important, they demonstrated that biological research in the area of human sexuality is possible. We hope that this landmark research will open the door to other work that will give us a better understanding of human sexuality (Self-Quiz 12.1).

THE HUMANISTIC APPROACH

Rollo May describes our society in his book *Love and Will* as a **schizoid society.** "My term 'schizoid,' " he tells us, "means out of touch; avoiding close relationships; the inability to feel." (10) The tendency for people to appear in control of all emotion has become a characteristic of our time. We stand aloof from one another and avoid any form of emotional display, but this lack of emotion is actually a repression of our longing for love. Rather than allow anyone to know how lonely we are and allow ourselves to be hurt by those who discover our vulnerability, we hide behind a veneer of detachment.

Our detachment forms an apathy that is peculiar to this mood of aloofness. It tells other people, "I do not want to be involved." And that lack of involvement is a more powerful deterrent to love than hate could ever be, for hate is not the opposite of love, apathy is. Both hate and love demand activity, passion, and commitment. We can only hate if we react to the world, become involved in it, and have passionate feelings about it. By contrast, apathy and detachment are more frightening. When we repress our feelings, we withdraw from all active involvement and close off our senses.

We do not need any great insight to understand why people, at this point in time, become withdrawn and apathetic. Just the normal contact with life—the barrage of sights and sounds provided by radio and television, the depersonalized demands from business and industry, the structured existence in most institutions—presses us to protect ourselves. As our identity is more and more treated as a number, we see our individuality constantly threatened. At times, we must protect ourselves by withdrawing emotionally from the threats of this depersonalization. And the withdrawal, as time passes, becomes more and more attractive (Self-Quiz 12.2).

Self-Quiz 12.2 — Sensuality

This test contains a number of statements about personal attitudes. Read each statement and choose the alternative that best describes your attitude by checking the proper box to the left of the statement. Answer all of the statements.

Often	Occasionally	Seldom	
☐	☐	☐	1. I think that members of the opposite sex will respect me more if I do not become too familiar with them.
☐	☐	☐	2. I only get sexually excited when things are "just right."
☐	☐	☐	3. I believe that women should never become sexually aggressive.
☐	☐	☐	4. I prefer having sex in the dark.
☐	☐	☐	5. I am not aroused sexually during the day.
☐	☐	☐	6. I do not make vocal sounds during intercourse.
☐	☐	☐	7. I would rather not engage in sexual foreplay.
☐	☐	☐	8. I would rather that people did not touch me.
☐	☐	☐	9. Physical attraction is not important to me.
☐	☐	☐	10. I believe that sex should only be used for procreation and never for pleasure alone.

This test cannot tell you how sensual you are, but it does tell you how you compare with others who took the same test. To total your score, give yourself 3 points for each time you checked "often" on the test, 2 points for each "occasionally," and 1 point for each "seldom." Add up the total number of points and compare that score with the following scale.

21–30 This high score shows that you undoubtedly have difficulty expressing your sensual feelings.
14–20 Most people fall within this range. You appear to have a healthy appreciation for sensuality.
10–13 You rank with those who consider the sensual side of their personality significantly important. You marked the test in a way that would indicate little to no sensual inhibition.

Rollo May.
(Peter Vandermark)

"**Apathy** is the withdrawal of will and love," Rollo May explains, "a statement that they 'don't matter,' a suspension of commitment."

> It is necessary in times of stress and turmoil; and the present great quantity of stimuli is a form of stress. But apathy, now in contrast to the "normal" schizoid attitude, leads to emptiness and makes one less able to defend oneself, less able to survive. However understandable the state we are describing by the term apathy is, it is also essential that we seek to find a new basis for the love and will which have been its chief casualties. (11)

Sex Without Love

In Victorian times, a great aura of secrecy surrounded the sexual act. Few people, if any, would talk about sexuality. Then, in the 1920s, a dramatic change in attitudes took place. A new openness permitted discussion of sex in even the most polite social groups. However, the openness was surrounded by a philosophy that suggested, "Talk will solve all problems of repression. We will discuss the sexual problem to death."

While the new freedom in sexual matters had many positive effects, there was also an insidious byproduct. Women no longer struggled with the question, "Will I or won't I go to bed?" They began to struggle with the inner anxieties connected with having the perfect orgasm. Men spent more time worrying about their performance. This great emphasis on technique and performance led Dr. John Schimel to report a dream one patient recounted. "I am in bed with my wife," the patient said, "and between us is my accountant. He is going to have intercourse with her. My feeling about this is odd—only that somehow it seemed appropriate."

Singles bars can help sustain the attitude that the goal of a relationship is sex without love. (© 1978 Eric Kroll/Taurus Photos)

The modern preoccupation with technique dovetails with the tendency to withdraw psychologically. A subtle way for the apathetic person to approach sex in a modern act of freedom is to become concerned with technique. "It often occurs to me," Rollo May says, "that there is an inverse relationship between the number of how-to-do-it books perused by a person or rolling on the presses in a society and the amount of sexual passion or even pleasure experienced by the persons involved." (12) Ironically, the small daily contacts involved in a relationship—sharing with one another, discussing dreams for the future, talking about past fears—make people more vulnerable to one another than going to bed with one another. They become more uneasy over tenderness than they do over sexual intimacy (Case 12.3). "The Victorian person sought to have love without falling into sex; the modern person seeks to have sex without falling into love."

● Case 12.3

My own experience as a therapist supports the theory expounded by Rollo May to an amazing degree. The people who come to me with sexual problems seem saturated with technical knowledge about sex. Most impotent males seem to have read several of the "how to be technically perfect" sexual manuals. Frigid women are aware of the literature that spells out easy answers to their problems, answers that do not work for them. All those struggling with sexual problems seem able to talk knowledgeably about the subject; but ironically, the more aware these sexually troubled people are, the more difficult their problems seem to be.

Andy was only one of many impotent men I have worked with over the past fifteen years. However, his problems seemed more significant when I discovered that he taught a course in human sexuality at a major university. I knew immediately that Andy did not lack any technical knowledge. His problem had to be psychological.

Andy's expertise in sexuality led to his own difficulties. He confided in me that after spending most of his day talking, thinking, and writing about sex, he easily became fearful over his own performance. That fear, more often than not, left him impotent.

Though I had not read Rollo May's book at the time, Andy and I came to a solution to his problem that could have been inspired by *Love and Will*. The more we talked, the more I could see that Andy's technical knowledge made him lose his spontaneity. He admitted that the thrill he once associated with sex was long ago lost. I told Andy that he might enjoy his sexual life more if he put more excitement and romance into the atmosphere. He agreed. I then probed him to discover what sorts of things would inspire the same fire he once experienced. He talked about candlelit dinners, romantic evenings before the fireplace, a battered cabin near the seashore. The more he talked, the more he came alive. That night he reached orgasm for the first time in nearly six weeks.

Andy was not cured overnight, although the talk of romance did put him on the right path. He became more aware of the passion missing from his life. One image stirred another, and his wife responded with enthusiasm. And little by little, over the course of the following year, Andy recaptured the flame of passion he had lost in his life.

The New Puritanism

Classical forms of **puritanism** equated sexuality with sin. The modern form, identified by Rollo May, equates sin with the full expression of one's sexual desires. The curious times we live in suggest that we can and must perform sexually as often as possible, but that we must make certain that we do not engage in any passion or allow ourselves any commitment.

> The new puritanism brings with it a depersonalization of our whole language. Instead of making love, we "have sex"; in contrast to intercourse, we "screw"; instead of going to bed, we "lay" someone or (heaven help the English language as well as ourselves) we "are laid." This alienation has become so much the order of the day that in some psychotherapeutic training schools, young psychiatrists are taught that it is "therapeutic" to use solely the four-letter words in sessions. . . . (13)

Inadvertently, this approach to sexuality only reinforces the growing tendency to reduce sexuality to the biological process. The various terms for intercourse that May discusses have the peculiar capacity to remove all passion and commitment from the sexual act. Our schizoid tendency to avoid feeling, contact, and intimacy with one another thus becomes encouraged by the modern therapist under the guise of freedom. That aloof-

From *Non-Being and Somethingness: Selections from the Comic Strip* Inside Woody Allen, by Woody Allen, drawn by Stuart Hample. Copyright © 1978 by IWA Enterprises and Hackenbush Productions, Inc. Reprinted by permission of Random House, Inc.

ness gradually grows into hostility, and our alienation from one another easily turns to anger. It seems no accident to find the passionless words for intercourse also used in various hostile phrases.

The problems of the men who came to W. Charles Lobitz and Elgan Baker at the University of Colorado Medical School for sex therapy support the theories of Rollo May. As May might have predicted, their sexual impotence went hand-in-hand with low scores on tests for self-esteem and self-concept. On other psychological tests, they avoided any sexual content in pictures that contained explicit imagery. They also made clear their low opinion of the male ability to gain sexual mastery. All the men were impotent, and some had never been able to sustain an erection long enough to have intercourse.

Lobitz and Baker did not turn to sexual mechanics to help these men perform sexually. Instead, they worked on the men's social skills and tried to diffuse their anxiety over their performance. The men talked to one another about their difficulties, which eased a good bit of the fear and anxiety in the group. In time, they could laugh about their own ineptness. The relief among the men was immediate. A female therapist came to the group for some role-playing sessions. The therapist helped the men see that women will not be insulted if a male has trouble sexually. Again, the released tension could be sensed. And finally, the men were trained in relaxation techniques that would help them search for their own sexual pleasure and thus become distracted from their need to perform. The results are striking. Among these men, who had all been to several therapists, nearly two-thirds have overcome their sexual difficulties. (14)

Eros

Rollo May's answer to the new puritanism for the individual, if not for society, lies in restoring **eros** or passion, to the sex act. No matter how risky, how fearful, or how threatening, we must begin to approach one another with openness and emotion. Especially in sexual matters, we can live once again if we leave ourselves vulnerable so that we can experience sexual love to the fullest, even though when we expose our feelings, we risk experiencing pain. Once men and women abandon their preoccupation with how well they perform, how often they reach orgasm, and how technically correct their performance is, they will have to look at one another. Then they may, once more, experience the eros, or passion, of the sexual act.

The biological sexual drive has the capacity of pushing us toward union with a sexual partner. Eros, on the other hand, attracts us. We are talking about eros when we say someone "allures" us or "entices" us. May explains his important concept of eros:

> In eros, we seek increase of stimulation. Sex is a need, but eros is a desire; and it is this admixture of desire which complicates love. In regard to our preoccupation with the orgasm in discussions of sex, it can be agreed that the aim of the sex act in its zoological and physiological sense is indeed the orgasm. But the aim of eros is not: eros seeks union with the other person in delight and passion, and the procreating of new dimensions of experience which broaden and deepen the being of both persons. It is common experience, backed up by folklore as well as the testimony of Freud and others, that after sexual release we tend to go to

Rollo May believes that the restoration of eros, or passion, to love relationships will help to lessen the modern emphasis on sexual performance. (The Bettmann Archive Inc.)

sleep—or, as the joke puts it, to get dressed, go home, and then go to sleep. But in eros, we want just the opposite: to stay awake thinking of the beloved, remembering, savoring, discovering ever-new facets of the prism of what the Chinese call the "many-splendored" experience. (15)

CONCLUSION

Our three psychological vantage points in this chapter have given us three distinct ways to look at our sexual behavior. Carl Jung helped us understand our personality in terms of his theory of inner psychological balance between our masculine and feminine traits. Society puts pressure on us to repress our opposite-sex traits, Jung warned us, but we can find a sense of unity if we ignore society and allow our natural harmony to emerge.

Two significant studies help us understand our sexual behavior better and thus let go of many myths. The first study (actually two studies), conducted by Alfred C. Kinsey, told us how common sexual activity is in our society. Kinsey also exposed the variety of sexual behavior performed by people generally. The other important study was performed by Masters and Johnson. Their look at sexuality was more biological. They studied the orgasm in the laboratory with a variety of people and under a host of conditions. Their results help us see what the orgasm is and what it is not. Again, the results help us dispel a great many myths and understand the natural course of our sexuality.

Finally, Rollo May tells us how unhealthy our preoccupation with the techniques of sex can become. In our anxiety to become liberated and open about sex, we have buried our need for passionate and loving sexuality. Unless we regain the passion in our sexual experiences, we will join the many people in our society who have allowed sex to become mechanical and empty.

SUMMARY

1. Carl Jung, an early psychoanalyst, saw us as a psychological composite of masculine and feminine tendencies. However, society creates conflict for us as it tries to press us into exclusively male or female roles. The only release from the pressure of the sex roles that society imposes lies in accepting our natural masculine and feminine balance.
2. In his massive reseach project Alfred C. Kinsey attempted to help us see the breadth of our sexual behavior. He pointed out to most people that they lived in a society much more diverse sexually than they had ever imagined. A later study by Masters and Johnson showed us how we perform biologically. By observing hundreds of people performing sexually, they helped us see the true nature of orgasm much better than

we ever had in the past. More important, they dispelled many myths that surrounded the sexual act.
3. Rollo May, a humanist, concerns himself more with our sexual attitudes. He became alarmed at our tendency to treat sexuality in terms of performance, technical skill, and athletic ability. This preoccupation with numbers and skill, he warned us, removes the emotion from sexuality. As long as we center our attention on the perfect orgasm, we lose sight of the passion that makes the sexual act meaningful. Only by a return to the eros, or passion, of sexuality can we once more inject love into our sexual lives.

KEY TERMS

anima
animus
persona
sex roles
homosexuality
transsexuals
orgasm
masturbation
petting
coitus
premarital sexual intercourse
schizoid
apathy
puritanism
eros

STUDY QUESTIONS

1. Can you think of one way in which you are trapped by a sex-role stereotype? Is your life less happy as a consequence? Discuss.
2. Have you ever discovered yourself pretending to be more calm, more knowledgeable, or more self-assured than you really are? Did such occasions suggest you might be experiencing the effect of what Jung called the persona?
3. Many people resisted the Kinsey studies on moral grounds when they were released. Does such resistance make sense to you? Explain.
4. Name some of the weaknesses in the Masters and Johnson studies. Pay particular attention to any lack of scientific objectivity.
5. Do you feel that we now have become so casual about sex that we fear falling in love? Explain.
6. Why might passionate love make us fearful? Try to be specific.

ADDITIONAL READING

Berne, Eric. *Sex in Human Loving.* New York: Simon and Schuster, 1970.
Jung, C. G. *The Development of the Personality.* New York: Pantheon, 1954.

Kinsey, Alfred C., et al. *Sexual Behavior in the Human Female.* Philadelphia: Saunders, 1953.

_____ *Sexual Behavior in the Human Male.* Philadelphia: Saunders, 1948.

Lowen, Alexander. *Love and Orgasm.* New York: Macmillan, 1965.

Masters, William H., and Johnson, Virginia A. *Human Sexual Response.* Boston: Little, Brown and Company, 1966.

_____ *Human Sexual Inadequacy.* Boston: Little, Brown and Company, 1970.

Mead, Margaret. *Coming of Age in Samoa.* New York: Dell, 1967.

Morrison, Eleanor, S., and Borosage, V. *Human Sexuality.* Palo Alto, Calif.: Mayfield, 1973.

Otto, H. (Ed.) *The New Sexuality.* Palo Alto, Calif.: Science and Behavior Books, 1973.

Reuben, David. *Everything You Wanted to Know About Sex But Were Afraid to Ask.* New York: McKay, 1969.

Shope, David S. *Interpreting Sexuality.* New York: W. B. Saunders, 1975.

Young, W. *Eros Denied: Sex in Western Society.* New York: Grove Press, 1964.

Chapter Thirteen

Marriage and Family

OUTLINE

Open Marriage
The Open Marriage
Open Relationships
Jealousy

Between Parent and Child
Praise and Criticism
Self-Defeating Patterns
Discipline and Permissiveness

Creative Divorce
Memories
Growth Through Mourning
The Creative Effect

LEARNING OBJECTIVES

After reading this chapter, you should be able to:

1. Discuss some differences between the open and traditional forms of marriage.
2. Explain George and Nena O'Neill's attitude toward jealousy in a loving relationship.
3. Understand some of the ways in which parents fail to communicate with their children.
4. Discuss the distinction between permissiveness and overpermissiveness according to Haim Ginott.
5. Explain at least one way divorce differs from most other crises in life.
6. Understand how mourning can have a creative effect on the newly divorced person.

Chapter Thirteen

When I first began teaching, married students were something of an oddity. Even in graduate teaching, the number of married men and women rarely constituted a significant minority. The vast majority of students in any classroom came directly up the education ladder and reserved marriage for after their final graduation.

Since then, the number of married students, students with families, and even divorced students has risen sharply. More sophisticated students, some of them reentering college after working or starting a family, fill the modern classroom with diversity. A chapter on marriage and family in a psychology book today, then, is a practical imperative.

I have organized most of the topics in this book according to three important and distinct psychological vantage points—the psychoanalytic, behavioristic, and humanistic. The material in the last three chapters, however, does not easily yield to those categories. In order to give experienced and inexperienced students a close look at marriage, family, and divorce, I have turned to three popular bestsellers in this chapter. They are all controversial. I do not expect any student to agree with the advice given in all these books. Instead, I hope that their unique approaches will press students to think reflectively about marriage, family, and divorce.

In the book *Open Marriage* George and Nena O'Neill discuss a new form of married relationship. Their open style of marriage asks partners to begin to treat one another as independent human beings. This open, as opposed to traditional, style of relationship turns from the couple approach to marriage. Men and women in an open marriage would not expect to meet life only as a couple, but would maintain their own separate areas of interest. Couples with an open relationship would attend concerts, go to sporting events, and even establish opposite-sex relationships completely independent from one another.

In the second book, *Between Parent and Child* by Haim Ginott, the author talks about the breakdown in communication between parents and their children. Parents often take the words their children use too literally and miss the underlying feelings that reveal hidden meanings. In a series of delightful examples, Haim Ginott helps parents listen to their children with new understanding.

The last book discussed in this section is titled *Creative Divorce.* In this book Mel Krantzler helps divorced couples see the creative ways in which they can handle divorce pain. He realistically accepts the fact of the painful divorce, but also believes that creative use of the pain can bring new insights to those enduring divorce turmoil.

OPEN MARRIAGE

In 1972, alternative forms of marriage abounded. Some people decided to live together without the traditional marriage ceremony; others chose to live in communal marriages. It appeared that marriage as an institution would soon be obsolete. At that point, George and Nena O'Neill wrote a book called *Open Marriage*. In that book, they defended the institution of marriage, but recommended a fresh approach that they hoped would save many marriage relationships.

The traditional form of marriage, they claimed, had stifled the growth and independence of couples. People's unhappiness with this stifled growth accounted for their tendency to abandon marriage and seek more awkward liaisons. Marriage had always pressed partners to form couple relationships, which inevitably restricted the individuality of the partners. When invited to a party, they were invited as a couple. No one ever thought of inviting Hal unless Sue tagged along. Yet, the truth often was that Hal enjoyed the kind of gathering Sue hated to attend. The same sort of example worked in reverse. One of Sue's favorite college chums married a complete bore, but to sustain Sue's friendship, Hal dutifully listened to what seemed an endless number of pointless stories every time the two couples got together.

The so-called couple demands on Hal and Sue did not all come from the outside. When they got married, Hal and Sue also adopted the couple mentality for themselves. They restricted themselves to activities that they could both enjoy. Hal abandoned his hope of continuing to attend professional football games because he realized how much they bored Sue. Sue did not consider attending a late afternoon college class because she would not be home to get dinner for Hal. The couple mentality dominated both of them. Nena and George O'Neill explain:

> In a closed marriage the couple does not exist in a one-plus-one relationship. Their ideal is to become fused into a single entity—a couple. Separate experiences, beyond those forced upon them by the fact that the husband goes to an office or a factory while the wife remains home to clean and shop, are not allowed, except for occasional, generally resented outings with "the Boys" (for the husband) and "the Girls" (for the woman). (1)

The Open Marriage

Many couples misunderstand the **open marriage** concept. They assume that an open marriage only demands that couples share everything equally. All of the housework, for example, is split down the middle by some couples in an attempt to open up their marriage. Men and women think that if the husband does his own laundry, and the wife works in the yard, they are building an open marriage. Others place their emphasis for an open marriage on a career for the woman. Any marriage where both partners work full time is assumed to be an open marriage (Self-Quiz 13.1).

While **equality** is an important factor in the open marriage, simple sharing of duties does not accomplish the task. Couples must work for more fundamental changes. The relationship must give freedom to each individual to strive for personal fulfillment. The equality and **role flexibility** that allows a man to do his own laundry helps build an open marriage, but the freedom and trust implicit in giving the same man a chance to attend a stage play his wife might not enjoy is more important to the open marriage. The woman who builds personal friendships without demanding that her husband be involved with them also helps an open marriage grow.

Another important part of the O'Neills' concept of the open marriage revolves around the concept of **privacy.** Traditional marriages breed the attitude that if a partner wants to be alone that decision implies some kind of rejection of the other partner. Yet, we all know we need psychological space at times. The concept of psychological privacy is well illustrated, by an example the O'Neills gave in their chapter on privacy. They told the story of the psychologist who, when he needed privacy at home, simply put on his golf hat. This **nonverbal signal** meant, "I just need to be alone for a while with my thoughts." His wife, when she was in a similar mood, wrapped a bandana around her head to signal her need.

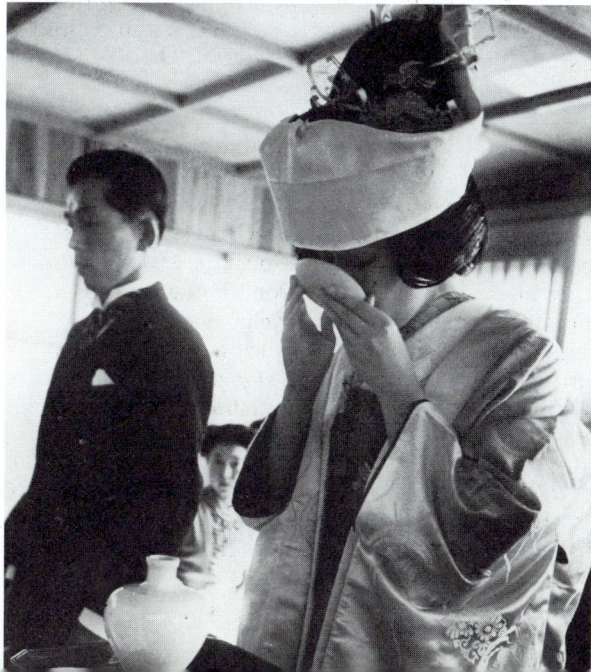

The O'Neills believe that the traditional marriage can stifle growth and independence. (Werner Bischof/Magnum)

Self-Quiz 13.1 — Open Marriage

Not everyone would find an open marriage fulfilling. This test is designed to help you decide how you would respond to that sort of relationship. Next to each statement place the number 1, 2, 3, 4, or 5 — depending on how characteristic each statement is of you. Continue the process for each of the statements. Then total your score.

5 strongly characteristic of me
4 moderately uncharacteristic of me
3 neutral
2 moderately uncharacteristic of me
1 strongly uncharacteristic of me

____ 1. Because many men are excellent cooks, both husband and wife should plan the meals together.
____ 2. Men should have at least one son to carry on the family name.
____ 3. Women should express sexual needs as openly as men.
____ 4. A husband and wife should, for the most part, be together when they meet with others socially.
____ 5. Only couples who remain "faithful" to one another can have a happy marriage.
____ 6. Both husband and wife must make decisions concerning home furnishings, or neither will be happy.

____ TOTAL SCORE

6–16 Your low score on this test suggests you need great freedom in marriage.
17–25 You score with most people who took this test.
26–30 Your score indicates you believe in great togetherness in marriage. Your attitude can help create a close relationship so long as you choose a mate with similar values.

Any couple who can set up a non-verbal signal to indicate the need for privacy will find it a great help in eliminating hard feelings and furthering their understanding of one another. If the relationship between two people is such that either one can openly say, "Don't bother me for a while," without the other being upset, they will have no need for a non-verbal system. But if either mate is likely to take such a statement as a form of rejection, or demand an explanation, then a signal system can be very useful. Verbal explanations or requests can be misinterpreted, but a golf hat makes itself instantly clear. (2)

The theory behind the open marriage may make a great deal of sense, but not all marriages open up easily. And the effects of opening a marriage may not be all positive, especially for the man. To study the effects of both partners in a marriage having a career, researchers Ronald Burke and Tamara Weir of York University in Canada compared the health and happiness of some working couples with some couples in more traditional marriages.

The study indicates that working wives are happier than their at-home counterparts. They communicate better with their husbands, report feeling better both physically and mentally, and are more satisfied with their work and their life generally. The results for their husbands is not so positive. They feel under greater work pressure, experience poorer health, and are more unhappy with their marriages.

> When a wife commits herself to work outside the home, the husband loses part of his active support system. In addition, the husband finds himself undertaking more of what was once considered the woman's work in the home while continuing to perform whatever tasks were traditionally his in the household. (3)

Open Relationships

A great many of the aids George and Nena O'Neill suggest for the open marriage are not new. Their emphases on open communication and role flexibility have been discussed by several other authors. Suggestions such as these are hardly controversial, but the O'Neills do open up a controversial topic when they talk about **open companionship.** The open marriage, according to the O'Neills, allows married partners to have intimate friendships outside their marriage, friendships that might very well lead to sexual intercourse. The O'Neills say that when couples are open to new friends of the opposite sex the marriage bond will grow stronger, but they also state:

> This is not to say that there are no risks in open companionship. This is not to say that extramarital relationships in an open marriage will never be sexual. That claim would be just as ill-founded as the claim made by those who defend the exclusivity of the closed marriage that every outside relationship would invariably lead to sex. Neither extreme is true. And it should be remembered that life is risky. We believe that the risk of failure in marital relationships is far greater in the closed marriage, with its forced exclusivity that denies individuality and growth, than in the open marriage with its open communication. (4)

Jealousy

Though the chapter on open companionship added fuel to the controversy that surrounded the O'Neills' book, the chapter on **jealousy** became the focus of the controversy.

> The idea of sexually exclusive monogamy and possession of another breeds deep-rooted dependencies, infantile and childish emotions, and

insecurities. The more insecure you are, the more you will be jealous. Jealousy, says Abraham Maslow, "practically always breeds further rejection and deeper insecurity." And jealousy, like a destructive cancer, breeds more jealousy. It is never, then, a function of love, but of our insecurities and dependencies. It is the fear of a loss of love and it destroys that very love. It is detrimental to and a denial of a loved one's personal identity. Jealousy is a serious impediment, then, to the development of security and identity, and our closed marriage concepts of possession are directly at fault. (5)

This chapter gave a great many people strong feelings of guilt. Many couples decided they were responsible for their own jealous feelings. Their guilt over honest feelings broke with the entire humanistic tradition stressing feeling expression. The entire book suggests openness and freedom, but in a concluding note the O'Neills condemn those people who happen to feel jealous. The O'Neills bless couples who feel the emotional need to look beyond their marriage for friendship and chastise those who experience jealousy, no matter how true and honest that feeling happened to be.

Many of the people who experienced great guilt over their jealous feelings after reading the O'Neills' book repressed those feelings. They pushed their strong jealous feelings into their unconscious where they could breed greater insecurities and more anger. The worst possible psychological results abounded. Couples hoping to achieve new levels of growth in their marriage by suppressing their jealousy began to put extra pressure on their relationships.

Few of the couples stopped to think of comparing the O'Neill's attitude toward jealousy to another emotion, say loneliness. Loneliness, too, can be called a sign of immaturity and insecurity. Yet we never think of condeming ourselves for feeling lonely. We might say, "I would rather not be lonely, but until the mood passes I guess I will have to live with it." We could approach jealousy in a similar way, by saying to our lover, "I would rather not be jealous, but until the mood passes I had better tell you how I feel and do my best to live with it. I love you and want you to have all the freedom necessary for your growth. Until my jealous feelings pass, however, I will also need to tell you about them." Such a statement expresses true feelings. The O'Neills would have served the humanistic tradition better had they followed the same path of open expression in their approach to jealousy as they suggested in their chapter on open communication (Case 13.1).

● Case 13.1

The O'Neills' have what some people consider an automated attitude toward jealousy. They act as if the person who wants to end jealous moments need only flip an emotional switch, and the troubling feeling will disappear. Yet, wanting to rid ourselves of an unpleasant emotion does not make that task easy. And for some the ordeal can create new tension.

For example, I remember Donna, a large and athletic-looking woman, who talked to me about her problems controlling jealous feelings. Her husband worked in an office filled with young women. Donna could not rid herself of the feeling that one of them would steal Kirk away from her.

"I know that's crazy," she told me. "But I just can't seem to get the thought out of my mind."

"Have you told Kirk about how you feel?" I asked sympathetically.

"Oh, no!" Donna drew back from me in surprise. "If I told Kirk how jealous I get, he would surely be upset."

"Maybe so, but now you resent Kirk. And he doesn't even know why."

"That's right." Donna looked down at the carpet. I can feel myself turning on Kirk and I don't want that."

"Then tell Kirk about your jealousy. Just be sure to let him know you would rather not feel that way."

I talked with Donna quite a while before she felt better about herself and her jealous feelings. In time, she did talk to Kirk about her jealous turmoil. At first, Kirk thought her attitude implied an accusation. Then he realized Donna's emotions caused her more pain than they ever could cause him. Jealousy still gives Donna some unhappy moments, but she finds relief in talking with Kirk about her feelings. And most important, both Donna and Kirk learned from the experience. They are now much more apt to discuss openly their inner conflicts.

BETWEEN PARENT AND CHILD

Dr. Haim G. Ginott suggested fresh lines of communication between parents and their children in his 1965 best seller, *Between Parent and Child*. For example, when a child becomes angry because rain spoils the promise of a picnic, a parent's response that, "There is no use crying over rained-out picnics," only makes matters worse. A closer look at the child's anger reveals it to be the same as an adult's anger. The child does not expect the anger to change the rain, but does need to release some feelings. The alert parent will give the child the opportunity to do so.

> Mother: "You seem very disappointed."
> Eric: "Yes."
> Mother: "You wanted very much to go to this picnic."
> Eric: "I sure did."
> Mother: "You had everything ready and then the darn rain came."
> Eric: "Yes, that's exactly right."
> There was a moment of silence and then Eric said, "Oh, well, there will be other days." (6)

This sort of respect for feelings sets the tone for Ginott's book. He feels parents often misunderstand their conversations with children because

Haim Ginott has helped many parents open lines of communication with their children. (Peter Vandermark)

they fail to hear the feelings involved. If a child were to tell parents that she was scolded in school, most parents would say, "What did you do to deserve the scolding?" Yet a moment's reflection will remind parents what an embarrassing thing a scolding can be. A child would undoubtedly not even mention the scolding unless she were quite troubled by it. Rather than taking sides for or against the teacher, the parents would do better to respond to the feelings with statements such as:

"It must have been terribly embarrassing."
"It must have made you furious."
"It must have hurt your feelings terribly."
"It was a bad day for you." (7)

Such responses are consistent with the best humanistic advice. A child's strong feelings will not disappear when parents tell that child such feelings are wrong. The child's emotional turmoil will ease only when the parents accept the child's feelings as valid (Case 13.2).

● Case 13.2

Haim Ginott gives a host of examples to illustrate how perceptive adults can translate childhood language in *Between Parent and Child*. The following excerpt is one of his examples.

"On his first visit to kindergarten, while mother was still with him, Bruce, age five, looked over the paintings on the wall and asked loudly, 'Who made these ugly pictures?'

"Mother was embarrassed. She looked at her son disapprovingly, and hastened to tell him, 'It's not nice to call the pictures ugly when they are so pretty.'

"The teacher, who understood the meaning of the question, smiled and said, 'In here you don't have to paint pretty pictures. You can paint mean pictures if you feel like it.' A big smile appeared on Bruce's face, for now he had the answer to his hidden question: 'What happens to a boy who doesn't paint so well?'

"Next Bruce picked up a broken fire engine and asked self-righteously, 'Who broke this fire engine?' Mother answered, 'What difference does it make who broke it? You don't know anyone here.'

"Bruce was not really interested in names. He wanted to find out what happened to boys who break toys. Understanding the question, the teacher gave an appropriate answer: 'Toys are for playing. Sometimes they get broken. It happens.'

"Bruce seemed satisfied. His interviewing skill had netted him the necessary information: 'This grownup is pretty nice. She does not get angry quickly, even when a pictures comes out ugly or a toy is broken. I don't have to be afraid. It is safe to stay here.' Bruce waved good-bye to his mother and went over to the teacher to start his first day in kindergarten." (8)

Praise and Criticism

Most parents expect praise to bring out the best in their children. In fact, children can and often do respond to praise with misbehavior. Why? Because children's lives are full of turmoil. They can, and often do, wish harm would come to their mother, sister, or friends. Even a casual comment that he is such a "good boy" can cause an eruption of misbehavior, because he sometimes needs to show others just how bad he thinks himself to be.

Parents would be wise, in praising children, to refer to the reason for their praise. If Debra cleaned up her room without prompting, the prudent parent will say, "How nice your room looks, Debra," rather than, "What a good girl you are." By pointing comments directly at the task accomplished, the child is left to make inferences about her personality. Haim Ginott uses the following example of this kind of communication.

> Mother: The yard was so dirty. I didn't believe it could be cleaned up in one day.
> Jim: I did it!
> Mother: It was full of leaves and garbage and things.
> Jim: I cleaned it all up.
> Mother: What a job!
> Jim: Yeah, it sure was.
> Mother: The yard is so clean now, it is a pleasure to look at.
> Jim: It's nice.
> Mother: Thank you, son.
> Jim: (with a mile-wide smile) You are welcome. (9)

The same principles should be used when we attempt to criticize children. When a child breaks an expensive vase, for example, it is appropriate to point out the damage, but to call the child who breaks the vase stupid, clumsy, or bad can only do harm. It also makes sense to allow the child an opportunity to help restore order. She can clean up after spills, help wash walls that have been marked, and even help buy new tablecloths that must be replaced.

We are so accustomed to attempting to control our anger, we feel we must never become angry with our children. What happens, then, is that our anger grows until we can no longer hold it in, and then we explode at our children in destructive ways. The truth is that anger can be an appropriate reaction to our child's words or actions. Our anger at a soiled tablecloth, a fight between children, or an accident with matches seems only reasonable. Furthermore, we have a right to our anger so long as we do not attack the character of our child when we express it. For example:

"It makes me angry to see you hit your brother. I get so mad inside myself that I see red. I start boiling. I can never allow you to hurt him."

"When I see all of you rush away from dinner to watch TV, and leave me with the dirty dishes and greasy pans, I feel murderous! I get so mad I fume inside! I feel like taking every dish and breaking it on the TV set!"

This approach allows parents to vent their anger without attacking the child. The outbreak can even be an important lesson for the child in proper expressions of anger. At the very least, the child can learn that personal expressions of anger will not result in catastrophy (Self-Quiz 13.2).

One way of dealing with a child's mistake is to have her do something to correct the error. (Peter Vandermark)

Drawing by Opie; © 1978 The New Yorker Magazine, Inc.

Self-Defeating Patterns

Parents and children can fall into a series of **self-defeating patterns** quite easily. The difference between a child's way of thinking and an adult approach to logic lead to serious difficulties in no time. Most adults, for example, cannot quite believe that when children hear the phrase, "If you do it once more . . .," they rarely hear the phrase, "If you," but only the words, "do it once more." Children often believe if they do not repeat the forbidden behavior, their parents will be disappointed. Far better, says Dr. Ginott, to give direct comands. "Please stop shouting in the living room." Then, if the command is not obeyed, punishment can follow.

Bribes lead to the same sort parent-child confusion: "If you are nice to your baby brother, then I'll take you to the movies." The very wording of the request suggests to the child that her parents do not believe she can be nice to her baby brother. She may believe that the only way to get rewards is to create problems. Teasing baby brother may be the best way for Susan to get an extra trip to the movies.

Another self-defeating pattern emerges over the lies children tell. Parents unwittingly set the pattern. When the child tells the truth that he hates his brother, his father will punish him. If the boy lies and says he loves his brother, the father gives him an extra hug. As parents, we may not want to hear truths like this, but accepting negative feelings is the only way to encourage honesty in children.

Parents have a way of questioning children that encourages them to lie. When a parent sees that a child has flunked an arithmetic examination, their line of questioning often begins with a question like, "Did you pass

Self-Quiz 13.2 — Parental Discipline

This test was designed for parents. However, students without children may want to take the test to see how their attitudes compare with the parents who took the test. A number of statements follow regarding personal attitudes. Read each statement and choose the alternative that best describes your attitude by checking the proper box to the left of the statement. Answer all of the statements.

Often	*Occasionally*	*Seldom*	
☐	☐	☐	1. I believe in the old saying, "Spare the rod and spoil the child."
☐	☐	☐	2. I believe in stopping disobedience before it becomes established.
☐	☐	☐	3. If my child appears to be faking an illness to avoid school, I would give him a good talking to and threaten punishment if he did not stop his act.
☐	☐	☐	4. I believe children should be seen and not heard.
☐	☐	☐	5. Most juvenile delinquency is caused by a lack of discipline in the home.
☐	☐	☐	6. Punishment is good for both parents and children.
☐	☐	☐	7. A good punishment for a child is to send her to her room and isolate her from others.
☐	☐	☐	8. Punishment can extinguish all bad behavior.
☐	☐	☐	9. Firmness is the key to effective toilet training.
☐	☐	☐	10. Children like to be dealt with by parents who are strict.

This test cannot tell you how strict or permissive you are or would be as a parent, but it can show you how you compare with others who took the same test. To total your score, give yourself 3 points for each time you checked "often" on the test, 2 points for each "occasionally," and 1 point for each "seldom." Add up the total number of points and compare that total with the following scale.

21–30 Few parents who took this test scored this high. Your attitudes toward discipline suggest you may be quite severe.

14–20 Most parents scored in this range. Your score suggests you have a balanced attitude toward discipline.
10–13 Your score was unusually low. Even by modern standards, your score indicates you may be a bit lenient.

---

your arithmetic test? Are you sure?'' Such a line of questioning only encourages defensive lying. The more appropriate response would be to state things directly: "Your arithmetic teacher tells us you failed your test. Is there anything we can do to help?" The approach not only encourages honesty, but also suggests to children that their parents are understanding and can be trusted with embarrassing material.

Discipline and Permissiveness

The term permissiveness has been used and abused for so long that it has lost most of its meaning. Dr. Ginott defines the term as the permission parents grant to children to express their feelings. **Permissive** parents allow children angry feelings. **Overpermissive** parents allow children angry acts Dr. Ginott feels parents make a grave mistake when they allow angry acts such as striking a parent, breaking household items, or other disruptive behavior. Naturally, circumstances make inflexible rules difficult to follow. For example, times of stress create new permissiveness for everyone, children included. However, the rule of thumb that allows children to express angry feelings but not commit angry acts gives parents a point of departure for their discipline.

Parents do children a favor when they set clear limits on behavior.

> It is preferable that a limit be total rather than partial. There is a clear distinction, for example, between splashing water and not splashing water on sister. A limit that states, "You may splash her a little, as long as you don't wet her too much," is inviting a deluge of trouble. Such a vague statement leaves the child without a clear criterion for making decisions. (11)

Vague rules give almost all young children a cause for anxiety.

Dr. Ginott outlines a plan for setting limits: "There are different ways of phrasing specific limits. At times the following four-step sequence may prove effective."

1. The parent recognizes the child's wish and puts it in simple words: "You wish you could go to the movies tonight."
2. He states clearly the limits on a specific act: "But the rule of our house is 'no movies on school nights.'"
3. He points out ways in which the wish can be at least partially fulfilled: "You may go to the movies on Friday or Saturday night."

Cathy by Cathy Guisewite. Copyright, 1978, Universal Press Syndicate.

4. He helps the child to express some of the resentment that is likely to arise when restrictions are imposed: "You wish there weren't such a rule." "When you grow up and have your home, you are sure going to change this rule." (12)

This approach to children, like so many that Dr. Ginott suggests, evolves from a close look at the world of children. Rather than imposing the adult world of logic and values on children, Dr. Ginott looks at children as people just learning to understand the world about them. His approach makes sense and helps parents grow toward a greater sense of harmony with their children.

A recent study done by a University of Delaware psychologist suggests that parents should pay attention to the way they discipline their children. As Haim Ginott suggests, children do pattern their behavior after parental discipline approaches. Dr. Suzanne Steinmetz studied 78 people between the ages of 18 and 78. Seventy percent of those studied remembered their parents engaging in verbal acts of aggression to end conflict in the family. Thirty percent recalled physical aggression being used to settle arguments. Generally speaking, the parental approach to discipline correlated with the way these subjects now dealt with their partners and how they disciplined their own children.

In more specific categories, the subjects showed the same adherence to their parents' behavior. Subjects whose parents had engaged in excessive physical abuse followed that approach. Those who came from families where both physical and verbal abuse abounded were apt to use both approaches to resolve conflicts. Children also imitated their parents whether the parents engaged in verbal abuse only or dealt with conflict without resorting to physical or verbal abuse. Children, then, learn more from their parents' actions than from their words. (13)

CREATIVE DIVORCE

Divorce is a significant crisis in the lives of the people it affects. For any two people who develop emotional ties to one another, the crisis means a significant amount of pain. The entire world changes overnight; every familiar means of coping seems to fail. Even the smallest details of life become overwhelming. Yet, the crisis period can only last for a limited amount of time. Then divorced people must learn new ways to deal with life. Since they must now approach the world in which they had had a partner without a partner, new patterns begin to emerge. And those patterns often force divorced men and women to develop their hidden potentials.

The crisis divorce thrusts upon an individual is similar to other crises in life. Crisis, whether it affects flood victims, cancer patients, or fired workers, does not vary significantly from one person to another. Society's attitudes do vary, however. Blankets, food, and messages greet those trapped in certain kinds of crises. "Unfortunately, society holds out no such helping hand to divorced men and women experiencing the loss that comes with the death of a relationship," Mel Krantzler says in his book *Creative Divorce*.

> Despite the fact that almost one out of two marriages in this country will eventually break up, our society clings to the belief that nice people don't get divorced. Divorce is accepted among the exotics of our society—film stars, TV performers, and the jet-setters—but it is not for "real people." (14)

Divorce among film stars is considered acceptable and even exciting, but the pain and loneliness of single parenthood is what many divorced people experience. (Rachemoni/Sygma, right; © 1979 Jim Harrison, below)

Memories

Divorce does not automatically end a marriage relationship: too many ties bind the couple together long after the physical separation occurs. Habit alone keeps reminding them of their life together. An unpaid bill, a faulty light switch, a song on the radio—all bring the relationship to mind again. Society allows the abandoned partner to yearn for the lost marriage and expects those who effect the separation from their marriage partners to breathe a sigh of relief. Such is rarely the case. No matter how painful the marriage might have been, divorce always carries pain.

The first reaction to the pain of divorce is normally extreme. Either the people affected try to remove themselves emotionally from all thoughts of a former spouse or continue, sometimes for years, to refuse to accept the reality of the separation. Both approaches are equally unrealistic. The only realistic approach Mel Krantzler calls the **reconfirmation effect**—the emotional process that allows us to accept the reality of divorce.

> Just because a relationship has ended in fact does not cancel the emotional needs it fulfilled, even if through hostility and anger. It is the fact that these needs are now unmet which gives rise to fond hopes for reunion and prevents us from letting go. By activating these hopes, meetings with a former mate provide the opportunity for us to test them against reality, and eventually to recognize them as fantasies born of emotional needs which our past marriage can no longer satisfy. This is what I term the reconfirmation effect, the process by which our emotions accept the fact that the marriage is over. (15)

Growth Through Mourning

The first shock period following a divorce often brings analogies of death to the people affected. Soon after separation people talk about "the house that feels like a tomb," "feeling like a part of me died," and "walking around like a zombie." Such feelings most commonly occur to those who received a good part of their identity as a person from their partner. Partners who, during their marriage, spoke of one another as "my life," "my soul," or "my better half" suddenly realize that part of them has been amputated. They naturally grieve for the lost part of themselves. This mourning period can be so painful that many people decide to repress their feelings and pretend no pain exists. Unfortunately, that decision also cuts them off from an important path to growth.

A significant number of problems face the newly divorced person. He or she must accept many cruel facts of life. Divorce ends former social relationships. A divorced woman may find it difficult to find work. Even new income tax brackets punish divorced people. Troublesome as these problems are, divorced people overdramatize them. Why? Because they must now face even the ordinary tasks of life alone; and to the extent that they had their personal identities tied up with a partner, that aloneness can seem particularly painful. They must now rediscover themselves and their relationship to every part of their world.

Many divorced people refuse to believe their marriage really has ended. In subtle ways, they cling to hopes that some miracle will happen, and they will be reconciled. So long as the distortion of reality does not become rigid, this denial can be an honest step for divorced people in the gradual process toward accepting reality. Part of their personality remains married mentally, while another part begins to redefine itself as a single person. In such a way, the mourning period gives divorced people a chance to slowly reestablish themselves as independent, both emotionally and mentally (Case 13.3).

> Denial permits us to test the reality of our new situation in pieces, absorbing only those aspects which do not threaten to destroy us completely. For most of us, reality eventually wins over; we come, slowly, to see our fantasies as just exactly that. Gradually we accept the fact that the relationship has ended, and that we now are single people. We all go through denial in one form or another when our marriage ends. (16)

● Case 13.3

At one point I was convinced that the tendency for newly divorced people to deny their fate was unrealistic. I believed that the sooner a divorce was accepted, the sooner psychological balance could return. In my conviction to help the divorced accept their lot, I pressed many of them to move more quickly than was healthy for them. In particular, I remember Karen, a middle-aged woman, who separated from her husband just before she came to me for therapy.

Karen could not, or would not, accept the reality of her divorce. She kept telling me that Neal would soon come to his senses. "He has to return," Karen told me one day. "I can't make it on my own." That bit of false logic upset me considerably. Up to that point I had listened patiently to Karen. However, I had to point out that she was functioning just fine on her own. I believed it my duty to show Karen how capable she was of acting as an independent woman. She responded to my support with anger. Her face turned scarlet as she vigorously denied her ability to function without Neal's support. I backed away emotionally and once more let Karen take the lead in her therapy.

After her therapy ended, and Karen finally did begin to function on her own, we talked of that emotional outburst. Karen explained her feelings to me.

"I did need to deny the reality of my divorce for a time," she said, able to see things in perspective now. "I gave up so much of my independence in order to live a happy married life. I could not turn around and immediately deny that my sacrifices were unnecessary. I had to believe, for a time at least, that I could not function on my own."

Karen's explanation made sense to me. The transition from marriage to divorce means accepting a new personal vision of ourselves. Such a transition cannot occur quickly; it takes time. Since Karen explained her struggle to me, I have been able, as Mel Krantzler suggests, to give divorced people more time to accept an entirely new image of themselves.

The Creative Effect

No one wants to experience the pain of divorce. However, there are positive, even creative, ways to handle that pain. The pain of divorce—lonely feelings, helpless feelings, abandoned feelings—all point out weaknesses in our personality. To accept the feelings of weakness, to the extent that is possible at any one time, is to begin to develop a more healthy and stable personality.

The divorced person who realistically accepts the new single state finally begins to live in the present. The ability to step beyond the blaming, the guilt, and the self-pity that are a necessary part of separation puts the divorced person on the road to personal growth. A new ability to achieve independence grows out of the pain: divorced people see the life around them in new ways, and their relationships with others take on new meaning. Krantzler explains **creative divorce:**

> A creative divorce, by tapping the feelings that emerged during the mourning process, makes it possible to maintain the momentum for change generated during the period and use it to continue your drive toward independence. Life then becomes a series of choices, not inevitabilities, and you can set about the challenging and exciting task of dealing with the realities of your new life, free from the traps of the past. Meeting these challenges is what I call living creatively in the present and is a far more rewarding prospect than living as if the present were a repetition of the unhealthy past. (17)

SUMMARY

1. George and Nena O'Neill published a book in 1972 titled *Open Marriage*. In that book, they suggested that couples should begin treating their partners more as individuals. Married partners should, according to the O'Neills, even be free to have intimate relationships with members of the opposite sex. Their most heartless attack is on those people who feel jealousy because a partner becomes intimate, even sexually intimate, with a friend.
2. Haim Ginott feels parents often miss the emotional truth behind the communications of their children. He further warns parents that they may communicate heavy emotional burdens to children by suggesting they are "good boys" or "good girls" when they do as they are told. Much better, says Dr. Ginott, to thank children for specific tasks completed and not overload children with moral implications. And finally, Dr. Ginott suggests that children ought to be free to express angry feelings, but not be free to commit angry actions.

3. Divorce, Mel Krantzler tells us, has painful overtones if the separated couple meant anything at all to one another. The realistic person can expect to mourn the loss of a loved one. But more important, this mourning can bring a divorced person new personal insights. When the painful feelings implicit in the separation process are met and experienced realistically, they can help a person achieve new emotional balance.

KEY TERMS

open marriage
equality
role flexibility
privacy
nonverbal signal
open companionship

jealousy
self-defeating patterns
permissive
overpermissive
reconfirmation effect
creative divorce

STUDY QUESTIONS

1. State one specific way in which you would want your present or future marriage to be open. State one way you would prefer your marriage to be closed.
2. Do you consider jealousy an unhealthy form of emotion? Explain your answer in some detail.
3. State one important way you feel parents could help children learn to communicate with them better.
4. State one thing a parent might do that you would consider overpermissive.
5. State one reason why you believe so many marriages wind up in divorce courts. How might that situation be corrected?

ADDITIONAL READING

Ackerman, N. *The Psychodynamics of Family Life: Diagnosis and Treatment of Family Relationships.* New York: Basic, 1958.
Bettelheim, B. *A Home for the Heart.* New York: Knopf, 1974.
Elkin, F. *The Child and Society.* New York: Random, 1960.
Gordon, M. (Ed.) *The Nuclear Family in Crisis.* New York: Harper, 1972.
Kagan, J. *Understanding Children: Behavior, Motives and Thought.* New York: Harcourt, 1971.
Otto, H. A. *The Family in Search of a Future.* New York: Appleton, 1970.
Sussman, M. B. (Ed.) *Sourcebook in Marriage and the Family.* Boston: Houghton Mifflin, 1963.

Chapter Fourteen

Work and Leisure

OUTLINE

Work Theories
Trait-and-Factor Theory
Need-Drive Theory
Developmental Theories
John Holland
Work-Motivation Theory
Theories of Management

Leisure
Playful Work
Other People

LEARNING OBJECTIVES

After reading this chapter you should be able to:

1. Identify the trait-and-factor theory of Frank Parsons.
2. Explain how Anne Roe thinks parental attitudes influence career decisions.
3. Discuss the developmental theories of Eli Ginzberg.
4. Describe John Holland's six categories for personalities and work environments.
5. Show how Frederick Herzberg applied Maslow's need hierarchy to work motivation.
6. Discuss McGregor's two theories of management attitudes—Theory X and Theory Y.
7. Compare and contrast leisure with work.

Chapter Fourteen

Tom looked unusually serious the day we talked over a cup of coffee at the school cafeteria. "Is something bothering you, Tom?" I asked, after I swallowed a mouthful of hot coffee.

"Yes and no." Tom's eyes seemed fixed on a spot some distance across the room. "It's just that I should pick a major pretty soon. I've been delaying that choice because I have no idea what I want to do with my life. But I had better make some decisions pretty soon. And I don't even know where to begin."

"Why don't you begin with yourself?"

"I'm not sure I understand." Tom looked at me quizzically.

"About the most important factor in deciding on a career centers on deciding who you are. Almost all psychologists tell us that by determining our personality we take a long step in discovering our career in life."

Tom was amazed to discover that the critical element in career choice was understanding himself. Like Tom, most students do not emphasize themselves enough when they think about their life work. Factors such as money, fame, or prestige seem to crowd out the personality factors that will help determine work as a success or a failure.

In this chapter we will see that one of the earliest theories of career development, the trait-and-factor theory, puts as much weight on the person as it does on the career as an aid for matching people to careers. Anne Roe (b. 1904) and the Freudians centered more specifically on personality factors. Like Freud, Anne Roe looks to early parental influence to find the seeds of career choices. Eli Ginzberg (b. 1911) also believes that personality development has the most important role in career choice. However, Ginzberg sees adolescence rather than childhood as the critical period for determining that choice. John Holland (b. 1919), another vocational theorist, felt personalities could be divided into six different categories. Once people can identify their personality category, they can more easily look for work that would satisfy them.

Frederick Herzberg has centered his attention on people's motivation to work. He decided that basic needs—money, job security, and so on—must be satisfied before higher needs can be met. Yet these higher needs—creative work atmosphere, chance for advancement, and a sense of responsibility—create satisfaction.

Instead of looking at the workers, Douglas McGregor examined employers to see what created healthy working conditions. He found sharp differences. Some employers thought of their workers as lazy, inept, and irresponsible. McGregor labeled this management attitude Theory X. By contrast, Theory Y management saw that workers are responsible, conscientious, and committed if given healthy work conditions.

A most critical element in healthy and happy life is a mature approach to leisure. Although leisure is important, most of us fail to give ourselves creative leisure time because we labor under an ethic that claims leisure is "sinful." The best idea, for those who can overcome the work ethic in our social atmosphere, would be to turn work into play. The most successful people in our society manage to blur the distinction between the two.

WORK THEORIES

Trait-and-Factor Theory

The **trait-and-factor theory** represents one of the first attempts by a psychologist to understand what makes a person choose one career rather than another. Why does one identical twin decide to become an airline pilot when the other twin wants to work as a clerk in a supermarket? Frank Parsons (1854–1908) felt we could only understand such diversity by exploring what he called a "crossroad" approach to vocational choice

Parsons believed the traits of the person and the factors of the job lead people into one career rather than another. (Peter Vandermark)

that he developed in 1908 in the book, *Choosing a Vocation*. People usually reach a crossroad in their life when they graduate from high school. At that point, they must begin to choose a career. Those who enter college have to think in terms of a major field of study, and those who end their studies with high school must begin to look for work.

How do we decide which way to turn at the crossroads? What does make the one identical twin turn to flying and the other turn to selling? Parsons believed two elements are involved in a good choice—the traits of the person and the factors of the job. We begin to understand a person's career choice when we understand the person. We look at that person's intellectual ability, mechanical aptitudes, special interests, ambitions, and inclinations. Once we have an intimate picture of that person, we can look at possible careers and occupations, studying them in much the same way we studied the person. We learn what special skills are necessary to perform the job. And finally, we match the person who has the necessary skills with the job that can satisfy the interests and ambitions of the person (Self-Quiz 14.1).

Need-Drive Theory

The trait-and-factor theory has left Freudians unsatisfied. The theory might work, they have said, if we could ignore the early childhood experiences of the individual. However, no true Freudian believes that parental influences can be ignored. Consequently, Freudians, most prominently Anne Roe, have studied the influence of parents on vocational decisions. Anne Roe created the Center for Research on Careers at Harvard University, where she and her colleagues have pursued the topic of career choice by studying early parental influences.

First of all, Roe suggested in her **need-drive theory** our parents made our childhood atmosphere either warm or cold. Those parents who maintain close contact with their children create a warm atmosphere. Through intimacy, they teach sons and daughters to satisfy their needs by contact with people. Children of these parents tend to choose occupations that involve people. They may teach, counsel, or do social work. Whatever they do, however, they try to work with people. Some parents, however, are aloof from their children, sometimes even rejecting. Children born into such families typically select jobs that keep them distant from people. They might become laboratory technicians, factory workers, or construction workers, as they turn to work that minimizes their contact with other people.

Besides distinguishing between warm and cold home atmospheres, Anne Roe looks at the way parents produce one or the other of the atmospheres. For example, parents can produce a cold atmosphere by **avoidance.** Some parents avoid children by shunning emotional contact. In such homes, physical closeness and even emotional conversations are kept

Self-Quiz 14.1 — Leadership

This test attempts to discover your attitude toward characteristics typical of strong leaders. Next to each statement place the number 1, 2, 3, 4, or 5—depending on how characteristic each statement is of you. Continue the process for each of the statements. Then total your score.

   5 strongly characteristic of me
   4 moderately characteristic of me
   3 neutral
   2 moderately uncharacteristic of me
   1 strongly uncharacteristic of me

_____ 1. If people who follow my instructions do not succeed at a task, I would think that I obviously did not explain that task in sufficient detail.

_____ 2. If asked by a group to lead them in a cause with which I am unfamiliar, I would accept the offer and seek the advice of someone familiar with the cause.

_____ 3. When a superior gives me an order, I am most likely to question that order and suggest alternative solutions.

_____ 4. When a strong leader takes charge in a chaotic situation in a foreign country, I think such steps are necessary. People must first be led before they can participate in decision.

_____ 5. I identify with people who relentlessly drive themselves and others until they reach their goal.

_____ 6. Leaders who never compliment anyone, watch every detail, create much fear, and become overwhelmingly successful draw my pity. I always think that with more sensitivity they might have been even more successful.

_____ TOTAL SCORE

22–30 You score with students who indicate strong leadership inclinations. You appear to have the potential for leadership in most areas of life.
14–21 Your score ranks with most people who took this test. It indicates that you have leadership potential, but that your taste for it is not as strong as for some people.
6–13 You score with those who indicate the least inclination to lead people.

---

to a minimum. The word "love" is avoided. In more dramatic examples of avoidance behavior, parents actually abandon their children. The critical factor in such avoidance for Anne Roe is the lack of effort on the part of parents to satisfy a child's needs.

An attitude parents can display toward their children to create a warm atmosphere is **acceptance.** As opposed to avoidance behavior, acceptance

Anne Roe believed a warm home atmosphere will eventually lead a child into a career choice involving people. (Peter Vandermark)

seeks to satisfy the needs of children. This behavior can be direct and loving, with a great deal of touching and embracing, or the approach can be more casual.

In contrast to both acceptance and avoidance, Anne Roe claims parents can also become **emotionally concentrated** on a child. This emotional concentration sometimes takes the form of overprotection. Parents who constantly worry about a child's health, for example, easily become overprotective. And while this overprotective attitude might help keep a child healthy, more important needs for independence are often frustrated. The emotional concentration on a child, in a cold atmosphere, can mean excessive demands will be made on the child. When parental intention may be to help the child strive for intellectual achievement, for example, independence may be sacrificed (Case 14.1).

Anne Roe's theories have never received much scientific validation, but they do suggest how Freud's theories might apply to the world of work. You must decide if the theories, despite their lack of validation, might help us understand ourselves in the field of work.

● Case 14.1

Anne Roe's thoughts about parental influences on career choice makes a good deal of sense. Most of us are influenced by the emotional warmth our parents show to us. We learn quite early how to handle a certain degree of intimacy and resist having people come any closer. Yet we grow anxious if we lose the contact we have come to expect. We seem to search constantly for just that amount of closeness we can comfortably handle.

Cheryl experienced a certain degree of intimacy with her family during her formative years. Her parents both loved her dearly, but they had some difficulty expressing their affection openly. They rejoiced with Cheryl over her accomplishments and talked about how much she meant to them. However, neither of them could use the word "love" or bring any sustained touching or embracing into their relationship with their child.

Her family life left Cheryl with a strong desire for more affection. She looked to her friends to supply what her parents could not. Yet, when a friend did try to draw close with words of intimacy, Cheryl drew back in panic. Although she wanted the closeness, she could not handle it when it was offered. It would not surprise Anne Roe or other Freudians to discover that Cheryl looked for a career that would give her some contact with people, but not too much. Social work, her first choice, left Cheryl exhausted by the overwhelming amount of emotional closeness the work demanded. Only after trying several work environments did she finally decide to become a bank officer. Her work in the bank put her in constant contact with people, yet the contact remained, for the most part, oriented to financial concerns. In that way, Cheryl could sustain just the exact degree of intimacy with other people that her early life had led her to expect.

Developmental Theories

The developmental theories of vocational choice, like the need-drive theories, focus on the personality of the person choosing a career. However, the **developmental theories** do not focus on the relationship between parents and children so much as they do on self-development during adolescence. Eli Ginzberg, for example, believes occupational choice develops along with the personality during adolescence. As young people begin to understand themselves, they also come to select a career that fits their personality.

This dynamic process of deciding "who I am" as well as "what I want to do with my life" Ginzberg says begins sometime before the age of eleven.

Cathy by Cathy Guisewite. Copyright, 1978, Universal Press Syndicate.

At that point, children live in a fantasy world that permits them to be whatever they want to be. The child who would like to be a police officer, a doctor, a pilot, or a lawyer can indulge those fantasies without restraint. However, by the time young people enter high school, some more realistic, though still tentative, choices must be made. The young woman struggling to finish high school, for example, cannot realistically expect a career as a research scientist. Finally, sometime after the high school years, young people make some realistic choices. These choices, according to Ginzberg, usually represent a compromise between the dreams of the person and the reality of the world and individual limitations.

It is important to note that the developmental theories of Ginzberg and others emphasize the development of the person as well as that person's career choice. As young people become more aware of themselves and who they are, they also have a better understanding of the career they want to follow. At the same time, the process of selecting a career gives young people a better understanding of themselves. The two tasks work so closely together, in fact, that it can be difficult to tell them apart at times (Case 14.2).

• Case 14.2

The developmental theories of Eli Ginzberg suggest that we move through the fantasy period of childhood and the tentative period of adolescence before we make a realistic career choice. Most of us can relate the theories when we remember the frequent question, "What do you want to be when you grow up?" Consequently, we have little problem relating to the special struggle that Greg faced with his career choice.

Greg was born into a family of surgeons. His father, graduate of a prestigious ivy league school, was a significant figure in the world of medicine. Greg's older brothers also entered medical schools across the country and gained outstanding scholastic reputations. Greg came along late in his father's marriage and was everyone's favorite. Naturally, Greg dreamed of a medical career, and his play during childhood almost always included some form of medicine or surgery on real or imaginary animals.

Greg's family realized quite early that a medical career was out of the young boy's reach. His struggle with his studies made such goals unrealistic. Fortunately, Greg's father soon recognized the boy's limitations and prepared him for less demanding careers. Adolescence was particularly painful for Greg as he slowly accepted his own limitations. He searched about for some skill that would keep him in contact with medicine but would not exceed his skill.

Greg finally decided on X-ray technology. The choice allowed him to remain intimately associated with medicine, but the role of technician did not demand skills that Greg did not possess. In the end, the choice helped Greg develop himself as a person as well as remain an intimate part of a medical family.

John Holland

John Holland looked at the trait-and-factor theory of Frank Parsons and decided it made a lot of sense. No matter how much research they do on vocational choice, in the end counselors and theorists match up people with jobs. Each theory, no matter how sophisticated or how simple, succeeds if it manages to give people jobs they can do well and at the same time enjoy doing. Yet Holland did not want to ignore the developmental theories of career choice. He also believed that people do see their careers in personal terms. Our career choice, Holland told us, is an intimate part of our growth as a person.

Holland believes that people act in response to both their personality and the environment they occupy. If their personality and their work environment agree, they will make stable career choices and become competent in and satisfied with their work. To help people understand themselves better, Holland categorized personalities into six groups.

Realistic. People in the realistic category think in concrete and tangible terms. Such people put a premium on status, whether gained through money or power.

Investigative. The investigative person likes to pursue problems with concrete answers. This individual has an intellectual orientation toward life and often finds work involving mathematics and science quite satisfying.

Artistic. The artistic person enjoys intuitive and expressive forms of work. The more original the expression of artistic people, the more fulfilled they are.

Social. Social people find fulfillment when they work with people. They often orient themselves to the ethical and moral activities in society.

Holland believes that people who find a work environment that agrees with their personality are happiest at their job. (© Joel Gordon, left; Peter Vandermark, center and right)

"We are gathered here today, gentlemen, to make money."

Enterprising. The enterprising person thinks in aggressive terms. Such people enjoy leading others and place a high value on political and economic achievement.

Conventional. The conventional person values conformity and order. Such people enjoy mechanical problems and value business achievement.

The principal task for most people, according to Holland, is to determine their personality type and find the environment in which they will be able to express that personality. The environments break down in Holland's theory into the same six categories of realistic, investigative, artistic, social, enterprising, and conventional. When we find our personality type and match it to an appropriate environment, our chances for a fulfilling career are good.

Until quite recently, John Holland's career theories were supported only by research on students choosing academic majors. Studies have showed that students do pick their majors according to their personality type. However, John C. Smart of Virginia Polytechnic Institute wanted to see if 1200 male college students would choose careers as well as academic majors based on their personality characteristics.

Smart's research suggests that students do select their careers according to their personality type. As Holland might have predicted, the conventional and enterprising types placed a great value on high earnings. The artistic types chose to work with ideas more than those who fit other Holland categories. The social types wanted to work with people.

Smart concluded that his results support John Holland's theory that people prefer occupations that suit their personalities. That result should interest career counselors, who can help students through testing and counseling to choose careers that fit their personality. (1)

Work-Motivation Theory

Frederick Herzberg helped us understand work satisfaction in terms of Abraham Maslow's **need hierarchy.** Maslow pointed out that we all must have our basic needs satisfied first: we cannot think of anything else until we have enough to eat and drink, are physically safe, and satisfy our basic sexual desires. Then we can turn to higher needs such as our need for esteem, love, and self-actualization.

Herzberg saw that Maslow's breakdown of needs could be applied to the world of work. For example, a worker's salary might well be considered a basic need. Money allows the worker to eat, to live safely, and to have a sense of security. Once workers satisfy such basic needs in a career, they then look to their higher needs. The higher needs that bring greater satisfaction to workers include the responsibility of the work, its importance, and the chances for advancement.

In an important study of accountants and engineers, Herzberg analyzed worker attitudes toward the lower and higher needs on Maslow's scale. Herzberg found that the lower needs such an adequate salary, reasonable working conditions, and healthy interpersonal relationships might best be described as *dissatisfiers*. That is, the worker who lacks a decent salary will be dissatisfied. Nothing else will matter to that worker until the salary becomes reasonable. Yet, though the proper salary will end the dissatisfaction, it will not bring satisfaction. The workers who finally receive what they believe to be an adequate salary will cease being unhappy; however, money alone will not create a happy atmosphere. To bring a sense of satisfaction to these workers, their jobs must also bring them some direction for their higher needs. Only work that offers a chance for advancement, a sense of responsibility, and a creative work atmosphere will bring workers long-term satisfaction (Self-Quiz 14.2).

Theories of Management

Just as Herzberg focuses his attention on the motivation of workers, Douglas McGregor looks carefully at the attitudes of management. A careful study of several different work settings led McGregor to divide management attitudes into two categories. In the first of these categories, which McGregor refers to as **Theory X,** employers have a series of negative attitudes toward their employees. They assume people dislike work and will avoid it at all costs. They feel people must be forced to do an adequate job.

Self-Quiz 14.2 — Job Satisfaction

Next to each statement place the number 1, 2, 3, 4, or 5—depending on how characteristic each statement is of you. Continue the process for each of the statements. Then total your score.

- 5 strongly characteristic of me
- 4 moderately characteristic of me
- 3 neutral
- 2 moderately uncharacteristic of me
- 1 strongly uncharacteristic of me

____ 1. I never watch the clock when I am working.
____ 2. On Monday morning, I am refreshed and ready to return to work.
____ 3. Though I might be tired at the end of the day, I usually feel satisfied.
____ 4. I rarely find my mind drifting during my work.
____ 5. I never think about changing jobs.
____ 6. I enjoy the people I work with.
____ 7. For me, a job is much more than a way to make money.
____ 8. I think of myself as ambitious in my work.
____ 9. I will talk about my work with anyone who seems interested.
____ 10. I never become bored with my work.

____ TOTAL SCORE

40–50 You score with people who appear most satisfied with their work. Your involvement with your work suggests you would probably do well in other occupations as well.

22–39 This score represents the average person's reaction to work. You enjoy your work well enough. Yet you probably wish for more money, for more interesting work, for a greater chance for promotion.

10–21 Your score indicates unhappiness in your work. You may be in the wrong job. You might look for work that better taps your skills and abilities. You should think seriously of working for less money if you can find work that will make life more pleasant for you.

Such employers further assume that their workers lack ambition and actually appreciate being goaded into working.

McGregor feels, at the other extreme, that some managers make dramatically different assumptions about the people who work for them. Such assumptions, called **Theory Y** by McGregor, include the belief that work can and ought to be as natural for people as play. These employers believe that if they can help workers achieve some sense of commitment to their job, they will exercise a great degree of self-control in reaching their goals. Theory Y assumptions also include the belief that people, under proper conditions, will not only accept responsibility but also seek it actively.

The management at the Kingswood office of the Legal and General Assurance Society of London tested Theory Y by giving its workers an opportunity to have more flexible working hours. The workers were allowed to punch in and out any time between 8:30 in the morning and 6:00 in the evening. They only needed to be certain that they worked 35 hours a week. Further, those who fulfilled their contract were given a free time bonus each month.

Dr. Martin G. Evans studied this flextime schedule to see the effects of such a Theory Y approach on workers. He studied these employees and compared their responses to those workers at Temple Court, another branch of the same company not exposed to the flexible system. The workers at Temple Court were asked to imagine how they would respond to such a flexible schedule.

Over 75 percent of the workers at Kingswood gave the experience rave reviews. They said flextime allowed them to integrate their lives on and off the job much better and that they appreciated the freedom the scheduling gave them. The Temple Court people, by contrast, imagined they would not like all the clocking in and out necessary for the system to work. However, 70 percent of the Kingswood people did not object to the procedure.

Comparing the two environments, the Theory Y approach to management appears validated. The employees functioning under flextime found the system more conducive to their effort as well as planning work and getting it done. The flextime employees also reported increased satisfaction in their work, both immediate and long range. They further said that they felt their capabilities, both on and off the job, were utilized more effectively. Evans concluded that the greatest overall effect was on the attitudes of the flextime workers. They reported that they enjoyed their work much more when given flextime freedom. (2)

LEISURE

So far this chapter has emphasized the work we do. To lead a fulfilled life, we cannot overstate the need for a career that gives us a sense of significance. However, work alone cannot bring us a balanced life. We need relief from work, no matter how fulfilling that work might be. Even the most rewarding activities eat up energy and put a strain on our bodies. Time away from the concentration, effort, and stress of work is critical.

The leisure that is so important to our mental and physical health is not easy to achieve. Most of us still labor under the **work ethic**. We believe it is a moral obligation to not "waste" any time at play; our leisure time, therefore, often contains feelings of guilt. We think of the many things we "ought" to do. Some students, no matter how little time they spend at leisure, spoil that time with worry about the reading they have yet to com-

Drawing by Lorenz; © 1978 The New Yorker Magazine, Inc.

plete or the exam that awaits them. Business people during a vacation often do nothing but think about the problems and conflicts they left at the office.

Compulsivity spoils leisure time and can turn play into work. The person who arrives at a party determined to have a good time will soon become exhausted. We have all experienced trying earnestly to fall asleep and being unable to do so. The more attention we give to counting sheep or watching our breathing, the more likely it is that we will remain awake. Sleep, like play, only occurs when we allow ourselves to be drawn into it.

While work commands attention, play demands spontaneity. We relax when we turn to those activities that come naturally to us. For example, the mystery novel that draws us back every evening has the qualities we need for leisure, and hobbies, exercise, and light reading can all be forms of leisure. However, we should also note that what is work for one person may be leisure for another. Some people can relax while reading heavy academic prose, writing serious articles, or performing intricate mechnical adjustments on an automobile. The critical factor appears to be that quality of spontaneity. We are not driven compulsively to play; it attracts us spontaneously.

Only spontaneity can turn activities into play. (Peter Vandermark)

Playful Work

While we all need relief from the attention work demands, most people must also keep searching for work that takes on the qualities of play. Work and play need not be opposites. Work does not need to hang as a burden over our head. In fact, the most successful people think of their work as pleasure. On one occasion, a reporter asked the great Italian movie director, Frederico Fellini, how long it had been since he took a vacation. Fellini replied, "Vacation? Vacation? I am always on vacation. My work is my vacation."

Drawing by Stevenson; © 1978 The New Yorker Magazine, Inc.

Many creative people find it difficult to distinguish between work and play. (Peter Vandermark)

As strange is it may sound, the most tedious work can be fulfilling for some people. Such people find ways to express themselves in even the most repetitious tasks: I can still recall talking to assembly line workers who found great fascination in their work. Many people, of course, cannot express themselves in certain work. These people who are frustrated in their jobs usually face a choice: they can find more fulfilling work at less pay or remain in work they grow to detest.

We might emphasize, once more, the path taken by many successful people. Often those who become most successful in their field have searched for ways to express themselves in their work. They enter jobs, often at low pay, that somehow allow them to reveal their personality. Those parts of the work they find boring, they manage to turn into games. This approach to work can help most people separate their work from its overtones of sin and burden. More and more, for such people, their work becomes another part of their play (Case 14.3).

● Case 14.3

All work can be turned into play, even academic work. And I suppose that truth was never more dramatically illustrated for me than during my college years by the two young men—Phil and Dan—who vied with one another for valedictory honors. As far as I or anyone else could see, they were about equal in talents and skills. They were both conscientious students with unusually high IQ's. The principal difference between them was their attitudes toward college study. Phil thought of college as work, while Dan treated his studies as play.

Phil began his day with study. He rose quite early in the morning, gulped down some breakfast, and began studying before most of the campus arose. Every break in his class schedule Phil spent studying. His only recreation came at rigidly spaced intervals. Even during his favorite recreation of tennis, however, Phil continued to worry about his classes. Phil could not seem to approach college in any other way.

Dan had a completely different attitude toward his work. He enjoyed his studies. Most of the things he read and thought about fascinated him. He found himself at odd times puzzling about a mathematical problem, the motive behind a medieval revolution, or the factors that cause an economic recession. His friends loved to kid Dan about the time he became so involved in the principle of the telescope that he walked out of the dorm on his way to the basketball courts without pants. Unlike Phil, however, Dan had no rigid schedule in his life. He simply took things as they came along.

Dan became valedictorian of our class. That, of course, does not mean he was the better student. I only mention it because it suggested to me, quite early, that those people who turn their work into play can be even more successful than those who make all work drudgery.

Other People

As social beings, we need other people to help us fulfill ourselves. An important part of our nature demands that we seek the company of others. Naturally, our need for love presses us to seek intimacy with some people more than with others. Whenever we spend too much time in personal isolation, this need for intimacy becomes urgent. Most of the time, however, our social needs remain more subtle, and we satisfy them without even becoming aware of their influence.

Besides pressing us to seek the company of others, our social needs also urge us to look for new companions. When our daily activities put us in the company of the same people for too long, we find ourselves talking with strangers. Bartenders, supermarket clerks, salespersons can all help us satisfy such needs. However, the desire for diversity is best met by reaching out beyond our immediate circle of friends and entering a new social atmosphere. We can join clubs, introduce ourselves to strangers, or take up new interests in an effort to expand our social horizons. Most often, life becomes more exciting as a result.

Our need for social contact does not negate the complementary need for solitude. Our desire to be alone is more than a reaction against too much social exposure. Privacy is necessary for people to maintain a balance in their emotional life. Each person satisfies this need in a unique way. For example, many people find solitude in long walks alone, in private meditations by the seashore, in a quiet evening before a fire. Such private experiences are never a waste of time. They are periods when we remind ourselves of our internal direction, reestablish our inner goals, and recall personal values. Those who find periods of solitude impossible usually have little personal direction, so they look to others for direction in their lives. Without others to turn to, such people soon become irritated and emotionally upset.

SUMMARY

1. Frank Parsons pointed out, in his trait-and-factor theory, that most people should choose a career by matching the traits of their personality with the factors implicit in the job they choose.
2. Anne Roe, a Freudian, felt that parental attitudes have the greatest influence on determining a child's later career choice. The first major influence parents have on their children occurs when they make the home atmosphere warm or cold psychologically. Beyond creating the degree of home intimacy, parents also help determine careers for their children when they either accept, avoid, or, in the extreme, emotionally concentrate their attention on their children.
3. Eli Ginzberg sees the career develop within a person dynamically in much the way Anne Roe does. However, Ginzberg thought of the career choice as something the individual decides during the period of adolescence.
4. John Holland looked at the personality of workers and the environment they occupy and decided that both could be categorized in six separate groups. The major task for those making a career decision, then, is to determine the characteristics of their own personality and then search for a career environment that satisfies that personality.
5. Frederick Herzberg felt that people have two kinds of needs. The first and most essential set of needs might be called basic. These needs for workers include enough money, decent working conditions, and reasonable interpersonal relationships. Only after these needs are satisfied can workers look to higher needs that will bring them satisfaction. Such higher needs include responsible work, a chance for advancement, and creative work.
6. Finally, Douglas McGregor studied types of managers and decided one approach to management, which he referred to as Theory X, believes that workers are lazy, dislike work, and must be constantly goaded to perform. The other approach to management, Theory Y, suggests that workers are, under proper conditions, responsible, hard working, and committed.
7. Most of us find leisure psychologically hard to separate from "sin." Even during leisure time, many people become so compulsive that they turn relaxation into strain. Yet, the ideal for success as well as the good life is to turn work into play. The most successful people have the capacity to make hard work seem like fun.

KEY TERMS

trait-and-factor theory
need-drive
avoidance
acceptance
emotionally concentrated
developmental theories
need hierarchy
theory x
theory y
work ethic
compulsivity

STUDY QUESTIONS

1. List a number of personality factors you possess that might direct you to one kind of work rather than another.
2. Do you believe your own personality development during childhood and adolescence presses you toward one kind of work rather than another? Explain.
3. Does you own personality fit into one of John Holland's categories? How about some of your friends?
4. Do you believe you would be more productive as a worker if you were working under a Theory X or a Theory Y employer?

ADDITIONAL READING

Ginzberg, E. S.; Axelrod, S. W.; and Herma, J. L. *Occupational Choice: An Approach to a General Theory.* New York: Columbia, 1951.
Haire, M. *Psychology of Management.* New York: McGraw-Hill, 1964.
Herzberg, F. *Work and the Nature of Man.* New York: World, 1966.
Herzberg, F.; Mausner, B.; and Snyderman, B. *The Motivation to Work.* New York: Wiley, 1959.
Holland, J. *Making Vocational Choices: A Theory of Careers.* Englewood Cliffs, N.J.: Prentice-Hall, 1973.
McGregor, D. *The Human Side of Enterprise.* New York: Macmillan, 1960.
Parsons, F. *Choosing a Vocation.* Boston: Houghton Mifflin, 1908.
Pietrofesa, J., and Splete, H. *Career Development: Theory and Research.* New York: Grune and Stratton, 1975.
Roe, A. *The Psychology of Occupations.* New York: Wiley, 1956.
Super, D. E. *The Psychology of Careers.* New York: Harper and Row, 1957.

Chapter Fifteen

Life Cycles

OUTLINE

Industry
   Inferiority

Identity
   Role Confusion

Intimacy and Isolation
   Genitality

Generativity and Stagnation

Ego Integrity and Despair

Death and Dying
   Denial and Anger
   Bargaining and Depression
   Acceptance and Hope

LEARNING OBJECTIVES

After reading this chapter you should be able to:

1. Explain how people meet the challenges of Erikson's last five life stages.
2. Illustrate how people might fail to meet such challenges.
3. Discuss Dr. Kubler-Ross's contribution to our understanding of death.
4. Explain why dying people should have the right to meet each stage of death in their own way.
5. Distinguish among the five stages through which the dying person must pass.

Chapter Fifteen

"I wish my parents would spend a little more time trying to understand me," Beth, a college sophomore, told me as we sat waiting for a college basketball game to begin. "Sometimes I feel like a complete stranger in my own home."

"What would you like your parents to know?" I turned away from the playing floor to face Beth.

"Everything. I wish they knew about what makes me happy, how I feel about myself, and what I want from life."

"I hear that a lot from young people." I chose my words carefully. "I think the desire to communicate is important. But I always wonder why young people like yourself don't begin first."

"Begin first?" Beth's eyes narrowed with suspicion.

"Yes. Why don't you first ask your folks about what makes them happy, how they feel about themselves, and what they want from life. If you showed them that sort of interest, they might be more likely to respond to you."

"Oh, I think I understand my parents pretty well." Beth smiled knowingly.

"That's the problem. They probably think they understand you pretty well also. The truth is that a pretty wide generation gap separates all of you."

Beth came to see that her demands of her parents were unrealistic. She would not offer them the same sort of understanding that she expected from them. Beth is far from alone with her problem. Most young people and their parents seem unable or unwilling to extend themselves to one another. Consequently, they rarely realize that more than personal misunderstanding stands between them. In fact, they live in two entirely different worlds.

In this chapter, we will examine the ages lying beyond the stages of life that Freud described in his work. Erikson comments on the later life stages and focuses on the task each stage presents. For example, during latency, children must either develop their personal skills or fall into feelings of inferiority. In our society, children feel adequate to the extent that they learn the skills of reading, writing, and arithmetic. Those who fail to master such skills develop inferiority feelings. The children who pass through that task successfully immediately encounter another. Puberty forces them to question their identity. They either answer the question, "Who am I?" or carry confusion with them for years to come. Young adults have still more challenges. With their identity intact, they look for others with whom they can share themselves intimately or face the terrible ordeal of isolation. People in the middle years have not ended their struggles. They must become creative with their lives or face a devastating stagnation. Erikson says that even people in old age must work to remain integrated or sink into despair.

The last section of this chapter centers on death and dying, particularly on the work of Dr. Elizabeth Kubler-Ross. This woman's work with dying patients has helped make us all a little more aware of death and its meaning in our lives. In particular she discerned stages that any dying person must endure before coming to an acceptance of fate. By letting us know that the denial, anger, bargaining, and depression are simply stages along the way, she gave all those who must struggle with death a new understanding. And her discovery that hope remains a lingering element in all death's stages helps us all gain a new respect for ourselves.

INDUSTRY

Since Sigmund Freud was convinced that personality development ends about the age of five (as we saw in chapter two), he did not address any changes in the personality beyond that point. For such discussions, we must look to Erik Erikson, the neo-Freudian. He studied the stages of life beyond childhood with insight. Even modern interpretations, notably Gail Sheehy's bestselling book, *Passages*, draw heavily from Erikson's original insights.

Erikson continues to study the child's development after the turbulent "oedipal" stage, five to six years of age. At this point, children no longer exhibit the extremes of turmoil. About the age of five, both boys and girls turn to a quiet period of schooling. During the **latency** period, between about seven and twelve, they learn the skills necessary for their entrance into society. And whether they learn the grade school skills necessary to function in an industrial society or the primitive skills critical for jungle survival, all cultures give children systematic training at this time.

Erikson uses the term **industry** to describe the goal for children during latency. Those who meet the challenge do learn the skills necessary for industry in their world. Not only are the skills necessary, however, but children must also realize the need and develop the desire to become industrious. Development of this goal occurs in the modern classroom that teaches children the fundamentals of arithmetic, reading, and writing. It also develops in the jungle where children learn to trap their own food, weave cloth, and find shelter. Erikson explains the stage:

During latency, children must learn the skills necessary for industry in the culture of their world. (Paul S. Conklin, left; © Daniel Anderson/Jeroboam, right)

Thus the inner stage seems all set for "entrance into life," except that life must first be school life, whether school is field or jungle or classroom. The child must forget past hopes and wishes, while his exuberent imagination is tamed and harnessed to the laws of impersonal things — even the three R's. For before the child, psychologically already a rudimentary parent, can become a biological parent, he must begin to be a worker and potential provider. (1)

Inferiority

Children who do not develop the skills necessary for survival in their society soon experience feeling of **inferiority.** Rather than learning to become industrious and productive, they fall into various forms of withdrawal. The child who develops serious feelings of inferiority during this stage often does so because his or her family life failed to provide adequate preparation for school life. Some families become so overprotective that their children cannot cope with the real world of sharing that grade school demands. Others give their children exalted notions of what to expect in school. These children, through disappointment, become equally inept at adapting themselves (Case 15.1).

● Case 15.1

Many parents with the best intentions become overprotective toward their children. Such parents often feel that they only have their children's best interests in mind, but children who are restrained from making personal discoveries will gradually come to think themselves inadequate and inferior. They can even learn to adopt their parents' attitude toward their lack of ability for making decisions.

Anita was one young woman who had suffered from an overprotective mother. Her mother had assumed that Anita was far too fragile to indulge in even the normal tasks and joys of childhood. Consequently, Anita rarely played with the other children in the neighborhood, helped her parents with household chores, or even formed friendships at school. Her days were filled with endless trips to the doctor. Anita had no time to be a child, to explore the world on her own, or to find her own sense of adequacy.

Anita carried her childhood attitudes into her adult life. The early impressions would not disappear. She failed miserably in the world of work, so her mother rushed in with a weekly stipend. Anita was a handsome woman physically and many men were attracted to her. However, her almost total lack of adequacy soon turned them all away. The same held true of her woman friends. Few even tried to penetrate her shy and withdrawn attitude. Those who did soon gave up in frustration.

Anita finally turned to therapy. The psychiatrist she visited suggested group therapy. In sessions with others, Anita not only discovered her problems were shared but also learned the skills necessary to relate in a group. Anita found a great deal of help in group therapy. However, she may always labor under the weight of her mother's overprotective attitudes.

During the years of latency, we can see the social consequences of the industry or inferiority that develops. Children who become socially oriented in their attempts to learn the work of the culture will round out their abilities realistically. However, many children focus too closely on the skills necessary for survival and do not integrate themselves socially. Such children can easily become slaves to technique and lose the human perspective on their life. Or, to use Erikson's words, "If he accepts work as his only obligation and 'what works' as his only criterion of worthwhileness, he may become the conformist and thoughtless slave of his technology and of those who are in a position to exploit it." (2)

IDENTITY

As children enter puberty with a good understanding of the basic skills of society, they are prepared for the new challenges of the next stage. The sexual turmoil of puberty causes them to question all their own values and the values of their world. Because of their limited experience, adolescents must look to others for their sense of **identity**. They place a great value on what other people, particularly their friends, think of them. In the midst of this turmoil, they must approach the world cautiously as they look for a place where they fit. Because the struggle to discover their home in the

The tasks for young people during adolescence are formidable. (Paul S. Conklin)

world can be filled with such frustration, adolescents often make enemies simply to vent that frustration. During this time, their parents can become particularly distasteful in their eyes. By contrast, most adolescents are also willing to make idols of public personalities in their attempt to find a model who will show them the way to appear to the world. They join "in" crowds and conform to group norms.

The task for young people during adolescence is formidable. They must somehow try to integrate their own attitudes, their parents' hopes for them, and their personal expectations into a consistent personality that will also be accepted in the world of work. For only when their personality blends with an acceptable career, can they begin to find peace in the world.

During adolescence, many young people join various "in" crowds. The various high school groups presumably have an impact on the conforming members and help shape them. At least, most people thought so until recently. A study by sociologist Jere Cohen suggests otherwise. He studied 1,040 students at a white, working-class suburban high school. By analyzing student responses, he determined which young people formed the leading group. He then compared the "in" crowd with the rest of the school.

The attitudes of the members of the leading clique toward studies, drinking, dating, athletics, and religion were virtually identical to those of the rest of the school. As opinion leaders, the "in" crowd also failed. By taking a second survey several months later to determine any shift in attitudes, Cohen found that the leading group had shifted their opinions right along with the rest of the school in the period of time.

Cohen concluded that the leading crowd has "virtually no impact in changing student values, attitudes and behaviors." So that while the "in" crowd may help young people gain the sense of identity they desire, it is virtually powerless to shape that identity in any particular direction. (3)

Role Confusion

When young people fail to discover their identity, they develop **role confusion.** The fundamental sense of who they are becomes fuzzy and unfocused. At times this lack of a sense of identity can become so acute as to demand psychological help, even hospitalization. For most young people, however, the confusion is painful but not overwhelming. The failure to find a personal identity, particularly a satisfying career choice, leads adolescents to overly identify with groups, cliques, and heroes.

The same hope to find a personal identity can lead to various forms of "puppy love." The experience rarely represents true love, but rather a new hope for self-discovery. One symptom of puppy love is an overwhelming emphasis on talk. Parents can testify to the hours that phones are tied up during this period. The talk often represents little more than an attempt to receive personal feedback from a trusted friend (Case 15.2).

The tendency of young people to form clans and exclude those who do not conform has many distasteful aspects. The most dramatic form of clannishness is racial prejudice. But skin color is not the only way youths can discriminate. Clothes, speech, and even mannerisms have been enough to exclude some young people from the conforming group. Because of personal confusion, adolescents are prone to set up categories of good and bad without fully recognizing the "gray areas" between categories. Unfortunately, many young people are hurt by the vicious way such categories are imposed on them.

● Case 15.2

Erikson points out that many people, in their search for a personal identity, become infatuated. This "puppy love" is held together by a weak bond because the young people are finding in one another only someone who will offer them feedback on their identity. At least that was the case with Dick. His relationship with Sherry was established on their willingness to be open with one another. Dick and Sherry would talk on into the night about their feelings, their hidden secrets, and their most important aspirations. Their relationship became so exhilarating that they eloped one evening on the spur of the moment. Everyone, including their parents, was overwhelmed. But Dick and Sherry just knew their relationship would last.

Not long after their marriage, Dick and Sherry began to have those intimate talks less and less frequently. The openness that had sustained their relationship previously now lost its great appeal. Each of them, almost simultaneously, came to a sense of personal identity. And once this personal identity took shape, the bond that held them together began to weaken. Neither wanted to admit their marriage was a mistake, so they lingered together for over a year. However, the hours they spent with one another became few and far between. Soon separation was the only sane approach to what now seemed so obviously a mistake. They were able to have one last talk together in which they thanked one another for a friendship that had meant so much. They also admitted that their love had had very shallow roots.

INTIMACY AND ISOLATION

The young person who acquires a sense of personal identity in the turmoil of adolescence is then prepared to bring that identity to relationships with other people. Once we know who we are, we long to form friendships with others. Even though such associations may cost young people some personal freedom, they want to make contact with others. They grow willing to sacrifice their privacy in order to establish friendships. In some cases, they find **intimacy** in relationships with members of the opposite sex. At other times, they make same-sex friendships. They begin to explore themselves in relationship to others. The sacrifices of such friend-

Young people must learn how to become intimate with others.
(© Joel Gordon)

ships become a part of their lives, as they enter, for the first time, into the give and take of love.

To the extent that young people fail to make intimate relationships with others work, they isolate themselves. The extreme of such **isolation** can result in withdrawing from friendships altogether. Many young people find the task of intimacy too threatening and pull back from relationships. They become shy, and others avoid their company.

Many other young people, however, avoid the challenge of intimacy by remaining superficial. They appear to enter into several relationships, and their conversation often seems quite personal. Yet, they never allow themselves to experience any true form of intimacy. If their problem is not resolved, such people do not allow themselves to become truly involved with anyone, even in marriage. For all their talk, their friendships, their parties, and their activities, they never permit anyone to become personal with them. Instead, they remain on a level so superficial that it only isolated them from others.

Genitality

In his discussion of adolescence, Erikson mentions that sexuality at that stage often only reflects the young person's search for identity and not any true form of love. The biological urges, so strong for adolescents, also dominate the sexual expression. Only after the search for identity has eased can young people truly begin to understand the genital relationship as they reach the goal Erikson calls **genitality.**

> Freud was once asked what he thought a normal person should be able to do well. The questioner probably expected a complicated answer. But Freud, in the curt way of his old days, is reported to have said: "Lieben und arbeiten" (to love and to work). It pays to ponder on this simple formula; it gets deeper as you think about it. For when Freud said "love" he meant *genital* love, and genital *love;* when he said love and work, he meant a general work-productiveness which would not preoccupy the individual to the extent that he loses his right or capacity to be a genital and loving being. Thus we may ponder, but we cannot improve on "the professor's" formula. (4)

Sexuality at this stage of development (approximately 18–35 years old) is usually a full genital experience, as the preoccupations with personal identity fall away and do not disturb the love experience. The young couple have the first opportunity to fully experience the pleasure of orgasm, which gives them a full discharge of tension. This experience can take the mind from the many personal preoccupations that block an intimate relationship. Between two mature adults, this intimate sexual relationship can be the ultimate form of intimacy. Partners who become involved in one another's lives and express this involvement sexually achieve the final goal of this stage.

"Well, I'm 21. I guess I'm through with all my stages."

GENERATIVITY AND STAGNATION

Successful completion of the intimacy task prepares people to begin to look to the goal of **generativity.** Our society's preoccupation with the needs of young people blocks us from understanding the equally important needs of older people. The mature person needs to be needed. All people need to exercise their ability to guide and to teach. If they do not feel that they are passing on important truths to a new generation, they would surely stagnate.

Mature adults commonly think of procreation as generativity. Parents express their need to teach and to guide with their own children. That does not mean that every person can or should think only of raising children as the way to express this need. Many people, because of special talents or particular circumstances, apply their generative energies in other ways. Many creative forms may fulfill this need.

The natural tendency for people who lose themselves in intimate relationships is to become deeply involved in the product of that relationship. The primary example of such involvement is the preoccupation loving parents have with their children. When that maturity between partners fails, however, an individual can turn the natural tendency to be involved

Loving parents express their generativity through their children. (Peter Vandermark)

with others inward. When they are no longer giving to others, such people become stagnant in personally destructive ways. The primary example of turning inward is the tendency to treat oneself as one's own child. Instead of turning to their own children at this stage, adults can turn to themselves physically or psychologically. Physical and mental illnesses that occur during this stage of life often suggest the **stagnation** of the generative urge by turning inward (Self-Quiz 15.1).

EGO INTEGRITY AND DESPAIR

The final stage of life contains all the others implicitly. Only those people who meet the challenges of each age can enjoy the triumph of old age. The terror that surrounds old age and death dominates people who have not gone about the job of living with courage and honesty. In the maturity of old age, people can see the order and meaning in their personal life cycle. They look out beyond themselves and gain a spiritual sense of the world. Such people also find themselves in harmony with ancient wisdom and truth, as they become more aware that their life represents only one way or one approach to meaning in the world. Yet they also see that their attitude had the integrity of its own meaning. This is what Erikson means by **ego integrity.**

Those who fail the challenges of life's stages become petrified by the thought of death. They despair that they have not lived life fully, they yearn to begin another life, and this time do it correctly. A host of small disgusts toward themselves, their friends, their family, and even the world of nature turn the final stage of life into an experience of **despair.**

Self-Quiz 15.1 — Psychological Age

Regardless of your chonological age, you probably recognize the importance of attitude in determining your psychological age. Some days you feel worn down and negative toward life, while others you feel reborn. This test attempts to give you an overall perspective on your psychological age. Choose the alternative to each of the following statements that best describes your attitude by checking the proper box to the left of each statement.

Often	Occasionally	Seldom	
☐	☐	☐	1. I am attracted to people who need me.
☐	☐	☐	2. Even though depressed during a social evening, I will try to stay with the mood of the evening.
☐	☐	☐	3. When I feel in a miserable mood, I would rather be left alone.
☐	☐	☐	4. I enjoy my own cooking.
☐	☐	☐	5. At the end of a difficult day, I love to go out and enjoy myself.
☐	☐	☐	6. My close friends need me more than I need them.
☐	☐	☐	7. Unexpected gifts make me wonder how I can return the favor.
☐	☐	☐	8. I love to pursue things that capture my interest.
☐	☐	☐	9. If a little extra money comes my way, I spend it on something special.
☐	☐	☐	10. I love activities that bring me into contact with others.

To total your score, give yourself 3 points for each time you checked "often" on the test, 2 points for each "occasionally," and 1 point for each "seldom." Add up the total number of points and compare that total with the following scale.

27–30 Your score ranks with the students who scored highest on this test. It suggests you are an adult at heart.

21–26 You score with the majority of students taking this test. Your psychological age ranks along with most students.

10–20 Your score indicates a strong need for emotional support and a degree of immaturity.

"Webster's Dictionary is kind enough to help us complete this outline in circular fashion," Erikson tells us.

> Trust (the first of our ego values) is here defined as "the assured reliance on another's integrity," the last of our values. I suspect that Webster had business in mind rather than babies, credit rather than faith. But the formulation stands. And it seems possible to further paraphrase the relation of adult integrity and infantile trust by saying that healthy children will not fear life if their elders have integrity enough not to fear death. (5)

Most of us have a narrow, prejudiced view of old age. Part of the reason lies in our limited contact with older people. The other part of the reason emerges from stereotypes. To help set the record straight, psychologists Marilyn A. Borges and Linda J. Dutton studied various age groups. They broke the ages six to sixty-five and beyond into seven age groups. Borges and Dutton then asked psychology students to contact one person they knew best in each of the age groups. The students asked their friends to fill out a questionnaire about their attitudes toward age and aging.

The results of the questionnaire pointed out several things. For example, it appears that those who have not yet reached twenty-four look forward to their best years, while those past twenty-four look back on their best years. In the context of old age, however, the results highlight our stereotypes. The young people questioned inevitably thought that life would be grim in old age. Yet those over sixty-five had no such attitude toward their life. "Happy, productive adulthood is not a state of existence on limited hold," Borges and Dutton tells us. "Rather it is a dynamic process in which problems are attacked and pleasures sought, with personal equipment whose powers and limitations, though changing with age, do not necessarily favor one age as opposed to another. Lust for life is available to all ages." (6)

Too many of us develop negative stereotypes of the elderly. (© 1978 Steve Meltzer/West Stock)

DEATH AND DYING

Not that many years ago, death was treated as part of the natural family life. Children saw their grandparents age and die in the context of the home. No one saw the need to protect children from anything so natural as death; the young people grieved right along with their parents. For a variety of reasons, we now hide death from children and even from ourselves. We ship aging parents off to nursing homes. We relegate dying patients to closed wards in hospitals. We attempt to hide the disturbing truth of death from ourselves and others.

Fortunately for all of us, a courageous woman psychiatrist, Dr. Elizabeth Kubler-Ross, has called our attention to our fear of death. She tells us how much of our life experience we are missing by hiding from the fact of death. She encourages us to look again at our attitudes toward death. She reminds us that if the plight of the dying person is not enough to make us interested in death, we might consider ourselves; our need to push all reminders of death away from us makes us less human.

Dr. Kubler-Ross spends most of her life with dying people. She does not test new electronic equipment on them, periodically take their blood pressure, or carefully monitor their heartbeat. Instead, she talks with them. She provides a human contact that other doctors rarely offer. That contact over many years has given her an understanding of the dying person that few people have achieved. In particular, she has distinguished five stages or attitudes the dying person encounters in the normal course of any terminal illness. Understanding these stages and their course can not only help us understand people who are facing death, but also give us a better understanding of ourselves in relation to our own inevitable death (Case 15.3).

● Case 15.3

Often people write books to make money or to gain fame. Consequently, everyone who writes a bestseller becomes suspicious. Before I met Dr. Elizabeth Kubler-Ross, I worried that this woman who had influenced the lives of so many people might fail to live up to my high expectations. I needed to know that the woman who so sensitively helped us all look more humanly at death was herself a warm and sensitive person. I was not disappointed.

Dr. Kubler-Ross did not try to overpower me with her presence. She did not use the penetrating look that is so popular with those who fancy themselves gurus. Instead, her voice was warm and her manner spontaneous. Yet, when she talked to me about her work with the dying, I could almost see her holding someone in pain. She told me about rocking a little girl whose mother was dying of cancer. Her fingers unconsciously responded as if the moment lived for her again. The more we talked, the more I left the room where we sat and mentally visited sick wards, hospices, and funeral parlors. Dr. Kubler-Ross *is* her work.

Denial and Anger

"Among the over two hundred dying patients we have interviewed," Dr. Kubler-Ross writes, "most reacted to the awareness of a terminal illness at first with the statement, 'No, not me, it cannot be true.' This initial denial was as true for those patients who were told outright at the beginning of their illness as it was for those who were not told explicitly and who came to this conclusion on their own a bit later on." (7) Dr. Kubler-Ross does not regret this initial stage of **denial**. She does not wish to force patients to become "realistic." Rather she sees denial as a natural reaction of the dying patient during the early stages of terminal illness. "Denial functions as a buffer after unexpected shocking news, allows the patient to collect himself and, with time, mobilize other, less radical defenses." Those of us who have occasion to talk with dying patients would do well to allow them to deny their impending death when they feel overwhelmed by the fact. Pressing someone to admit "reality" can, at times, be most unrealistic.

Patients who are allowed to deny their fate commonly pass through that stage and begin a second stage, **anger.** Once terminally ill patients accept the reality of their state, they inevitably react in rage, anger, and resentment over their condition. Because their family and friends cannot cope with the anger that justifiably emerges, the dying patient often becomes angry with anyone and everyone. They vent their rage on doctors, nurses, friends, and relations. With the best of intentions, those close to the dying person try to soothe the anger. Instead, Dr. Kubler-Ross tells us, we ought to give dying people permission to vent all their anger—rational and irrational. For only when dying people have expressed all their pent-up anger can they expect to move on to a more realistic attitude.

Bargaining and Depression

The third stage the dying patient encounters is called **bargaining.** The person tried to strike a bargain—with God, with the fates, with the unknown—to be spared. This bargain is not unlike the bargains children pose to parents. The child who is told she may not attend the movies with a friend may become quite angry at first. Then, after a period of sulking, the child poses some bargains to the parents. "If I clean my room without being asked all this week, may I go to the movies?" Parents can and often are swayed by such requests. The dying person may remember such childhood success and try the same sort of pleas with God.

The patient who is given the freedom to pass through the first stages finally enters a depression. When the illness makes its mark with longer hospitalizations, more severe pain, and complex surgeries, depression is inevitable. Loss becomes an intimate part of the patient's life. People lose parts of themselves to surgery, their life savings to hospital care, and their ability to perform even the normal life functions. Such losses lead to what Kubler-Ross calls a **reactive depression.** Dying patients become depressed in reaction to the many losses they must suffer.

No matter how painful the reactive depression might be, it is not the serious depression that represents the fourth stage. The final depression is called the **preparatory depression** because it prepares the patient for final losses. The dying person must become prepared to give up everything including love, life, and experience itself. The worst reaction to this final depression would be to try to end it. Those who ask the dying person to cheer up during a preparatory depression also ask that person to stop preparing for death—a cruel and heartless request. Our need to have dying friends or family come out of their depression only points out our own fear of death and inability to tolerate its reality.

> In the preparatory grief there is no or little need for words. It is much more a feeling that can be mutually expressed and is often done better with a touch of a hand, a stroking of the hair, or just a silent sitting together. This is the time when the patient may just ask for a prayer, when he begins to occupy himself with things ahead rather than behind. It is a time when too much interference from visitors who try to cheer him up hinders his emotional preparation rather than enhances it. (8)

Acceptance and Hope

"If a patient has had enough time (i.e., not a sudden, unexpected death) and has been given some help in working through the previously described stages," Kubler-Ross tells us, "he will reach a stage during which he is neither depressed nor angry about his 'fate'"

> He will have been able to express his previous feelings, his envy for the living and the healthy, his anger at those who do not have to face their end so soon. He will have mourned the impending loss of so many meaningful people and places and he will contemplate his coming end with a certain degree of quiet expectation. He will be tired and, in most cases, quite weak. (9)

The patient who comes to this natural **acceptance** of the end spends a great deal of time in sleep. The patient's sleep does not represent a "giving up." Rather the person simply rests for the ordeal of facing death realistically. The stage is not a happy or unhappy one. It is devoid of feeling. The dying person does not want to talk, particularly about the world and its affairs. Most of the time, quiet communication seems most appropriate. A moment with a patient in this stage of acceptance is usually a reflective time in which we simply say, "I am here." Opportunities to stay with dying people in this stage of acceptance should not be lost. Our presence not only communicates our concern, but also gives us a realistic view of death. Such moments can teach us a great deal about our life as well as our death.

Dr. Kubler-Ross found hope among most of her patients right to the end. Sometimes this hope came in the form of unrealistic expectations for a miracle cure. At other times, the hope abounded when everyone around the dying patient—friends, family, and doctors—seemed incapable of further hope. Naturally, they all faced periods of despair as well. But the highest human aspirations sustain even those in the depths of painful and destructive illness. And the hopes that sustain those facing their last days say more about life than any other experience.

SUMMARY

1. Erik Erikson discussed the stages of life that extend past early childhood. For each he suggests a task that characterizes the stage. During latency, for example, each child struggles to become industrious according to the norms of the society. Failure to achieve industry leaves children with feelings of inferiority.
2. Successful completion of the latency task immediately plunges young people into a struggle with personal identity. They begin to ask themselves the question, "Who am I?" Failure at this task results in role confusion and leaves the young people uncertain about who they are and how they fit into society.
3. Those young people who find their identity face another task. They must take that personal sense of definition and look for friendship. They seek intimacy with one another. They sacrifice their privacy to establish friendships. Those who fail to make intimate contacts during this period soon fall into isolation.
4. Adults need to become generative or face stagnation. They may express their need by becoming parents, or they may find other creative ways to satisfy this need. And finally in old age, people must integrate the various parts of their life into a meaningful whole or fall into despair.
5. Dr. Kubler-Ross helps us all see death as an integral part of the life process. She points out that it is normal for the dying people to first deny that their illness is terminal. Just as normal is their fury at the discovery that the doctors were telling the truth and that fate had struck them a cruel blow. We do such patients no favor by encouraging them to forget their feelings. We should help them then by allowing them their period of denial and giving them freedom to vent their anger.
6. Dying people also quite naturally enter into periods of bargaining with the "fates" to save them. A sustained depresssion is also a normal and natural part of the dying process. Only after all the stages have run their course can the dying people accept their fate. This is a period of resignation. But hope prevails through all the stages. Contact with that hope in a dying person can give us all a greater hope for ourselves.

KEY TERMS

latency	stagnation
industry	ego integrity
inferiority	despair
identity	denial
role confusion	anger
intimacy	bargaining
isolation	reactive depression
genitality	preparatory depression
generativity	acceptance

STUDY QUESTIONS

1. Did you personally face a crisis of identity during your adolescence? If so, do you consider it the most important turning point in your life? Explain.
2. Do you believe your own attempts to find intimacy in your life are more or less difficult than those of your friends? Explain the differences.
3. Imagine you were told you would soon die. What would you like your friends to say to you? Would you say those same things to people you know are sick and dying?
4. Kubler-Ross says dying people must go through a period of deep depression and that we interrupt an important process when we try to cheer them up. Do you believe this is true? Explain.
5. Kubler-Ross also tells us that we must let dying people become angry before they can accept their fate. How do you feel about this? Explain.

ADDITIONAL READING

Blos, P. *On Adolescence: A Psychoanalytic Interpretation.* New York: Free, 1962.
Bowley, J. *Separation.* New York: Basic, 1973.
Erikson, E. H. *Childhood and Society.* New York: Norton, 1963.
_____. *Identity: Youth and Crisis.* New York: Norton, 1968.
Jung, C. G. (Aniela Jaffe, ed.). *Memories, Dreams, and Reflections.* New York: Vintage, 1965.
Kubler-Ross, E. *Death: The Final Stage of Growth.* Englewood Cliffs, N.J.: Prentice-Hall, 1975.
_____. *On Death and Dying.* New York: Macmillan, 1969.
Levinson, D. J. *The Seasons of a Man's Life.* New York: Knopf, 1978.
Moody, R. A. *Life After Life.* New York: Bantam, 1976.
Neugarten, B. L. (Ed.) *Middle Age and Aging.* Chicago: University of Chicago Press, 1968.

NOTES

Chapter One

1. Calvin S. Hall and Gardner Lindzey, *Theories of Personality* (New York: John Wiley and Sons, 1970), p. 515.
2. An interview with James D. Papsdorf, Department of Psychology, University of Michigan at Ann Arbor. *Human Behavior* 7 (1978): 50–51.
3. Hall and Lindzey, p. 30.
4. An interview with Roger Bennett, School of Journalism, Ohio University, Athens, Ohio. *Human Behavior* 7 (1978): 34–35.
5. Duane Schultz, *A History of Modern Psychology* (New York: Academic Press, 1975), p. 317.
6. Russell Noyes, Jr. et al., "Depersonalization in Accident Victims and Psychiatric Patients," *The Journal of Nervous and Mental Disease* 164 (1977): 401–407.
7. B. F. Skinner, *About Behaviorism* (New York: Vintage, 1976), p. 184.
8. Edward C. Tolman, *Behavior and Psychological Man* (Berkeley and Los Angeles: University of California, 1966), p. 49.
9. An interview with Ronald Nelson, Executive Vice President, Consumer Response Corporation, New York, New York. *Human Behavior* 7 (1978): 49.
10. Skinner, p. 51.
11. Ibid., p. 208.
12. Marianne W. DeVoe, "Cooperation as a Function of Self-concept, Sex and Race," *Educational Research Quarterly* 2 (1977): 3–8.
13. Carl R. Rogers, *On Becoming a Person* (Boston: Houghton Mifflin, 1961), p. 315.
14. Hadley A. Cantril, "A Fresh Look at the Human Design," in *Challenges of Humanistic Psychology*, ed. James F. T. Bugental (New York: McGraw-Hill, 1967), p. 13.
15. James F. T. Bugental, *Challenges of Humanistic Psychology* (New York: McGraw-Hill, 1967), pp. 1–2.
16. John S. Dunne, *The Way of All the Earth* (New York: Macmillan, 1972). p. x.

Chapter Two

1. Erik H. Erikson, *Childhood and Society* (New York: Norton, 1969), p. 249.
2. Bonnie W. Camp, "Verbal Mediation in Young Aggressive Boys," *Journal of Abnormal Psychology* 86 (1977):145–153.
3. Jonas Langer, *Theories of Development* (New York: Holt, Rinehart and Winston, 1969): p. 40.
4. Hall and Lindzey, *Theories of Personality*, p. 52.
5. A. Nicholas Groth and Ann Wolber Burgess, "Sexual Dysfunction During Rape," *The New England Journal of Medicine* 297 (1977): 764–766.

6. Sigmund Freud, *New Introductory Lectures on Psychoanalysis* (New York: Norton, 1965), p. 110.
7. Hall and Lindzey, p. 479.
8. Anita Woolfolk, Robert I. Woolfolk, and G. Terrence Wilson, "A Rose by any Other Name . . .: Labeling Bias and Attitudes Toward Behavior Modification," *Journal of Consulting and Clinical Psychology* 45 (1977): 184–191.
9. Langer, p. 51.
10. Skinner, *About Behaviorism*, p. 64.
11. Tanya Grieger, James M. Kauffman, and Russell M. Grieger, "Effects of Peer Reporting on Cooperative Play and Aggression of Kindergarten Children," *Journal of School Psychology* 14 (1977): 307–313.
12. Skinner, p. 64.
13. Rollo May, *Man's Search For Himself* (New York: Signet, 1967), p. 138.
14. Rogers, *Person*, p. 189.
15. Thomas Gaines, Jr., Paul M. Kirwin, and W. Doyle Gentry, "The Effect of Descriptive Anger Expression, Insult, and No Feedback on Interpersonal Aggression, Hostility, and Empathy Motivation," *Genetics Psychology Monographs* 95 (1977): 349–367.

Chapter Three

1. Adelaide Bry, *A Primer of Behavioral Psychology* (New York: Mentor, 1975) pp. 22–23.
2. Ibid. p. 24.
3. Ibid. pp. 24–25.
4. Skinner, *About Behaviorism* p. 44.
5. Wolfgang Kohler, *The Mentality of Apes* (New York: Harcourt, Brace and World, 1925) p. 174–175.
6. Edward C. Tolman, "Cognitive Maps in Rats and Men," *Psychological Review* 55 (1948): 189–208.
7. B. T. Gardner and R. A. Gardner, "Two-way Communication with an Infant Chimpanzee." In A. Schrier and F. Stollnitz (eds.), *Behavior of Non-human Primates* (New York: Academic Press, 1971).
8. Edward C. Tolman and C. H. Honzik, "Introduction and Removal of Reward and Maze Performance in Rats," *University of California Publications in Psychology* 4 (1930): 257–275.
9. Robert Rosenthal and Lenore Jacobson, *Pygmalion in the Classroom* (New York: Holt, Rinehart and Winston, 1968), p. 177.
10. Jerome S. Bruner, *The Process of Education* (Cambridge: Harvard, 1961), p. 55.
11. Carl R. Rogers, *The Freedom to Learn* (Columbus, Ohio: Merrill, 1969), p. 126.

Chapter Four

1. Frieda Fordham, *An Introduction to Jung's Psychology* (New York: Penguin, 1953), pp. 29–30.
2. Anthony Storr, *C. G. Jung* (New York: Viking, 1973), p. 63.
3. Ibid., p. 61.
4. Rodger W. Griffeth and Ronald W. Rogers, "Effect of Fear-Arousing Components of Driver Education or Students' Safety Attitudes and Simulator Performance," *Journal of Educational Psychology* 68 (1976): 501–506.

5. Storr, p. 63.
6. Daniel J. Levinson et al., "Periods of Adult Development of Men: Ages 18 to 25," *The Counseling Psychologist* 6 (1977): 21–25.
7. Skinner, *About Behaviorism*, p. 174.
8. Ibid., p. 175.
9. Ibid., pp. 177–178.
10. Alexander Tolor, Bryan R. Kelly, and Charles A. Stebbins, "Altruism in Psychiatric Patients: How Socially Concerned Are the Emotionally Disturbed?" *Journal of Consulting and Clinical Psychology* 44 (1976): 503–507.
11. Rogers, *Freedom*, pp. 108–109.
12. Carl R. Rogers, *Carl Rogers on Encounter Groups* (New York: Harper & Row, 1970), p. 18.
13. Ibid., p. 104.
14. Ibid., p. 175.

Chapter Five

1. Calvin S. Hall, *A Primer of Freudian Psychology* (New York: Mentor, 1954), p. 61.
2. Ibid., p. 63.
3. Freud, *Introductory Lectures*, p. 73.
4. Hall, pp. 65–66.
5. David Spiegel, "A Group Approach to Treating Metastatic Breast Cancer" (Paper presented at the 85th Annual Meeting of the American Psychological Association, San Francisco, California, August, 1977).
6. Hall, p. 68.
7. Ronnie Janoff Bulman and Camille B. Wortman, "Attribution of Blame and Coping in the 'Real World': Severe Accident Victims React to Their Lot," *Journal of Personality and Social Psychology* 35 (1977): 351–363.
8. Skinner, *About Behaviorism*, p. 68.
9. Pat Stitch, An interview in *Human Behavior* 7 (1977): 34.
10. Skinner, p. 69.
11. Bry, *Primer*, p. 25.
12. Ibid., p. 29.
13. Peter H. Waxer, "Nonverbal Cues for Anxiety: An Examination of Emotional Leakage," *Journal of Abnormal Psychology* 86 (1977): 306–314.
14. May, *Man's Search*, p. 31.
15. Ibid., pp. 13–14.
16. James J. Lynch, An interview in *Human Behavior* 7 (1978): 61.
17. May, p. 35.
18. Ibid., p. 35–36.
19. Ibid., p. 39.

Chapter Six

1. Sigmund Freud, *The Ego and the Id* (New York: Norton, 1920), p. 11.
2. Erich Fromm, *The Anatomy of Human Destructiveness* (New York: Holt, Rinehart and Winston, 1973), p. 15.
3. D. Kaplun and R. Reich, "The Murdered Child and His Killers," *The American Journal of Psychiatry* 133 (1976): 809–813.
4. Hall and Lindzey, *Theories of Personality*, p. 39.

5. John Dollard et al. *Frustration and Aggression* (New York: Yale, 1939), p. 1.
6. Albert Bandura and R. H. Walters, *Social Learning and Personality Development* (New York: Holt, Rinehart and Winston, 1963), p. 47.
7. Albert Bandura, Dorothea Ross, and Sheila Ross, "Imitation of Film-Mediated Aggressive Models," in *Confrontation: Psychology and the Problems of Today*, ed. Michael Wertheimer (Glenview, Ill.: Scott, Foresman, 1970).
8. Stanley Milgram, "Behavior Study of Obedience," *Journal of Abnormal and Social Psychology* 67 (1977): 371–378.
9. Rogers, *Person*, p. 194.
10. Rollo May, *Power and Innocence* (New York: Delta, 1972), p. 182.
11. Ezra Stotland, "Self-Esteem and Violence by Guards and State Troopers at Attica," *Criminal Justice and Behavior* 3 (1976) 85–96.
12. Anthony Storr, *Human Aggression* (New York: Bantam, 1968), p. 48.
13. Richard J. Borden and Gordon M. Homleid, "Handedness and Lateral Positioning in Heterosexual Couples: Men are Still Strongarming Women" (Paper presented at the 48th Annual Meeting of the Midwestern Psychological Association Chicago, Illinois, May, 1976).
14. George R. Bach and Peter Wyden, *The Intimate Enemy* (New York: Avon, 1970), p. 17.

Chapter Seven

1. Hall, *Primer of Freudian Psychology*, p. 55.
2. Ibid., p. 14.
3. Sigmund Freud, *The Complete Psychological Works of Sigmund Freud* (New York: Norton, 1976), p. 83.
4. Edward F. Foulks "A Sociobiologic Model of Schizophrenia" (A paper presented at the American Anthropological Association Annual Meeting in San Francisco, California, December, 1975).
5. Joseph Wolpe, "The Systematic Desensitization Treatment of Neuroses," *Journal of Nervous and Mental Diseases* 132 (1961): 189–203.
6. Stephen Brand, "Personal Management of Growth: Productivity, Decision-Making, Emotion, and Social Behavior in My Senior Year," *Adolescence* 10 (1975): 549–562.
7. Hall and Lindzey, *Theories of Personality*, p. 463.
8. Albert Bandura, E. B. Blanchard, and B. Ritter, "Relative Efficacy of Desensitization and Modeling Approaches for Inducing Behavioral, Affective and Attitudinal Changes," *Journal of Personality and Social Psychology* 13 (1969): 173–199.
9. Lawrence V. Harper and Karen M. Sanders, "The Effect of Adults' Eating on Young Children's Acceptance of Unfamiliar Foods," *Journal of Experimental Child Psychology* 20 (1975): 206–214.
10. David Knox, *Marriage Happiness* (Champaign, Illinois: Research, 1972), p. 26.
11. Rogers, *Person*, p. 34.
12. Iradj Siassi and Stanley B. Messer, "Psychotherapy with Patients from Lower Socioeconomic Groups," *American Journal of Psychotherapy* 30 (1976): 29–40.
13. Rogers, *Person*, p. 52.
14. Ibid., p. 22.

Chapter Eight

1. Calvin S. Hall and Vernon J. Norby, *A Primer of Jungian Psychology* (New York: Mentor, 1973), pp. 39–40.
2. Hall and Lindzey, *Theories of Personality*, pp. 84–85.
3. Fordham, *Jung's Psychology*, p. 49.
4. Raymond E. Rainville and Edward McCormick, "Extent of Covert Racial Prejudice in Pro-Football Announcers' Speech," *Journalism Quarterly* 54 (1977): 20–26.
5. Hall and Lindzey, p. 86.
6. Roger A. Woudenberg, "The Relationship of Sexual Attitudes, Attitudes about Women, and Racial Attitude in White Males," *Sex Roles* 3 (1977): 101–110.
7. Thomas R. Clark, "Homosexuality as a Criterion Predictor of Psychopathology in Non-patient Males (Paper presented at the Western Psychological Association Convention in Sacramento, California, April, 1975).
8. R. H. Abrams, "Residential Propinquity as a Factor in Marriage Selection: Fifty Year Trends in Philadelphia," *American Sociological Review* 8 (1943): 288–294.
9. Theodore Caplow and Robert Forman, "Neighborhood Interaction in a Homogeneous Community," *American Sociological Review* 15 (1950): 357–366.
10. Leon Festinger, S. Schachter, and K. Back, *Social Pressures in Informal Groups* (New York: Harper & Row, 1950).
11. Bernard Steinzor, "The Spatial Factor in Face to Face Discussion Groups," *Journal of Abnormal and Social Psychology*, 45 (1950): 552–555.
12. Festinger, p. 132.
13. Donn Byrne, "The Influence of Propinquity and Opportunities for Interaction on Classroom Relationships," *Human Relations* 14 (1961): 63–69.
14. Morton Deutsch and Mary E. Collins, *Interracial Housing* (Minneapolis: University of Minnesota Press, 1951).
15. G. R. Thornton, "The Effect of Wearing Glasses upon Judgments of Personality Traits on Persons Seen Briefly," *Journal of Applied Psychology* 28 (1944): 203–207.
16. Mark J. Jones, An interview in *Human Behavior* 4 (1975): 55.
17. A. J. Smith, "Similarity of Values and Its Relation to Acceptance and the Projection of Similarity," *Journal of Psychology* 43 (1957): 251–260.
18. Abraham Maslow, *Toward a Psychology of Being* (New York: Van Nostrand, 1968), p. 149.
19. W. F. Dove, "A Study of Individuality in the Nutritive Instincts," *American Naturalist* 7 (1935): 469–544.
20. Maslow, p. 169.
21. Abraham H. Maslow, *Motivation and Personality* (New York: Harper & Row, 1954).
22. Frank Goble, *The Third Force* (New York: Pocket, 1970) pp. 92–93.
23. Abraham H. Maslow, "Eupsychia–the Good Society," *Journal of Humanistic Psychology* 2 (1961).

Chapter Nine

1. Hall, *Primer of Freudian Psychology*, p. 86.
2. Ibid., p. 89.

3. R. L. Monroe, *Schools of Psychoanalytic Thought,* New York: Holt, Rinehart and Winston, 1955), p. 254.
4. Julius Fast, *Body Language* (New York: Pocket, 1970), p. 42.
5. Carol Werner and Lee Hanchett, "Eye Contact as an Inhibitor of Responsibility Diffusion" (Paper presented at the Rocky Mountain Psychological Association Convention at Salt Lake City, Utah, May, 1975).
6. Fast, pp. 80–82.
7. Rogers, *Person,* pp. 339–340.
8. Fast, pp. 340–341.
9. Lewis Brodsky, "Anger Provocation as a Crisis Intervention Technique," *Hospital and Community Psychiatry* 28 (1977): 533–536.
10. Rogers, p. 342.
11. Ibid., pp. 330–331.
12. Ibid., p. 331.
13. Ibid., pp. 332–333.

Chapter Ten

1. Karen Horney, *The Neurotic Personality of Our Time* (New York: Norton, 1937), pp. 20–21.
2. Ibid., pp. 88–89.
3. Martin L. Hoffman, "Altruistic Behavior and the Parent-Child Relationship," *Journal of Personality* 31 (1975): 937–942.
4. Eric Erikson, *Identity: Youth and Crisis* (New York: Norton, 1968), pp. 155–156.
5. J. F. Dashiell, "Experimental Studies of the Influence of Social Situations on the Behavior of Individual Human Adults," *Handbook of Social Psychology* (Worcester, Mass.: Clark University Press, 1935).
6. Marvin Dunnette, John Campbell, and Kay Jaastad, "The Effect of Group Participation on Brainstorming Effectiveness for Two Industrial Samples," *Journal of Applied Psychology* 30 (1963): 30–37.
7. K. Lewin, R. Lippit, and R. K. White, "Patterns of Aggressive Behavior in Experimentally Created 'Climates,'" *Journal of Social Psychology* 10, (1939): 271–299.
8. Mazafer Sherif, *The Psychology of Social Norms* (New York: Harper, 1936).
9. Solomon E. Asch, *Social Psychology* (Englewood Cliffs, N. J.: Prentice-Hall, 1952).
10. Maryla Zaleska and F. Askevis-Leherpeux, "Influence of the Style of Presentation of a Contingency Series on the Choice of a Strategy," *Année Psychologique* 2 (1976): 501–513.
11. Carl R. Rogers, *Carl Rogers on Encounter Groups* (New York: Harper and Row, 1970), pp. 7–10.
12. Ibid., p. 19.
13. Ibid., p. 27.
14. Morton A. Lieberman, Irvin D. Yalom, and Matthew B. Miles, *Encounter Groups: First Facts* (New York: Basic, 1973).

Chapter Eleven

1. Erich Fromm, *The Art of Loving* (New York: Bantam, 1956), pp. 3–4.
2. Ibid., p. 5.

3. Ibid., p. 92.
4. Ibid., p. 107.
5. Abraham Tesser and Michael Brodie, "A Note of the Evaluation of a 'Computer Date,'" *Psychonomic Science* 23 (1971): 300.
6. Elaine Walster et al., "Importance of Physical Attractiveness in Dating Behavior," *Journal of Personality and Social Psychology* 4 (1966): 508–516.
7. Ellen Berscheid et al., "Physical Attractiveness and Dating Choice: A Test of the Matching Hypothesis," *Journal of Experimental Social Psychology* 7 (1971): 173–189.
8. Dennis Krebs and A. Adinolfi, "Physical Attractiveness, Social Relations, and Personality Style," *Journal of Personality and Social Psychology* 31 (1975): 245–253.
9. Harold Sigall and David Landy, "Radiating Beauty: The Effects of Having a Physically Attractive Partner on Personal Perception," *Journal of Personality and Social Psychology* 28 (1973): 218–224.
10. Zick Rubin, "Measurements of Romantic Love," *Journal of Personality and Social Psychology* 16 (1970): 265–273.
11. Elaine Walster et al., "'Playing Hard to Get': Understanding an Elusive Phenomenon," *Journal of Personality and Social Psychology* 26 (1973): 113–121.
12. Frederick S. Perls, *Gestalt Therapy Verbatim* (Moab, Utah: Real People Press, 1969), p. 3.
13. Joseph Simons and Jeanne Reidy, *The Risk of Loving* (New York: Seabury, 1973), p. 13.
14. Ibid., p. 31.
15. Ibid., p. 52.
16. Ibid., p. 142.

Chapter Twelve

1. Hall and Nordby, p. 46.
2. Hall and Norby, pp. 46–47.
3. Deanna Kuhn, Sharon Nash and Laura Brucken, "Sex-role Concepts of Two- and Three-year-olds. A paper presented at the Western Psychological Association in Los Angeles, California. April, 1976.
4. Carl G. Jung, *The Development of the Personality* (New York: Pantheon, 1954), p. 198.
5. Hall and Norby, *Jungian Psychology*, p. 48.
6. Elaine Crovitz and Arthur Robbins, An interview in *Human Behavior* 7 (1978): 40–41.
7. Alfred Kinsey et al., *Sexual Behavior in the Human Male* (Philadelphia: Saunders, 1948).
8. Alfred Kinsey et al., *Sexual Behavior in the Human Female* (Philadelphia: Saunders, 1953).
9. William H. Masters and Virginia A. Johnson, *Human Sexual Response* (Boston: Little, Brown, 1966).
10. Rollo May, *Love and Will* (New York: Dell, 1969)., p. 16.
11. Ibid., p. 33.
12. Ibid., p. 12.
13. Ibid., p. 47.

14. W. Charles Lobitz, An interview in *Human Behavior,* 7 (1978): 49.
15. May, p. 73.

Chapter Thirteen

1. Nena O'Neill and George O'Neill, *Open Marriage* (New York: Avon, 1972), p. 39.
2. Ibid., p. 92.
3. Ronald Burke and Tamara Weir, "Relationship of Wives' Employment Status to Husband, Wife, and Pair Satisfaction and Performance," *Journal of Marriage and the Family,* 38 (1976): 279–287.
4. O'Neill and O'Neill, p. 173.
5. Ibid.
6. Haim G. Ginott, *Between Parent and Child* (New York: Avon, 1965), p. 26.
7. Ibid., p. 27.
8. Ibid., p. 22–23.
9. Ibid., p. 46.
10. Ibid., p. 59.
11. Ibid., p. 116.
12. Ibid., p. 118.
13. Suzanne K. Steinmetz, "The Use of Force for Resolving Conflict: The Training Ground for Abuse," *The Family Coordinator* 26 (1977): 19–26.
14. Mel Krantzler, *Creative Divorce* (New York: Signet, 1973) p. 40.
15. Ibid., p. 54.
16. Ibid., p. 81.
17. Ibid., p. 118.

Chapter Fourteen

1. John C. Smart, "Distinctive Career Orientations of Holland Personality Types," *Journal of Vocational Behavior* 8 (1976): 313–319.
2. Martin G. Evans, "A Longitudinal Analysis of the Impact of Flexible Working Hours," *Studies in Personnel Psychology* 6 (1975): 1–10.

Chapter Fifteen

1. Erikson, *Youth and Crisis,* pp. 258–259.
2. Ibid., p. 261.
3. J. Cohen, "The Impact of the Leading Crowd on High School Change: A Reassessment," *Adolescence* 11 (1976): 373–381.
4. Erikson, pp. 264–265.
5. Ibid., p. 269.
6. M. A. Borges and L. Dutton, "Attitudes Toward Aging: Increasing Optimism Found with Age" (Paper presented at the 56th Annual Meeting of the Western Psychological Association, Los Angeles, California, April, 1976).
7. Elizabeth Kubler-Ross, *On Death and Dying* (New York: Macmillan, 1969), p. 38.
8. Ibid., pp. 87–88.
9. Ibid., p. 112.

GLOSSARY

Acceptance 1. Carl Rogers' term for a therapist's warm, unconditional regard for a client. 2. Dying people's final acceptance of their fate and the reality of their condition.

Acceptance of feelings The humanistic attitude and philosophy that we should acknowledge that our feelings exist and not try to repress them.

Aggression Behavior through which we intend to harm another person.

Altruism Unselfish interest in the welfare of others.

Anal stage The second of Freud's psychosexual stages of development, characterized by concern with the control of one's bodily functions.

Anger Kubler-Ross' technical term for the second stage of death in which people vent their hostility at the "fates" that chose them to die.

Anima The feminine side of a male's personality.

Animus The masculine side of a female's personality.

Anxiety A state of apprehension or uneasiness resulting from an indefinite cause.

Apathy A lack of emotion.

Archetype Jung's term for our inherent predisposition to perceive and react to the world in certain ways.

Assertiveness Positive, direct behavior.

Assertiveness training A type of conditioning through which assertive responses are reinforced to help people overcome passivity.

Authoritarian leader A group guide who dominates his or her group with instructions and commands.

Autokinetic illusion Apparent, but not actual, movement of a single stable light after a person has stared at that light for a period of time.

Aversive stimuli Painful or unpleasant stimuli.

Bad-me A term used by Sullivan to suggest the negative attitudes we develop toward ourselves when others disapprove of us.

Bargaining Kubler-Ross' third stage in the dying process, during which dying people try desperately and irrationally to change their fate.

Behavior control Alteration of behavior through the systematic application of rewards and punishments.

Bisexuality Possessing characteristics of, or sexually oriented toward, both sexes.

Castration anxiety Freudian term for a boy's fears that he will be castrated by his father.

Charismatic A personal quality of leadership arousing special popular loyalty or enthusiasm.

Classical conditioning A basic form of learning in which stimuli initially incapable of evoking certain responses acquire the ability to do so through repeated pairing with other stimuli that are able to elicit such responses.

Cognitive psychologists Psychologists who emphasize the role of thought in determining behavior.

Cognitive structure The organization the mind uses to recall whatever is learned.

Coitus Sexual intercourse.

Collective unconscious Jung's term for the inborn portion of the unconscious that is common to all people.

Conditioned stimulus A stimulus that acquires the capacity to evoke particular responses through repeated pairing with another stimulus capable of eliciting the responses.

Coping A method of direct problem solving for

personal problems, usually contrasted with defense mechanisms.

Death instincts Freud's term for our destructive tendencies and life's impulse to return to the inorganic state through death.

Defense mechanisms Various techniques we use, including denial, repression, projection, displacement, and intellectualization, to reduce or avoid anxiety by distorting the source of our conflict or by obscuring the conflict entirely.

Democratic leader A group guide who encourages his or her group to make shared decisions.

Denial Kubler-Ross' term for the first stage of dying in which dying people need to avoid the truth of their condition.

Desensitization A technique of behavior modification intended to gradually ease a person's fear or phobic responses.

Developmental theories Career-choice theories that focus on the self-development of adolescence.

Diagnostic formulations Technique for identifying mental illness by looking at its symptoms and signs.

Discovery learning The process through which a person learns by doing.

Discrimination The process by which an organism distinguishes between closely related items and responds to each item distinctly.

Dream interpretation An analysis of dream material in the process of psychotherapy.

Ego Freud's term for the conscious, logical part of our mind that keeps us in contact with reality.

Electra complex A Freudian term for a girl's love for her father and hostility toward her mother.

Emotion The experiencing, organizing, and interpreting of the bodily sensations accompanying a stimulus or event.

Emotional maturity The psychological balance one can achieve after a certain period of time and experience.

Encounter groups A type of group therapy with encouragement of open expression of feelings as its main emphasis.

Environmentally formed A term often used by behaviorists to suggest that our personality is determined by our environment.

Ethical relativism The theory that ethical concerns are never absolute.

Extinction The disappearance of a conditioned response when reinforcement is withdrawn.

Extroverts People who are more concerned with the world around them than with their inner world of experience.

Facade A false, superficial, or artificial appearance.

Facilitate To make easier or smoother.

Fair fights Fights in which the participants avoid blaming one another.

First impression The influence that results from an initial encounter.

Free association A person's attempt to report without modification whatever comes into his or her awareness.

Free choice The theory that we determine our own destiny rather than our destiny being imposed on us by forces beyond our control.

Freudian slip A confusion of speech patterns that Freud thought originates in the unconscious and reveals the thoughts in the unconscious.

Frustration Circumstances that block or interfere with our achievement of goals.

Generalization The process in which organisms respond similarly to stimuli that resemble one another.

Generativity Erikson's seventh stage of growth, which has generativity, or the need to be needed, as its goal.

Genetics The study of heredity.

Good-me A term used by Sullivan for the positive attitudes we develop toward ourselves when others approve of us.

Group dynamics The nature and sequence of interaction among individuals in groups.

Group therapy A therapy that attempts to treat several patients simultaneously.

Guilt Anxious feelings arising from behavior or desires contrary to one's ethical principles.

Hallucination A sense experience without the appropriate stimuli.

Hard-to-get An attitude some women adopt to make themselves appear more desirable to men by pretending to be an elusive prize

Hollow people Rollo May's term for people who lead empty or meaningless lives because they are out of touch with their feelings.

Homeostasis The organism's attempt to achieve a balance that will allow it to function at its best.

Homosexuality Of, relating to, or exhibiting sexual desires toward members of one's own sex.

Human potential The ideal toward which humans can grow.

Hypnosis The process of inducing a trance state.

Hysteria A nervous disorder marked especially by defective emotional control.

Id Freud's term for the unconscious part of the personality composed of primitive, instinctive forces toward sexuality and aggression.

Identity The goal for adolescents during Erikson's fifth stage of life of discovering who they are and their place in the world.

Imitation learning Behavior in which we copy the actions of another.

Impotence Powerlessness.

Incongruence Rogers' term for a lack of harmony between the mind and the emotions.

Individuation The process through which we search for a sense of personal unity.

Industry The goal for children during Erikson's fourth stage of life of learning the skills necessary to succeed in their culture.

Inferential Deduced.

Inferiority Withdrawal experienced by children who fail the task of Erikson's fourth stage.

Insight The sudden discovery of the essential elements necessary in the solution of a problem.

Interpersonal Related to or involving relations between people.

In the now The state of complete absorption with the present moment.

Intimacy The young adult's close relationship with others that develops after the young adult's successful search for personal identity, according to Erikson.

Introverts Those people who, particularly in times of stress, tend to withdraw into themselves and avoid other people.

Isolation Erikson's term for the withdrawal from all relationships by the young adult who fails to find intimacy.

Kinesics Nonverbal and primarily unconscious communication through body movements.

Laissez-faire leader A group guide who allows his or her group to do whatever they decide they want to do.

Latency According to Freud, the period of psychosexual development (about ages six to twelve) during which sexual urges are dormant.

Latent learning Learning that takes place when it is unnecessary or undesirable and which remains unexpressed behaviorally until it becomes necessary at a later time.

Learning A relatively permanent change in behavior as the result of experience or practice.

Life instincts Those instincts, according to Freud, that serve the purpose of individual survival and racial propagation.

Loneliness The emotional state of feeling isolated, without any recognized concern or care for others.

Love scale A test that attempts to distinguish between the attitudes of liking and loving.

Manic-depression Psychotic condition characterized by dramatic mood swings from the extremes of elation to the extremes of depression.

Mask An assumed behavior or attitude used to hide our feelings from ourselves and others.

Masturbation Stimulation of the genital organs to a climax of excitement by contact exclusive of sexual intercourse.

Mechanical mirror A behavioristic term for illustrating how we are formed by the environment: the child enters the world and reflects what is going on around him or her.

Monogamy Marriage with only one person at a time.

Moral anxiety The apprehension that arises

from conflicts of conscience, experienced as guilt or shame.

Naturalistic Innate.
Need-drive theory A theory that explains career choice in terms of unmet needs and drives originating in the personality.
Need hierarchy An expression used by Maslow to suggest that until one group of needs is met, for example, our physical needs, we cannot begin taking care of the next group of needs, for example, our safety needs.
Neurotic anxiety A person's fear that arises from unconscious conflicts.
Nocturnal orgasm Orgasms that occur spontaneously in sleep.
Not-me Sullivan's term for our disgust with ourselves when others become openly hostile to us.

Oedipus complex The Freudian theory that a young boy develops sexual attraction toward his mother and feelings of hostility toward his father.
Open marriage Marriage focused on individual growth by encouraging free communication, role flexibility, and activities and relationships outside of the marriage.
Operant conditioning The process by which voluntary behavior becomes attached to a specific stimulus.
Oral stage The first of Freud's psychosexual stages of development, characterized by dependence on the mother and her nipple.
Organism An individual animal, either human or subhuman.
Orgasm A climax of sexual excitement.
Overpermissive A parental attitude that grants children freedom to express angry feelings in destructive acts.
Overt Observable.

Paranoia A psychotic condition characterized by feelings of grandeur and persecution.
Penis envy A Freudian term for the young girl's envy of the penis that she thinks was removed from her.
Permissive A parental attitude that grants children the freedom to express their feelings and emotions except in destructive acts.

Persona The mask we wear to affect conformity.
Personal identity Our ability to describe ourselves accurately.
Personal space The area around us that we protect from the intrusion of others.
Petting Sexual stimulation between partners, usually short of intercourse.
Phallic stage The third of Freud's psychosexual stages of development, characterized in part by the child's sexual attraction to the parent of the opposite sex.
Phobia An irrational apprehension which the victim, though aware of its irrational nature, cannot overcome.
Pleasure principle Freud's term for the demand of our unconscious id for immediate and total satisfaction of all desires.
Projection The mechanism through which people assign their own undesirable traits to another person.
Propinquity Nearness in place or time.
Punishment A negative incentive, capable of producing pain or annoyance.
Puritanism One who practices or preaches a stricter moral code than the current one prevailing in society.

Reaction formation The mechanism that protects a person from an attitude by giving strong expression to its opposite.
Reactive depression In Kubler-Ross' fourth stage of dying, the depression felt by dying people as a reaction to the physical and economic losses of their illness.
Reality anxiety The apprehension that arises from objective dangers in the real world.
Reality principle The principle on which the conscious ego operates to delay gratification demanded by the id because of the demands of reality.
Reconfirmation effect The emotional process that allows divorced couples to accept the reality of their divorce.
Reflex behavior An automatic reaction to a stimulus.
Repression The defense mechanism that denies an impulse or memory that might provoke anxiety.
Reward A positive incentive to behavior capable of arousing pleasure or satisfying a drive.

Risky shift The tendency of group members to take chances as a group that they might never take as individuals.

Role confusion Erikson's term for the unfocused feelings about themselves that adolescents experience if they fail to discover a sense of their personal identity.

Role flexibility The ability to behave outside the norms society thinks proper for us.

Schizoid Rollo May's term for a person who avoids close relationships because of an inability to experience emotion.

Schizophrenic A psychotic who is plagued by thought disorders and often endures emotional disturbances and even motor disturbances.

Search for security An expression Horney uses to explain the basic drive in life, the need for security, especially in contrast to Freud's emphasis on the sexual drive.

Self The central reference point in our personality around which experience and actions are organized.

Self-actualization Maslow's term for the process of fulfilling one's potential as a person.

Self-defeating patterns Patterns of behavior that have the opposite effects of those intended.

Self-esteem Feelings of personal worth.

Sexologist A psychologist whose primary professional interest concerns sexual matters.

Sex roles The behavior society thinks proper for an individual based on his or her sex.

Shadow Jung's term for the archetype of the animal side of our nature.

Sign learning Learning that helps us understand how one thing can signal another.

Simple assertion A direct statement of fact, a method used in assertiveness training.

Snake phobia An unreasonable fear of snakes.

Social learning Learning that occurs as a result of social interaction.

Sounds of silence Those thoughts and feelings we would like to express to others but fail to reveal.

Spontaneous recovery In conditioning, the reappearance of a response after a period during which the response appeared to have extinguished fully and a rest period.

Stagnation Erikson's term for the inward-turning of adults who fail to achieve the goal of the seventh stage, generativity.

Standing in love The permanent state of being in love.

Subjective What arises in our mind as opposed to objective fact.

Superego The largely unconscious part of our personality that threatens punishment for transgressions and offers rewards for perfection.

Supernaturalism Relating to phenomenon beyond or outside of nature.

Symbols Something that stands for something else, as a red light is a symbol that tells us to stop.

Theory X Employers who have a Theory-X attitude toward their workers have a pessimistic outlook and feel they must force their employees to perform.

Theory Y Employers with a Theory-Y attitude feel that, given the proper working conditions, people can and will enjoy their work and work well as a result.

Transference The psychoanalytic patient's unconscious attempt to make the therapist the object of emotional responses meant for someone else important in the life of the patient.

Trait-and-factor theory A theory that explains career choice in terms of personality traits and job factors.

Transsexuals A person who psychologically exhibits characteristics of the opposite sex.

True self A term often used by humanists to suggest that core part of our self that contains no pretense.

Trust The feeling we have about someone when we place confident hope in his or her character, strength, or honesty.

Unconditioned response A response by an unconditioned stimulus.

Unconscious The motives, feelings, memories, and thoughts that we are not aware of and that are assumed to affect our behavior.

Unstructured atmosphere The attitude in a group that allows the members a maximum amount of freedom.

Violence Physical force intended to injure or abuse.

INDEX

acceptance, 174, 332, 363
acceptance of feeling, 41
aggression, 41
Allport-Vernon Scale of Values, 198
altruism, 240
anal stage, 33–34
anxiety, 4–5, 107–115, 126
anima, 190–193, 284
animus, 190–193, 284
apathy, 295–297
archetypes, 185–193, 205, 284–290
art of loving, 266–269
artistic, 336
assertiveness, 148–150, 170–172
anger, 362
authoritarian leader, 244
autokinetic illusion, 248
autonomy, 34
aversive stimuli, 115

bad-me, 241
Baker, E., 300
Bandura, A., 144, 168
bargaining, 362–363
behavior control, 15
behavior shaping, 60–61
behavioristic school, 5
Bennett, R., 7
bisexuality, 190
body language, 212, 217–224
Borden, R., 150
Borges, M., 360
Breuer, J., 162
Brodsky, L., 225
Bruner, J., 70–71
Brucken, L., 284
Bry, A., 57, 117
Bugental, J., 21
Bulman, R., 114

Burgess, A., 35
Burke, R., 311

Camp, B., 32
Cantril, H., 20
castration anxiety, 34–36
Charcot, J., 158, 162
childhood development, 8, 30
Clark, T., 191–192
classical conditioning, 56
clitoral orgasm, 295
cognitive psychology, 63–68, 73
cognitive structure, 63, 64, 74
Cohen, J., 353–354
coitus, 292
collective unconscious, 184–193, 205
compulsivity, 341
concentration, 264
conditioned response, 56, 117
conditioned stimulus, 56
conformity, 245
congruence, 226
control, 15, 24
conventional, 337
creative divorce, 324
criticism, 315–316
crossroad approach, 331

Daniel, S., 271
Dashiell, J., 243–244
death instinct, 134–138
defense mechanism, 11, 213
democratic leader, 244
denial, 362
depression, 362–363
desensitization, 158, 167
despair, 358–360
developmental theories, 334–335
DeVoe, M., 15

381

discipline, 264
discovery learning, 70–71
discrimination, 57–58
dissatisfiers, 338
Dove, W., 200
dream interpretation, 162–164
dream symbols, 162
Dunne, J., 23–24

ego, 9–11, 24, 107, 114
ego integrity, 358–360
Eichmann, A., 204
Einstein, A., 100
Ekman, P., 5
Electra complex, 36–37, 51
emotion, 17, 24, 30, 47
emotional maturity, 177
emotionally concentrated, 333
encounter groups, 96, 251–256
enterprising, 336
environment, 39
equality, 309
Erikson, E., 32, 242–243, 256, 350–360
eros, 300–301
ethical relativism, 203–204
Evans, M., 340
excitement phase of intercourse, 294
extraverts, 80–83

facade, 227
facilitate, 72, 173
fair fight, 151
faith, 267
falling in love, 262
Fast, J., 223
feeling expression, 252–254
first impression, 195–196, 205
Fordham, F., 80
Foulks, E., 163
free association, 158, 162
free choice, 20, 44, 51
Freisen, W., 7
Freud, S., 6–11, 31–37, 80, 107–115, 127, 128, 133–138, 152, 153, 158–166, 177–178, 211–217, 224, 230, 256
Freudian slip, 164
Fromm, E., 137, 261–267, 278
frustration, 140–143, 153

generalization, 57–58, 117, 196
generativity, 357, 358
genitality, 356
Gentry, W., 47
Ginott, H., 313–20, 324
Ginzberg, E., 334–335
Goble, F., 204
good-me, 241
Grieger, R., 41
Grieger, T., 41
Groth, A., 35
group dynamics, 243–244
group pressure, 245
group therapy, 96
Griffeth, R., 86
growth, 21–22
guilt, 107, 114

Hall, C., 4, 6–7, 34, 37, 108, 109–110, 111, 114, 138, 159, 160, 168, 185, 186, 190, 213, 215, 184, 288
Hanchett, L., 221
hard-to-get, 272
Harper, L., 169–170
Hemingway, E., 100
higher order conditioning, 118
Hitler, A., 203–204
Hoffman, M., 240–241
Holland, J., 336–338
hollow people, 121
homeostasis, 84–86
homosexuality, 190–191, 288–290
Horney, K., 36–37, 238–241, 256
Hornleid, G., 150
humanistic, 5–6
hypnosis, 158–162

id, 9–11, 24, 107, 114
identity, 242, 352–354
imitation, 143–144, 153, 168–170
impotence, 35
incongruence, 224–225
individuation, 86–87
industry, 350–351
inferiority, 351–352
insight, 63–64
instinct, 134–138
interpersonal, 262
intimacy, 355–356

introverts, 80–83
intuition, 83
investigative, 336
isolation, 355–356

Jacobs, H., 221
jealousy, 311–313
Johnson, V., 283, 293–295, 302
Jones, M., 196
Jung, C., 80–88, 89, 101, 183–191, 205, 283–290, 302

Kaplun, D., 137
Kauffman, J., 41, 92
kinesics, 218–219
Kinsey, A., 192, 283, 290–293, 302
Knox, D., 170
Kohler, W., 63, 103–104, 155–156
Krantzler, M., 307, 321–325
Kubler–Ross, E., 361–364
Kuhn, D., 286

laissez-faire leader, 244
Langer, J., 33, 39
latency, 350
latent learning, 67
leadership, 244–245
learning, 167
leisure, 340–344
lie detector, 13
life instinct, 134
Lindzey, G., 4, 34, 37, 138, 168, 190
listening, 228–229
Lobitz, W., 300
loneliness, 121
love scale, 272

manic-depressive, 91
Maslow, A., 50, 184, 198–206, 338
masturbation, 292
Masters, V., 283, 293–295, 302
May, R., 44, 120, 121–123, 124–125, 127, 147, 283, 295–303
McCormick, E., 188
McGregor, D., 338
mechanical mirror, 39
Messer, S., 174
Monroe, R., 217
Milgram, S., 145

moral anxiety, 114–115
mourning, 322–323

Nash, S., 286
near-miss, 141
need-drive theory, 331–333
need hierarchy, 338
neurotic anxiety, 110, 114, 127
noncontingent reinforcement, 61–62
Norby, V., 185, 284, 288
not-me, 241

Oak Park study, 69, 73
Oedipus complex, 34–35, 51
Oliver, W., 196
O'Neill, G. & N., 307–313, 324
open companionship, 311
open marriage, 308–313
operant conditioning, 59–60
oral aggression, 32
oral stage, 31–32, 51
organism, 44
orgasm, 294
overpermissive, 319–320

panic reactions, 111
paranoia, 91
Parsons, F., 330–331
patience, 264
Pavlov, I., 56–58, 73, 74
peace, 276
penis evny, 36–37
Perls, F., 273
permissive, 319–320
persona, 284
personal space, 221
personal unconscious, 184
petting, 292
phallic stage, 34–35, 36
phobias, 108, 110, 112, 158, 169, 177–178
plateau stage of intercourse, 294
plain people, 269–270
praise, 315–316
potential, 21–22
predict, 15, 24
prejudice, 190
premarital intercourse, 292
privacy, 309
projection, 214–215

propinquity, 193–195
punishment, 115
puritanism, 299–301

Rainville, R., 188
rape, 35
reaction formation, 216
realistic, 336
reality anxiety, 109–110, 127
reality principle, 10
reconfirmation effect, 322
reflex behavior, 60
refractory stage of intercourse, 294
Reich, R., 137
repression, 11, 47, 213
rewards, 13, 40–41
risk, 49–50
risk in loving, 275
risky shift, 250
Roe, A., 331–313
Rogers, C. R., 17, 45–47, 72–73, 74, 80, 86, 93–94, 96, 101, 145–146, 173–178, 212, 224–231, 251–256, 257
role confusion, 354
Rubin, Z., 271

Saunders, K., 169–170
Schimel, J., 397
schizoid, 295
schizophrenic, 38, 91, 163
Segal, E., 271
segregation, 195
self, 4
self-actualized, 50, 200, 204
self-defeating patterns, 317–319
self-esteem, 15–16, 147
shadow, 187–188
Sheehy, G., 87, 350
Sherif, M., 245
Siassi, I., 174
sign language, 64–66
silence, 275
simple assertion, 171
Smart, J., 337
social, 336

social learning, 143–144, 168–170
Spiegel, D., 112–113
spontaneous recovery, 57
stagnation, 357–358
Steinmetz, S., 320
Stitch, P., 115–116
Storr, A., 85, 86
Stotland, E., 147
subjective, 19
Sullivan, H., 241–242, 256
superego, 9–11, 24, 107, 114
superstition, 62

theory X, 338–340
theory Y, 338–340
Tolman, E., 13, 64, 66, 67
Tolor, A., 91
toilet training, 33–34, 51
trait-and-factor, 330–331
transference, 166
transsexual, 290
trust, 176

unconditioned response, 56
unconditioned stimulus, 56
unconscious, 6–7, 158, 159

vaginal orgasm, 295
violence, 147–148
Volpan, 13

Washoe, 66
Watson, J., 12
Waxer, P., 119–120
Weir, T., 311
Werner, C., 221
Wilson, G., 38
Wolpe, J., 167
Woolfolk, A., 38
Woolfolk, R., 38
work ethic, 340
work motivation, 338
Wortman, C., 114
Woudenberg, R., 190–191

Zaleska, M., 250